TWENTIETH CENTURY LINCOLNSHIRE/   5

£19.95

D1351334

AD 01008892

HISTORY OF LINCOLNSHIRE

Edited by
MAURICE BARLEY

VOLUME XII

TWENTIETH CENTURY LINCOLNSHIRE

Edited by
DENNIS R. MILLS

HISTORY OF LINCOLNSHIRE
XII

Twentieth Century Lincolnshire

edited by
DENNIS R. MILLS

Lincoln
HISTORY OF LINCOLNSHIRE COMMITTEE
for the Society for Lincolnshire History and Archaeology
1989

Published by
THE HISTORY OF LINCOLNSHIRE COMMITTEE
JEWS' COURT, STEEP HILL, LINCOLN

© 1989 THE HISTORY OF LINCOLNSHIRE COMMITTEE
ISBN 0 902668 14 5

British Library Cataloguing in Publication Data
History of Lincolnshire.
Vol. 12: Twentieth century Lincolnshire.
1. Lincolnshire, history
I. Barley, M. W. (Maurice Willmore), *1909–*
II. Mills, Dennis R. (Dennis Richard), *1931–*
III. Society for Lincolnshire History and Archaeology
IV. History of Lincolnshire Committee
942.5'3
ISBN 0-902668-14-5 — 5

Produced for the Committee by
Yard Publishing Services, Lincoln
Printed by Billing & Sons, Ltd, Worcester

To all those men and women
of Lincolnshire and in Lincolnshire
who served their county and country
during the wars of this century

CONTENTS

FIGURES

TABLES

See also Appendix

PREFACE AND ACKNOWLEDGEMENTS

This is the tenth volume to be published in the Committee's twelve-volume chronological series on the History of Lincolnshire, but its appearance represents a departure from the previous practice of single-person authorship. So my first duty is to thank the History of Lincolnshire Committee for asking me to edit the book, and I hope the results will justify this trust.

The selection and definition of topics to be included in the book and the recruitment of authors were challenging processes in which the Committee made many valuable suggestions. Once recruited, the authors worked loyally and enthusiastically towards the goal. Although there has never been a single complete meeting of authors, there has been a great deal of cooperation and commentary around the team. We are all conscious of presenting a partial view of our subject, conditioned by our experience of Lincolnshire as well as by the state of the existing literature on the county in our period. There is much to do yet, not least by extending the topics of enquiry, but we hope we have erected some useful signposts for those who follow.

As General Editor of the series, Professor Barley relaxed the canon of conventional history which emphasizes the idea of a seamless web of events, personalities, and trends; and this has allowed us to pursue subject specialisms for their own sake, as well as for their part in the totality of experience. However, in contributing a postscript, he has offered an interesting corrective to our approach, since his description of some cultural changes rounds out the view presented, indicates further avenues of enquiry, and helps to give unity to our text.

We are also grateful to those who have read and commented on the whole or parts of the text. Mrs M. E. Armstrong, editor of a similar book on Scunthorpe, Dr K. Warren, fellow of Jesus College and lecturer in geography in the University of Oxford, and Mr F. T. Baker read the whole text, making many valuable comments and saving us from inaccuracies. Dr D. Gunby and Mr R. L. Stirling read the chapter on planning, which is something of a pioneer in its field. Miss Joyce Skinner and Mr George Cooke are among those who read the chapter on schools. Mr Terry Hancock helped with the chapter on the RAF. Many others have helped in matters of detail, but as authors we take responsibility for any remaining blemishes. Miss F. A. R. Murray made a valuable suggestion relating to captions.

The bibliographical notes suggest our indebtedness to libraries, both within and without Lincolnshire, to the Lincolnshire Archives Office, and to specialized archives such as those held in planning offices, and the library of the RAF College at Cranwell. Finding illustrations for the book has involved a wide range of institutions and individuals, as indicated in captions. For their committed co-operation, we would like to thank collectively the owners of the photographs used, and in those few cases where we have been unable to trace holders of copyright we would like to apologize for any unintentional infringement of their rights. The final versions of line drawings, and the total creation of some of them, has been the responsibility of Mrs Jayne Peacock of the City of Lincoln Archaeological Unit. We would like to acknowledge her careful attention to detail under the arrangement made by Mr M. J. Jones, Director of the Unit. We are again indebted to Mr Max Marschner for his creative work in designing the dust jacket.

Mrs Elizabeth Nurser, as production editor, assisted by Miss Helen Palmer, Mrs Christina Houghton, and Mrs Penny Fogg, has undoubtedly had the most arduous task of all. The book has been printed from her computer-generated text. In dealing with the countless details of consistent house style, proof corrections, cross references, sub-headings, figure numbers, the realignment of tables, and most of all the page lay-out of this complex book, Mrs Nurser has maintained high standards with great cheerfulness and courtesy.

Last, but definitely not least, we acknowledge with gratitude the help of our financial sponsors. On the centenary of the setting up of the county councils, it is fitting that the Lincolnshire County Council has offered a loan to the Committee in connection with a book that deals with a large part of that hundred-year period. We hope the volume will justify continued confidence in the Committee's ability to interpret and represent Lincolnshire's history and identity. Additionally we are most grateful to the Trustees of the Marc Fitch Fund for a grant specifically intended to help us with the heavy costs of the illustrations.

Dennis R. Mills
Chairman, History of Lincolnshire Committee
Society for Lincolnshire History and Archaeology
23 January 1989

NOTE ON THE ILLUSTRATIONS

The twentieth century being an age of photography, we have tried to use this medium as an historical source in its own right, rather than merely as a means of enlivening the text, which we hope the illustrations also do. One consequence of this objective is that we have concentrated on scenes of the first half of the century, now lost or much altered. Another consequence is that we have attempted to include representations of different parts of the county and of different kinds of photo collections. In particular, we would like to draw attention to the work of the Lincolnshire and Humberside Film Archive in Spalding, who have rescued precious early cinematograph films from oblivion and have developed an expertise in their conservation, which is no straightforward matter. Stills from three films are printed as Figs. 9.10, 11.4, and Postscript Fig. 1, not so much for their quality, but more to give readers some insight into the use of film as an archival source.

Captions are fuller than is usual, partly because the illustrations are an extension of the text and partly because, at least for younger readers, old photographs require a little explanation if they are to be fully appreciated. Acknowledgements as to the sources of our illustrations are given as fully as possible within their respective captions. Although we have taken care to ascertain the names of copyright holders wherever possible, it is in the nature of the task for some doubts to remain. Any copyright holders not acknowledged or recompensed are asked to contact the Secretary, History of Lincolnshire Committee, Society for Lincolnshire History and Archaeology, Jews' Court, Steep Hill, Lincoln, LN2 1LS.

Several photographs, not used in the text, appear as part of the cover design. The steam traction engines and the Hornet tank have been taken from *The tank: its birth and development* (Wm Foster and Co. Ltd), and Ruston Gas Turbines Ltd kindly provided the photograph of the turbine. We are grateful to Balliol College, Oxford, for the photograph of the young Francis McLaren. We also acknowledge with thanks the assistance of the Libraries' staff of the Recreational Services Department of Lincolnshire County Council in locating the photographs of the Lancaster bomber and the William Foster machines.

D.R.M.

CHAPTER 1

INTRODUCTION

by Dennis Mills

Abstract *This introduction comprises three sections, in the first of which a sketch of Lincolnshire life about 1900 has been drawn. The second section discusses some geographical features of Lincolnshire, especially those related to local government. The last section comments on the problems of writing the history of our own century and on the structure of this volume of essays on twentieth-century Lincolnshire.*

LINCOLNSHIRE LIFE c. 1900

The lives of most Lincolnshire people at the beginning of the twentieth century were still bounded largely by their locality, an area perhaps comprising a market town and the circle of villages it served. This emphasis on locality began at birth, for most babies were born at home, and those surviving, a higher proportion than in the Victorian period, entered a local school at the age of about five, possibly earlier if family circumstances made this favourable. This was the period of all-age elementary schools, even in towns, and most children, therefore, stayed in the same school until the leaving age of thirteen or fourteen.

A few children went to a grammar school, sometimes as boarders if they could not walk to school each day, or travel by train. Going away to any kind of college was the privilege of a tiny minority. Outside the industrial towns, however, leaving home to get a job was very common; domestic service for girls, farm service and apprenticeships for boys. Local newspapers were the main source of information on jobs other than word of mouth and, in some areas, the hiring fairs.[1] Consequently most youngsters did not go very far, and carriers' carts (Fig. 1.1) were at least as important as the railways when it came to getting them and their tin boxes to places of work. Many girls and some boys had to stay at home to help mother with her big family and inconvenient house, or to work with father in the shop or workshop, or on the farm. Parents played a much bigger part in determining what children should do with their lives than they can attempt today.

Fig. 1.1 The Folkingham carrier. Carriers' carts were still popular with country people in the Edwardian period. The carrier took people to market, did their shopping for them, and transported young people with their tin boxes when they went into service. Here is Mr Simpson of Folkingham, who linked that railway-less place with Grantham, Sleaford and Bourne on their respective market days. Source: Lincoln Central Library.

Since the collapse in corn prices in the late 1870s the movement of people out of Lincolnshire villages had increased, some going to the expanding towns of Cleethorpes, Grimsby, Lincoln, Scunthorpe and Skegness in particular, others further afield in Britain, others still to the colonies, encouraged by tales of cheap land and agricultural opportunities. The coalfield areas west of Lincolnshire were favourite destinations within England, although not always for employment in the pits. An interesting and successful example is Walter Scrimshaw, who walked from his farm labourer's job in Mareham-le-Fen to Doncaster just before the turn of the century, where he took advantage of expanding opportunities in the distribution of potatoes and made the fortune he could never have amassed at home, even if he had been lucky enough to take a farm.

Town and country were quite sharply distinguished in the Edwardian period, and the subsequent blurring of these distinctions is an important theme in parts of this book. Commuting to work was still very limited, townspeople were packed tightly together in terraced streets and lived a quite different life from their country cousins (Figs. 1.2, 1.3, and 1.4). Street lights and cooking by gas were commonplace, running water and sewerage systems could be taken more or less for

Fig. 1.2 Edwardian street scene in Grantham. The terraced streets of the towns, with their orderly uniformity and modern amenities, presented a sharp contrast to the informal and old fashioned atmosphere of the typical village scene (as seen, for instance in Figure 1.3). This example is a postcard view in Manthorpe Road, Grantham. Source: D. N. Robinson Collection.

granted, though a typhoid epidemic in 1905 showed limits to Lincoln's progress. In the villages one still stumbled about in the dark, fetched water from a pump or well, and used the garden privy.

Developments of the previous century and a half had produced some large enterprises and important specializations within the county. Agriculture was the leading employer. Many Lincolnshire farms were well above the national average size, and partly because of its broad acres, the county made a notable contribution to the nation's larder, especially in wheat and barley, and new crops, such as the potato and field-grown vegetables. Agricultural engineering works, especially in Gainsborough, Grantham and Lincoln, included some which were large by national standards, their products leading their field worldwide. Grimsby's fishing fleet ranked among the most important in Europe, and Scunthorpe's new ironworks were thoroughly modern in scale and efficiency.[2]

In other walks of life, however, enterprises, services, and institutions were on a small scale, in keeping with local self-sufficiency. As those who read the names on manhole covers will know, even small towns often had their own foundries. Departmental and chain stores had made their appearance, but village and street-corner shops still had a very large share of trade. Milk sales were still unregulated and most dairies were very small, often producer-retailers with cowsheds close to, or actually in, the towns where customers lived. Much the same conditions applied to bread, except that milling had become a big business which put many windmills out of work. Although the railway companies were large, they were to get much larger in the 1920s, and again on nationalization after the second world war. The carriers' carts were usually one-man businesses, as were many contractors, except where steam-traction called for more capital.

Until 1902 the local school board, typically controlling only a handful of small schools, was the main medium through which education was organized. Although the parish had long since ceased to be an important element in local government, even in rural areas, both the scope of local government and the sizes of the authorities were much smaller than today. Poor relief, taken away from the parish overseers in 1834, was still in the hands of local Boards of Guardians until 1930,

Fig. 1.3 Saltfleet's memorial to a Boer War soldier. The Boer War was shattering the long Victorian Pax Britannica as the century began. In villages where a pure water supply was still wanting, there was no more fitting tribute to a fallen son than a brand new pump. This is the scene at Saltfleet at the foot of The Hill and the top end of Pump Lane. The memorial was erected to Frederick Allen Freshney, trooper, wounded at the Battle of Colenso, 15 December 1899, as a consequence of which he died 20 May 1906. The shop behind sold Ovum dog biscuits and Thorley's Foods, but is now a unisex hairdressing salon. Note the workmen's wooden wheelbarrow, and T-handled shovels manufactured in Sheffield for the Lincolnshire market. Source: Lincoln Central Library.

when the county and county borough councils took over, only to be replaced by an impersonal central government department after the second world war.

Although the Football League and the FA Cup competition brought some important first and second division teams to the county, most entertainment was organized on a local and amateur basis. The churches and chapels still played a very prominent role in this field; their choirs and organs were the basis of many secular musical events, and Sunday school treats were among the high points of the social year in many a rural and urban community organized around a place of worship.

Older people regret the fading of the sense of community which they remember. It is quite difficult to measure. Less regretted is the tightening up of environmental control which has gone on more or less continuously since the last quarter of the nineteenth century, bringing with it town planning as one of several new professional disciplines. Least regretted is our loss of the relatively primitive medical and dental services which prevailed in the early part of the century.

Fig. 1.4 Traditional cottage interior at Reepham. Mr Cridge, of Kennel Lane, Reepham in the mid-1970s. The house interior is little different from the period before 1914. The 'range' includes a side oven and a water boiler heated by the living room fire. Mr Cridge continues the old habit of sitting indoors wearing his outdoor clothing. House interiors of this period can be seen at the Scunthorpe Museum, the Church Farm Museum, Skegness, and the Museum of Lincolnshire Life, Lincoln.
Source: Mrs C. M. Wilson.

I find it quite difficult to believe that it was my own father who, in the early 1920s, pushed his father in a wheelbarrow over a mile across fields after a nasty accident with an axe in the woods near Thorney. This effort was followed by a two-mile cycle ride to Saxilby to alert the doctor, who was out on his rounds, and only turned up about six hours after the accident. It was a marvel that gangrene did not develop. Nowadays such an accident would have led to a 999-call and the patient would have been in hospital inside half an hour. The difference, however, is not only the result of technology, but also of the success of stronger trades unions in their campaign for better health and safety regulations at work.

LINCOLNSHIRE AS A COUNTY

In recent centuries Lincolnshire has had a small population relative to its size: only about 800,000 in 1971, out of a total of over 48 millions in England and Wales, compared with several millions each in Lancashire and the West Riding, and a million in the single city of Birmingham. Lack of numbers and relative isolation from the main highways of England help to explain why so many people know so little about Lincolnshire.

A common description is that it is a large flat area with few trees, and while this contains an element of truth, it neglects the variety of landscapes to be found within the county. For example, it distracts attention from the 27.5 million trees planted on the Brocklesby estate between c. 1780 and c. 1920.[3] The Wolds, the Cliff and the Heath provide some thrilling hilltop views, often taking in the great landmark of Lincoln cathedral on its own hill, a walk up which can put most pedestrian visitors distinctly out of breath. Also, somewhat incredibly, the highest point (347 ft above sea level) on the whole of the King's Cross–Edinburgh line is to be found just south of Stoke tunnel, south of Grantham.[4]

Lincolnshire is the second biggest of the ancient counties of England, but with an area of 2,791 square miles it comes far behind Yorkshire (6,067), and is closely followed by Devon (2,605). The road distance is about 80 miles from Stamford to the Humber Bridge, the two most important entry points for visitors, while Lincolnshire stretches about 50 miles east–west from the Trent through Lincoln to the coast (see Fig. 1.5 for some important geographical features of historic Lincolnshire).

These distances are the main reason why Lincolnshire has never been administered as a single county; Holland, Kesteven, and Lindsey Divisions were each an administrative county. This arrangement was replaced in 1974 by a Lincolnshire County Council administering the

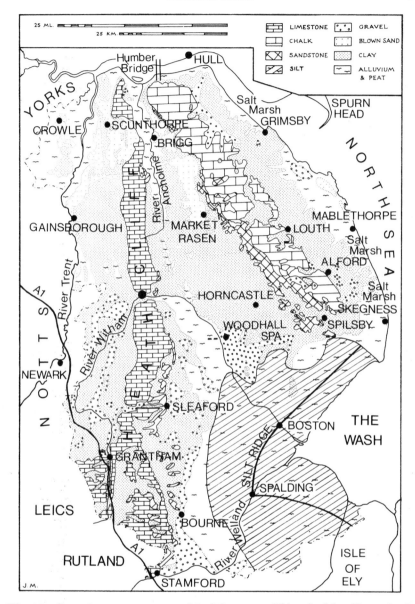

Fig. 1.5 Some important geographical features of Lincolnshire. Drawn by J. Peacock, based on History of Lincolnshire, Vol. I, fig. 2.

southern two-thirds or so of the historic county, and a Humberside County Council taking in the remainder, along with the East Riding and Kingston-upon-Hull. Since these essays have little to say on the

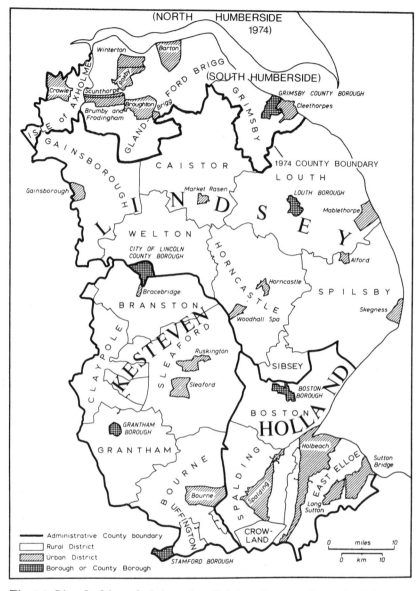

Fig. 1.6 Lincolnshire administrative divisions in 1900. Drawn by J. Peacock, based on History of Lincolnshire, Vol. X, fig. 6.

period from 1974, the reader should understand that Lincolnshire is taken to mean the historic county, unless the context makes another interpretation clear. (Compare Figs. 1.6 and 1.7.)

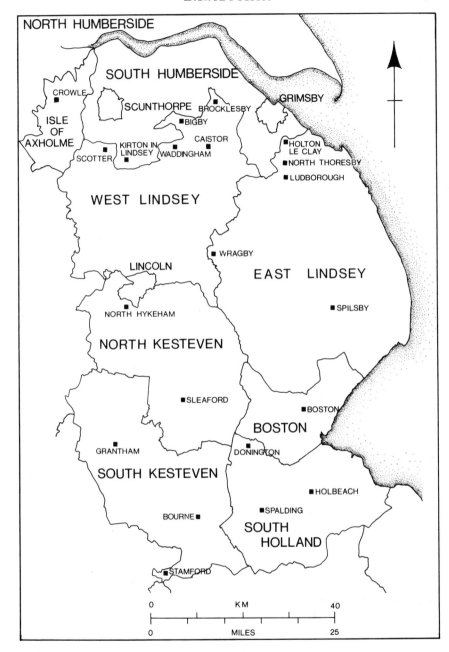

Fig. 1.7 Lincolnshire administrative divisions in 1974. Drawn by J. Peacock, based on 1981 Census of England and Wales.

Although Lincoln stands centrally on the county's long north–south dimension, its influence as a city has never extended over the whole county in the way that towns like Leicester, Nottingham, Bedford, Oxford, Durham, and Hereford can claim. There was never any challenge to its authority as head of the diocese, nor as the meeting place of the county assizes, because the Divisions enjoyed a measure of jealously guarded independence. In the case of Holland, distance from Lincoln was reinforced by the difficulties of movement in an undrained fenland environment.

Lincoln has also been a small town relative to the size of the county, for example, about 57,000 in 1901, compared with over a quarter of a million in Nottingham and Hull, 120,000 in Norwich and 80,000 in York. Its commercial influence is correspondingly weaker, and while large neighbouring towns such as Hull, Doncaster, Sheffield, Nottingham, Leicester, Peterborough, and even King's Lynn have spread their influence into Lincolnshire, there has also been a compensation in that such medium-sized towns as Stamford, Grantham, Gainsborough, Louth, Spalding, and Boston have a lively independence of Lincoln's and other outside influences. In the north, Scunthorpe and Grimsby developed to a point where their open challenge to Lincoln was one of the reasons why they were included in a different administrative county after 1974.

The first county and county borough councils were elected in January 1889, and had their first meetings on 1 April 1889, following a series of meetings of provisional councils.[5] Grimsby (from 1891) and Lincoln were the only two towns ever qualifying for county borough status, but they both extended their boundaries. They were all-purpose authorities since, unlike the administrative counties, they shared local government functions with no other councils of lower status.

Scunthorpe, which had long been an 'Excepted District' for educational purposes, that is, had a measure of independence from the Lindsey Education Committee, was actively seeking county borough status in the early seventies, but this initiative was overtaken by general reorganization.

Lindsey County Council chose Lincoln as its headquarters, giving a southern bias to an area where the thrust of population growth was further north in Scunthorpe and in the environs of Grimsby, perhaps unconsciously sowing seeds of later dissension. Holland set up offices in Boston; Kesteven avoided the ancient borough of Grantham and made Sleaford its administrative centre,[6] but the arrangements for meetings were more complex.

Each of the administrative counties was divided into urban and rural areas (see Fig. 1.5 and Appendix, Table 1). One complication with the urban group is that the ancient boroughs of Boston, Grantham, Grimsby (to 1891), Louth and Stamford kept the higher status of municipal borough, and were joined by Cleethorpes and Scunthorpe in 1936. They therefore possessed wider powers than the more lowly urban and rural district councils, with particular implications for education, police, and the maintenance of roads.

In 1900, six years after the Act that had set them up, the urban district councils numbered 24. As time went by, promotions to the status of municipal borough, amalgamations with other urban authorities, or absorption into the surrounding rural district reduced their number by half. The same fate befell some of the early rural district councils, of which there were initially 20. Some were anomalies from the beginning, but there were still 16 RDCs in 1974, saved in the trend towards larger authorities by suburban population growth and, in some cases, by the absorption of small urban areas.

Within the rural districts there was, and is, a still lower tier of local government: parish councils, or parish meetings in smaller parishes, with very limited formal powers. They have enjoyed a status of some distinction, especially in more recent decades over matters of planning in which they are consulted by higher authorities.

Finally, a word needs to be said about the prosperity or otherwise of local authorities in Lincolnshire. Very few of them have been known for high spending, although in individual fields and in particular places exceptions from a policy of restraint can be found. For example, Grimsby was very forward-looking in education at the turn of the nineteenth century, Lincoln spent heavily on council housing over long periods, and both Lindsey County Council and Scunthorpe Borough spent heavily in that town in the face of phenomenal population growth, though perhaps not always enough to keep up with that growth. The Lincolnshire road system has on the whole been well maintained, taking advantage of its heritage of wide, straight roads across thinly populated areas, which make the crowded, winding local roads of the rich Home Counties seem very inadequate.

Low spending may have been more a matter of choice than of necessity. It has sometimes been suggested that Lincolnshire suffered disproportionately from the derating of agricultural land in 1896 (by one half), 1923 (by a further quarter), and 1929 (the final quarter). However, what is not so well appreciated is that some attempt was made by central government to offset this loss by raising the level of grant appropriately at least in 1923–4 and 1929–30. Nor is it well known that the present system of giving grant aid to local authorities

goes far back into the nineteenth century. By 1884–5 grants constituted 12 per cent of the local authority income in England and
Wales derived jointly from rates and grants (but excluding income
from investments). By 1932–3 the proportion was 45 per cent, thus
approaching the post-1945 level of more than a half. In the earlier
part of the century, as now, there must have been argument about
whether the rate-support system was fairly administered.[7] This is a
question, however, which must be left for future writers on Lincolnshire local government to investigate.

CONTEMPORARY HISTORY – A FIRST ATTEMPT

The notion of writing contemporary history has developed only in our
century and has been strongest in the fields of national and international history. Many volumes have been devoted to topics such as the
causes and events of the two world wars, the problems of the depression years, the reasons for the decline of Britain, and the development
of the welfare state. Diaries and official records have figured very
prominently, just as they have in the history of previous centuries.
What is new is that discussions have started within the lifetimes of
the participants, and with their active involvement. It is, of course,
accepted that these histories will have to be rewritten as new perspectives emerge, a practice already well established in the history of
earlier centuries. Nevertheless this is not a reason for doing nothing
now, for to leave the writing of history entirely to succeeding generations is to abandon our duty at least to capture factual records made
and the views of events and periods held by those who lived through
them.

These general principles apply equally to writing at the levels of
local and county history, but with the difference that while the range
of topics is much wider than for times earlier than the Victorian
period, much less has already been done to collect, sift, and sum-
marize the available evidence. This is especially true of oral evidence
and personal recollections, which we have, nevertheless, attempted
to use.

A number of reasons can be put forward in partial explanation of
this state of affairs. Relatively few decision-makers at the local level
have thought it necessary to set their own records straight. Apart
from a few businesses and some local authorities, very little money
has been invested in the professional writing of contemporary history
at the local level, compared with the vast sums which have gone into,
for example, the official histories of the second world war. One Lincolnshire historian has gone so far as to suggest that 'To have those

who were actors in the scene safely dead is the limiting and liberating condition of the trade of a local historian'.[8]

Consequently, historians who have written on recent local topics have had a relatively poor framework within which to write. The published material on which we have been able to draw tends, therefore, to lack comparative perspectives and conceptual bases that would have made it so much more useful. Furthermore, a significant proportion of authors in this field have been writers whose work has been commissioned and published by the institutions concerned. One is grateful for what has been accomplished, but there is a need to be wary of conscious and unconscious bias.

A comparison of the sources available for the twentieth century on the one hand and the sixteenth to nineteenth centuries on the other reveals some factors which inhibit research into certain aspects of twentieth century history, particularly at the local level. For the sixteenth to eighteenth centuries probate inventories give us a better record of the contents of the homes of many social groups than the historian can acquire for the twentieth century, despite photographs and government social surveys.

There is nothing comparable in our own times to parish registers, although census material is superabundant at an aggregrate rather than a personal or family level. The census enumerators' books are not available until after a century has passed, owing to the rules of confidentiality which still cover some other modern records. We know far more about the distribution of landownership from the land tax assessments, tithe surveys, and enclosure awards of the eighteenth and nineteenth centuries than it is possible to find out about contemporary ownership. Even the valuation records made as a result of Lloyd George's 1910 Finance Act have only recently become available for academic study, and since the Ballot Act of 1868 it has been impossible to determine how individual electors voted.

There is a hint also in the last paragraph of a sharp difference in character between the records of the present century and those of earlier times. Statistical material abounds along with planning documents and local authority minutes. They do not attract local historians accustomed to the human scale and evocative qualities of wills, inventories, parish registers, overseers' accounts, and householders' census schedules. Many people turn to local history as a hobby, perhaps also as a profession, in order to turn their backs on the problems of present day life. Hunger marches of the twenties, planning decisions of the forties, and arguments about the nationalization of public utilities remind us rather too pointedly of current unemployment, the present blight of inner cities, and the privatization of government utilities.

All these difficulties add up to an argument that a start must be made somewhere to create a conceptual and factual framework for the history of Lincolnshire in the twentieth century. The authors will be well pleased if their work is used as a springboard for further research and publications, leading to a revised view of the subject more trustworthy than our own. It is hardly surprising that the team is made up of writers who are mostly professional practictioners or, broadly speaking, social scientists, rather than mainstream historians. Indeed, when I approached one mainstream historian with a very good knowledge of Lincolnshire his response was that he was a historian, and did not come past 1914! The reader cannot expect us to have written the same kinds of history as can be found in earlier volumes in this series; but we hope that the volume is as enlightening, informative, thought-provoking, and attractive.

In striking a course across poorly charted territory we have evolved a few rudimentary rules of navigation, one of which was that individual chapters were conceived as making significant contributions to their own disciplines or subjects on the national plane, as well as in a Lincolnshire context. We wished to break new ground in both directions. Within the covers of one volume of modest size there had obviously to be some restriction on the number of chapters, to allow authors sufficient space to develop their topics. Sadly, a number of important topics have not been touched at all, except in the most incidental ways, including law and order; sport; health, welfare and medicine; the press; and the distributive services. Some fell by the wayside because we did not know of any academic historical research being done in these fields. Professor Barley's Postscript attempts to give some indications of the cultural life of the county, particularly in relation to the performing arts, adult education, and the developing interest in local history and archaeology, but all of these topics deserve more attention by scholars.

We also faced a considerable problem in attempting to give equal attention to all parts of the county. For example, in the field of early planning, some areas simply did not figure. Moreover, our need to rely exclusively on secondary sources inevitably led to gaps in our geographical treatment of the county. Owing to considerations of space, we had to place restrictions on the breadth of the material discussed in individual chapters. Here, conversely, we have sometimes avoided going over ground already well cultivated, notably the history of the Royal Air Force and of Scunthorpe. But it is mainly for lack of space that there is no discussion of adult education alongside the history of our schools and their administration, and nothing on the Army to keep company with the RAF in Chapter 6.

Another rule of navigation was that no restrictive view should be taken about how individual authors were to find starting and finishing points within the twentieth century. Starting points for some were more or less fixed by what had already been written in Volumes VIII, X, and XI, and what is expected in Volume IX, while in others particular events or watersheds, such as the Education Act of 1902 and the outbreak of the first world war, focused attention. A consensus emerged across several chapters that the decade 1965–75 was a period of marked change in Lincolnshire, as in the life of Britain as a whole.

In agriculture, entry into the Common Market in 1973 was a major turning point, while in secondary school education Circular 10 of 1965 set off projects of comprehensive reorganization. Soon after these dates traffic management plans, including pedestrianization schemes, began to alter the face of our towns rapidly, while the principles of conservation slowed down change in other ways and in other areas.

Finally, where a choice had to be made about space within a chapter, priority was given to the earlier decades of the century, rather than later ones, thus giving scope for continuity between this volume and earlier volumes, while relying to some extent on the reader's knowledge of present day society and recent years to fill in significant gaps. In our choice of illustrations, we have concentrated on the earlier part of the century.

Before moving into the main body of the volume, it might be useful to appreciate how the chapters have been written and arranged to flow into each other. Chapter 2 sets the scene for much that comes later by giving prominence to the considerable changes which have occurred in our places of work and the influences those changes have had on the distribution of Lincolnshire's population. Chapters 3 and 4 discuss agriculture and manufacturing industry, two of the most important sources of employment. The service industries, which constitute the third sector of employment, are briefly touched upon in Chapter 2, and one of them, transport, is the subject of Chapter 5. Here the concentration on passenger transport gives the chapter strong links with our discussion of changes in residential patterns, and with several later chapters. For example, one of Chapter 6's important topics is the reliance of the RAF during the 1939–45 war on the county's rail network for the movement of very large numbers of personnel. And in Chapter 7, the importance of rail links from the large towns of the Midlands and South Yorkshire to our seaside resorts is given due prominence. The growing popularity of the Lincolnshire coast in the 1920s was marked by the appearance of a rash of week-end chalets, disused railway coaches, and other forms of chaotic and unsightly development that led to Lindsey County Council's pioneering Sandhills Act. On this cue, Chapter 8 moves on to a comprehensive discussion of the early days of town and country planning in Lincolnshire. And from planning to politics is but a short step, since the growth of their planning activities brought local authorities ever more into the lives of ordinary people. In Chapter 9 the link between planning and politics is reinforced by the inclusion of a case study of politics and housing. Similarly the transfer of responsibility for education to local education authorities in 1902 again led the politicians on the county and county borough councils into the lives of parents and children, teachers, and governing bodies (Chapter 10). With the final chapters we move more consciously into the spiritual and qualitative aspects of Lincolnshire life. Chapter 11 discusses religious life and church organization, while Chapter 12 draws together strands from many earlier discussions by focusing on changes on the quality of life in a single village. The last chapter, a Postscript by the General Editor of the series, briefly sketches out some of the developments in the cultural life of Lincolnshire. Finally, please note that the more complex tables for all chapters appear as appendixes at the end of the book.

Bibliographical note

The contributors to this book hope that they will have opened up the main sources of twentieth century history for those who follow. Each chapter contains a note on sources specific to its subject, in addition to footnote references, and there is a collective A–Z bibliography on pp. 373–85. Here it is appropriate to make a few more general points. First, the Central Libraries at Grimsby, Lincoln and Scunthorpe contain extensive local collections indexed by place and subject, and many of the items have a twentieth century content, while a smaller number are devoted specifically to the present century. Town libraries administered by the Lincolnshire County Council have smaller local collections and at the time of writing they are being connected to the county's bibliographical computer database. In such a large county, it is impossible for a book of this kind to deal with individual places except as illustrations of trends and experience general to a significant part of the county. Nevertheless, there is a considerable amount of purely local material to which the historian can turn, notably five kinds of items:

1. The county directories of Lincolnshire down to the 1937 edition of Kelly, and later editions of directories for a few of the larger towns.

2. In a similar vein, the guides issued by local authorities, often of 1950s vintage, but sometimes of earlier or later dates.

3. Town and village histories, typically centred on earlier periods of history, frequently finish with accounts of their localities in the Edwardian period or even later.

4. The monthly magazine *Lincolnshire Life* contains a considerable amount of interesting information on a wide range of topics and places, and several indexes have been published. In almost the same bracket one can include items from local newspapers, which for the most part have not been indexed, and for that reason still remain largely unquarried by historians.

Notes to Chapter 1

1. Lincoln hiring fair was still in operation in 1924 (*Lincolnshire Life*, April 1987, p. 24) and Brigg hiring fair is mentioned as still being in operation in Kelly's 1922 *Directory of Lincolnshire*, but they may have been largely a matter of entertainment by these dates.

2. C. Ekberg, *The story of the Port of Grimsby and the decline and fall of the deep water industry*, Buckingham, 1984 and M. E. Armstrong (ed.), *An industrial island: a history of Scunthorpe*, Scunthorpe, 1981.

3. C. Brears, *A short history of Lincolnshire*, Hull 1927, p. 187.

4. S. Vessey, *The other side of the track*, Reepham, Lincoln, 1986 (unpaged).

5. J. Varley, *The parts of Kesteven*, Kesteven Co. Council, 1974, pp. 104–7.

6. R. J. Olney, *Rural society and county government in nineteenth century Lincolnshire*, History of Lincolnshire, vol. X, Lincoln, 1979, p. 139.

7. G. Gibbon, 'The expenditure and revenue of local authorities', *Journal of the Royal Statistical Society*, vol. 99 (1936), pp. 457–515, especially pp. 460, 481–4, 488; and J. Sykes, *A study of English local authority finance*, London, 1939, especially p. 72.

8. E. Gillett, *A history of Grimsby*, Oxford, 1970, p. 291.

CHAPTER 2

THE REVOLUTION IN WORKPLACE AND HOME

by Dennis Mills

Abstract   *This chapter begins with a description of the shift of employment out of agriculture into, first, manufacturing industry, then more latterly the service occupations. These changes have been accompanied by increases in the numbers of women in paid employment. The next section shows that employment changes have led to a movement of population towards the principal towns, and especially towards the north of the county. The class structure of country areas, once dominated by manual workers, now shows a clear preponderance of the middle class, or white-collar workers. The final section pursues this theme in describing how housing developments have suburbanized villages near large towns at the same time as many villages have suffered from a stagnant population.*

THE FARM WORK FORCE DECLINES

Lincolnshire still thinks of itself as an agricultural county. In several senses this is appropriate; it contains very large areas of high grade arable land, and by national standards a relatively high proportion of its people still work on the land – about 1 in 10 of the county's workforce in 1971, compared with the national average of only about 1 in 36 of the employed population (Figs 2.1 and Table 2.1). A relatively large number of Lincolnshire people work in occupations providing services to agriculture or processing its products. Finally, in so far as 'agricultural' and 'rural' are interchangeable, it is relevant that, even as late as 1971, 44 per cent of the county's population lived in 'rural districts', a proportion twice the national average.

Nevertheless, the most important change in Lincolnshire's economy has been a marked continuation of the fall in the numbers and proportions of those working on the land, which began in the previous century. In this key sense, Lincolnshire is no longer dominated by agriculture as it was in 1901 when almost one worker in three was still engaged in farm work. For those remaining on the land there has also been a bigger change in the style of work than for many of those working in factories. The winter scene of several teams of horses ploughing together in one field has been replaced by one lone driver in a huge machine listening to audio- cassettes instead of to the peewits and the creak of harness. The same man in summer sits masked and goggled on his combine harvester, visited only by satellite tractors and trailers, the memory of crowded harvest fields fading rapidly.

Table 2.1   *Changes in the main occupational groups in Lincolnshire, 1901-71, by percentages*

	1901 Lincolnshire			GB	1971 Lincolnshire			GB
	Male	Female	All	All	Male	Female	All	All
Agriculture, forestry, fishing	36.6	3.9	29.2	8.7	12.8	5.9	10.6	2.9
Mining, manufacture, construction	30.2	18.5	27.5	46.3	44.7	22.3	37.4	37.9
Service occupations	27.7	76.9	38.8	45.1	42.1	70.4	51.3	56.6
Not classified	5.5	0.6	4.4		0.4	1.4	0.7	2.6

Sources: Economically active population tables in 1901 and 1971 Censuses; see also Lee, *British Regional Employment Statistics*, Deane and Cole, 1962, pp.142, 166; Mitchell, *European Historical Statistics 1700-1975*. NB, about 5% of those in the Agriculture, Forestry, and Fishing sector were in the two latter categories.

While agricultural employment was falling, both manufacturing and service occupations were gaining between 1901 and 1971, but their experience since the later date has diverged, as employment in manufacturing has fallen considerably. Prominent among the rapidly growing industries were iron and steel manufacture, and the making of chemicals and petroleum products, all located predominantly in the northern half of the county. More evenly spread across the county were above-average increases in employment in textiles, electrical engineering, printing and publishing, and the food and drink industries.

Despite periods of serious unemployment between the wars, the important traditional foundry trades more than kept pace with average increases in manufacturing employment 1901–51, but from the later date remained stationary. Considerable activity in house building, to which we return below, along with other construction work, allowed the growth in employment in the building trades to keep up with the county average. Among rapidly waning occupations between 1901 and 1971 was the manufacture of finished clothing and footwear, as local tailors, dressmakers, milliners, and shoemakers

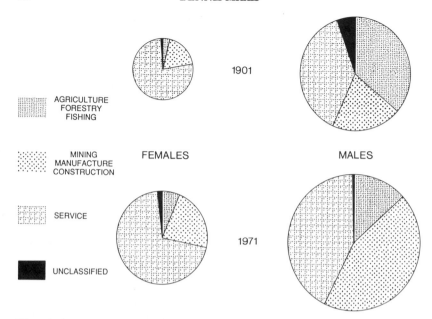

Fig. 2.1 Lincolnshire people at work: the circles are proportional to the male and female workforces in 1901 and 1971, and are divided to show the proportions engaged in the main types of employment. Source: D. R. Mills based on Table 2.1.

literally died out, or were put out of business by factory concerns elsewhere in the country.[1]

Many of the new industries are located in correspondingly new factories, single-storey buildings, often on industrial estates and dependent on good road access, rather than, as in the nineteenth century, using canal or rail transport. The replacement of steam power by electricity has been a major factor in allowing the dispersal of industry. However, it is important to notice that one of the main attractions of Humberside, including the lower reaches of the Trent, has been accessibility to deep water, making it possible to use bulk container ships and tankers. Typically, the modern factory employs a larger proportion of girls and women than was the case in 1901 (Fig 2.2). Women have gone out to work in increasing numbers as the century has passed by, while few of them now enter domestic service, which became unpopular owing to social isolation, low wages, and long hours. The two wars were also responsible for sharp increases in the employment of women in factories (Fig. 2.2). With the use of more sophisticated machinery, the need for long apprenticeships (a male preserve) has declined and women have proved themselves in assembly work, where manual dexterity is more important than strength.

The service occupations already claimed almost two-fifths of work people in 1901, and by 1971 the proportion had risen to over a half, many of the newcomers being women in shops and offices, banks, hospitals and nursing homes. Expansion over the 70 years was especially rapid in finance, which includes banking, insurance, and building society work; in the many kinds of professional and scientific services, such as teaching and medicine; in local and central government departments, and in the provision of electricity and water services. In transport and communications, however, increases of employment in road haulage and on the telephone network were more than cancelled out by losses in railway employment and, from the 1950s, in bus operations. Subsequently, there have been redundancies in the telephone network brought about by large-scale automation.

Fig. 2.2 A Grimsby jam factory. One alternative to domestic service was to work in a factory, as with these women in Tickler's jam factory in Pasture Street, Grimsby built 1899. It processed fruit grown on the firm's own farms at Laceby and Bradley. Thomas Tickler was MP for Grimsby 1914-22. The photo was taken during the first world war, which may explain the Union Jack. Source: Grimsby Central Library, caption based partly on D. Boswell and J. M. Storey, *Grimsby As It Was*, Vol. I (1974).

GB 82 47 bc
mit GB 82 48 bc
Nur für den Dienstgebrauch
Bild Nr. 427 L 81
Aufnahme vom 3. 9. 39

Lincoln
Dieselmotorenfabrik „Ruston and Hornsby Ltd."
Werk Ost (GB 8247), Werk West (GB 8248)
Länge (westl. Greenw.): 0° 32′ 18″   Breite: 53° 13′ 30″   Bildmitte
Mißweisung: − 10° 48′ (Mitte 1941)   Zielhöhe über NN 5 m
Maßstab etwa 1 : 15 800

Genst. 5. Abt. Oktober 1941
Karte 1 : 100 000
GB/E 14

Fig. 2.3 The Luftwaffe's view of Lincoln. A vertical aerial photograph of Lincoln taken by the Luftwaffe and issued as being correct at the outbreak of war, 3 September 1939. For the German General Staff the locations of Ruston and Hornsby's oil engine works were of paramount interest, but the view captures for us the extent of the built-up area in 1939, when the city was still mainly a creation of the pre-1914 period. Most of the streets are terraces running at right angles to the major thoroughfares. The different and more spacious pattern of the inter-war council housing estate at St Giles is visible on the right hand side of the top edge of the photo, while the beginnings of similar private developments can be seen to the left (west) of this area, on either side of Nettleham Road, which runs north eastwards out of the city. The north sign has been

Table 2.2 *Main changes in Lincolnshire's population 1901–1971*

Area	1901	1971	Increase	
			No	%
Whole county	500,022	809,148	309,126	61.8
Holland	77,610	105,690	28,080	36.2
Kesteven	103,962	158,280	54,318	52.2
Lindsey	206,528	375,369	168,841	81.8
Grimsby	63,138	95,540	34,402	51.3
Lincoln	48,784	74,269	25,485	52.2
Scunthorpe (in Lindsey figures)	*11,167	70,907	59,740	535.0
Boroughs and Urban Districts**	261,129	448,900	187,771	71.9
ditto, excl. Scunthorpe	249,962	377,993	128,031	51.2
Rural Districts*	238,893	360,248	121,355	50.8
England and Wales (1000s)	*32,528*	*48,750*	*16,222*	49.8

*Based on M. E. Armstrong (ed.), *An industrial island*, p. 203.
**Using the local government boundaries in force in 1901 and 1971.

Source: Censuses of England and Wales, 1901 and 1971.

JOB OPPORTUNITIES MOVE TOWNWARDS AND NORTHWARDS

Britain as a whole has gone through a broad cycle of change, with falls in agricultural employment, a rise and fall in manufacturing, and a continuous increase in service occupations. Perhaps surprisingly, Lincolnshire's population increased at a rate substantially above the national average between 1901 and 1971 (Table 2.2). The main reason for this must be that industrial development began late compared with many areas in the Midlands and the north, and continued in a relatively healthy way until well into the twentieth century, benefitting from good labour relations, and from locations suitable for expanding industries. Since the late sixties, Lincolnshire's economy has been less buoyant, because the absence of a large regional city means that many service activities are difficult to attract, while the county is too far north to have obtained large shares of what is now commonly called hi-tech employment. The accent is, rather, on

placed near the prison, over an open area of allotments and old quarries. In the south-west (bottom left) corner the estate village of the Ellisons at Boultham, west of the R. Witham, has succumbed to suburban development. In the south-east corner, the Sibthorps' village at Canwick is still countrified (see also Fig. 2.4). Source: Luftwaffe, courtesy Ruston Gas Turbines.

Fig. 2.4 Canwick residences 1969. Oblique aerial view of part of Canwick village 1969, facing south, i.e. the opposite way to Fig. 2.3. In the centre, houses had been built in the Dower House grounds and other new houses of the previous 15 years are seen especially on the top and bottom edges of the photo, in large plots sold off by Jesus College, Oxford, who followed the Sibthorps as owners in 1938. Other houses have now filled up practically all the empty spaces, including the Canwick Hall kitchen gardens near the church, rented by A.W. Mills as a market garden 1945-65, following the conversion of the Hall (off photo left) into flats. Source: *Lincolnshire Echo*.

tourism and retirement. In the latter context, one of Lincolnshire's attractions has been its relatively low house prices, but this situation has been modified in the last few years, owing to the extension of long-distance commuting to the south-western corner of the county as train services to the south have improved.

In addition to comparing Lincolnshire and the whole country, Table 2.2 shows the generally northward drift of population within the county. Holland's low population increased by only 36 per cent, Lindsey's bigger population by 82 per cent. Kesteven's average increase owes much to rapid growth in the villages around Lincoln, counterbalancing declines in some rural areas. Lindsey also combines villages that have actually lost population with areas of very rapid increase, notably Scunthorpe, which achieved five-fold growth between 1901 and 1971. Uneven population change has been one of the many problems faced by local government administrators, as is shown in the field of education (chapter 10), where falling roles and overflowing schools

Fig. 2.5 Grimsby council houses c. 1921. Houses under construction in Milton Road, Grimsby about 1921, marking the birth of Nunsthorpe municipal estate, planned to have 1,000 houses, schools and recreational services. The 128-acre site had been bought from the Earl of Yarborough in 1919 for £19,200, a project typical of large councils striving for economies of scale. Notice that slates were still being used on roofs and that the scaffolding is still wooden, but the concrete fence post had made its appearance. Source: Grimsby Central Library; caption: based partly on Boswell and Storey, Vol. I.

have sometimes been almost simultaneous problems in different areas.

Rapid industrial growth in north Lincolnshire has also led to rapid urban growth, but the latter is difficult to measure for lack of clear definitions of 'urban' and 'rural'. The one exception is the Scunthorpe area, where phenomenal growth of population occurred within boundaries which effectively remained the same over the seven decades. In other areas, however, a very large part of the growth associated with a town's expanding employment opportunities was absorbed in nearby areas defined as 'rural' for local government and census purposes.

This explains why in Table 2.2 'rural' population growth is almost the same as 'urban' growth, Scunthorpe excepted. Several towns, notably Boston, Cleethorpes, Grantham, Grimsby, Lincoln, and Louth (Appendix, Table 1), were able to extend their boundaries for purposes of suburban growth, but commuting has effectively extended the residential areas of all towns far out into the countryside (Figs 2.3, 2.4 and 2.5). This has led to crises of identity for many rapidly expanding villages, which have clung to their historically separate and self-sufficient image in the face of absorption into the economy of the nearby town. This absorption has been a two-way process, with inhabitants born locally exchanging rural for urban jobs, and townspeople moving out into 'the country' in preference to contiguous suburbs.

Table 2.3 summarizes some of the evidence for the growth of commuting. As early as 1921, 8.6 per cent of the workforce made their way into the town from a rural home each day on foot, by bicycle, by bus or train, or rather rarely in their cars. Despite considerable extensions to town boundaries, the comparable 1971 figure was 34.6 per cent, four times as high, while the absolute figures had increased by nearly five times, and very large numbers of people were now travelling by car. The highest proportions were found in the case of Sleaford, where large numbers worked at the headquarters of the Kesteven County, East Kesteven Rural District, and Sleaford Urban District Council offices, while no boundary extensions had occurred. Scunthorpe's case is also interesting, its industrial growth setting up very substantial inflows of workpeople as early as 1921, despite an enormous growth of housing within the town boundaries.

Table 2.3 *Journeys to work in 1921 and 1971: selected towns*

Town	1921		1971	
	Workers enum'd outside town	As % of workforce	Workers res. outside town	As % of workforce
Boston	1,368	17.8	5,330	38.7
Gainsborough	763	9.1	2,250	29.2
Grantham	1,126	13.2	3,500	27.0
Lincoln	2,623	8.6	13,860	35.1
Louth	259	6.7	1,430	28.0
Scunthorpe	2,761	20.3	14,620	34.6
Skegness	255	8.0	1,370	24.6
Sleaford	331	3.7	1,870	45.0
Spalding	498	8.4	3,650	37.0
	9,984	median 8.6	47,880	median 34.6

Sources: Census of England and Wales 1921: Workplaces; Census 1971 England and Wales: Workplace and Transport to Work tables.

In addition to these inward flows, reverse flows outwards from a town have also become part of modern life, and are well represented in the Grimsby area, where large numbers of commuters have travelled from Cleethorpes to Grimsby and from Grimsby to Immingham and the Humber Bank over many years.[2] More recently,

Peterborough has drawn for its growth on work people in such south Lincolnshire towns as Stamford, Bourne, and Market Deeping. Furthermore, in this age of car travel, it is no longer possible to think even of an isolated town like Horncastle being self-sufficient in employment terms: as early as 1966, 22 per cent of the working population of Horncastle was employed outside the town, two-thirds of the 350 people concerned going outside the large area within the boundaries of Horncastle Rural District.[3]

Table 2.4 *Late Victorian male occupations in three rural areas*

Occupational group	Pinchbeck 1881 No	%	Heckington 1871 No	%	Barnetby 1881 No	%
Farmers, cottagers bailiffs, mkt gdners, etc	144	15.9	73	14.5		
Agricultural labourers, shepherds , horsemen, etc.	493	54.3	250	49.7	(incl. farmers etc.) 301	63.2
Trades/craftsmen	146	16.1	133	26.4	90	18.9
Professions, managers	15	1.7	12	2.4	9	1.9
Railway workers	21	2.3	*	*	46	9.7
General labourers	40	4.4	9	1.8	*	*
Miscellaneous	49	5.4	26	5.2	30	6.3
Totals	908	100.1	503	100.0	476	100.0

*Not separately distinguished

Sources: Reworked from Barnetby-le-Wold WEA, *Aspects of the history of Barnetby-le-Wold 1766-1901*, 1983, p. 100 (includes Barnetby, Kirmington, and Melton Ross); Pinchbeck Local History Group, *Pieces of Pinchbeck, No. 2*, WEA Spalding Branch, 1984, pp. 26–7; M. Woods (ed.), *Heckington in the 1970s*, Heckington Village Trust, 1981, p. 3.

Changes in the relationship between workplace and home have brought about corresponding changes in the class structure of urban and rural communities, the former traditionally the home of the middle classes, supplemented in the nineteenth century by factory artisans. By contrast, the country areas were the home of the gentry, farmers, country craftsmen, and, above all, a large mass of agricultural labourers. This early twentieth century urban-rural contrast can be discerned in the county directories, with their long lists of professional men in towns, to be compared with no more than the parson, schoolmaster, and a few retired farmers listed as 'private residents' in each village, and the squire where there was an estate big enough to sustain such a position. The census enumerators' books give a more accurate picture for the period up to 1881, the last date for which they are available. In the absence of fundamental changes between 1881 and 1900, they may be taken as a broad indication of the position at the beginning of our period, if we allow for a faster fall in the numbers of village trades/craftsmen and farm labourers than of farmers.

Despite some inconsistencies of classification, the figures in Table 2.4 demonstrate very clearly the occupational and social structure of three large Lincolnshire villages, one each in Holland, Kesteven, and Lindsey, in the late Victorian period. Agriculture dominated the scene even more than its near two-thirds share of the male workforce suggests, since many of the trades/craftsmen were also servicing it in such occupations as blacksmithing, wheelwrighting, and the building trades. At the other extreme was a mere two per cent of males who Pinchbeck 1881 could be classified as middle class. Even if one adds a proportion of the more prosperous farmers and tradesmen, it is clear that the higher income groups were very modestly represented.

For the recent period it is impossible to obtain comparable local data, owing to the 100-year confidentiality rule relating to census forms, but the contrast can be made clear in other ways. For example, for Mareham-le-Fen and Corby Glen local surveys indicate the proportions of occupied people working outside their parishes. The Parish Council survey at Mareham, carried out at the time of the 1971 census, recorded 133 men and women in full- time jobs in the parish or within half a mile of the boundary, compared with 139 working outside, many of whom would be professional or managerial workers.[4] Similarly, David Steel's survey at Corby in 1975 revealed that 52 per cent of working men and 36 per cent of working women were employed outside the parish.[5] As neither Mareham nor Corby is a typical 'commuter village', being remote from large centres of employment, there must be far greater proportions of commuters in many large dormitory villages.

Data on car ownership provide a clearer indication of the changes in class structure. Thus, for instance, in Table 13 of the 1966 census, 68 per cent of Grimsby households did not possess a car, compared with only 40 per cent in the Rural Districts of Lindsey. Some of this contrast would be due to differences in the availability of public transport, but a larger part was probably due to income differentials, a point borne out by parallel differences in the distribution of two-car households. Whereas 9.7 per cent of the rural households had more than one vehicle, the figure was only 3.9 in Grimsby. Similarly in Holland 11 per cent of rural households had more than one car, compared with only 6.5 per cent in Boston and Spalding. In these two towns 53 per cent of households had no car, but in the surrounding countryside only 37 per cent were without, a remarkably low figure given the number of elderly and other persons not able to drive.

It is even possible to trace a class difference between villages of different size. Thus, in the Women's Institute survey of car ownership in rural Lindsey in 1971, an average of about 12 per cent of households owned two cars in 75 small villages containing 70 or fewer households, whereas in 18 larger villages the percentage was only about seven.[6] These differences can be related to the poor bus services of many small villages, and to the absence there of large housing estates containing properties in the lower price brackets.

The most direct contrast to the information on class structure given in Table 2.4 is to be found in Table 2.5, which summarizes the distribution of the population between the manual and non-manual classes, i.e. between the 'working' and 'middle' classes. Local authorities have been arranged in rank order by the percentage of their male employed populations classified as non-manual, and it will be seen that all the rural areas appear higher up the table than all the urban areas.

Table 2.5 *Class composition of Lincolnshire populations, 1971*

Local Authority areas	Percentages of employed population	
	Non-manual	Manual
Kesteven Rural Districts	36.0	64.0
Lindsey Rural Districts	33.5	66.5
Holland Rural Districts	33.0	67.0
Kesteven towns (MBs and UDs)	31.8	68.2
Holland towns (Boston, Spalding)	31.4	68.6
Lincoln (County Borough)	29.1	70.9
Lindsey towns (MBs and UDs)	26.4	73.6
Grimsby (County Borough)	24.0	76.0

Source: Economic Activity County Leaflets, Lincolnshire, Census 1971, reworked and summarized from Table 4. Males by area of usual residence and socio-economic class (10 per cent sample).

Far from the rural areas having a manual-class preponderance as in 1900, the trend has actually carried them not merely to comparability with urban areas, but has taken them to a point where they are now more middle class than the towns. In so far as the process of suburbanization is one of the movement of the middle classes away from town centres, this table supports other evidence that the process has gone far out into the countryside, as defined by the Rural District boundaries in use up to 1974. It is also one of the principal reasons

why the new local government structure minimized the old distinction between urban and rural. Finally, this table and other evidence
assembled in this chapter suggest that social change since 1900 has
been much greater in the the rural areas than in the towns.

HOUSING CONTRASTS

These changes in class structure are now followed through into a
study of housing, the growth of commuter villages, and the related
changes in household structure that have taken place since 1901. In
Lincolnshire, as generally throughout the country, this century has
seen a very large growth in the owner-occupation of homes, even
before the sales of council houses began in more recent years. There
has been a corresponding decline in the amount of privately rented
accommodation. In 1971 the proportion of houses in owner-occupation hardly differed between the urban areas of Lincolnshire, where
it stood at 52.5 per cent, and the rural districts, where the figure was
slightly higher at 54.7 per cent. However, these figures do not provide
an indication of trends, which can be studied interestingly from the
rather different standpoint of the Housing Returns.

Up to 30 June 1966, the Ministry of Housing and Local Government
published returns of the construction of new houses, including
cumulative figures from the starting point of April 1st, 1945. The accent in the first few post-war years was on building by local
authorities. Despite this boost to the stock of council houses, by 1966
wide disparities had grown up between different local authorities in
the proportions of new houses being built in the local authority and
private sectors respectively. Taking all the Lincolnshire urban
authorities together, 60 per cent of houses built between 1945 and
1966 were constructed by or for local councils. In the Rural Districts
the situation was almost exactly the reverse, 59 per cent of new houses
having been built by the private sector. While the match between
owner-occupation and private sector building was not exact, the
relationship is close enough to sustain the conclusion that the wave
of building in commuter villages was very largely associated with a
faster spread of owner-occupation than in the towns, as also certain
rural areas less affected by commuting (see Appendix, Table 3).

Thus, for example, in Grimsby. 60 per cent of new houses were built
for the council, compared with 41 per cent in middle class Cleethorpes, and only 26 per cent in the Grimsby Rural District, where the
decline in the farm work force was depressing the demand for working class housing to rent, tied cottages being provided for many of
those remaining on the farms. A similar situation developed in the
Lincoln area, where only 22 per cent and 26 per cent, respectively, of

new houses built between 1945 and 1966 in the Welton and North Kesteven Rural Districts were council houses, compared with the massive proportion of 72 per cent in the city. Here the council built enthusiatically, and there was a shortage of building land before the sites of brickyards on Bracebridge Lowfields (Brant Road) and the site of Skellingthorpe aerodrome became available. In some rural areas, however, private housebuilding failed to reach the same levels as that of district councils, including the Caistor and Isle of Axholme districts in Lindsey, East and West Kesteven, and all three rural districts in Holland. An interesting future study could be based on the interaction between housing and political life: did country areas reinforce the habit of voting Conservative by accepting middle-class housing, or is the story more complicated than that?

Table 2.6 *Growth of population in Grimsby and Lincoln areas*

| Area | Population | | Increase 1901–71 | |
	1901	1971	No	%
Grimsby	63,138	95,540	32,402	51.3
Cleethorpes	12,578	35,837	23,259	184.9
Grimsby and Cleethorpes	75,716	131,377	55,661	73.5
Villages within six miles of centre of Grimsby	5,502	34,238	28,732	552.2
Lincoln	48,784	74,269	25,485	52.2
Villages within six miles of centre of Lincoln	13,590	48,980	35,390	260.4

Source: Census Reports 1901 and 1971.

The growth of the commuter villages in the Lincoln and Grimsby areas deserves some further analysis, and is summarized in Table 5, with more detail in Appendix, Table 4. A six-miles-radius from both main town centres has been used, but this is purely arbitrary. Some villages outside this limit, such as Metheringham, near Lincoln, experienced rapid growth. Conversely, some villages such as Riby, near Grimsby, witnessed a decline despite being within the limit. Out of a total population increase of nearly 85,000 in the Grimsby area between 1901 and 1971, nearly 29,000, or one third, occurred in the villages not absorbed within town boundaries. This rural growth, however, was from a very low base, with the result that the population at the later date was over six times that at the earlier date. The impact was felt especially at Immingham, which absorbed a growth of 10,000 people, but this is largely due to the semi-independent growth of economic activity on Humberside. Waltham and Humberston added about 6,000 each, and between 500 and 2,000 were added at Healing, Holton-le-Clay, Keelby, Laceby, and Tetney. The other nine villages in the area either lost population or grew much more modestly, owing largely to an absence of services, and an unwillingness of landowners to part with land, followed in post-1945 years by planning controls.

The Lincoln area was rather different because here rural growth exceeded urban growth in absolute numbers, although since it started from a higher base percentage change was about half as great as in the Grimsby villages. Nevertheless, North Hykeham, like Immingham reached the size of a town, with 9,551 people in 1971, where there had been only 551 in 1901. Bracebridge Heath, Cherry Willingham and Nettleham absorbed over 2,000 each; and Branston, Dunholme, Heighington, Saxilby, Skellingthorpe, Washingborough, and Welton all experienced population growth of over 1,000. Scampton and Waddington can be added to this list if families in RAF married quarters are included. A further 21 villages absorbed lesser amounts of growth, except for South Carlton and Burton which declined.

In other parts of the county there are further examples of large scale suburban growth, such as the increase in population from 162 in 1901 to over 1,000 at Londonthorpe, near Grantham; and from 627 to 3,385 at Wyberton, near Boston. However, apart from the special case of Scunthorpe, where there was also a massive percentage increase within the town boundaries, it was villages in the Lincoln and Grimsby areas which bore the brunt of suburbanization, which began after the first world war, but took on a new dimension after the second, with the growth of car and home ownership.

Away from the larger towns, a falling behind in population rather than suburbanization has been the trend over many decades of this century. Actual depopulation has been limited to a relatively small number of villages; much more widespread has been the problem that population has not grown at a rate equal to the national and county increases in population. The consequences have been that while larger populations are now required to sustain a village grocery store or a village school than was the case in 1901, many villages have suffered from relative decline. This is an important background factor in the context of the location of new factories, problems of passenger transport, education, the RAF as employers, and the quality of rural life, all of which are discussed in later chapters.

Outside the towns, much of the planning effort in the post-1945 period went either into the development of commuter villages in a

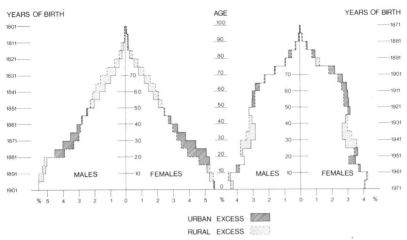

Fig. 2.6 Lincolnshire population pyramids, 1901 & 1971. The broad base and regular shape of the 1901 pyramid represent a population containing many children and few old people, and reflect gradual declines in birth and death rates over several preceding decades. The rural population is ageing, as shown by the stippling at ages above 50, but the towns are youthful and are especially attractive to girls and young women who lacked jobs in rural areas. By 1971 the broad base had gone and the upper reaches of the pyramid have widened out as more people survive into old age. The 'waist' effect is the result of sharp falls in the birth rate between the wars, partly attributable to the loss of many young men in the first world war. Following the second world war there were 'bulges' in the birth rate, notably in 1946-51 and 1961-66. The towns had an aging population in 1971, as young married couples born between *c.* 1925 and *c.* 1945 established themselves in new housing in rural districts in disproportionately high numbers. Source: drawn by J. Peacock, based on an original by Mrs J. A. Mills from data in the 1901 and 1971 Census Reports for Lincolnshire.

coordinated fashion, or into the problems of rural depopulation. Thus, for instance, in 1966 the Lindsey Planning Department carried out a special study of south-east Lindsey, where low and declining population levels were identified as a major problem for many villages: indeed, in the whole of the Spilsby Rural District there was a net loss of 710 people between 1955 and 1965, representing 3 per cent of the population at the earlier date. South East Lindsey, which had a civilian population of 90,000 in 1955, gained by only 2 per cent over the next decade, and one consequence of this stagnation was to be seen in the age structure of the population, in which 40.6 per cent were 45 and over, compared with only 35.9 per cent in Lindsey as a whole. A stagnating population is also an aging population, with less vigour, enterprise, and productivity.7

At first it may seem difficult to reconcile this picture of stagnation with another picture of very widespread house-building throughout the peacetime years of this century, at least outside the very smallest villages and hamlets. One reason is that the housing stock is in constant need of renewal, and with the general rise in standards of housing in this century, this process has become more conspicuous, as cramped terraces of workers' cottages, often with small gardens, were replaced by large semi-detached council houses on the outskirts of villages, set in large gardens. Increased national prosperity has led to an increase in the number of families with two homes, the second one commonly situated in a rural county like Lincolnshire, thus potentially increasing the demand from the permanent population of the county for additional housing, though often in a different location.

Moreover, there was a fall in the average numbers of persons per household, from 4.4 persons per inhabited dwelling in Lincolnshire in 1901, itself a fall on the Victorian national averages of 4.5 to 5.0 persons. In 1971 the comparable figure for the county was 2.9 persons per household, a decline of two-thirds on 1901. Put another way, had the population not increased, there would still have been a need to build half as many houses as stood in 1901.

This dramatic fall in household size was brought about by falls in both the birth and the death rate, a decline in the number of domestic servants and living-in employees, and an increase in the number of young people and others setting up house as single persons. Figure 2.6 summarizes some of the effects of changes in birth and death rates and brings out the contrasts between urban and rural areas. The age-sex pyramids of 1901 are much more broadly based than those of 1971, indicating large numbers of children rather than large numbers of people over 65, many of the latter living in one- and two-person households. The irregular shapes of the 1971 pyramids also reflect fluctuations in the birth rate, with very low rates in the inter-war period followed by two post-1945 'bulges'. Urban-rural comparisons show that the rural population of 1901 was already ageing as compared with that of the towns, but in the 1971 pyramids this trend in areas of stagnating population has been more than offset by the outward flow of young families from towns proper into the semi-urban commuter villages.

This chapter has summarized some changes in the distribution of employment in Lincolnshire. Demand for labour led to increases in the total population at a faster rate than the national average, and its location has redistributed it, with most gains occurring on south Humberside and around the larger towns of central and south Lincolnshire, notably Lincoln, Grantham, and Boston. Improvements in living standards, including the decline in the size of households, have also contributed to an outward growth of the towns, both in contiguous suburbs, often embraced by towns through boundary changes, but also on a very large scale in commuter villages, whose geographical separation from towns has been assured by the structure plans of the county planning authorities. Town and country are no longer almost different worlds as they were when Victoria died, but although agriculture is no longer such a dominant form of employment, it is logical to look at it next.

Bibliographical note

Population and employment statistics form the basis of this chapter, but it has made use of only a tiny fraction of the data available. The main employment sources are listed in note 1, where the data are available on a national basis, county by county. The Census of Great Britain, undertaken every tenth year since 1801, with the exception of 1941 and with the addition of 1966, is available in a series of national reports, supplemented by county reports and, in the case of the 1971 and 1981 censuses also by small area datasets available in a machine-readable form. Census schedules filled in by household heads include questions about age, sex, marital status, employment, journey to work, educational qualifications, migration and housing, and the data generated from the answers finds its way into many planning reports, which are also to be found in the Central Libraries at Grimsby, Lincoln, and Scunthorpe.

Notes to Chapter 2

1. Based on Appendix, Table 1 and C. H. Lee, *British regional employment statistics 1841–1971*, Cambridge, 1971. Other important sources in this field are P. Deane and W. A. Cole, *British economic growth 1688–1959*, Cambridge, 1962; B. R. Mitchell, *European historical statistics 1750–1970*, New York, 1976; B. R. Mitchell and P. Deane, *Abstract of British historical statistics*, Cambridge, 1962; and B. R. Mitchell and H. G. Jones, *Second abstract of British historical statistics*, Cambridge, 1971. In using these sources I have attempted to provide as much direct comparison as possible over the period 1901–71, but readers should be aware of the differences between those listed in censuses and elsewhere as 'economically active' and the insured or employed population. The difference is especially wide in agriculture because of the large number of farmers, who are economically active, but self-employed. The building industry is also much affected. See also Chapter 3, p. 51 for additional assessment on agricultural employment.
2. See, for example, Lindsey C.C., *Report of the Survey, Town Map Areas: Immingham and Humber Bank and Cleethorpes, Humberston and Waltham*, nd. but c. 1953, p. 17.

3. Lindsey C.C., *South-East Lindsey Study*, 1967, p. 38.

4. *ex info.* Peter M. Trafford.

5. D. I. A. Steel, *A Lincolnshire village: the parish of Corby Glen in its historical context,* London, 1979, p. 220.

6. *Ex info.* Mrs. C. Elcoate, Linwood, Market Rasen: 3,030 households surveyed in the smaller villages, 3,529 in the larger villages.

7. Lindsey C.C., *South-East Lindsey Study,* 1967, *passim.*

CHAPTER 3

AGRICULTURE

B. A. Holderness

Abstract *After a general introduction the author discusses trends in Lincolnshire farming up to c. 1973 (the date of Britain's entry into the Common Market) on the basis of abstracts from the returns of crops and stock. Attention is particularly focussed on the period up to the second world war, the latter being the subject of the third section, followed by the new or 'third agricultural revolution'. In the fifth and sixth sections, the agricultural workforce is described and the organization of their interests in and by the NUAW and the NFU is discussed. A brief section on the tenure of farm land precedes a final section on the marketing and processing of agricultural produce.*

Agriculture is easily the largest industry in Lincolnshire. In the first three-quarters of the century its characteristics changed substantially, but since Lincolnshire has remained essentially a rural county, cultivation of the soil is still the main activity. Among the most astonishing changes has been a vast increase in output. In real terms agricultural production increased perhaps fivefold between 1901–05 and 1971–75. This expansion occurred in a period when employment in the industry declined by 50 per cent.[1] These changes did not occur at a steady rate. Indeed the period can be divided broadly into two phases, *before* and *after* 1940. Before the second world war production did expand, but very modestly, partly as a result of wartime measures in 1914–19 not entirely lost in the following recession, and partly as a result of adjustment in production schedules, emphasizing wheat, potatoes, sugar-beet, and vegetables after 1920. But the greatest change occurred after 1940, in the era sometimes called the Third Agricultural Revolution, when price guarantees, improvement grants, mechanization and scientific research together with better advisory and educational opportunities and a better-constructed system of marketing, combined to bring about both agricultural prosperity and consumers' plenty.[2]

The experience of agriculture in Lincolnshire depended upon the condition of the soil and the utilization of the land (Fig. 3.9, p. 66). The broad differences that existed between upland, clays, and fenland from very early times became less pronounced after the second world war when almost all farms prospered under the plough, but in the earlier period it was of great significance to farmers whether they occupied good silt, heavy Oxford clay or thin, parched chalk. Rider Haggard, who toured the country in 1901, found that many landowners, farmers, and bankers in Lincolnshire were as despondent as their fellows in other arable counties. Wherever he went on Heath, Wold or heavy clay similar complaints about the profitless present and uncertain future of agriculture were voiced; but on the peat and silt soils prospects were evidently better.[3] He cites several cases of farmers diversifying their production to meet new opportunities. Haggard's tour occurred after the worst years of the late Victorian depression had passed. It was still evident that farming in the old way in the uplands was frequently unremunerative but difficult to change, since basic fertility depended upon the combination of sheep and turnips to produce adequate crops of barley, which in a good year could still pay, because of demand from the maltsters, but which was a very limited crop not easily replaced by any alternative.

Apart from the changes wrought by war conditions between 1915 and 1920, these complaints from the old cereal-growing heartlands of eastern England continued until the late 1930s.[4] Nevertheless, as we shall see, adjustments did take place in the uplands during the long depression. Haggard confirmed that land was easier to let to small farmers than to the large capitalist entrepreneurs who had dominated the region before 1880. This trend was still apparent to John Bygott a generation later, but he added that on several remote, light-soiled holdings the opportunity to break them up did not exist and deep in the middle Wolds there were farms that had deteriorated since their mid-Victorian hey-day.[5] Part of the answer therefore was to reduce commitments, to spend less on labour and to allocate more of the routine work of farming within the family. The hard-working two-horse farmer on the uplands may have remained poor, but he survived better, even when the opportunity for diversification was restricted.[6]

In the lowlands also, working, as distinct from managing, landholders seem to have enjoyed better prosperity than the relatively few large occupiers. The advantages that the lowlands enjoyed were in the wider choice of marketable crops and in more productive permanent grass, which in some parts of the clays led to a revived interest in commercial dairying. But the best way to examine these adjustments to Lincolnshire agriculture is by way of the annual agricultural returns.[7]

TRENDS IN LINCOLNSHIRE FARMING TO c. 1973

The change in crop preferences through time are set out in Table 3.1. In the pre-war period the drift away from arable production was muted. The area devoted to arable declined between 1903 and 1937, from 0.97m. acres to 0.93m., but the trend was upward after 1937 and the gains made for tillage during the war were largely retained afterwards. In 1953 there were 1.2m. acres in arable production, a level more or less maintained during the next twenty years. Cereal production declined before the war, but by less than the fall in the area sown to wheat, barley, oats, and rye owing to somewhat improved yields. After the war the cereal acreage expanded steadily from the high point already reached by 1944.

Table 3.1 *Selected agricultural statistics, Lincolnshire 1903–73*

	1903	1925	1937	1953	1965	1972
Arable crops ('000 acres)						
wheat	136.6	183.6	235.6	248.7	245.7	366.3
barley	211.3	174.3	101.3	200.5	384.7	388.9
oats	139.2	114.1	83.3	78.1	27.1	32.8
rye	3.0	n.a.	n.a.	n.a.	n.a.	n.a.
potatoes	75.2	119.1	112.2	106.6	111.5	88.7
sugar beet	n.a.	7.2	54.9	72.7	84.9	89.9
perm. meadow	104.7	98.6	120.5	(perm. grass)		
temp. meadow	95.2	94.9	90.9	332.9	250.0	193.8
perm. pasture	400.1	411.0	424.5	(temp.grass)		
temp. pasture	89.6	60.8	43.4	153.6	145.1	107.9
Livestock ('000s)						
cattle	249.9	259.4	238.7	266.1	241.9	207.7
sheep	1,012.0	672.9	536.7	308.3	483.9	279.8
pigs	134.8	139.3	208.9	175.7	242.3	291.8

Source: *Annual Agricultural Returns (Statistics) of England and Wales* (HMSO for MAFF for dates as above)

The figures suggest that Lincolnshire adjusted painfully but successfully to new patterns of demand after 1880. New opportunities favoured the fens, but even in the uplands there was some movement in response to these new markets. John Bygott, whose connections with the substantial Victorian yeomanry of the county were close, recognized that adversity was a flexible term and that in 1928,

Fig. 3.1 Spalding cattle market c. 1900, when it was an informal business still carried on in the street, a practice that was beginning to disappear. Cows at this date still kept their horns, as they were still to do for another half century. This photo was issued as a postcard. Source: D. N. Robinson.

approaching the nadir of the twentieth-century recession, diversification could still be achieved in some light-soiled districts.[8] The decline of barley production and of the number of sheep, in a county long famous for both, underlines the slow decay of traditional upland regimes. The increase in the acreage under wheat, especially in Lindsey, even before some protection was introduced in 1935, suggests that even the most embattled farmers were trying to change strategy, since it occurred in the middle Wolds and on the northwestern sands as much as on more suitable soils. Some land fell out of production between 1922 and 1936 and there was a particularly marked increase in 'fallowing' in 1931–33, but the effects of the depression were less acute than many contemporary farmers and landowners professed. It is true that wheat yields and the quality of cereal crops were often poor in the uplands.

The aggregate figures disguise substantial differences between Lindsey and Holland that were exaggerated by the stubborn preference of wold farmers for wheat instead of rye or maslin, which could have been grown more successfully. Moreover poor yields also resulted from the need for upland farmers to economize on fertilizers in the inter-war years, when they possessed fewer sheep. Wheat was preferred because most farmers had few profitable alternatives. Neither sugar beet nor potatoes were believed to thrive in shallow, chalky soil, and the demand for malting barley had declined considerably since 1914. In the circumstances, upland farmers were compelled to maintain a rotational system, including grass leys and roots. Thus they still kept some sheep, although many were increasingly interested in feeding store bullocks as an alternative. The more moisture-retentive soils were often allowed to fall into permanent grass, although the total acreage given over to pasture and meadow only increased by 20,000 between 1903 and 1937, or by just over 10 per cent between 1919 and 1933.

On the fen soils, where much of the new acreage dedicated to fruit and vegetables was to be found, it is difficult to find convincing evidence of depression except briefly between 1930 and 1933. Elsewhere in Lincolnshire, moreover, there were farms that exploited the opportunities of inserting new crops into alternating systems. On the deeper soils of the north Wolds and the Kesteven Heath, potatoes, sugar beet and some other vegetables were grown in the inter-war years.

The clays also retained a considerable proportion of their high Victorian arable acreage in tillage, growing much the same variety of crops as on other good soils: wheat, roots, potatoes, sugar beet, beans and ley-grass. Mixed husbandry on the heavy soils was less dependent upon sheep than upon bullocks and dairy cattle, but except perhaps in a few districts where the liquid milk trade flourished, in the inner marsh and the middle Trent valley, interest in most kinds of livestock does not seem to have increased in the first forty years of the century.

Sheep numbers fell by almost one-half between 1903 and 1937, from over one million to 600,000; cattle of all kinds fell from 250,000 to 239,000 while the number of milking cows remained at about 50,000 throughout the period. Agricultural horses declined slowly from 57,000 to 52,000 (Table 3.1 and Fig. 3.7). On the other hand the number of swine notably increased, from 135,000 in 1903 to 210,000 in 1937. Poultry-keeping was even more buoyant. In 1924, when first recorded, there were about 1.5 million fowls; by 1937 the number had increased to 2.7 millions (although ducks, geese, and turkeys actually declined). The egg trade especially seems to have grown and poultry-keeping provided a living for many small farmers, often on the weakest of soils, as around Woodhall Spa. Until the late 1950s the increase in poultry was not associated with any large-scale demand for fowl meat, which in 1937 was a by-product of the industry. Altogether the livestock statistics do not indicate any substantial transference towards pasture-farming before 1940, for both swine and poultry made minimal demands upon grassland. Some considerable enterprises indeed were actually conducted upon smallholdings.

The shift of advantage towards the small farmer was also reflected in other lines of business. The fenland bulb trade, for example, which had become quite significant by the 1930s, required only about 3,000 acres before the war, but there were apparently several hundred participants in south Holland. The production of fresh vegetables was also closely associated with market gardening, although there were some more substantial landholders interested in growing brassicas and roots. In 1937, however, the total acreage devoted to vegetables other than peas and potatoes did not exceed 4,800 in Lindsey, 3,350 in Holland and 500 in Kesteven. The only considerable enterprises in this area of business were involved in growing peas for canning (13,300 acres) and early potatoes (12,300 acres).[9]

On the eve of the second world war the evidence for renewed prosperity in Lincolnshire was patchy. It was certainly not confined to the silts, but one has to make some allowance for lowered expectations. Farmers who had passed through the depression of 1930–33 were disposed perhaps to feel satisfied with modest improvements in the late 1930s, especially since the government had introduced a series of measures to protect agriculture and remedy some of its defects, such as the completion of de-rating following the Act of 1928, improvements in the flow of agricultural credit and experimental marketing schemes.

Nevertheless, hope and despair were still essentially personal reactions. For some, adversity was a matter of indebtedness or the result of lingering extravagance; for others it was the consequence of a breakdown in the relationship between landlord and tenant; and for others again, it came about through incompetence, disability, or family commitments. By post-war standards, farming in the 1920s and 1930s was a thankless, unremunerative way of life, the average family farmer with 150 acres earning about as much as a skilled industrial worker, but given expectations, it was not uniformly depressed in Lincolnshire.

THE SECOND WORLD WAR

The war wrought profound changes in the practice of agriculture and its social bearings. Preparations to increase the supply of carbohydrate foods had been made before the war in the light of experience gained between 1914 and 1919. In addition, the initiatives of the 1930s in agricultural protection and marketing were exploited to promote and regulate production and distribution when control of the nation's food supply was assumed by the central government. The problem of setting priorities in agriculture was compounded by the dispersed, individualistic character of farming enterprises; it was necessary to bring both the producers and their work-force into the process of planning. The NFU and the NUAW were drawn into the regulation of agriculture to such an extent that the NFU, in particular, almost became an arm of government. Farmers and landowners were allowed to regulate the industry in an unprecedented way, especially through the War Agricultural Committees, which had draconian powers of coercion and sequestration in the wider national interest.

The Lincolnshire committees, farmer-directed and very conscious of the county's importance in the drive to increase the food supply, used their powers sparingly, but farmers who refused or were unable to convert designated land into tillage or to grow particular crops were usually compelled to do so. The so-called 'War Ags.' also controlled much of the subsidy offered for improving or modernizing farm

Fig. 3.2 Land Army girls making silage, Bardney in 1941. As often in this period, the cart has been modernized by replacing the wooden wheels with an old lorry axle and wheels. Two of the women are treading down the hay unloaded from the cart, while the fourth woman is probably carrying molasses to pour on to the hay, as a means of turning it into silage. Molasses was used to sweeten the very green hay that was then turned into silage, whereas today the hay is dried slightly before going into air-tight containers, making molasses unnecessary. Uniform overalls are being won, but the headgear is various. Source: *Lincolnshire Echo.*

undertakings and allocated drainage-pipes, machinery and fertilizers. The necessity of economizing upon many purchased materials, from imported feeding stuffs to chemical fertilizers, in itself imposed limits upon agricultural expansion. Dairying was encouraged because of the great importance of milk in the national diet, but with no great success in Lincolnshire, and other branches of stock-keeping had to be modified or cut back, partly because grassland was converted into arable and partly because purchased feeds were scarce and rationed. The county's feed mills ran at less than half capacity in the war and then only by dint of utilizing whatever could be found to grind; the oil mills were equally underemployed and the maltings depended upon barely adequate and often poor quality supplies of barley.

Another problem was the scarcity of labour. Those employed in agriculture were mostly excused from military service, although there was a steady leaching of farm workers into the Services or into the towns where wages were higher, especially in munitions factories. In this respect Lincolnshire suffered quite badly. Regular hired labour, for example, hardly changed in numbers between 1939 and 1944, although women's full-time employment increased, and the almost 20 per cent increase in land in tillage had to be attended to by mechanization and an expansion of casual labour of which there was an increase of 4,000. The force was augmented by almost 2,000 members of the Women's Land Army (Fig. 3.2) and 1,850 prisoners of war. By 1944, however, farmers all over eastern England were regularly complaining of insufficient manpower to maintain or extend high acreages under the plough or given up to dairy farming.[10]

Agriculture in Lincolnshire prospered, however, and those engaged in the industry gained as much from the combination of protected production and steady inflation of food prices as any group within the economy. Only the 'rentier' landowner had some reason to grieve, since his income from land in tenancy was tightly controlled and did not keep pace with inflation: hence in part the tendency to sell estate land or to take vacant holdings in hand.[11]

The effects of the war in detail can be discovered by comparing the agricultural returns of 1939 and 1944. Arable acreage increased by 17.5 per cent at the expense of permanent grass. There was no great loss of fodder output because of the difficulty of obtaining purchased feeds, but the main change in arable production was in the cultivation of crops for human food. The wheat area increased by 9 per cent; barley 47.5 per cent; sugar beet 36 per cent; potatoes 32 per cent, and other field vegetables 212.5 per cent. In terms of output, the increase between 1937–39 and 1944–46 can be estimated at about 60 per cent

Fig. 3.3 An early combine harvester at Wellingore. Combine harvesters (i.e. reaping and threshing combined) did not make their appearance in real force until c. 1950, but here an early Caterpillar model is at work in 1931 at Wellingore. It is pulled by a Caterpillar tractor, self propulsion coming at a later stage, and three men are necessary to work it, but the 'leading' of corn (Fig. 3.7) and the building of stacks (Fig. 3.5) have been eliminated. The practice of emptying grain into a following tractor trailer had not been adopted, and the sacks on the ground indicate that a heavy lift awaited someone when they were collected. Source: *Lincolnshire Echo.*

for commodities for human consumption. For livestock the pattern is equally clear. Only the number of cattle, including cows in milk (not specifically dairy cows) remained more or less stable during the war at about 250,000. Sheep fell by 220,000; swine, where the decline was steep, from 206,000 to 83,000; fowls almost halved from 2.75 to 1.47 million, sacrificed to tillage and import-saving. But to illustrate the importance of dairying in war-time, milking machines increased from 279 in 1942 to 417 in 1944 and had probably trebled since the war began. As a measure of mechanization in general in the middle years of the war, the number of tractors increased from 7,119 in 1942 to 9,667 in 1944 (Fig. 3.3).[12]

THE 'THIRD AGRICULTURAL REVOLUTION'

The experience of 1920–21, when some farmers believed that they had been betrayed by government after receiving promises of post-war protection, figured largely in the negotiations between the government and the farmers' lobby late in the war and in the early years of peace.[13] But economic circumstances reinforced the will of the Labour administration to retain much of the apparatus of control after 1945. In effect the 1947 Agriculture Act laid down the principles of agricultural planning which continued many war measures into the age of austerity. Production was believed to be vital at almost any cost, partly for strategic reasons but chiefly because shortage of dollars reduced the British consumers' ability to buy abroad. Farmers responded enthusiastically and within five years problems of glut rather than dearth were causing anxiety to the Ministry of Agriculture. In the next twenty years until Britain joined the Common Market in 1973, successive governments attempted to adjust or regulate supply according to need and financial constraints, but the essential promises of the post-war plan were unchanged: to maintain cheap food for the consumer, to guarantee prices to the farmer to secure his prosperity and to provide incentives to modernize, reconstruct or adapt agriculture to new conditions.

Two major initiatives only can be mentioned: in the later 1950s policy switched from price guarantees towards improvement grants in fixing subsidies; and after 1965 the government tried to introduce more extensive social changes by buying out small-scale or elderly farmers in favour of amalgamation, encouraging the spread of cooperation, and extending the range of advisory or supervisory agencies within the industry. One consequence of the end of rationing in 1953–4 had been the resurgence of marketing boards and the creation of new ones, so that the commissions of the late 1960s to oversee home-grown cereals and meat and livestock, although not marketing boards, fitted in a long-established tradition. After the mid 1960s also there was a gradual shift of policy towards EEC objectives, which differed in several respects from the approach of the British government since the war.[14]

Against this background a new agricultural revolution took place. The much more intensive 'high' farming standards encouraged by the war were retained throughout the whole post-war period. The chief constraint upon arable production in the 1940s had been labour shortages. This problem continued into the 1950s, but was gradually resolved by mechanization and amalgamation. This was so successful that the labour force began to decline once more after 1953. Moreover, agriculture in the age of plenty left its mark on the landscape more profoundly than at any time since the early nineteenth century. Very little of the pre-war grassland ploughed in the 1940s fell back into turf. Mechanization and amalgamation, and to a less extent perhaps the decay of the *rentier* estates, encouraged the realignment of farmsteads and hedgerows, countless miles of which had been stubbed out by 1970 in order to promote operating efficiency.

Lincolnshire farmers certainly increased the productivity of their soil and of their livestock to an unprecedented degree. Cereal yields at least trebled in twenty years, milk yields doubled and even the energy value of forage crops went up by perhaps 150 per cent. Chemical fertilizers, pesticides, plant-breeding, the genetic manipulation of livestock and engineering all played a significant part in this revolution. Agricultural chemistry was so highly developed by 1970 that it was capable of producing specific formulations to satisfy the needs of farmers in almost any circumstances, although the temptation remained to rely upon general prescriptions on the grounds of cost and convenience, and this created numerous environmental problems in all the rural districts (Fig. 3.4). Mechanization not only displaced horse- and man-power, but also had become so sophisticated by the late 1960s that specialized machines were employed in virtually every aspect of agriculture.[15]

Changes in crop selection reflect some modification of war-time priorities as new demands, built up after the abolition of controls, allowed farmers more latitude in producing most arable crops. The area

Fig. 3.4 An early crop sprayer near Market Rasen. Crop-spraying is mostly an introduction of the post–1950 era, but there were earlier innovators. Here Mr C. Starbuck, of Payne and Starbuck, agricultural chemists of Market Rasen, is inspecting the spraying of a crop of Redback potatoes with his own product, probably before 1914. There is an example of a horse-drawn sprayer of a different type in Church Farm Museum, Skegness. Source: Lincoln Central Library, Starbuck Collection.

under wheat fell slightly between 1944 and 1953, but despite the re-establishment of world markets in the commodity in the 1950s and its falling international price, the Lincolnshire acreage remained fairly stable until the later 1960s when it began to rise sharply. Output, however, was almost three times greater in 1965 than it had been in 1944. The rising trend in favour of barley that set in after 1939 continued for upwards of twenty years after the war. The area more than doubled between 1944 and 1965, when it approached 400,000 acres, and there it remained until after 1972. Acreages of the other chief crops, potatoes and sugar beet, changed from year to year but remained fairly stable on the trend, which implied a steady increase in output, between the later 1950s and 1972. One explanation of this is the controlled market for both commodities: in the case of beet the British Sugar Corporation imposed quotas on acreage that were usually enforced strictly; and for potatoes the Potato Marketing Board exercised a rather more erratic control over output.

Field vegetables usually occupied between 80,000 and 90,000 acres after 1950. Much of the production was still sent fresh to market, especially brassicas, early potatoes, salad crops, and roots. Canning was a major market, particularly but not exclusively for peas, until it was overtaken by deep-freezing in the 1960s. By that time a good part of the acreage under vegetables had been transferred from the fens to the north Wolds and neighbouring clays around Grimsby. The culture of peas for freezing introduced a new dimension into the business that was soon extended to other appropriate crops. Virtually all the crop was grown upon contract and the large deep-freeze undertakings controlled the harvest to suit their own requirements. By 1970 peas, broad beans, green beans, cauliflowers, brussels sprouts, and some carrots were cultivated for freezing.[16]

Most of the forage or compost crops invaluable to pre-war agriculture had declined by the 1960s and the attempt in the war to stimulate the cultivation of flax had been abandoned before 1950. Bulbs and flowers, which had been replaced with food crops in the war, regained lost ground in Holland by the early 1950s and rose from 6,000 to 9,000 acres between 1953 and 1965 and to 11,500 in 1972. With this important exception, the dominant role of arable farming in post-war Lincolnshire was still to produce high-energy food or feeding-stuffs. The old pattern of mixed husbandry had been modified under pressure of demand for cereals, sugar beet, and potatoes, and livestock tended to play a different role in agriculture, although on some farms the combination of roots, cereals, and sheep remained very tenacious.

Sheep indeed regained some of their popularity on the uplands after 1947. By the mid 1960s there were about 480,000, one fifth fewer than in the mid 1930s, but well up on their number in about 1950. The size of the Lincolnshire cattle herd for long remained on a plateau of 250,000 head, but from the mid-1960s there set in a steady decline to about 200,000 in 1972. Pigs and poultry showed the greatest increase, rebounding quickly from their wartime levels. In the case of poultry the revival began with an expanded demand for eggs, but by 1960 this had already passed its peak and a new impulse was provided by the broiler trade, in both fowls and ducks, which was buoyant throughout the 1960s.

By 1965 Lincolnshire contained 5.75 million fowls and 375,000 ducks which increased by 1972 to 6.5 million and 470,000 respectively. Much of this poultry was managed in large enterprises, and several substantial arable farmers were equipped with great broiler houses in the same way as they operated extensive indoor piggeries or calf-feeding installations. The 1960s was the great age of barley-fed beef, produced from young animals held in confined boxes. Livestock, in other words, remained a major part of high-farming techniques even though the traditional method of field-grazing or close-folding had been superseded or modified by the constant cropping of barley, the surplus of which could be used to fatten the stock and achieve early maturity. To an extent the policy of subsidizing farm building by government grant, extended after 1958, led in the same direction. In the 1960s many farmsteads were partly reconstructed to accommodate both grain storage and drying and new facilities for livestock-keeping. This in turn added another dimension to the fashion for amalgamation, since many of the new 'prairie' farms could be managed from a more or less purpose-built steading.

Needless to say, mechanization of agriculture also progressed very rapidly after the late 1950s. It is not necessarily true that machines displaced men, because in areas near the towns or close to alternative forms of employment, it was the shortage of farm labour that precipitated mechanization. However, once the process had begun it became irresistible. County data on agricultural machinery have seldom been published and are ambiguous in any event, since the number of implements in use is less informative than the horse-power available or the comparative cost of machinery against labour.

Mechanical reaper-binding was already commonplace in Lincolnshire by 1955 although many horse-drawn implements were still in use. Harvesting, however, was not transformed as an operation until combined harvesters, especially the powerful and capacious machines available after about 1960, had become prevalent. Equally, milking machines had been taken up by at least three-quarters of commercial dairymen in Lincolnshire by the end of the 1950s, but numbers actually declined in the next fifteen years as the smaller dairy farms gave up the business. Nevertheless in capacity the remaining equipment was very much more powerful in 1972 than had been the case twenty years before.

Finally, the information about tractors disguises important qualitative changes, including a large increase in horse-power per machine between 1942–44 and 1972–73. Indeed a new machine bought in 1973 was technologically so different from a wartime tractor that we should think of them as distinct kinds of equipment. Hydraulic transmission was the chief means of bringing about this revolution. Altogether the 7,200 tractors in the county near the end of the war delivered at most 100,000 horsepower; at the end of the period there were probably 23,000 farm tractors in use with a capacity of at least 1.6 million h.p. The cheapness of hydrocarbon fuels for most of the post-war period obviously stimulated the demand for diesel-powered traction, which above all else accounts for the immense increase in labour productivity after 1953.[17]

AGRICULTURAL MANPOWER

The manpower of agriculture declined considerably in the first three quarters of the century. It is, however, not easy to measure this

Fig. 3.5 Women harvesters at Kirton End, Boston. A harvest scene photographed for a postcard *c.* 1900, a time when the cult of the sun was still well in the future. The head gear also kept fragments of straw and hay, and insects out of the long hair then fashionable. Skirts were protected by sack bags cut open to wear in a single thickness. Behind the women is a straw/hay elevator used to speed up stack building.

change with precision since the methods of collecting information altered between 1901 and 1971–2. The Agricultural Returns reported on holdings, not occupiers, although there was usually a more consistent method of counting the hired labour force through time. The Census Office has changed the terms of reference for occupations at various times since 1901, and the aggregate figures usually quoted for employment in agriculture, fishing and forestry are particularly misleading for Lincolnshire, given the importance of Grimsby as a fishing port. Total employment in June 1972, full-time and part-time, is set out in Table 3.2.

Table 3.2 *Agricultural employment in Lincolnshire, 1972*

		Full-time	Part-time & casual
A	Farmers	8,520	2,372
	Managers	227	–
B	Family workers M	1,714	339
	F	423	884
C	Hired workers M	11,676	1,114
	F	973	2,038
D	Seasonal workers	–	5,003
Totals		23, 533	11,750

See text for explanation

Leaving aside seasonal workers, fewer than 30,000 people were engaged in farming at the end of the period, and in all probability the necessary work was performed by the employment of less than 25,000 whole-time workers.[18]

For the Edwardian period the categories were rather different, but it is possible to give an estimate of employment equivalent to full-time at about 48,000 people. The unadjusted figures are obviously higher, since many individuals did not work a six-day week of at least 60 hours and some there were, still classified as farmers, who were retired: 1901, farmers, 11,347; their relatives assisting on the farm, 4,198; regular labourers of all kinds, 38,820; machine proprietors and attendants, 715; gardeners and nurserymen, 2,558 (Figs. 3.5 and 3.6).[19]

The figures suggest that the number of hired workers fell further than the farmers. The steady decline in the number of holdings from the 1960s was beginning to show in the records by the early 1970s, but for a long period down to the sample census of 1966 the population

Fig. 3.6 Potato picking at Ashby, Scunthorpe. Gangs are an old established feature of Lincolnshire seasonal farm work. Here a gang of varied ages and both sexes are potato picking at Ashby, now part of Scunthorpe, before 1914. Note the baskets, the sack aprons and the ubiquity of head gear, even if it meant borrowing father's old cap. The man on the right is wearing binder band or leather thongs round his trousers to keep their bottoms off the soil. Source: Scunthorpe Central Library.

of landholders in Lincolnshire ebbed slowly from the high tide of the 1860s, that is to say from over 16,000 to about 12,000.[20]

Even among the agricultural labourers the rate of decline increased from the later 1950s. Mechanization wrought its changes including a simplification of the categories of labour. As the horse disappeared, so the complex classification of horsemen, from the head wagoner downwards, lost its point. Confined service, still largely intact in 1914 and still viable through the inter-war years, vanished after 1940. A big mixed farm in the Edwardian period had been as hierarchical as a man-of-war and labourers who obtained employment on a regular basis differed considerably in the perquisites, terms of contract and payment that they could expect to enjoy.

Tied cottages may already have been a bone of contention, but they also served as one of the more valuable perquisites offered to the confined men. But much of the *raison d'être* of high farming evaporated after the first world war and many farms were economizing substantially upon this labour force after 1922, not least because the farmers and their families did more of the work themselves. Yet until machines made it possible to reduce manpower, or in some instances to substitute casual for full-time labour, the decline in employment could be seen as merely the consequence of depression that would be reversed with the revival of arable production. We have already noted that anxiety about labour supplies surfaced in the second world war, but this proved to be a short-lived problem, as industrial and scientific methods of husbandry developed.

Mechanization, in a sense, reduced the variety of farming operations and therefore made specialization in the old style less necessary. Most hired farm workers were general operatives, except perhaps dairymen, competent to handle machines of several different sorts. The tendency to equality was also encouraged in its first decade or so by the national Agricultural Wages Board, constituted in 1948, since the National Union of Agricultural Workers was opposed to differentials except by age. The real solvent of exclusiveness however must have been the decline in numbers, since a farm that had employed 20 men and boys in 1890 may have had only about 3 regular hired men in 1970. The social change which thus occurred was far-reaching, especially when the farmer himself, his sons and even his wife found it necessary to work as well as to manage their enterprise.[21]

The men (and occasionally women) described as farmers in Lincolnshire have always been diverse in both social and material terms.[22] Throughout the centuries they shared in common a characteristic mobility. Being rooted in a particular place is regarded as a feature of agrarian life, but this is very misleading. Neither the farmsteads nor the families occupying them have been changeless through several generations. There have always been recruitment into the profession, and emigration out of it. Sample surveys of various estate rentals between 1680 and 1914 have shown a turnover exceeding 70 per cent within three generations and of about 40 per cent within two. The historical record suggests that adversity affected the constancy of farm populations, for in periods of low prices, such as 1720–55 and 1815–30, and again after 1880, the turnover of tenancies notably increased.

Given the economic problems of the inter-war years therefore we should expect inconstancy rather than fixity in the occupation of farms. Most of the evidence points in that direction, although there were some fluctuations along the trend. Using information from estate records, directories, and electoral rolls, change in farm occupations was greater in 1879–1902 than it was between 1902 and 1921; it increased again between 1922 and 1935; stabilized until the early 1960s, but then returned to its previous high levels owing chiefly to amalgamations. Much of the evidence for these fluctuations is impressionistic, and cannot be quantified, but for most of the period

until 1961, decline in the aggregate farming population was small.
But before 1960 the changeability of tenures was overlaid by a regular
influx of new men.

Nevertheless, although particular farms changed hands frequently, the filling of vacancies provided little opportunity for real
newcomers into agriculture, since the same farming families populated particular neighbourhoods over long periods, and seem to have
supplied the majority of applicants for vacant farms. This was especially marked at times of land hunger, but it also occurred when
landlords or vendors found it difficult to dispose of land, above all in
the early 1930s, when suasion was needed to convince men that there
were advantages in amalgamation or the exchange of places. But
whereas Lincolnshire farmers may have been geographically mobile,
most remained faithful to the profession of their forebears. A marked
discontinuity in this tradition is noteworthy at the end of the
nineteenth century, when even stable estates such as Lord
Yarborough's and Lord Brownlow's parted company with a high
proportion of their tenants, many of whom belonged to families that
had occupied holdings for upwards of a century. Many writers observed the 'shake-out' of the well-found, rather gentrified
agriculturists of the high Victorian era around 1900, but commented
on the better survival of plainer, less affluent families.[23]

Perhaps the small farmer managed better than the capitalist in the
depression because he had nowhere else to go, except into poverty or
into another form of drudgery. The real determinant of success after
1880, as in the 1920s and 1930s, however, was entrepreneurial competence and adaptability as well as sheer tenacity. Lowering one's
sights, retrenching on personal expenditure, increasing one's own
part in routine husbandry hardly appealed to those reluctant to consider themselves as workers of the soil – for whom 'farmer' was a title
as honorific as that of 'yeoman' in the seventeenth century – and yet
few prospered who did not adopt a more professional way of business
in agriculture.

The large farmer certainly did not disappear between 1880 and
1940. Indeed it was often the case, as in the 1930s, that poor returns
of profit would encourage consolidation in the hope of economies of
scale or at least in the knowledge that land let at virtually any price
was better than land in hand or falling into disuse. A survey of several
villages in the southern Wolds between 1921 and 1940, however, suggests that whereas the number of holdings declined by 10–12 per cent,
there were very few amalgamations except on a temporary basis.[24]
In some instances the large farm remained quite prosperous, for example Riby Grove, where first John Dudding and then Ernest

Fig. 3.7 'Leading' corn at Kettlethorpe. A harvesting scene in the hot summer of 1947. The vehicle is a hermaphrodite cart-wagon, better known as a moffrey. After harvest the front pair of wheels and the platform above would be removed, converting the vehicle into a two-wheeled cart, more suitable for winter's heavy loads, such as farmyard manure and sugar beet. There are examples in the Museum of Lincolnshire Life, Lincoln and the Scunthorpe Museum. Source: *Lincolnshire Echo*.

Addison, continued to attract international attention for the quality of its breeding stock until the early 1950s. But elsewhere great Wold farms, as at Stenigot, Withcall and Lambcroft, survived intact because the land was too poor and the buildings insufficient to permit their dissolution, although tenancies were often difficult to maintain and some land tumbled into rough grazing.[25]

Several fenland farmers expanded into other districts between the wars, no doubt partly because upland farms were cheap, but also because the move offered greater scope for diversification. When potato and sugar beet growing were extended outside the fens, several of the innovators were fenlanders looking for ground not infested with pests such as eelworm.

The difference between 'holdings' and 'enterprises' makes it difficult to discern trends in the pattern of landholding in twentieth-century Lincolnshire. It seems evident that multiple holdings were quite commonplace from comparison of the Census Returns and the Agricultural Statistics but the connection is inexact. Moreover in the 1972 survey of occupation and employment there were seemingly

1000 more 'farmers' than there were 'holdings' in the county. On the other hand, analysis of the unprinted parish returns to the Ministry tends to reinforce the anecdotal evidence that there were fewer enterprises than holdings. For two of the National Agricultural Advisory Service's districts, No. 126 in north-east Kesteven and No. 132 in southern Lindsey (not areas of large farms), the relationship between 'holdings' – the unit of compilation in the returns – and 'enterprises' – i.e. individual undertakings of partnerships – changed from a ratio of 92 enterprises to every 100 holdings in 1922 to 87 to 100 in 1937 and stood at 79 to 100 in 1956. This only changed significantly in the late 1960s by which period the method of compilation had altered again.[26]

Recruitment from outside farming families was always possible but always infrequent. Historians make light of the opportunity for advancement out of wage labour into business. While it is true that few labourers became farmers, Lincolnshire can show several examples of the change at work, particularly on fen soils or in the clays where farms were small and dairying revived at the end of the nineteenth century.[27] Even so, no more than five per cent of Lincolnshire farms under 150 acres, at any period before the first world war, was occupied by men from wage-earning backgrounds. The ancient ladder of opportunity offered by the institution of farm service was partly rotten in the rungs but it could still be scaled with care and good fortune, while the comparative abundance of holdings or plots of ground under 10 acres also provided some assistance to upward mobility.

To what extent the position altered in the inter-war years when sales of farm land increased is difficult to establish. It does appear certain however that many formerly tenanted holdings were acquired by their occupants or by men who chose to farm them in hand. There is no evidence that wage-earners benefited from these changes. Indeed many of the farmers who had bought land before 1921 were hit by the subsequent recession, and with most upon or over the edge of bankruptcy, the enthusiasm for land purchase among agriculturists evaporated. There was, however, a problem, since many of the old land-owning gentry were shedding their estates and tenants found that freeholding was at least a safeguard of their way of life.

Given that land was relatively cheap between 1922 and 1936 in Lincolnshire, especially in the early 1930s when farmers were severely embarrassed by debts and losses, we should expect outsiders to enter the market. Leaving aside the remaining *rentier* estates that changed hands as going concerns, the intervention of newcomers seems to have followed a pattern. Other farmers, either from more prosperous districts like the fens, or from Scotland and the north, are to be found in many parts of the county, buying farm land not always with steadings attached. There was also of course still some amalgamation of holdings by farmers in the neighbourhood. It required courage and foresight to take on upland arable or unimproved clay in the depths of depression, and prices mirrored the uncertainty. Several holdings in the southern Wolds, for instance, changed hands between 1928 and 1936 for £8–16 per acre freehold, a discount of one-half to two-thirds upon prices in average conditions. Land not sold was equally difficult to dispose of. In the same area farms were let sometimes for years without change of rent. In such circumstances the opportunities for outsiders foolhardy enough to try their luck in agriculture were better than at any time in the recent past.

For Lincolnshire we lack an angle of vision from which to estimate the appeal of the land and its deficiencies, for there is no equal of Adrian Bell or Henry Williamson to give expression to this problem.[28] Nevertheless, men whose fathers were clergymen, land-agents, solicitors, businessmen, auctioneers and military officers were drawn into farming in the early twentieth century. Village tradesmen such as innkeepers or blacksmiths were also represented. At the highest level there were a few who became farmers whose fortunes originated in industry or large-scale commerce, although they seldom survived a decade on the land, probably because its social appeal did not match up with harsh reality. It is necessary to point out that more than half the apparent newcomers into agriculture are of unknown origin and no doubt many of them were farmers' sons. However the instability of the farming population is clear enough, as Kelly's Directories for 1922 and 1937 indicate, since the change of surnames exceeded 30 per cent.

In the late 1930s things settled down and during the war control of transactions and a good rate of profit encouraged landholders to remain in business. Indeed most of those who had fallen into debt, not least for land purchase, had been recompensed for their pre-war speculation or folly by 1945. There is little evidence relating to changes of tenure in this period, but from what is known of land sales it seems probable that fixity was characteristic of the 1940s, although the decommissioning of aerodromes after 1945 brought about some changes compared with 1939.

Otherwise little altered until after the end of controls in 1952–3, and the common feature of the next two decades, overriding the trend of consolidation, was the increasing difficulty for outsiders to break into farming. The spread of owner-occupancy and amalgamation reduced to virtually nothing the number of holdings available for new men to settle upon. The evolution of laws protecting agricultural tenancy after 1941 was also important in confirming families in possession of their holdings. Prosperity and confidence after 1940 recreated the conditions of land hunger that were more or less unrequited. If farming in Lincolnshire had not become a closed caste by 1972 recruitment into the ranks of landholders was severely restricted, usually to other farmers' sons or to affluent businessmen.

THE NUAW AND THE NFU

The farmers had always been a more diverse group than is allowed in the conventional division of agrarian society into three classes of landowners, landholders and labourers, in which the social and political lead was taken by the first group which held the second more or less in dependency. Even in the mid-nineteenth century there was by no means a coherently organized Agricultural Interest capable either of speaking in unison or of influencing policy. In any event the old reciprocity of interest changed with the dissolution of the gentry estates. By the Edwardian period it was painfully apparent that farmers would need to organize a lobby on their own behalf. In 1908 a farmer on the border of Lincolnshire and Nottinghamshire, Colin Campbell, was instrumental in founding the National Farmers' Union, which was intended to be more than a shield against organized labour or political interference, but which cut its teeth in meeting these challenges. The Union was more than a Lincolnshire farmers' club by 1914, but its membership and social composition were patchy until the war provided the boost necessary to mobilize agricultural opinion and enthusiasm. The NFU learned much about the politics of agriculture before 1920, but it could not yet speak as the mouthpiece even of Lincolnshire farmers, and its inexperience and slow-footedness were disclosed when the Corn Production Act was repealed in 1921. On the other hand, the Union did play some part in securing the peace-time protection of sugar-beet growing in Lincolnshire and East Anglia. Uncertain as the future may have been, the NFU had established itself successfully by the early 1920s.[29]

By 1925, Lincolnshire was divided into two county branches, rather oddly named Lincolnshire and Holland, and with rather uncertain territorial limits. Membership was high by comparison with Norfolk (2,500 members), Kent (2,600) and Essex (3,767), with 3,625 in Lincolnshire and 1,800 in Holland. Only in the pastoral west of England was membership as dense or more dense as a proportion of all the farmers in each county, since Somerset had 5,578 members and Devon 5,210. It was often alleged of the Union in its first quarter-century that domination of eastern arable interests offered little in the way of advantage to grassland farmers. This is an opinion that requires testing, but the evidence from yearbooks published in the period after the first world war does not support the implication of pro-arable bias. So far as Lincolnshire is concerned, groups interested in cattle and in horticulture provided lively and persuasive lobbies within the organization.

Virtually all new developments in agriculture attracted the interest of the two branches in the country during the inter-war period; support of agriculturists struggling to come to terms with depression was clearly expressed and enacted so far as it lay within the power of the NFU. At county level the work of the NFU was usually advisory or protective of individuals, but the meetings of local branches probably also acted as a means of transmitting new ideas.

The golden age of the NFU was during the 1940s, when in partnership with government and other interest groups it was able to influence or determine policy quite successfully. Membership certainly increased, though whether from enthusiasm or self-protection is difficult to judge. By 1951 the number of members in Holland had doubled since 1925 to 3,921 and in the Lincolnshire County Branch the increase was also substantial, from 3,625 to 5,994. The 1951 census recorded 12,000 farmers in the whole county, so that support for the Union was impressive. This was the high tide of Union membership, although numbers held up very well until the late 1960s when the spate of amalgamations and retirements affected the association quite severely. Lincolnshire farmers, though loyal to the NFU, are regarded, not least by its agents in the county, as especially independent and even self-willed. The NFU retained much of its influence with government until the end of rationing and the 'liberalization' of agricultural policy in the mid 1950s. Since then the Union has resumed as its principal role the professional representation of farmers at various levels from Whitehall to the rural district council, although in presentation of policy the branches have become more reticent than they were in the inter-war years.[30]

Farmworkers too were organized into a trade union by the early years of the century. Nineteenth-century attempts to unionize the agricultural labourer, even including the initiative of some of the larger industrial unions in Lindsey in the 1890s, had proved inconsequential. When in 1906 Norfolk was moved to begin again and in the following three years laid the foundations of the successful National Union of Agricultural Workers, there was some support from Lincolnshire. Richard Winfrey M.P. became treasurer and W. B. Harris was elected to the Committee, but there is little evidence of organization within the county until the first world war. No doubt part of the interest in Holland emanated from the Committee's determination to include smallholders. Domination by Norfolk of the union continued thoughout the war and into the 1920s.

The war saw a great upsurge of membership from 4,300 in 1913 to 53,000 in 1918, although fewer than 10 per cent were apparently situated in Lincolnshire, where the so called Workers' Union was also recruiting energetically. The rather favourable climate for union membership changed after 1920 and the NUAW was eventually driven to strike in Norfolk in 1923 to protect hours of work and defend wage levels under pressure of post-war deflation. In Lincolnshire there were at least two lock-outs in 1922–23, but no large-scale unrest in the county, despite an offer towards the end of the Norfolk strike to bring out Lincolnshire members in sympathy. The failure of the union to beat the employers in 1923 was underlined by its stagnant membership before 1939. On the other hand, the Labour administration of 1923–4 enacted an Agricultural Wages Act to stabilize farm wages and make them more uniform.[31]

The second world war, like the first, stimulated union membership. Nationally it trebled between 1940 and 1947 and the campaign of recruitment was even more successful in Lincolnshire than elsewhere. The late 1940s, however, were the high-water mark in total membership. By 1956 numbers had already fallen to 135,000 and in 1971 the NUAW claimed to have only 100,000 members nationally. Nevertheless this decline was less steep after 1956 than the fall in numbers of agricultural workers, so that in 1971 unions perhaps represented 28 per cent of the agricultural workforce in Lincolnshire by comparison with 22 per cent in 1947.

So far as the county is concerned, the NUAW has lacked the radical cutting-edge apparent for a long period in Norfolk. Disputes have been small and easily contained since the 1930s. Campaigns to restrict the use of toxic chemicals, to reduce accidents on the farm and against the tied cottage certainly touched Lincolnshire, especially in the 1960s, but seldom caused serious turbulence. The NUAW was effective in organizing legal and provident services for its members but the old problem of penetration into a scattered, conservative and individualistic workforce limited the union's influence on affairs. Unlike in Norfolk, its effect on parliamentary representation was negligible and even at county and rural district level NUAW-sponsored councillors were overshadowed by the farmers and landowners.

Wage-rates and hours of employment were certainly contentious, but with the institution of county and, after 1947, of national wage boards, the contest became ritual rather than strenuous, with the employers and employees being concerned to sway the votes of the independent members. It is of course very difficult to generalize about wage trends, especially in agriculture before the war. Too many variables are involved. At different periods there were estimates of average or standard wage rates, not all of which are strictly comparable. However, Lincolnshire farm labourers were reputed to earn 14s 3d per week in 1898, a decline since the heady 1870s but still among the highest rates of pay in England. This had risen to 16s 6d by August 1914, although this did not fully match increased prices. In the war terms of employment were eventually fixed by the administration, so that by October 1919 workers were paid a basic rate for a 50-hour week, which in Lincolnshire was 40s 6d.

Conditions deteriorated in the next five years, the hours of work were bitterly contested and wage levels fell to 31s in Holland and 28s in the rest of the county. The Agricultural Wages Act in the same year tried to correct this downward slide by fixing wages at 36s for a 48 hour week in Lincolnshire (national average 33s), but it was some years before the statute was widely accepted and applied. By 1938 a tendency for wage-fixing to become more standardized within the arable counties resulted in some erosion of the Lincolnshire advantage, for the county rate was 37s 6d against an average of 36s. Wages, like farmers' profits, rose more than the average rate of price inflation during the war and this benefit was continued after 1945. According to the Agricultural Wages Act of 1947 rates were set at 90s throughout the country. There remained some differences in the grades of employee, but the unions were keen to reduce the differentials enshrined in tradition and it was a decade before the debate on incentive payments for skill or responsibility was won by the farmers and their allies. Although the Wages Board prevented a recurrence of 1920–24 it could stop neither emigration from the land nor the steady erosion of agricultural wages as a proportion of industrial rates of pay.

FARM TENURE

One of the most striking features of agrarian society in the twentieth-century has been the increase of owner occupation. At the end of the nineteenth century about 15 per cent of both holdings and land were owned by their occupants. By 1972, 3,432 holdings under one tenure were owned (54 per cent) and the proportion of holdings under multiple tenure in which more than half the land was owner-occupied amounted to 55 per cent. Altogether more than 471,000 acres were owned and 537,000 acres were rented by the farmers of the county at the end of our period. Moreover by 1972 a substantial, but unknown, percentage of the rented land was out of the hands of the old *rentier* or gentry estates. In Edwardian Lincolnshire well over half of the farm land in Lincolnshire was owned by the gentry, perhaps more than three-fifths, and a considerable portion of the remainder belonged to ancient institutions. At the end of the period many of the landowners were business corporations, insurance or financial institutions, public bodies, including the National Trust, as well as family trusts, speculative investors, and the kinsfolk of the occupants.

Several important gentry estates survived throughout the period, almost all much smaller than they had been before 1880, such as Brocklesby, Belton, Grimsthorpe, Hainton, Hackthorn, and Scawsby, where some land was still let out to occupying farmers. In many instances, however, surviving or previous gentry estates, not wholly broken up, were farmed in hand. Several ancient families converted their estates into 500–2,500 acre farms and their business from estate management to practical agriculture, and as such became almost indistinguishable from the richer of the new men who acquired freehold farms in the present century.[33]

The change to owner occupation as the salient feature of modern agriculture was not swiftly accomplished. Several influences were at work after 1880 when the first batch of dispersal sales was set in motion. Landownership retained its social cachet before 1914 but lost many of its political and economic benefits for the *rentier* aristocracy. Yet before the first world war at least as many estates were sold to aspiring millionaires or sportsmen as to their sitting tenants; the institution of landlordship, though diminished, maintained its essential character.

The new Liberalism, manifest in government after 1906, and the constraints and regulations of war-time began to alter attitudes among both landlords and tenants, but the inflation in real estate prices towards the end of the war was the main solvent of the system. Between 1918 and 1920 a great deal of land was sold and many tenants adventured their savings to acquire the freehold of their business. They did not always obtain a good bargain in the heady enthusiasm of the period. When prices broke in 1921 the mortgage debts of many Lincolnshire freeholders became intolerable and some of the gains in owner occupancy were lost even before the locust years in 1930–34. Nevertheless, for many non-occupying proprietors the low prices of the 1920s and early 1930s were in themselves sufficient incentive to dispose of even more land. Tenants and others hoping to enter agriculture were still able to buy farms, albeit sometimes reluctantly, throughout the depression.

The second world war added another dimension since the public accountability of *rentier* estates was even more closely supervised, landlords were under further pressure from the Agricultural Tenancy

Act of 1941 and rents were deliberately restrained by comparison with other agricultural prices. The disjunction between rent and agricultural profitability both increased the tendency for owners to farm on their own account and impelled landlords to get rid of tenanted property. This process of elevating the occupier's interest above the *rentier*'s continued through austerity and into affluence after the war because the chief beneficiaries of the managed economy in agriculture were the producers, at least until the later 1960s. The process had not been completed by 1973. Indeed in some sense it was inhibited by the intervention of outside corporations which invested in land, sometimes for fiscal reasons, and often had the resources to outbid local purchasers. Lincolnshire, however, has several examples of the alliance between corporate finance and farming experience that was a kind of equitable partnership, through which ambitious men starved of capital to expand in agriculture were able to advance themselves and join the circle of large-scale occupiers. Local sampling suggests that by the late 1960s about one-quarter of 'tenanted' land in the county was owned by new corporate investors of various sorts.

MARKETING AND PROCESSING

There is more to agriculture than working the land. Most farmers with mixed enterprises produce food for human consumption, of which much requires processing: cereals, vegetables, sugar, milk, meat, eggs; animal feeding-stuffs, offal, forage crops, feed grain, fodder beet, possibly vegetable oils; industrial raw materials, wool, hide, hoof and horn, possibly flax or hemp; even perhaps specialized products such as animal semen or seeds for nursery use. But farmers are also consumers of a multiplicity of goods and services, veterinary, mechanical, chemical and biotechnical, all of which must be accessible to a dispersed and often specialized market. Agriculture has always maintained close links with other segments of the rural economy such as metal-work and cart-building. Thus at the end of the nineteenth century after a century of industrialization, there were still many services provided for agriculture in all but the smallest of villages.

The twentieth-century agricultural revolution extended the scope of this interdependence by bringing farmers even more intimately into contact with industry and scientific research. The development of large-scale manufacturing based on agriculture commenced even before the beginning of the nineteenth century but the chain was not complete until after the second world war. It is obviously not necessary to locate mills, workshops, or research institutes remote from the farms, for many have been established in villages, but the trend in the agricultural service industries in the past century has been towards national organization. Many small, eminently local firms did survive competition from the giants and in recent years some revival in their fortunes has taken place, but the industries ancillary to agriculture have become dominated by firms such as Spillers, ICI, Fisons, or Associated British Maltsters (ABM). Their network of distribution spread across almost every county in Britain. In other branches a degree of local autonomy or diversity remained even in the 1960s: the Milk Marketing Board, for example, sub-contracted its monopoly in milk distribution to several local firms, and a multitude of potato merchants continued to deal in the produce under the auspices of the Potato Marketing Board.

Before the first world war Lincolnshire contained several manufacturing or processing enterprises that served agriculture in a national context. Agricultural engineering in the age of steam was especially well represented in the eastern arable region with major firms located in Lincoln, Gainsborough, and Grantham. They had already passed the meridian of their prosperity, since demand in farming for heavy and expensive implements of the type produced by Ruston's, Foster's, or Hornsby's was not sustained during the depression after 1880, but most continued in profit at least until 1914. Part of the problem was technological obsolescence. Steam power gradually gave way to other forms of energy such as internal combustion, heavy oil engines, and electric motors and the Lincolnshire firms were comparatively slow to adapt.

It would be unfair to suggest that they were unaware of the changes around them, for almost all responded in some way to new opportunities or by concentrating upon areas of production in which they retained an advantage. In the context of agriculture, Marshall's of Gainsborough was probably the most successful after 1920 since the firm gradually moved over to produce track-laying tractors and other modern agricultural implements. With that exception, it has to be said that in agricultural engineering Lincolnshire moved from the centre to the periphery of the industry before 1939 and the great Lincoln firms at best maintained a vestigial interest in agriculture on the eve of the second world war.[34]

Milling and malting had become organized on an extensive scale by 1914. Flour milling was already largely concentrated in the sea ports, including Grimsby, because of its dependence upon overseas supplies of bread grain. Equally substantial feed processing firms also emerged in the Edwardian period, and further concentration followed. Bibby's from Lancashire and Pauls' of Ipswich were

Edwardian successes with their feeding compounds. In Lincolnshire the long-established oil-crushing mills around the Humber played their part in the development of the new industry. Nevertheless there remained dozens of small mills grinding cereals and pulses for farmers and many farmers also still ground their own surplus grain.

Malting underwent a similar process of concentration in the later nineteenth century. The driving force was the breweries' desire to control their own supplies. Lincolnshire was particularly attractive to the Midland brewery companies such as Bass, Ratcliffe and Gretton which established a large malting at Sleaford. Maltsters unconnected with brewers, however, also flourished in Edwardian Lincolnshire and firms such as Sandars of Gainsborough and Lee & Grinling of Grantham had enviable reputations for the quality of their produce (Fig. 3.8).[35]

Another trade ancillary to agriculture of long standing in Lincolnshire is plant-breeding. W. W. Johnson & Son Ltd of Boston claims to have been founded in 1820 and others made their appearance in the early twentieth century. Equally interesting is the enterprise set up by William Dennis of Kirton which exploited the Edwardian craze for developing new varieties of potato and built up a substantial trade

Fig. 3.8 The Corn Exchange, Lincoln (built 1879), probably in the 1930s. The corn merchants at their desks are considering samples of corn brought in by farmers, who had the chance of going from desk to desk to strike the best bargain. The telephone has changed all that. The room was also used as a cinema, later a roller skating rink, and stands over the fruit market. Source: *Lincolnshire Echo*.

Fig. 3.9 Lincolnshire farming regions. Source: adapted by Dr J. Thirsk, *English Peasant Farming* (Routledge and Kegan Paul 1957), p. 50, from L. D. Stamp, *Land of Britain: The Report of the Land Utilisation Survey of Britain*, pts 76, 77, Lincolnshire, 1942, pp. 481 and 506.

in the product, not least by changing attitudes to the root in British households.[36]

Even as late as 1930 many branches of agricultural production remained fragmented and dispersed. Milk, meat, eggs, and field vegetables and flowers were disposed of piecemeal or by individual enterprise, and the wool trade was very much under the control of West Riding factors whose first consideration was the price and supply of Australian wool. Indeed it could be argued that much of the farm produce of the county was subordinated to international supplies in an era when cheap food was an object of public policy and free trade the preferred means to achieve it.

There were new developments in the inter-war years. Before 1937 sugar refining, canning and jam making made an appearance. According to *Kelly's Directory* for that year, there were five considerable canners or vegetable driers in Holland and at Bardney and three preserve-makers at Louth, Brigg, and Grimsby (Fig. 2.2). Canning was the most significant development. In the fens the various firms processed several different kinds of fruit and vegetables, not necessarily locally grown, while at Bardney the Fosters concentrated on tinning peas, most of which were grown by the family and their neighbours.

The 1937 *Directory* gives a good indication of the range of agricultural service trades available in the county. Everywhere there were still smiths or agricultural engineers who repaired machinery, milksellers, carcass butchers, meal-men and poultry higglers (dealers). Among processors there were still 16 brewers dispersed about the county, all quite small and local, 12 substantial maltsters, situated chiefly in Grantham, Lincoln, Sleaford, and Gainsborough and about half a dozen industrial millers. In addition there were the seedsmen with local trial grounds: Johnson's of Boston, Elsom's of Spalding and Sharp's of Sleaford. Dennis of Kirton was still flourishing and several other produce merchants are recorded in the market towns. Implement-makers and boiler-makers had not disappeared but they were relatively unimportant in the old centres of engineering, despite the success of Marshall's and the profitability of Blackstone's at Stamford. In 1937 finally there were several small-scale processors of veterinary medicines or chemical fertilizers but no firm with a national reputation.

By the 1970s the picture had changed again.[37] The seedsmen were still in place, but much of their produce was imported from abroad or from other parts of Britain, although on a narrow front some plant-breeding continued in the county. Malting had contracted and the whole capacity of the industry was in the hands of ABM at Louth and

Pauls and Sandars at Gainsborough and Grantham. There was only one cannery at Long Sutton, another at Bardney, one preserve-manufacturer at Brigg and two breweries. One new development, the quick-freezing of food, poultry, vegetables, fruit and fish, had taken root all over the county. It originated in Hull and Grimsby, where firms such as Ross Foods began by processing sea fish. Ross and its chief competitors, Birdseye, Findus, and Christian Salvesen, progressed to other kinds of freezing during the 1960s. The culture of field vegetables obviously lent itself to the industry's expansion, since it was not difficult to adapt crops intended for canning or fresh sales to be frozen. Peas were first to be exploited, but they were soon followed by green beans, broad beans, Brussels sprouts, carrots and cauliflower.

In addition, the deep-freeze companies began to preserve manufactured meat products with the same technology. Here again they were well placed in Lincolnshire to obtain suitable raw materials from the wholesale butchers, some of whom began to specialize in the supply of beef, pork, and mutton for manufacturing. Yet the most striking new departure in quick-freezing related to poultry. Although the buoyant broiler trade did not depend upon freezing it gained much from the new technique in the 1960s. Firms such as Cherry Valley Farms Ltd, which had a very large share of the market in frozen ducks, and G. W. Padley & Co. Ltd, which specialized in broiler fowls, played a great part in the consumer revolution of the post-war period. They naturallly enjoyed no monopoly of the frozen poultry trade: firms elsewhere in the country were effective competitors and the large general freezer companies quickly joined in, once the potential of the demand for table poultry had been appreciated.

By the 1960s moreover several of the previously fragmented branches of agricultural production had been organized for large-scale marketing.[38] The Milk Marketing Board after 1955 achieved domination of the liquid milk trade. In Lincolnshire several firms were involved in collecting, pasteurizing, manufacturing and distributing milk and milk products, since the Board preferred not to become directly involved within Lincolnshire. But Clover Dairies Ltd of Grimsby and Willoughby controlled most of the milk supplies from the eastern dairy district along the inner marsh. All sugar was processed by the British Sugar Corporation in factories at Brigg, Bardney, and Spalding (or at Kings Lynn, Newark, or Ely just beyond the county boundaries). An increasing volume of the meat trade was in the hands of the Farmers' Meat Corporation, an example of NFU business enterprise that was highly successful in the 1960s. Finally the bulb and flower business fell more and more under the control of a small group of specialists, often Dutch, who improved the organization of the industry and modernized its chain of supply.

Among the most interesting of Lincolnshire firms on the periphery of agriculture is the Geest Organization of Spalding, which like so many of the businesses set up in Holland (Lincs) in this century floated upon Dutch enterprise and Dutch capital. Jan van Geest began to exploit the demand for Dutch horticultural produce in England in the mid-1930s as an outlet of the family firm in 's Gravenzand. He developed the trade in Spalding before being marooned in Britain during the war, when he had to diversify in order to make up the deficiency of Dutch supplies from what was locally available. Other members of the family were drawn into the business after 1945 and the company flourished and expanded into fields remote from the Lincolnshire fens. The Geest Organization has always been involved in horticulture, even though much of the capital and enterprise were applied to exotica such as the Windward Islands banana trade in the post-war period. Nevertheless the firm is still based at Spalding and the Geests are deeply interested in all aspects of local horticulture and retain vital links with the Low Countries through various east coast ports including Boston.[39]

The links in the chain that connects Lincolnshire agriculture with the economy at large, with manufacturers on the one hand and consumers on the other, have become fewer but stronger in the course of the present century. It is an important part of the new agricultural revolution to consider changes in the relationship between agriculture and other parts of the economy, not least because that indicates how far the sector, through declining in terms of employment and gross national product all this century, still has a central role to play in the process of production and distribution. In Lincolnshire agricultural services loom so large in the structure of the county's economy that their viability is as much a measure of prosperity as the fate of farming itself.

On balance, we may conclude that the national perspective in which we now view the cluster of trades concentrated upon agriculture has not been to the advantage of the county, which has lost more than it has gained in the process of reorganization around a small number of great firms. Every considerable town in the county could show an empty factory, derelict malting, or shuttered mill as a sign of the craze for concentration in the 1960s. It would be more to the point, however, to compare the fortunes of growing and declining segments of the service industries. Upon that calculation Lincolnshire did rather well in the twenty years before 1973.

Bibliographical note

The sources for agricultural history tend to fall into two broad categories: statistical and descriptive/analytical. Among other places, statistics of output are dealt with on p. 36 and in footnote 1; statistics of acreages and livestock in Table 3.1 and footnote 7; and statistics of employment in Table 3.2 and footnotes 20–22. The descriptive sources are many and varied and the reader is recommended to follow them through in detail from the text, but footnote 2 includes some good general starting points; a study of the Edwardian period could start with Haggard and Turnor (footnote 3), that of the inter-war period with sources quoted in footnotes 4 and 5, and that of the early post-war period with those given in footnotes 16 and 17.

Notes to Chapter 3

1. The difficulties of estimating value added output in agriculture cannot be exaggerated since a portion of the product was not or was seldom calculated in the agricultural statistics. A national figure is perhaps reliable, but the changing basis of collection makes an estimate for a mere county very uncertain. In many branches of the industry, for milk yields, the proportion of milk produced that was thrown on the market, the number of livestock delivered for slaughter each year, their dead weight, and the value of several arable crops such as vegetables, flowers and fruit, the data are either non-existent or incomplete. However, I have attempted to compare the means of 1901–05 and 1971–75, imputing production values where necessary, and then deflating the result by reference to the average of prices in the early period. The result is an index number of 530 (1901–05, 100), which may be a slight overstatement. As for employment, similar problems occurred since the bases for calculation were not exactly the same in 1901 and in 1971, but a decline in full-time or full-time-equivalent employment from 100 to 54 is quite probable. There was apparently an increase in horse-power per man at least tenfold in the interval.

2. For the general background no one book is adequate, but the measure of changes in the period can be taken from P. J. Perry (ed.), *British agriculture, 1875–1914* (London, 1973); E. H. Whetham, *The agrarian history of England and Wales, VIII, 1914–39* (Cambridge, 1978); B. A. Holderness, *British agriculture since 1945* (Manchester, 1985). A brief but quite useful survey is J. Brown, *Agriculture in England. A survey of farming 1870–1947* (Manchester, 1987). Additionally, J. Brown, 'Agriculture in Lincolnshire during the Great Depression, 1873–96', unpublished PhD thesis, Manchester, 1978, is excellent for the late nineteenth century.

3. H. Rider Haggard, *Rural England, 1901–02* (London, 1902), vol. II, pp. 144–244 *passim*. Cf. C. Turnor, *Our food supply: perils and remedies* (London, 1916), for a view by a Lincolnshire landowner.

4. See, e.g. R. M. Carslaw, 'The economic geography of the eastern counties', *Agricultural progress*, XI, 1934; *The land of Britain. Report of the Land*

Utilisation Survey: 69, 'Lincolnshire: Holland' (by C. I. Smith); 76, 'Lincolnshire: Lindsey' (by L. D. Stamp); 77, 'Lincolnshire: Kesteven' (by L. D. Stamp); O. Hamilton, *The Lincolnshire landscape* (London, 1939).

5. John Bygott, *Eastern England* (London, 1923), pp. 171ff; Bygott, 'Lincolnshire,' A. G. Ogilvie (ed.), *Great Britain: essays in regional geography* (Cambridge, 1928) pp. 184–99, esp. p. 194.

6. See, e.g. J. Thirsk, *English peasant farming* (London, 1957), pp. 333 f.; Haggard, *op. cit.*, pp. 145, 210; J. Bygott, *Lincolnshire* (London, 1952), p. 147; M. W. Barley, *Lincolnshire and the Fens* (London, 1952), p. 183.

7. *The Agricultural statistics of England and Wales* (Board, afterwards Ministry, of Agriculture and Ministry of Agriculture, Fisheries and Food at various times) annually from 1867. They have been exhaustively used by historians and geographers, see e.g. *Victoria County History, Lincolnshire*, vol. II, p. 409; E. M. Ojala, *Agriculture and economic progress* (London, 1952), J. T. Coppock, *An agricultural geography of Great Britain* (London, 1971), *passim*.

For Lincolnshire the returns have been arranged to cover each of the three administrative counties, which is useful, but does not give a true picture of local diversity. That can be obtained from the unpublished evidence collected for each holding and then sorted into coherent agricultural districts, as by J. T. Coppock, *An agricultural atlas of England and Wales* (London, 1964, 2nd ed. 1975). Nevertheless, for the sake of simplicity we shall concentrate on returns for the whole county and discuss differences or different trends as occasion arises.

8. J. Bygott, 'Lincolnshire', Ogilvie, *op. cit.*, pp. 192 ff. Cf. L. D. Stamp, 'Lindsey' and 'Kesteven', *op. cit.*, *passim*.

9. The evolution of vegetable and fruit growing in the county is discussed by S. R. Haresign, 'Agricultural change and rural society in the Lincolnshire Fenlands and the Isle of Axholme, 1870–1914', unpublished Ph.D thesis, East Anglia, 1980, ch. VI, pts iv, v, vi; E. C. Eagle, 'Some light on the beginning of the Lincolnshire bulb industry', *Lincs. Historian* 6, 1950, pp. 220–9; J. C. Wallace, 'The Development of Potato Growing in Lincolnshire', *Jnl. Royal Agricultural Society of England*, 1954.

10. H. M. D. Parker, *Manpower. History of the second world war, Civil Series* (London, 1957), pp. 128–9; K. L. Murray, *Agriculture. History of the second world war, Civil Series* (London, 1955), *passim*.

11. See, e.g. S. G. Sturmey, 'Owner farming in England and Wales, 1900–50', *Manchester School*, XXIII, 1955; Holderness, *op. cit.*, pp. 127–28; Bygott, *Lincolnshire*, pp. 139 ff.

12. *Agricultural Statistics 1940–44: England and Wales*, pt I.

13. E. H. Whetham, 'The Agriculture Act 1920 and its repeal – the great betrayal', *Agric. Hist. Review* XXII, 1974, pp. 36–49. But see also, A. F. Cooper, 'The transformation of British agricultural policy, 1912–36', unpublished D.Phil. thesis Oxford, 1980, ch. III, which interprets events differently.

14. See B. A. Holderness, *op. cit.*, chs 2, 3; P. Self and H. J. Storing, *The state and the farmer* (London, 1962) *passim*; I. R. Bowler, *Government and agriculture* (London, 1979).

15. Holderness, *op. cit.*, pp. 103–6, 110 ff; K. C. Edwards, 'Lincolnshire', J. Mitchell (ed.), *Great Britain: Geographical essays* (Cambridge, 1967), pp. 308–29; J. T. Coppock, *Agricultural geography*, pp. 98.

16. Coppock, *Atlas*, pp. 123 ff; *Geography*, ch. 13.

17. These are estimates of my own, drawn from various reports in *Power farming* magazine. See also, *Agricultural statistics, England and Wales*, 1972, pp. 106–07 which gives no numbers for particular counties.

18. *Agricultural statistics, England and Wales*, 1972, pp. 63 ff. Cf. Coppock, *Geography*, pp. 80–106; R. Gasson, 'Labour', in A. Edwards & A. Rogers (eds.), *Agricultural resources* (London, 1974), pp. 107–33.

19. *Census of England and Wales, 1901, County Report, Lincolnshire*, Table 35.

20. From 1951 the census of occupations was constructed on a 10 per cent sample rather than by counting the whole population. Post-war figures therefore are estimates based on the sample, on unpublished parish statistics at M.A.F.F. and the annual return of holdings. These data contrast somewhat with those cited in chapter 1, above, p. 19, but all the figures are questionable.

21. See e.g. Holderness, *op. cit.*, pp. 122–32.

22. The following paragraphs are based on unpublished collections of my own which will eventually appear in *The English farmer, 1700–1940. A social history*.

23. See e.g. J. Bygott, *Lincolnshire*, ch. VI.

24. These estimates are part of my wide-ranging investigation of the social history of the farmer.

25. Bygott, *Lincolnshire*, p. 142.

26. For the dimensions of the districts mentioned, J. T. Coppock, *Atlas,* who has a map p. 43.

27. Haggard cites some examples from the late nineteenth century when conditions were far from easy for aspiring labourers, pp. 220 ff; Holderness, *British agriculture*, pp. 128–31.

28. It is instructive to compare, say, Adrian Bell's *Corduroy* with some such work as Geoffrey Robinson, *Hedingham Harvest* (London, 1977); but Owen Hamilton, *The Lincolnshire Landscape* (1939) has its literary merits as an evocation of the county's rural scene.

29. There is a useful perspective on the early years of the NFU with its divisions and uncertainties in A. F. Cooper's thesis cited above.

30. No history of the NFU has yet been written and the yearbooks are patchy as a source of information, but apart from Cooper there is a discussion of the Union's changing role in Self and Storing, *op. cit. passim*; P. Wormell, *The anatomy of agriculture* (London, 1978), ch. 14.

31. Reg Groves, *Sharpen the Sickle* (London, 1949) is an official history which is still very scholarly but it does not take the story far enough in time. W. A. Armstrong's *Farm Labourers* will supply this deficiency (Batsford, London, 1988). Otherwise, cf. F. D. Mills, 'The National Union of Agricultural Workers', *Jnl Agric. Econ* 16, 1964.

32. See, e.g. R. Groves, *op. cit.*, pp. 252 ff; Gasson in Edwards and Rogers, *op. cit.*, pp. 116 ff. E. Mejer, *Agricultural labourers in England and Wales* (Univ.

of Nottingham, 1949); C. S. Orwin & B. I. Felton, 'A century of earnings and wages in agriculture', *Jnl. Roy. Agr. Soc. England*, 1931.

33. Sturmey, *loc. cit*; Holderness, *British agriculture*, pp. 138–45; P. Wormell, *op. cit.*, pp. 153–199; Edwards and Rogers, *op. cit.*, pp. 87–101.

34. M. Pointer, *Hornsby's of Grantham* (Grantham, 1977); J. W. F. Hill, *Victorian Lincoln* (Cambridge, 1974) pp. 201–3; J. Bygott, *Lincolnshire*, pp. 160–64; N. R. Wright, *Lincolnshire Towns and Industry 1700–1914*, ch. 6; R. H. Clarke, *Steam engine builders of Lincolnshire* (Norwich, 1955). See also chapter 4 below.

35. I have written an unpublished history, *Pauls of Ipswich: a business and family history* (1981) on behalf of the firm of Pauls and Whites plc; H. Bibby, *The Miller's Tale* (London, 1981); H. W. Brace, *History of seed crushing in Great Britain* (London, 1960); Bygott, *op. cit.*, pp. 164–9.

36. See, T. Kime, *The Great Potato Boom, 1903–04* (Horncastle, 1917); E. H. Grubb and W. S. Guildford, *The Potato* (New York, 1912).

37. *Lincolnshire Industrial Directory* (Lincolnshire County Council, Gloucester, n.d.).

38. Holderness, *British Agriculture*, ch. 5; Wormell, *op. cit.*, chs. 26, 27.

39. R. Stemman, *Geest 1935–85* (published by the company, 1987) is a clear account of the firm's development.

CHAPTER 4

THE VARIED FORTUNES OF HEAVY AND MANUFACTURING INDUSTRY 1914–1987

by Neil Wright

Abstract *The chapter begins with Lincolnshire engineering industry during the first world war, carrying forward the story from Volume XI in this series. The second section describes the great contrast in the years of post-war depression, followed by discussions of mineral extraction and iron and steel manufacture. In the next sections engineering responds again to wartime demands, but after 1945 the long-term decline in mechanical engineering reappears with many closures and takeovers. In the final section, the theme is one of diversification in manufacturing industry and its spread from the traditional centres of Lincoln, Gainsborough, and Grantham, but does not include the most recent hi-tech industries.*

MUNITIONS OF WAR

By 1914 several engineering firms in Lincolnshire had risen to considerable size, employing thousands of workers and dominating the economic affairs of Gainsborough, Grantham, and Lincoln. These Victorian firms had prospered on the manufacture and export of steam thrashing sets, but they had also developed the heavy oil or diesel engine and diversified into other lines. Although the great Lincolnshire firms responded to the unprecedented demands of the first world war they were unable afterwards to regain their paramount position in overseas markets, and it seemed in retrospect as though 1914 had marked the end of an epoch. Seventy-five years later most old firms had disappeared or were much reduced in size and they worked alongside a diversity of new and small firms. No single company dominated a town in the way that Marshall, Sons & Co. Ltd had earlier held sway over Gainsborough. By 1988 many of the largest works in Lincolnshire were those related to oil or chemical industries built by national or multi-national companies on green field sites near

Fig. 4.1 First world war aircraft manufactured at Lincoln. An almost completely assembled Sopwith Camel aircraft pictured on Lincoln Cattle Market, with the abattoir in the background, later the site of the 'Tech' extension, now the North Lincolnshire College. These women workers were known as munitionettes, cf. the suffragettes of pre-1914 days. Their sailor-like cap ribbons read 'Ruston Proctor and Co. Ltd.' Was the hatless woman one of the female inspectors of whom the male shop stewards complained? Source: John Walls, *Ruston aircraft production.*

the north coast. Even long-established businesses saw a loss of local control as they became parts of companies with headquarters outside the county.[1] (See Appendix Table 2 for details of employment in Lincolnshire and Table 5 for a summary of industrial mergers and takeovers.)

From 1914 Lincolnshire's engineering works went over to the production of munitions for the war effort. To ensure rapid and uninterrupted production, the government controlled the supply of raw materials and sent military engineers into the works to oversee contracts. Volunteers left the engineering works to join the armed forces, nearly 2,000 from Marshalls alone, and women took over many jobs previously thought unsuitable. L. B. Barley, a shop steward at Ruston, Proctor & Co. Ltd during the war, said that the use of female labour brought 'all kinds of sticky possibilities and we skilled engineers had to assert ourselves', particularly as some women were given Inspector's duties. The shop stewards' organization developed into an aggressive movement, said Mr Barley. 'We were called Syndicalists then, Communism had not been thought of.' The shop stewards adopted the sit-down strike as a very effective method of

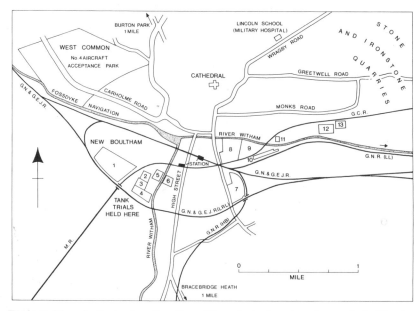

Fig. 4.2 Lincoln factories. Location of the principal engineering works in Lincoln during the first world war. *Clayton & Shuttleworth's works*: **9** Stamp End; **10** Titanic; **11** Electric Power Station; **12** Abbey; **13** Tower. *Wm Foster's works*: **3** Wellington. *Robey's works*: **7** Globe. *Ruston, Proctor & Co.'s works*: **1** Spike Island; **2** Boiler; **4** Boultham; **5** Woodyard for Sheaf Wood Works; **6** Sheaf Wood Works (later Anchor Street); **8** Sheaf Iron Works. Drawn by J. Peacock from material supplied by N. R. Wright and J. T. Turner.

getting their way. Shop Stewards Committees were formed in each Lincoln works, and became more effective than the branches of each union spread across the city. The shop stewards' movement declined after the end of the war.[2]

Between 1915 and 1919 Lincoln became one of the largest centres of aircraft production in the world. Women fitted and painted the textile coverings to the fuselage and wings while men made the engines and assembled the finished military aircraft. However, the majority of the aircraft built in Lincoln were not designed in the city, and it was because of this lack of design facilities that the local aircraft industry collapsed when the war ended and military contracts were cancelled. Robeys had designed some prototype aircraft themselves, but not with much success; one test flight in September 1916 ended disastrously when the biplane caught fire and crashed on to the roof of the county lunatic asylum, causing £50-worth of damage.[3]

Ruston, Proctor & Co. Ltd were the first Lincolnshire firm to start making aircraft. They became the largest producer of aircraft engines in the kingdom and one of the five leading British firms, employing about 3,000 men and women in 1918 on aircraft production alone. They built over 2,000 aircraft, over 3,000 engines, and spare parts amounting to a further 800 engines. The first order for 100 B.E.2c two-seater biplanes was placed with Rustons on 15 January 1915 and new buildings were quickly erected alongside the Witham at Boultham and Spike Island near their existing Boiler Works and Wood Works (Fig. 4.2).

During 1915, 129 acres of the West Common racecourse at Lincoln became No. 4 Aircraft Acceptance Park with turf landing strips, hangars and accommodation for test pilots under the grandstand. Two of the four brick hangars were on the site of the present tennis courts and the other two were alongside Alderman's Walk. The Common was also used to test aircraft made by three other firms: Robeys, Clayton & Shuttleworth, and Marshalls of Gainsborough. In 1916–17 Rustons produced 350 of the Sopwith 1$\frac{1}{2}$ Strutters and then in 1917–18, 1,600 of the famous Sopwith Camels (Fig. 4.1), more than any other manufacturer. Robey & Co. Ltd received a contract from the Admiralty on 21 May 1915 for 30 Sopwith Gunbuses; new aircraft shops were already being built in Coultham Street near their main Globe Works in Lincoln. In November 1915 many firms received orders for the Short 184 Seaplane and by 1919 Robeys had made more of these seaplanes than any other firm, producing 256 out of the 800-odd built. They were delivered by road to various seaplane bases for testing, including Inverkeithing in Fife, Calshot near Southampton and Killingholme on the Humber.

In May 1916 Robeys received an order for the Maurice Farman 'Longhorn' aircraft, and established an aerodrome on Bracebridge Heath near the county lunatic asylum. The aerodrome was also used for testing aircraft manufactured by Clayton & Shuttleworth Ltd, who had a small field of their own between the Witham and the Great Central Railway. In 1917 Bracebridge Heath was enlarged to 125 acres for test-flying larger aircraft and service use by the Royal Flying Corps. The seven large brick hangars with truss roofs built to take the Handley Page bombers still exist, though used as factories and vehicle workshops.

Clayton & Shuttleworth, formed in 1842, had long been the main firm in the county. Early in 1916 their Stamp End Works started producing tail stabilizers for airships which patrolled the coast for submarines. Later their Titanic Works made 40 Sopwith Triplanes followed by 522 Sopwith Camels in 1917–19. In 1916 a prisoner-of-war camp was built west of Clayton's Abbey Works; prisoners built aircraft shops at the Abbey and Tower Works where 46 large Handley Page 0/400 bombers were built in 1917–19.

The only other Lincolnshire firm to build aircraft was Marshalls of Gainsborough, who received an order in November 1917 for 150 Bristol F.2B aircraft for reconnaissance work. They were built in the Carr House Works on Lea Road, near the G.N.R. station, W. T. Greaves being transferred from Rustons as works manager. Two Lincolnshire aircraft were still on permanent display in 1988, a Ruston-built B.E.2c in the Imperial War Museum in London and a Clayton & Shuttleworth-built Sopwith Camel in the Musée de l'Armée et d'Histoire Militaire in Brussels. Parts of some others have also survived.[4]

On 9 April 1918 King George V and Queen Mary visited Lincoln to tour the works of Ruston, Clayton & Shuttleworth, Robeys, and Wm Foster Ltd. Foster's were making the weapons of war for which Lincoln is perhaps most remembered, the tank. Some people had been thinking about mechanized fighting vehicles since the early days of the war with the advocacy of Winston Churchill and Col. Ernest Swinton. Lieut. W. G. Wilson, and William Tritton, the managing director of Fosters, developed the first such British weapons, which were manufactured in Lincoln. A development contract was placed with Fosters on 24 July 1915 and three weeks later construction began of a prototype known originally as the Tritton and in a modified form as 'Little Willie'. These armour-plated vehicles on caterpillar tracks

Fig. 4.3 Tank manufacture at Lincoln. Tanks of the 'Mother' type in the course of erection at the Wellington Works of Wm Foster Ltd in the district of Lincoln now crossed by Tritton Road, named after Sir William Tritton, managing director of the firm during the first world war. Machines like these were tested on ground deliberately made to represent the conditions of trench warfare; now cash-and-carry warehouses and their car parks occupy some of the site. Source: *The tank: its birth and its development*, p. 64 published by Fosters, reprinted by Tee Publishing, Hinckley, 1977.

were known as 'tanks for Mesopotamia' for security purposes and the name has persisted.

'Little Willie' was tested in Burton Park near Lincoln on 3 December 1915. Although problems were found with its tracks, it was invaluable as an experimental model and even while it was being built in August, Wilson was sketching the design for a completely different machine, rhomboid shaped with caterpillar tracks around the hull and guns mounted in 'sponsons' on the sides. This was named 'Mother' or 'Big Willie' and on 19/20 January 1916 was tested at Burton and fired its two naval six-pounder guns for the first time. Secret demonstrations took place at Hatfield Park on 29 January and 2 February, the latter attended by Lord Kitchener and Lloyd George, and by 12 February an initial order for 100 'Big Willies' had been placed. The first tanks arrived in France by 30 August, and on 15 September they went into battle on the Somme. They were able to cross barbed wire and trenches and to deal with machine-guns, and by the time of the Armistice in November 1918 they were an essential weapon in breaking the trench stalemate; Britain alone had built 2,500. For his part in the development of the tank William Tritton received a knighthood in 1917. In the latter part of the war, unarmed tanks to carry supplies to the front line were also made by Marshalls of Gainsborough at the rate of ten a week (Figs. 4.3, 4.4).[5]

THE TANK "EGBERT" AND ITS CREW

Fig. 4.4 A tank at Scunthorpe. The tanks were all given individual names. Here is 'Egbert' and its crew at Scunthorpe in 1918, presumably on a fund-raising/public relations exercise. Note the officer's cavalry uniform and the graffiti on the tank, including its name, to the left of the left hand soldier's cap. Source: Scunthorpe Central Library.

Aircraft and tanks were not the only munitions to be manufactured by Lincolnshire firms. Hornsbys of Grantham concentrated on naval requirements – gun mountings, submarine mines, machine-gun tripods, and high-explosive shells as well as ships' fittings and marine oil engines – while Blackstone & Co. Ltd of Stamford made machinery for submarines and were solely responsible for all spare parts for the Admiralty's fleet of motor launches. Similarly, Marshalls of Gainsborough produced naval gun mountings, shells and shell fuses in the Britannia Works and over 8,000 military vehicles from their Trent Works, as well as aircraft, tanks, boilers, chemical and engineering plant and five-ton traction engines. Rustons produced 8,000 Lewis guns and Claytons made crawler tractors for the War Department in the western half of the Titanic Works; one of these is preserved in the Museum of Lincolnshire Life. Fosters also built many 12-inch heavy howitzers with 98-100 h.p. traction haulage equipment. Those Lincoln works which had previously produced thrashing machines now made great numbers of general service wagons, limbers, field kitchens and other wooden equipment. At Grimsby minesweepers were repaired in the shipyard of John S. Doig, and with peace they were reconverted to trawlers; his yard undertook similar work in the second world war.

As chemicals could no longer be imported from Germany, Lincoln, Boston, and other town gas works installed plants to produce toluol and benzol for high explosives. Dawsons Leather Works in Lincoln produced all kinds of leather goods including fittings for army vehicles and bayonet scabbards, and T. G. Tickler Ltd of Grimsby made tins of jam for the troops.[6] (See Ch. 1, Fig. 1.2).

THE DEPRESSION

When the war ended in November 1918 it had drastically altered world economic relationships; any hopes that the Lincolnshire engineering firms had of returning to the comparative stability of the pre-war years were to be bitterly disappointed. A boom in trade immediately after the war encouraged false hopes and Ruston & Hornsby raised a further £1 million capital in ordinary shares for necessary restocking. But the boom ended after about eighteen months and for nearly 20 years the firms went through great difficulties which brought much suffering to those dependent on them.[7]

The biggest pre-war markets of most leading Lincolnshire firms had been overseas but after four years customers had found other sources of supply. Russia had been a major market for several firms before and during the war, and Hornsbys had even established a branch factory in Odessa to assemble and service machines. But as a result of the economic dislocation following the Revolution outstanding debts were unpaid, money in Russian banks was lost, and Hornsby's Odessa factory was confiscated.

The return to the gold standard in 1925 made British goods more expensive in foreign markets, and to reduce costs, firms cut wages and reduced employment. Economic and political upheavals in other European countries reduced their ability to buy British goods. From 1920 to the late 1930s Britain suffered a depression worse than any before and while Linconshire was not as badly affected as some areas, the effects in Lincoln, Gainsborough, and Grantham were painful. In Lincoln the number of unemployed reached a peak of 6,600 in 1922 and though the number dropped to 1,000 in 1927–28 things then rapidly worsened and in 1933 there were 7,800 unemployed in the city (which had a population of 66,243 in 1931). Job creation projects such as the reconstruction of Bracebridge Gas Works in 1932–33 were of little help. The Workers' Educational Association was involved with facilities for unemployed men to repair their family's footwear. Not until the late 1930s did the employment situation improve.[8]

The great Lincolnshire engineering firms struggled to survive the depression with varying degrees of success. Even before the war ended the directors of Richard Hornsby & Sons Ltd had anticipated future difficulties and approached Ruston, Proctor & Co. Ltd who, after initial doubts, agreed to an amalgamation that took place on 11 September 1918. David Roberts of Hornsbys was a Joint Managing Director until 1920, when George Ruston Sharpley became sole managing director until he succeeded his cousin Col. Joseph Seward Ruston as Chairman in 1939. The Ruston family remained in a senior position in the company until 1961. At Clayton & Shuttleworth Ltd the family involvement had ceased in 1919 when Alfred Shuttleworth resigned as Chairman, while at Marshalls, family control effectively ceased in 1934. In 1933, Mr. L. B. Barley's mother, widow of a boiler-maker at Marshalls, wrote to her son that 'people are leaving Gainsborough fast'. For all firms, survival in the depressed conditions of the 1920s and 1930s depended on adaptability and careful management of restricted finances; it involved not only the development of new products but also arrangements with other companies.[9]

The government had ended some munitions contracts very abruptly and firms were left with materials, factory space and workers, but with no orders. Ruston & Hornsby used the skills and equipment in their Lincoln aircraft factory to start producing the high quality Ruston car in 1920, but the national trend was towards the mass-production of cheaper cars, so Rustons made their last car in 1924.

John Henry Pick had been making cars in Stamford since 1898 and he also ceased about 1924. A few Lincolnshire firms made bodies for cars and buses between the wars, and some firms such as Clayton Dewandre were still making motor vehicle components in the 1980s.[10]

By purchasing their rivals, firms could acquire patents, skilled staff, and customers and perhaps transfer work to their own under-used premises, a good example being William Foster's acquisition of Gwynnes Pumps Ltd of Hammersmith, London in 1927. Fosters continued to make thrashing sets, traction engines, and showmen's road locomotives at the Wellington Works, but hydraulic pumps for docks and other installations were made at both Lincoln and Hammersmith. The sale of such subsidiary companies could also be used on occasions to raise fresh capital as in 1930 when Ruston & Hornsby sold their controlling interest in Ransomes, Sims & Jefferies Ltd of Ipswich to which they had transferred the production of Ruston steam engines and thrashers. To raise capital for the expansion of their mechanical excavator business they transferred it in 1930 to Ruston Bucyrus Ltd, a new company formed jointly with Bucyrus-Erie of the USA. Three years later Ruston & Hornsby provided space at Grantham for the new firm of Aveling-Barford Ltd which in 1933–34 transferred over 45,000 tons of plant and stock from Rochester in Kent to Grantham. Ruston & Hornsby had a controlling interest and supplied engines for their road rollers.[11]

The world economic situation in the 1930s brought the collapse of most Lincolnshire engineering firms and large scale unemployment. Ruston & Hornsby were the only substantial firm to avoid either a take-over or the appointment of a Receiver. The first and perhaps most serious disaster was the collapse of Clayton & Shuttleworth Ltd. Since 1910 the firm had considerably expanded, with the erection of the Titanic, Abbey, and Tower works near the original Stamp End Works, but after the war found it impossible to keep them fully occupied. From 1924 to 1932 the Stamp End boiler works were used by a Scottish firm, Babcock & Wilcox, who designed and built for the government huge mooring masts which were erected at Cardington in Bedfordshire, Ismailia in Egypt, and Karachi in India for an airship route to serve the Empire.

During the 1920s Claytons were heavily committed to the production of steam wagons, but that market only lasted a decade. They built over 1,200 wagons between 1912 and 1929, many being made by Clayton Wagons Ltd which was formed to handle that side of the business. A Liquidator was appointed in February 1930 and Claytons was finally wound up in December 1936. The *Lincolnshire Chronicle* reported in 1932 that 'the disastrous end to so magnificent a business has had a tragic effect in the homes of the many former employees who are now workless'. Some of the company's products and plant were viable on their own, and were sold to other firms, including the Clayton Dewandre Co. Ltd, formed in November 1928 'to carry on the business of the Motor Engineering Section of Clayton Wagons Ltd, and take over the Titanic Works'. They occupied the Titanic Works until 1988. In 1929 Thomas Smith of Coventry purchased the Clayton Forge as a ready means of undertaking larger types of work, and Clayton & Shuttleworth's other patent rights were sold to Marshalls of Gainsborough and to Babcock & Wilcox so they could produce thrashing machines and other products with the Clayton name. The Shuttleworth family invested their money in what are now the Shuttleworth Agricultural College in Bedfordshire and the nearby Shuttleworth Aeroplane Collection.[12]

Other firms managed to survive after restructuring, for example Penney & Porter were reorganized in 1932 and W. Rainsforth & Sons and Robey & Co. Ltd the following year. The family-controlled firm of Marshalls of Gainsborough had developed several new products including steel-framed thrashing machines, oil-driven tractors, central heating boilers and road rollers, but in 1934 they became associated with Thomas W. Ward Ltd of Sheffield and were reorganized in 1936. The diesel engine makers Blackstone & Co. Ltd of Stamford became associated with R. A. Lister in 1936 and the smaller Lincoln firm of John Cooke & Sons Ltd ceased business in 1937. In the late 1930s rearmament started to lift the depression and firms were more secure. Rose Brothers (Gainsborough) Ltd kept in full production by developing automatic food-processing machinery. In 1937 R. H. Neal established a crane-making business in Grantham and the following year the armaments firm, British Manufacturing and Research Ltd, built a factory there.[13]

MINERAL EXTRACTION

Mineral extraction developed as an important Lincolnshire industry in the nineteenth century, and by 1914 its chief product was Frodingham ironstone for the iron and steel works around Scunthorpe. Ironstone mining from open-cast pits there increased considerably during the first world war and continued to grow until 1961 when over 5.5 million tons were extracted, but then declined as more foreign ore was used in the steelworks. The iron content of the Frodingham ironstone was low, only about 22 per cent in the exposed or lightly covered beds in 1918. To counteract its high lime content it needed either to be carefully sorted or mixed with the siliceous Northampton ironstone, which was quarried in deposits scattered through Northamptonshire and into Lincolnshire as far north as Greetwell near Lincoln.

During the first world war supplies of foreign haematite ores were much restricted so more Frodingham ironstone was used. Increased war-time demand and labour shortages led to improved mechanization of quarrying, and it later became feasible to re-mine some areas previously considered to be worked out. The demolition or rebuilding of the ironworks also allowed ore to be quarried from beneath them. An underground mine opened at Santon in 1938 was soon closed because of labour shortages but reopened after the war, and a new mine was opened at Dragonby.[14]

Exploitation of the Frodingham ironstone had been initiated in 1860 by Rowland Winn, later created Baron St Oswald, and by 1917 the 2nd Baron was the largest single producer in the kingdom, supplying over one twelfth of the nation's total output of iron ore. Between 1948–53 the separate leases of Lord St Oswald's Frodingham Ironstone Mines, the Frodingham Iron & Steel Co. Ltd, and the more recently formed Santon Ironstone Mining Co. were amalgamated, and they later became the Ore-Mining Branch of the United Steel

Fig. 4.5 Iron ore extraction. Iron ore miners at work in 1905, probably at Dragonby, north of Scunthorpe. The shovels have the T-handles of the Lincolnshire tradition. This is long before workplace shower baths and the men would go home with yellow faces. Source: Scunthorpe Central Library.

Companies.[15]

At Greetwell (which closed in 1939 after about 66 years) and in Kesteven ironstone quarries were operated either by smelting companies or separate mining companies. Wartime demand led to excavation in Denton Park and the construction by the GNR. in 1915–16 of a mineral branch line from their main line south of Grantham to a quarry at Stainby. In 1935 the quarries around Grantham were producing about 200,000 tons each year but they closed at various times and mining did not resume there until the mid-1970s. Underground mines for the Claxby ironstone were opened at Nettleton near Caistor in 1929 and reached peak production in 1967 but closed suddenly in February 1969.[16]

For centuries there had been quarries for Lincolnshire limestone in Kesteven and though Stamford quarry closed in 1915–16 there is still one working at Wilsford near Ancaster. Brickyards around many towns and along the Humber bank have also closed during the present century and by 1988 only those at Barton-on-Humber were still working. By now, gypsum is no longer dug on the Isle of Axholme and agricultural lime kilns on the Wolds have also ceased, but there are still large quarries on the Wolds producing lime, chalk, and whiting for agricultural and industrial purposes. Lime quarries can also be found in the limestone areas of Kesteven, e.g. Blankney and Leadenham. The quarry at Melton Ross supplies burnt and hydrated lime and graded limestone to the British Steel Corporation and others serve cement works at South Ferriby, Kirton Lindsey, and Tallington. The Whisby–Hykeham area near Lincoln, Messingham near Scunthorpe, the Bain Valley near Horncastle, and Tallington and Langtoft on the fen edge near Bourne are important sources of sand and gravel for Lincolnshire and adjacent counties.[17]

Exploitation of the modest oil reserves under Lincolnshire began in 1959 when 1,211 tons were pumped from beneath Gainsborough in an extension of the Nottinghamshire oilfield. Production increased to 3,958 tons in 1960 when pumping also started in adjacent Corringham and later other areas further east were explored. In 1985 the Welton oilfield near Sudbrooke went into production and 17 wells supply a central gathering station at Reepham from which oil was first sent by train to British Petroleum's refinery in south Wales and then, in 1986, to Humberside.[18]

IRON MAKING AT SCUNTHORPE

The iron-making community in Frodingham and Scunthorpe was about fifty years old in 1914: the first blast furnace had started

producing iron in 1864 and steel making began in 1890. The
nineteenth-century iron and steel works had been erected by companies formed for the purpose, but after 1900 firms from outside
Lincolnshire started taking control, so that by 1914 only the Froding-
gham Iron & Steel Co. Ltd and the North Lincolnshire Iron Co. Ltd
were still independent. The Appleby Iron Works had closed in 1912
and had been leased by Frodingham Iron & Steel and the Steel Company of Scotland; the first of the Appleby or North Ironworks blast
furnaces was restarted in 1912, but the erection of a steel works was
not completed until 1927.

During and after the first world war there were further takeovers
so that by 1920 there were just three companies, each owning an integrated iron and steel works: the Frodingham company (which
became part of the United Steel Companies of Sheffield in 1917 and
was renamed Appleby-Frodingham Steel Co. Ltd in 1934), Guest,
Keen, and Nettlefold, who acquired Lysaght's Normanby Park works
in 1919, and Richard Thomas & Co. who started steel production at

Fig. 4.6 The Scunthorpe strike, 1909. Distribution of beef and bread outside Boots
in Scunthorpe, during the strike of 1909 which lasted for four weeks. The blast furnacemen failed to gain wage increases, but the employing firms conceded recognition
to the National Federation of Blast Furnacemen in Scunthorpe. Isaac Mitchell, a Board
of Trade official, and Sir Berkeley Sheffield (see also Fig. 9.1), a local royalty owner
and MP, were instrumental in bringing about the truce. Source: Scunthorpe Central
Library; caption: Armstrong, *Industrial Island*, pp. 72–3.

Redbourn Hill works in 1919. There were also the North Lincolnshire Iron Co. which was owned by Stewart and Lloyds and the Trent Iron Co. Ltd owned by John Brown & Co. of Sheffield.[19]

During the inter-war period there was a dramatic increase in the production of both pig iron and crude steel, despite national strikes in 1921 and 1926 (Fig. 4.6). Scunthorpe was the country's lowest cost producer and its share of pig-iron production rose from 6 to 14 per cent in the period, and steel production from 3 to 10 per cent of national production. The iron content of the Frodingham ironstone was so low that Scunthorpe produced more slag per ton than any other centre in the world, but after 1914 commercial uses were found in agricultural fertilizers and road building materials. Similarly, crude tar and crude benzol from the coke-ovens were distilled locally to produce road tar, creosote, chemicals, and other products. The Appleby-Frodingham and Normanby Park works were each substantially modernized after the second world war, and in 1958 British Oxygen Engineering Ltd opened a plant in Scunthorpe to pipe gaseous oxygen direct to the steel works. Foundries and steel fabrication plants were established in the town to use the steel. Nationalization in 1951 had little time to affect the industry before being denationalized in 1953, but the Redbourn works as part of Richard Thomas & Baldwin remained in public ownership.

Between 1952 and 1968 Scunthorpe's share of national steel production rose from 10 to 11.8 per cent and the population of the town rose by 15,000 between 1951 and 1966. In the mid-1960s the United Steel Companies decided that major new capacity should be provided in north Lincolnshire, as part of a national plan to concentrate bulk steel-making in a small number of large coastal plants. The possibility of developing a green-field site on the bank of the Humber was rejected in favour of redevelopment of the Appleby-Frodingham works at Scunthorpe.[20]

Under nationalization in 1967 the three integrated plants at Scunthorpe passed to the British Steel Corporation, who during the next three years created minor operating links between them. In 1969 BSC chose the town as the site for the Anchor Project, based on the USC plan, and combined existing and new plant to increase total steel capacity to 4.4 million tons at a cost of £232.8 million. The project included a terminal on the Humber at Immingham at an additional cost of £5.7 million and new ore reception and blending facilities which supplied the separate Normanby Park works as well as the main Anchor complex. Iron from the existing Appleby-Frodingham blast furnaces and from Redbourn Works supplied Anchor's three basic oxygen converters which had replaced all the old open hearth and rotary furnaces at those two works. The huge new facilities also included a mile-long mill for the production of steel billets, a medium section mill and a continuous casting plant for slabs. Work on the project started in 1970 and it was officially opened by Queen Elizabeth II in 1973. Scunthorpe became one of BSC's five main steel producing centres, and by 1974 it produced over 16 per cent of the country's steel and nearly 24 per cent of the pig-iron output.[21]

The development of the Scunthorpe works was reflected by an increase of workers in metal manufacture in Lincolnshire from 4,106 in 1901 to 21,050 in 1971, when nearly 10 per cent were women, but as output from Anchor expanded, so the old furnaces and some rolling mills were taken out of use and up to 3,500 jobs lost. The production of light plate at Scunthorpe ceased in 1971–72, when BSC concentrated that work on Teesside. By that time Scunthorpe had a population of 70,907, almost the same as Lincoln, but was dangerously dependent on a single industry. After the commissioning of Anchor there were further substantial developments costing £210 million at Normanby Park and Appleby-Frodingham. In 1978, 33 per cent of employees in the Scunthorpe area were employed in the coal, chemicals, or metals group, compared to only four per cent nationally. Anchor had seemed a satisfactory compromise between the retention of an existing inland site and development of a new coastal site near deep water, but the effects of international market forces and domestic depression during the 1970s meant that BSC was unable to sell all the steel it produced and retrenchment became necessary.

Iron and steel making ceased completely at Corby (Northants) in 1980 and Scunthorpe also suffered severely. In 1979 the Scunthorpe Works Rationalisation Plan led to the loss of 1,700 jobs as the three blast furnaces at Redbourn, seven coke ovens and four sinter plants were closed, and steel making capacity was reduced to 3.1 million tons. Two years later the Normanby Park works was closed completely (later demolished). The original rod mill at Appleby-Frodingham was also abandoned; the surviving rod mill was BSC's contribution to a new joint venture with Guest, Keen and Nettlefold known as Allied Steel and Wire. At the same time the closure of the Nypro chemical works at the ill-fated Flixborough site led to the loss of nearly 400 jobs. These closures gave Scunthorpe serious economic and social problems as unemployment rose from 8.6 per cent in 1980 to 16.4 in 1981 compared with 7.3 and 11.1 nationally. In an effort to attract new manufacturing and service industries to the town, the government established Enterprise Zones at Flixborough and Scunthorpe in 1983–84, with financial and planning inducements. After 125 years the future of Scunthorpe is uncertain since not even the remaining steel plant can be regarded as secure, although there is much diversification and some hi-tech industry.[22]

WORLD WAR II

During the second world war Lincolnshire industry was once more geared to the war effort as government allocated labour and raw materials, but changes in production were not so great as during the first world war. Many of the products coming out of the factories were developments of their peace-time lines.[23]

Ruston & Hornsby made thousands of diesel engines which provided power for a bewildering multiplicity of military establishments, including barracks in south east Asia, war-damaged Russian factories, and Winston Churchill's underground bunker. Such was the quality of the work that the Germans even used a Ruston engine at their underground HQ near Paris! Rustons engines drove refrigeration plants in the North African desert, electrical, hydraulic, and compressed air machinery for guns and searchlights at the Singapore naval base, and small naval vessels like minesweepers and landing craft. Ruston's diesel locomotives were used in Admiralty depots, underground bomb dumps, coal mines, quarries, and on the important railway across Iran which gave access to Russia from the Persian Gulf. Ruston & Hornsby built 400 Matilda tanks, following this with a prototype Cavalier, which superseded the Matilda, and then manufactured a run of 220 Cavaliers. They also made 400 armoured tractors to tow 17-pounder guns and Ruston-Bucyrus made a further 200.

Other munitions produced in Lincoln included mines, war-heads for midget submarines, parts for radar and searchlights, crankshafts, and Bofors guns. One of the first secret projects at Lincoln was the development of 'Nellie' during the early months of the war, almost a repeat of the development of the tank in the first war. Nellie was also a brain-child of Winston Churchill, a huge trench-digging machine designed to attack Germany's Western Wall and to avoid the stalemates of the first world war. It was produced in great secrecy by Ruston-Bucyrus but by the time it was ready France had fallen and it was useless.[24]

In Grantham, Ruston & Hornsby made more than a million parts of naval equipment, Aveling-Barford built machine-gun carriers and tanks, and British Manufacture and Research Co. Ltd made 98,000 aeroplane cannon and 52 million rounds of ammunition. In Gainsborough, Marshalls produced naval gun mountings, anti-aircraft guns, anti-tank guns and ammunition hoists for use on land

and, in 1942, amidst great secrecy, made the midget submarines which were used against the German fleet at Narvik in Norway. To increase home production of food, Marshalls also made over 2,000 thrashing machines, more than half of the total produced in Britain during the war, and maintained older machines. They also continued to make and develop diesel tractors and road rollers, the latter being used overseas in the construction of airfields and landing strips, and developed a class of portable steam engine for use by the Forestry Department in the collection of home-grown timber. The subsidiary, Marshall Richards Machine Co. Ltd, found steel and copper wire drawing machines in great demand as Swedish supplies were cut off.

Rose Brothers of Gainsborough produced guided-missile equipment, pom-pom directors, gun-sights and similar items and established a number of small 'dispersal factories' in villages nearby as well as other workshops in Gainsborough. For one order they built and equipped a factory at Saxilby in 30 weeks. Roses' works became almost an extension of the Air Force workshops in No. 5 Bomber Group and they produced gun turret fittings for the Lancasters involved in the Dambusters raid. H. Leverton & Co. Ltd of Spalding converted and repaired many Caterpillar tractors which were supplied to the British and U.S. Armed Forces. Food canning factories, of which there were three in Boston and others elsewhere, were at full pitch to meet civilian needs and military contracts and a new factory was built in Marsh Lane, Boston to produce dried potato, 'Smash'.[25]

The targets of the first German air raids on Lincolnshire in June 1940 were aerodromes, the docks at Grimsby and armament factories at Grantham. A raid on Gainsborough in November 1942 missed Marshall's Britannia Works but destroyed most buildings on either side of Market Street and seriously damaged the Town Hall. During the war 87 people were killed by bombing in Grantham and 133 in Grimsby, but Boston with 12 fatalities and Lincoln with 11 escaped more lightly.[26]

BRANCHES OF BIG BUSINESS

Since 1945 there have been dramatic changes in Lincolnshire's industries, both in terms of ownership and products, as indicated in Appendix Table 5. All the main engineering firms were acquired by larger companies during the following 25 years and some changed hands several times but only the medium-sized firm of Richard Duckering Ltd, which closed in 1962, disappeared completely. Allen-Gwynnes Pumps, successors to Foster & Co. Ltd, were the only major firm to leave the county but many reduced the size of their operations here.[27]

Several Lincolnshire firms had ceased making steam engines before 1939 and the traction engine which left Foster's works in 1942 was probably the last made in Britain, but Marshalls made steam rollers until 1954; they, together with Robeys and Aveling-Barford, were still making stationary steam engines in 1955. Marshalls had continued to develop diesel tractors during the war, so in 1945 they could immediately start deliveries of the Field Marshall Mark I with a revolutionary single-cylinder two-stroke engine. Few people then envisaged that by 1975 there would have been a significant reduction in the range and number of diesel engines being made in Lincolnshire. By the early 1950s thrashing machines had largely been replaced by combine harvesters (Fig. 3.3). Marshalls produced tractor-drawn models which Lincolnshire farmers bought rather than the more expensive self-propelled combines imported from Canada and the U.S.A. Marshalls made their last thrashing machines in 1956, after 102 years, and in 1960 Fosters made the last to be built in Britain.[28]

By the end of 1944 the managing director of Ruston & Hornsby, Victor Bone, whose son worked for Power Jets Ltd, became convinced that there was a future for the gas turbine in industry. Design work started in 1945 and the following year a separate gas turbine design department was established under G. B. R. Fielden who had worked closely with Sir Frank Whittle in developing the jet aircraft. Within three years a successful prototype was produced and in 1952 full-scale production began in the Anchor Street works of a twin-shaft engine designated the TA, with an output of 750 KW when close-coupled to an alternator. Ruston and Hornsby were launched as the leading British manufacturers of industrial gas turbines and by 1973 over 500 had been made in the Lincoln works.[29]

In 1956 British Thomson-Houston, later the English Electric Valve Co. Ltd and part of the General Electric Co. (GEC), adapted a joinery factory in Lincoln and started to make valves and semi-conductors for industrial and military electronic equipment. About the same time Allied Electrical Industries Ltd (AEI) also started to produce semi-conductors in Lincoln, and by 1971 there were 3,210 people working in electrical engineering throughout Lincolnshire.[30]

In contrast to the above, most national and multi-national companies came into Lincolnshire by taking over local firms. Early firms to be taken over were Clarke's Crank & Forge Co. Ltd of Lincoln in 1948 and R. H. Neal & Co. Ltd of Grantham in 1959, and the remaining Lincolnshire engineering companies lost their independence during the 1960s. Since 1945 there has been a steady decline in manufacturing employment in Lincoln mainly due to losses in mechanical engineering (a nationally declining sector) offsetting job-growth elsewhere in manufacturing industry. In 1966 mechanical engineering produced 51 per cent of jobs in manufacturing in Lincoln but by 1975 this had declined to 35 per cent. Of the six great engineering firms of Edwardian times only Rustons, as Ruston Gas Turbines, are still a major company in 1988. The Smith-Clayton Forge at Lincoln preserves part of one name, but Marshalls, Robeys, Fosters and Hornsbys are now historic memories.[31]

In 1950 Ruston & Hornsby Ltd had 9,248 employees in seven factories including five in Lincoln, the Spittlegate works in Grantham and their Paxman subsidiary in Colchester. They produced diesel engines, boilers, diesel-electric locomotives, smaller items, and industrial gas turbines. Castings for most of their Lincoln works came from the large Beevor Iron Foundry built in 1946–49 at a cost of £500,000 and opened on 5 January 1950 by Field Marshall Sir William Slim, Chief of the Imperial General Staff.[32]

Rustons was taken over in 1961 by the English Electric Co. Ltd, who closed the Grantham works two years later; the Grantham premises were purchased in 1971 by local businessmen who let the buildings for various industrial uses. In 1966 all companies in the English Electric Group were purchased by GEC and there followed a period of major alterations at Lincoln. The gas turbine activities of Ruston & Hornsby were formed into a separate company and the design and manufacture of turbochargers by D. Napier & Sons Ltd was transferred to Lincoln from Newton-le-Willows in Lancashire. The diesel interests became Ruston Paxman Diesels Ltd, which moved to Newton-le-Willows in 1973. Ruston Gas Turbines and Napier Turbochargers shared Ruston's original Iron Works site and as the successors to Ruston & Hornsby needed less space, the old Anchor Lane Works, the Boiler Works and Foster's Wellington Works (latterly occupied by Ruston-Bucyrus) were demolished in 1983–84.[33]

Marshalls of Gainsborough suffered a series of crises in the 1970s and 1980s, each leading to a reduction in the workforce and changes in ownership. Since the 1930s they had been associated with Wards, who merged them in 1969 with Fowlers of Leeds, but in 1975 Wards withdrew and there were mass redundancies before Marshall-Fowler was acquired by British Leyland Special Products Group who renamed it Aveling Marshall Ltd. That only lasted until 1979 when BL withdrew; there were 700 more redundancies, and local businessman Charles J. Nickerson purchased part of the Britannia works for the production of crawler tractors by Track Marshall Ltd. In 1982 he acquired the wheeled tractor business of Leyland Vehicles

Ltd from Bathgate, Scotland and transferred that to Gainsborough as Marshall Tractors Ltd, but in September 1985 the Marshall group was put into receivership and its parts were sold into different owner-ship. Track Marshall stayed in part of the Britannia works with less than a hundred employees but Marshall Tractors moved in 1986 to Scunthorpe and took with them the company's collection of historic products.[34]

Many other firms had similar experiences in the 1960s. Fisher Clark & Co. of Boston were purchased in 1960 by Norcross Ltd and in 1968 were merged with Tickepres Ltd to form Norprint, the largest producer of labelling products and systems in the world. Rose Brothers of Gainsborough were taken over in 1961 by Baker Perkins Ltd and in 1967 were merged with the Forgrove Machinery Co. Ltd to form the largest manufacturer of wrapping and packaging machinery in the world but their Gainsborough factory closed in 1987.[35]

LIGHT INDUSTRY AND THE HUMBER BANK

As employment in agriculture and mechanical engineering declined during the century, central and local government bodies sought to at-tract new industry which would provide jobs for Lincolnshire people. Even before 1914 Bourne UDC and Grantham Corporation had been trying to lure light industry to their towns, but during the Depression there was not much new industry to be established – the factory opened by Smiths Potato Crisps in 1938 was the first to be built in Lincoln for twenty years. This was in the Lincolnshire tradition of food processing factories such as ketchup, sauce, and jam factories es-tablished in the late nineteenth century and pea-picking and canning factories in Edwardian times. Large factories to process sugar beet were built with government assistance at Spalding, Bardney and Brigg in 1926–28. Smethursts opened the first fish freezing plant in Grimsby in 1928 and after 1950 other freezing plants were opened in the county (see above, Chapter 3, pp. 66–7 and Fig. 4.7).[36]

Over the country as a whole, unemployment was lower in centres of light or mixed industry. The Barlow Commission reporting in 1940 advocated the decentralization of industry and population, the development of existing small towns and the creation of new towns and trading estates. After the war, the Town Development Act 1952 was passed as part of government policies to plan the physical and economic development of the country. In 1968 Grantham and Gainsborough provided industrial estates and factories, some built for particular firms but others built in advance of demand. By 1977 Grantham had received 1,300 Londoners and two migrant factories,

Fig. 4.7 Boston advertises canned vegetables. Food processing represents both diversification of Lincolnshire industry and an extension of farming. This advertisement of the mid 1950s was a manicured hand to emphasize the convenience of canned vegetables, available throughout the year. Source: *Official Guide to Boston,* 1957, p. 50, Boston Borough Council.

while only 400 people and 20 small factories had moved to Gainsborough. Local authorities in Louth, Spilsby, Skegness, Mablethorpe, Sleaford and elsewhere provided industrial estates with electricity (via the national grid), drainage and other services and the Development Commission (later English Estates) provided small advance factories with the aim of stemming rural depopulation as jobs disappeared in agriculture. In 1914 only six Lincolnshire towns had a public electricity supply, but by 1939 it was available in all towns and large villages (either from the national grid or their own power station) and after the second world war was extended to the countryside.

By the early 1960s mobile firms in cost-conscious industries such as underwear, hosiery, and footwear had established factories employing female workers in Brigg, Gainsborough, Alford, Sleaford, and other towns. The Leicester firm of N. Corah (St Margarets) Ltd employed several hundred women in hosiery and clothing factories in Brigg and Scunthorpe by 1963, and during the 1960s Wolsey Ltd established factories in Gainsborough and Grantham. E. Fogarty & Co. Ltd took over feather factories in Boston and Billingborough (before becoming part of Coloroll in 1987), and started to use man-made fibres in its bedding and furnishing fabrics. By 1971 there were 5,430 textile workers in Lincolnshire. Other small firms produced plastic, polythene and fibreglass in Market Rasen, Wragby, Louth, and elsewhere.[37]

However, by the 1980s there was still high unemployment, relatively few women in jobs, a limited range of job choice and dependence on a small number of firms. By 1983, English Estates owned 119 factories and workshops with a total area of 275,000 square feet at 18 locations in Lincolnshire (new county), but many small towns still had little industry apart from the processing of farm produce and the servicing of agricultural machinery. The arrival of new clothing and footwear factories in the 1950s and 1960s did not compensate for the decline of local shoemakers and dressmakers who used to exist in every town and village; the number of workers in those categories of employment in Lincolnshire fell from 9,748 in 1901 to 2,180 in 1971. The closing of local tanneries reduced the number of people working in leather. Although the closure of breweries was for some time compensated by the opening of canneries and freezing plants, after 1971 these food factories were shedding workers and the closure of Lockwoods cannery in 1982 led to the establishment of the Boston Centre for the Unemployed.[38]

Until the second world war there was little manufacturing industry in Grimsby, a fishing port, apart from jam and biscuit making; but during the second half of the century Immingham Dock (opened 1912) became the busiest dock on either bank of the Humber, and the north Lincolnshire coast between there and Grimsby became a major growth area for heavy industry. Immediately before the war Grimsby RDC began to purchase land for industrial development and Grimsby Corporation purchased 222 acres in 1943 and financed the laying down of railway sidings. The advantages offered were flat, cheap land, a pool of labour in Grimsby in the early post-war years, good rail communications, access to the ports of Grimsby and Immingham, water from boreholes into the chalk, and ease of disposal of effluent into a tidal river.[39]

British Titan Products Co. Ltd of Teeside (now Tioxide) established a plant north of Grimsby in 1949 and when Laporte Titanium Ltd built a factory at Stallingborough in 1953 these two factories made the Humber bank the world's largest producer of titanium oxide. Courtaulds Ltd acquired a 500-acre site at Great Coates in 1954 and in 1957 opened a factory to produce viscose rayon staple. A second plant opened in 1959 to produce 'Courtelle', the first British acrylic fibre, and by 1971 employed over 1,900 people. Other new works included CIBA Laboratories Ltd (1951) and Dunlop Rubber Co. (1955) at Pyewipe, west of Grimsby, Fisons nitrogen fertilizer factory (1950) and ICI ammonia installation (1966) at Immingham Dock with Daverstand Ltd making synthetic rubber (1963) and the plant established by Kemps Biscuits Ltd at Great Coates. Other chemical plants were built at Barton-on-Humber (Allbright & Wilson) and Flixborough (Nypro). The latter was reconstructed after destruction by explosion and fire in 1974 but closed again in the early 1980s and in April 1984 the government made the site an Enterprise Zone.[40]

Although oil terminals were opened at Hull in 1914 and 1958, the real growth of oil imports has been on the south Humber bank since the 1960s. Crude oil imports were worth £13 million in 1965, but with two oil refineries (Conoco and Lindsey-Total/Petrofina) at North Killingholme and improved jetties at Immingham and Killingholme, £70 million worth of oil was imported in 1970. After the discovery of natural gas under the North Sea in the 1960s the whole of Britain was converted from town gas and the British Gas Corporation established a national grid. The Viking Gas Terminal was established on the coast at Theddlethorpe (Fig. 4.8) by Conoco to receive gas from several fields in the southern North Sea. In 1986 Conoco employed 260 people at Theddlethorpe, through which came 10 per cent of Britain's gas needs, and they announced plans to spend £650 million on developing three more North Sea gas fields to be connected to Theddlethorpe. In 1970 the British Steel Corporation opened a

Fig. 4.8   The Viking North Sea Gas Terminal at Theddlethorpe, built by CON-
OCO Ltd in 1973 and designed by Robert Cullen of Architects Design Group, repre-
sents the new large-scale industrial developments of the second half of the 20th century.
Such installations require a cooling pond, visible in the foreground. Source: D. Bower.

terminal at Immingham and in 1971 joined with the National Coal
Board and British Transport Docks Board to extend it to handle iron
ore for Scunthorpe as well as coal. By then the main imports through
Immingham were bulk materials for the steel and chemical industries, and crude oil and other liquids associated with the oil
industry. Exports comprised mainly coal, coke, steel, and the other
products of the petro-chemical industries.[41]

With this industrial development since 1945 north Lincolnshire experienced greater growth in population and employment than any
other part of Lincolnshire or the East Riding of Yorkshire. In 1901
there were only 570 people employed in chemical, petroleum and
allied industries in Lincolnshire but by 1971 there were 8,760, most
of them in the northern part of the county. The population of Immingham rose from 2,803 in 1951 to 10,259 twenty years later, acquiring
the amenities of a small town.[42]

Lincolnshire in the 1980s still has large industrial plants but only
Ruston's works in Lincoln shares continuity with the great engineering firms of the nineteenth century. The other huge Victorian
companies have closed, left the county or shrunk to a fraction of their
former size. In this they are following the national trend in mechanical engineering, and they have left a task for industrial archaeologists
to record their remaining buildings as evidence of a phase of British
history that is passing. Lincolnshire's Victorian firms were as much

a part of world trade as are the multi-nationals of the late twentieth century, but whereas the former had grown from local roots, the latter have come into Lincolnshire from elsewhere. Local people have continued to form new manufacturing firms, but they are small or medium-sized compared with the largest industrial sites in the county, mainly located on the Humber bank, which have been set up by firms from beyond Lincolnshire. In recent years probably more locally produced fortunes have been made in agriculture-related businesses rather than from manufacturing industry and in the future, prosperity may come from service industries and tourism.

Bibliographical note

A more detailed account of industry in twentieth-century Lincolnshire will make more use of company records than has been done in this general survey. Even using such material it will be necessary to place it in a wider context, and for this the various documents produced by the County and County Borough planning authorities for the Development Plans and later Structure Plans will be invaluable. For the first half of the century the general picture may be obtained from extensive usage of the various editions of *Kelly's Directory of Lincolnshire*.

For more local information the reference libraries in the main towns have some industrial material, and the town and county guides published in the middle years of the century had quite extensive sections on industry. Local histories such as those published by Barracuda Books sometimes contain industrial material, but sometimes not. Few Lincolnshire companies have had their own history written, apart from Ruston and Hornsby's by B. Newman, though there are quite extensive references to Lincolnshire steam engineering firms in the fairly numerous books on steam power.

Notes to Chapter 4

1. Wright, *Industry*, pp. 153–4, 156–7; P. Gregg, *A social and economic history of Britain 1760–1965*, London, 5th edn 1965, p. 419.
2. Gregg, *op.cit.*, p. 417; H. W. Brace, *Gainsborough, some notes on its history*, Gainsborough, 1965, p. 88; Reminiscences of L. B. Barley, Esq. per Prof. M. W. Barley.
3. B. Newman, *One hundred years of good company*, Lincoln, 1957, p. 95; Lincoln Central Library MS, Industry II, p. 50; S. E. Squires, *West Lindsey yesterday 1880–1980*, Gainsborough 1983, p. 32; J. Walls, *Ruston aircraft production*, Lincoln, 1974, pp. 3, 7, 11, 14, 21, 22; J. Walls, *Robey aircraft production*, Lincoln, 1974, pp. 2, 5, 11, 13 15.

4. This and the four preceding paragraphs include material from Walls, *Ruston, op.cit.*, pp. 3, 5, 19; J. Walls, *Clayton & Shuttleworth and Marshall aircraft production*, Lincoln, 1977, pp. 3, 6, 10, 12, 16, 17; Walls, *Robey, op.cit.*, 3, 4, 7, 13, 15; Wright, *Industry*, p. 84; Brace, *op.cit.*, p. 88.

5. This and the preceding paragraph include material from Walls, *Clayton, op.cit.*, p. 12; *Lincolnshire Echo*, 25 September 1946; K. Macksey, 'The tank story', in *A modern illustrated military history – land power*, London, 1979, pp. 90, 91, 94; Wright, *Industry*, p. 155; Squires, *ibid.*; C. Chant, ed., *How weapons work*, London, 1976, p. 86; Lincoln Central Library MS, Industry II, p. 155

6. This and the preceding paragraph include material from Newman, *op.cit.*, p. 95; N. C. Birch, *Stamford – an industrial history*, Lincoln, 1972, p. 7; Brace, *ibid.*; Walls, *Ruston, op.cit.*, p. 8; Lincoln Central Library MS, Industry II, p. 50; P. White and A. Tye, *An industrial history of Grimsby and Cleethorpes*, Grimsby, 1970, p. 26; D. E. Roberts, *The Lincoln gas undertaking 1828–1949*, Leicester, 1981, p. 31; M. B. Hodson, *Lincoln then and now*, Lincoln, 1982, p. 27; D. Boswell and J. M. Storey, *Grimsby as it was*, Nelson, 1974, p. 40.

7. Newman, *op.cit.*, p. 116; P. Gregg, *A social and economic history of Britain 1760–1965*, London, 5th edn 1965, p. 419.

8. This and the preceding paragraph include material from Gregg, *op.cit.*, pp. 417–19, 423, 426, 427; Newman, *op.cit.*, p. 115; Lincoln Central Library MS, Industry I, p. 121; Roberts, *op.cit.*, p. 41.

9. Newman, *op.cit.*, pp. 30, 88, 95–97, 121; Lincoln Central Library MS, Industry II, pp. 61, 71; J. Walls, *Clayton & Shuttleworth and Marshall aircraft production*, Lincoln, 1977, p. 13; H. W. Brace, *Gainsborough, some notes on its history*, Gainsborough, 1965, p. 91.

10. Newman, *op.cit.*, pp. 101–3; Wright, *Industry*, p. 221; G. Brooks, 'The motor car manufacturers of Lincolnshire' in *Lincolnshire Industrial Archaeology*, 5 no. 2 (1970), p. 24; P. White and A. Tye, *An industrial history of Grimsby and Cleethorpes*, Grimsby, 1970, p. 30.

11. Lincoln Central Library MS, Industry I, p. 3; Lincoln MS, Industry II, pp. 51, 148, 153; Newman, *op.cit.*, pp. 103–7; R. H. Clark, *Steam engine builders of Lincolnshire*, Norwich, 1955, pp. 1, 103; M. Honeybone, *The book of Grantham*, Buckingham, 1980, p. 116.

12. This and the preceding paragraph include material from P. Gregg, *A social and economic history of Britain 1760–1965*, London, 5th edn 1965, p. 419; J. Walls, *Clayton & Shuttleworth and Marshall aircraft production*, Lincoln, 1977, p. 13; L. Colsell, ed., R. Brooks and M. Longden, *Lincolnshire built engines*, Lincoln, 1986, pp. 4, 8; Lincoln Central Library MS, Industry II, pp. 51, 110; E. S. Mawer, *Lincoln Engineering Society 1923–73 Jubilee exhibition catalogue*, Lincoln, 1973, pp. 10, 21; *Kelly's Directory*, 1937, p. 202.

13. Lincoln Central Library MS, Industry I, pp. 32, 38, 45; H. W. Brace, *Gainsborough, some notes on its history*, Gainsborough, 1965, pp. 88, 89, 91; N. C. Birch, *Stamford – an industrial history*, Lincoln, 1972, p. 8; Gregg, *op.cit.*, p. 419; A. Muir, *The history of Baker Perkins*, Cambridge, 1968, p. 123; Honeybone, *op. cit.*, p. 116.

14. This and the preceding paragraph include material from M. E. Armstrong, ed., *An industrial island: A history of Scunthorpe*, Scunthorpe, 1981, pp. 48, 49, 52, 53, 54, 111, 113–15; Wright, *Industry*, pp. 158, 173; *Kelly's Directory* 1937, p. 26; *Lindsey – an official guide*, London, 1963, p. 54; I. J. Brown, 'Gazetteer of Ironstone Mines in the East Midlands' in *Lincolnshire Industrial Archaeology*, 6 nos 2 and 3 (1971), p. 46.

15. Wright, *Industry*, pp. 163, 173, 298; Armstrong, *op.cit.*, p. 113.

16. Wright, *Industry*, 170–71; *Kelly's Directory*, 1937, pp. 22, 26, 845; Brown, *op.cit.*, pp. 46–47; H. B. Hewlett, *The Quarries – ironstone, limestone and sand*, Stanton, 1935, reprinted Market Overton 1979, pp. 22, 25; *Consultation document* para. 3.130; D. N. Robinson, 'Nettleton Iron Mine' in *Lincolnshire Life* 11, no 2 (April 1971), pp. 31–32

17. Wright, *Industry*, p. 207; *Kelly's Directory*, 1937, pp. 1, 26, 723–24; *Lindsey – an official guide*, London, 1963, pp. 58, 59; *Lincolnshire county handbook*, London, 1971, pp. 59, 87

18. *Lindsey – an official guide*, London, 1963, p. 56; *Lincolnshire Echo*, 28 May 1985

19. This and the preceding paragraph include material from Wright, - *Industry*, pp. 172, 174; M. E. Armstrong, ed., *An industrial island: a history of Scunthorpe*, Scunthorpe, 1981, pp. 52, 53, 115, 120; *Kelly's Directory*, 1913, pp. 202, 515; G. R. Walshaw and C. A. J. Behrendt, *The history of Appleby-Frodingham*, Scunthorpe, 1950, pp. 103, 108, 135; A. Clark, 'Investment and closure in the nationalised iron and steel industry of the East Midlands, South Humberside and South Yorkshire, 1967 to 1983' in *The East Midland Geographer*, 8, part 4, no. 60 (December 1983), p. 100; *Kelly's Directory*, 1937, p. 489.

20. Armstrong, *op.cit.*, pp. 53, 90, 115, 117, 119, 121, 122; Manners, *et al.*, *Regional development*, 324, 325; *Lindsey – an official guide*, London, 1963, pp. 54, 55, 57; Clark, 'Investment', p. 103.

21. Clark, 'Investment', pp. 100, 104–5; Manners, *et al.*, *Regional development*, p. 325; Armstrong, *op.cit.*, pp. 115, 117, 120, 125–26.

22. This and the preceding paragraph include material from Lee, *Statistics*; Manners, *et al.*, *Regional development*, p. 325; Clark, 'Investment', pp. 104–10; T. Geraghty, 'Expanding enterprise in Humberside' in *County Councils Gazette* (June 1986), p. 66.

23. P. Gregg, *A social and economic history of Britain 1760–1965*, London, 5th edn 1965, p. 447.

24. This and the preceding paragraph include material from R. H. Clark, *Steam engine builders of Lincolnshire*, Norwich, 1955, p. 111; B. Newman, *One hundred years of good company*, Lincoln, 1957, pp. 121, 122, 127, 149, 156, 163–67, 170–75; J. Walls, *Clayton & Shuttleworth and Marshall aircraft production*, Lincoln, 1977, p. 15; J. T. Turner, *'Nellie': the history of Churchill's Lincoln-built trenching machine*, Society for Lincolnshire History and Archaeology, Occasional Papers in Lincolnshire History and Archaeology 7, 1988.

25. Newman, *op.cit.*, p. 165; M. Honeybone, *The book of Grantham*, Buckingham, 1980, p. 116; H. W. Brace, *Gainsborough, some notes on its history*,

Gainsborough, 1965, p. 92; S. E. Squires, *West Lindsey yesterday 1880–1980*, Gainsborough, 1983, p.32; A. Muir, *The history of Baker Perkins*, Cambridge, 1968, pp. 123, 124, 126; *Lincolnshire County Handbook*, London, 1960, pp. 10, 13; M. Middlebrook, *Boston at war*, History of Boston, vol. 12, Boston, 1974, pp. 47, 56.

26. Honeybone, *op.cit.*, p. 116; Middlebrook, *op.cit.*, pp. 52, 54; Squires, *op.cit.*, pp. 32, 54.

27. Lincoln Central Library MS, Industry II, p. 145; *Lincolnshire Chronicle*, 2 September 1960; *Lincolnshire Echo*, 9 February 1963; Lincoln Central Library MS, Industry I, p. 3.

28. R. H. Clark, *Steam engine builders of Lincolnshire*, Norwich, 1955, pp. 3, 36, 79, 100; S. E. Squires, *West Lindsey yesterday 1880–1980*, Gainsborough, 1983, pp. 15, 37, 38; H. W. Brace, *Gainsborough, some notes on its history*, Gainsborough, 1965, pp. 92, 93.

29. S. Strandh, *A history of the machine*, London, 1984, p. 184; B. Newman, *One hundred years of good company*, Lincoln, 1957, pp. 184–86, 239, 254; E. S. Mawer, *Lincoln Engineering Society 1923–1973 Jubilee exhibition catalogue*, Lincoln, 1973, p. 18.

30. Lincoln Central Library MS, Industry II, p. 87; Mawer, *op. cit.*, pp. 6, 12; Lee, *Statistics*.

31. Lincoln Central Library MS, Industry II, p. 94; M. Wilson and K. Spink, *Coles 100 years*, Uxbridge, 1978, p. 37; P. Gregg, *A social and economic history of Britain 1760–1965*, London, 5th edn 1965, pp. 549, 551–52, 558; *Consultation document*, para. 3.55.

32. Lincoln Central Library MS, Industry I, pp. 61, 80; B. Newman, *One hundred years of good company*, Lincoln, 1957, pp. 237, 239, 242, 244, 246–47, 250.

33. M. B. Hodson, *The quarries – ironstone, limestone and sand*, Stanton, 1935, reprinted Market Overton 1979, p. 23; M. Honeybone, *The book of Grantham*, Buckingham, 1980, p. 116; E. S. Mawer, *Lincoln Engineering Society 1923–1973 Jubilee exhibition catalogue*, Lincoln, 1973, pp. 11, 12, 14, 20; Newman, *op.cit.*, p. 111; *Lincolnshire industrial directory*, Gloucester, 1985, p. 59.

34. S. E. Squires, *West Lindsey yesterday 1880–1980*, Gainsborough, 1983, p. 7; Marshall, Sons & Co. Ltd, *A brief history*, Gainsborough, 1985, p. 3; *Lincolnshire Echo*, 19 April 1986.

35. J. Anderson, '130 Years of label making', in *Lincolnshire Life*, 20, no. 7 (1980) p. 31; A. Muir, *The history of Baker Perkins*, Cambridge, 1968, pp. 169, 171, 173, 206.

36. *Employment and industry; consultation document*, paras 3.66, 67; Wright, *Industry*, pp. 215–17; Lincoln Central Library MS, Industry I, p. 104; P. White and A. Tye, *An industrial history of Grimsby and Cleethorpes*, Grimsby, 1970, p. 35; *Lindsey – an official guide*, London, 1963, p. 58.

37. This and the preceding paragraph include material from P. Gregg, *A social and economic history of Britain 1760–1965*, London, 5th edn 1965, pp. 429–31, 448, 565; *Employment and industry*; Manners, *et al.*, *Regional development*, p. 198; *Consultation document*, paras 3.53, 56, 58, 67; *Lindsey*

– *an official guide*, London, 1963, pp. 56–58, 64; Wright, *Industry*, pp. 250–51; *Kelly's Directory*, 1930, pp. 194, 422; N. R. Wright, *Spalding – an industrial history*, Lincoln, 1973, p. 76; *Kelly's Directory*, 1937, pp. 236, 749, 765; *Lincolnshire county handbook*, London, 1971, pp. 29, 63, 65, 75, 76, 93; *Lincolnshire Echo*, 2 February 1987; Lee, *Statistics; Lincolnshire industrial directory*, Gloucester, 1985, pp. 30, 35.

38. *Consultation document*, para. 3.67; *Lincolnshire industrial directory*, Gloucester, 1985, p. 25; Manners, *et al.*, *Regional development*, pp. 198, 320; *Employment and industry*; Lee, *Statistics*; *Lindsey – an official guide*, London, 1963, p. 58.

39. Manners, *et al.*, *Regional development*, 323, 325; *Lindsey – an official guide*, London, 1963, pp. 61, 62; *Lincolnshire county handbook*, London, 1971, p. 47.

40. Manners, *et al.*, *Regional development*, pp. 323–24; *Lindsey – an official guide*, London, 1963, pp. 61, 62; *Lincolnshire county handbook*, London, 1971, pp. 75, 91; T. Gerahty, 'Expanding enterprise in Humberside' in *County Councils gazette* (June 1986), pp. 66–67.

41. P. White and A. Tye, *An industrial history of Grimsby and Cleethorpes*, Grimsby, 1970, p. 24; Manners, *et al.*, *Regional development*, pp. 323–25; E. S. Mawer, *Lincoln Engineering Society 1923–1973 Jubilee exhibition catalogue*, Lincoln, 1973, p. 27; 'Conoco Humber Refinery' in *Lincolnshire Life*, 26, no. 6 (1986), pp. 36–37; *Lincolnshire Standard*, 27 February 1986; *Lincolnshire county handbook*, London, 1971, p. 47.

42. Manners, *et al.*, *Regional development*, p. 323; Lee, *Statistics*.

CHAPTER 5

ROADS REPLACE RAILWAYS

by Peter R. White

Abstract   *The century opened with the railway network at its zenith, but within twenty years it was in severe competition from buses, including municipal transport. Between the wars there was stagnation of the railways; and during the second world war they were under acute pressure. After 1945 the railways were drastically reshaped, while the buses enjoyed only a brief period of great activity before they, too, began to suffer severely from competition from the car.*

The history of transport development in the twentieth century is a complex one, involving at least four modes (road, rail, air and sea) and two major markets (passenger and freight). Within this chapter, the story is traced through one main theme, the changes in public passenger transport, but where appropriate, references to other modes and markets are made, both in this and other chapters.

At the beginning of the century the transport system was dominated by the railways, the only mechanized land-transport mode. Neil Wright's previous volume in this series has documented the growth of the rail network up to its maximum extent, reached in 1913 with the opening of the Bellwater Junction–Coningsby line.[1] Much of the seaport development to this date was also associated closely with the rail companies.

This reflected the pattern in Britain as a whole at that time. Mechanized road transport based on steam traction had failed to develop, and in 1900 the internal combustion engine was still largely experimental. Turnpike trusts had been wound up. Roads functioned largely as feeders to rail, and for local traffic. However, the technology of 'heavy' standard-gauge railways was often inappropriate for lower density, short-distance movement. Attempts had been made through the introduction of 'rail motors' and simple halts to provide local stepping services over links such as Grimsby to Louth.

The narrow-gauge rural tramway was a common solution to such problems in other countries, notably Belgium and the Netherlands, but the Alford and Sutton line, which was open 1884–1889[2] was almost unique in mainland Britain, let alone Lincolnshire. Several similar schemes were proposed, but none built.[3] However, the 'Light Railway' concept – routes built under simplified powers of the Light Railways Act 1896 – was applied to several lower-cost standard-gauge lines built around the turn of the century, such as the Isle of Axholme and North Lindsey routes (Fig. 5.1).[4]

Although one thinks of the railway companies of this period as generally profitable before the onset of road competition, such was not necessarily the case. Of the two major companies in Lincolnshire, the Great Northern (operating mainly in the south and east) remained reasonably profitable, averaging a dividend of about 3 per cent for many years, but attained this only by minimizing its investment. Development of the resort at Skegness and the port at Boston had been left to local landowners and councils. Many of the branch lines worked by the Great Northern were in fact separate local companies, which were later purchased by the GNR for a sum substantially less than they had cost their local promoters to build.

In contrast, the Manchester, Sheffield & Lincolnshire Railway, serving the industrial northern part of the county, invested on a lavish scale in associated projects such as the resort of Cleethorpes, the docks at Grimsby, and biggest of all, the port of Immingham, which

Fig. 5.1 Turning of the first sod at Epworth, for the Isle of Axholme Light Railway. Opened in 1905, this section was one of the last lines to be built in the county, using powers under the Light Railways Act of 1896. However, passenger services succumbed to bus competition as early as 1933. Source: Scunthorpe Central Library.

opened in 1912. While some of these, notably the docks at Grimsby, helped to generate traffic, others went well beyond the financial interests of the company, such as the extension to London of the network in 1897. No dividend was paid on deferred ordinary stock from 1889 until the end of the company in 1923. However, the company's approach to investment certainly stimulated industrial development at a much earlier stage than might otherwise have been the case. In short, private returns were poor, but public benefit was considerable.

Rail technology also existed in the form of the street tramway. Horse-drawn lines had opened in Grimsby in 1881 and Lincoln in 1883. However, even in these urban areas the vast majority of local movement was on foot. Even quite long journeys in rural areas were made in this fashion. Anecdotal evidence suggests that pedal cycles had played a major role in increasing mobility from around 1890, but unfortunately little documentary confirmation is available. Most people rarely travelled further than the nearest market town or large village except, perhaps, for pleasure cycling.

Fig. 5.2 Dogdyke Station in the early 1920s. What did six men find to do here, in a village of only 174 people? These were the days of mixed goods trains carrying materials that now go by road: coal, timber, fertilisers, parcels, to the rural areas; agricultural products from the farms to their markets. Dogdyke station was on the GNR Lincoln–Boston line, which followed the east bank of the River Witham. The village was connected by ferry to its station on the opposite bank, a location which meant that other fen hamlets such as Scrub Hill and New York could make use of it. Note the Skegness excursion poster. The line was closed in 1963. Source: E. Croft postcard collection.

The approximate hinterlands of the market towns in 1896 can be derived from lists of local carriers in directories such as Kelly's and White's. Typically, a radius of up to about 15 miles was covered, but in some areas of traditionally poor communication decayed market towns could be found, such as Wainfleet and Wragby. Central villages such as Epworth acted as urban-like centres. Several were found in the area around the lower Trent, where river communication was easier than land movement. Hull thus retained some dominance even into the twentieth century, served by daily or weekly ferries from points on the Trent and south shore of the Humber, in addition to the main railway-operated ferry at New Holland.

Newer towns, whose growth had been promoted by the railways, such as Scunthorpe or Skegness, did not serve the surrounding area as a market centre, and even Grimsby, by 1901 the largest town in the county with 63,000 inhabitants, had a much smaller hinterland than the older market town of Louth. These observations illustrate the principle of historical inertia, or the difficulty which new institutions have in dislodging long-established competitors.

THE RISE OF THE BUS

The history of railways and tramways is generally well documented, because their construction required legislation. Tracing the history of bus services is much more difficult. Their ownership was greatly fragmented, and few written records remain. Before the Road Traffic Act of 1930, local authorities were able to exercise some powers of regulation, but these were not consistently used or recorded. Before the 1920s, only Grimsby, Cleethorpes and Lincoln councils provide complete records, and little is known of early operations outside these towns.

The county's first known regular bus service was also one of the first in Britain. During the summer of 1900 T. H. Barton operated a half-hourly service in Mablethorpe from the Pullover to The Cross public house, using a Benz single-cylinder ten-seater. He had purchased this vehicle at the Imperial Exhibition in London and in three days drove it to Mablethorpe under its own power.

Barton subsequently moved to Nottinghamshire, establishing the large independent bus company which still bears his family name and runs cross-country services to the Lincolnshire coast. In June 1900 a company started a service with two vehicles running between Arboretum and West Parade in Lincoln, but it ceased on 6 July 1901.

It was in the Grimsby area, the largest centre of population, that the major early bus operating initiatives occurred. In 1906, the Mail

Motor Company of Grimsby, financed by several prominent local residents, began running between Grimsby and Caistor on 10 July. The introduction of a service some twelve miles long over hilly country at such an early date is surprising, although perhaps explained in part by a wish to provide a link for Caistor, which had never gained a railway. Four weeks later, a second bus was delivered, and local services commenced from Grimsby Market Place to the villages of Waltham and Laceby, five times a day, the latter also served by the Caistor route. This attempt to utilize so intensively the primitive vehicles then available was not successful, and three more were purchased in an effort to maintain services, the share capital of £1,250 being increased by £2,000. A revised Caistor service, running three times a day was advertised in December 1906 and Laceby and Waltham services in February 1907, but by June of that year all five vehicles were unroadworthy and a Receiver was appointed. Sustained operation did not resume.

The Provincial Tramways Company – owner of the Great Grimsby Street Tramways – began to operate motor buses over the same route in 1909, the first vehicle being one of Mail Motor's, which they had purchased in 1907. Bus operation was based at the tramways depot in Cleethorpes, and largely initiated by H. Orme White, son of the then Grimsby tramways manager. After a short-lived tramway-feeder service, the vehicle was used to establish a service from Grimsby Old Market to Waltham on 22 July 1909; there has been continuous operation of public bus services in Lincolnshire from this date. A service to Laceby followed soon afterwards, and in December 1912 the Caistor service was reintroduced.

The Provincial Tramways Company also established charabanc hire and excursion services, which grew rapidly from 1911. Destinations included Woodhall Spa, Louth, and Skegness, and by 1913 a day trip to the Dukeries was not exceptional. Tours resumed after the first world war, and in 1921 were operated as far as Wales and Scotland. A rural bus service south from Grimsby along the coast to North Somercotes was introduced in 1915.

Other local operators appeared. In 1913 William Appleby of Conisholme, near Louth, started a carrier's service with a horse and cart, but one year later took to the road with a Ford model T. Today his grandson, Stuart Appleby, controls the county's largest independent bus and coach fleet, totalling around 70 vehicles. Another early rural operator was G. E. Jubb of Upton, near Gainsborough, who began his Woodland Bus Service around 1916. The first services in Scunthorpe began in 1914, running between the town and the other local centre about two miles away at Ashby, and to Gainsborough and Lincoln on market days. The operations were *from* Scunthorpe, which although already a substantial town, did not act as a centre for the carriers from the surrounding area, who ran instead to Brigg, Gainsborough and Winterton.

From 1918 onwards a steady stream of operators emerged, including many ex-servicemen. Others included the existing country carriers who switched over to motors during the early 1920s, and other local tradesmen, such as the blacksmith who had acquired some mechanical knowledge. The running of a bus service was often combined with some other activity, such as road haulage or garage ownership. Many local services were established initially by such concerns, but were later taken over by large companies, notably during the 1930s, although others have remained independent throughout.

In many cases, however, routes between towns were established from the outset by larger companies with access to greater capital. Within the independent sector, small firms acquired others to build up to fleets of 15 or so, either remaining in that form (such as Delaine of Bourne[7]), or being swallowed up later by bigger companies. It is also important to realize that there was a continual turnover of small operators, some of whom simply went out of business when faced by competition from a larger concern, rather than being acquired. As the network density grew, new small operators set up who had begun as drivers for larger concerns, as Fred Hunt of Alford, who set up an Alford–Spilsby–Boston service in 1930.

At first, the bus services simply repeated the pattern of carriers' carts, forming networks focused on existing market towns, although often at much higher frequencies than the carriers' services. By the mid 1920s, almost all villages had some sort of bus service, if only once or twice weekly. Timetables of the period reveal that these were geared largely to shopping and entertainment travel, with the first arrival in the town being too late for work (except for nearby villages, which started to become suburbs), but late evening departures were offered, especially on Saturdays, from theatres and the newly established cinemas. Villages continued to provide employment, but the range of shopping and entertainment facilities easily accessible to country people was vastly increased. Inevitably this eventually had major implications for the location of retailing and other services.

From the mid 1920s, daily routes between the major towns were established as the speed and reliability of vehicles improved, and competed effectively with railways. Villages en route gained a much better service than local traffic alone would have justified. These inter-urban services were often set up by larger companies, such as the Silver Queen company, established at Lincoln in 1922, and

Fig. 5.3 A 1930s Bedford bus of Enterprise and Silver Dawn at Scunthorpe bus station. Small vehicles such as this were used both on urban services – as in this case –
as well as on low-density rural routes. Note the excursion posters. Source: *Bedford
Magazine*, 1938.

renamed the Lincolnshire Road Car Company in 1928. Operations
covered much of east and south Lincolnshire by 1931, largely through
direct innovation by the company. Around Louth, Fred Wright began
services in 1925, creating a network to Lincoln, the coast, Spilsby and
Boston. In Holland, the Progressive company established services
linking main towns, and in 1922 this company set up a branch at
Scunthorpe, creating most of the inter-urban routes from that town.

Progressive was acquired, along with the Scunthorpe-based
Enterprise and Silver Dawn company, by a larger group in 1925.
However, both operations in the Scunthorpe area were repurchased
by Arthur Drury, proprietor of Enterprise & Silver Dawn, in 1927,
forming the basis for a company covering much of north Lincolnshire.
The Holland area services of Progressive eventually passed to Lincolnshire Road Car in 1930. In 1929 the Road Car company became
part of the BAT-Tilling group of bus companies, receiving capital investment from the railway companies.

Express coach services were set up from around 1928, including
many seasonal routes from the East Midlands to the coastal resorts,
and from Grimsby via Lincoln to London.

In 1931 a national system of regulation for bus and coach services
was introduced, under the Road Traffic Act 1930. Area Traffic Commissioners licensed operators, vehicles and services, Lincolnshire

falling within the East Midlands area, apart from a small area around Holbeach which was in the Eastern area. The role of local authorities in bus regulation was greatly reduced, and largely confined to that of objecting to fare or service proposals they disliked. Three authorities, Lincoln, Grimsby and Cleethorpes, operated their own services. The licensing system had the effect of protecting existing operators from newcomers, and also of protecting the railways from further competition, especially that from express coaches.

Larger operators were able to take over smaller ones with little fear of newcomers emerging on the routes gained. Thus Lincolnshire Road Car acquired many companies in the south and east of the county, notable examples including Skegness Motor Services and Friskney of Horncastle in 1934, Scunthorpe United Motor Services (a grouping of small independents who had sought to avoid takeover by Enterprise), and the two independent express services to London in 1936. Similarly, Enterprise and Silver Dawn acquired many local operators in an area stretching from Scunthorpe to Grimsby, Market Rasen, the Isle of Axholme and Goole. However, small independents continued to play a substantial role, and the domination of territorial companies was by no means as strong as in some other parts of Britain. The low-density rural nature of much of the area served is a partial explanation of this (Figs 5.4, 5.5).

By 1939 a comprehensive network served all parts of the county. Travel between towns was easier, as well as from village to town. Most routes offered evening and weekend services, although morning journey-to-work facilities were not universal, even on daily routes. Larger market towns came to dominate wider areas as speeds increased and certain minor settlements such as Caistor, Wainfleet, and Winterton ceased to act as local centres. Skegness became the centre for an area extending toward Boston, Spilsby and Alford. In addition, the flexibility of buses compared with railways encouraged a spread of the coastal resort development further from the limited areas around the railheads at Mablethorpe, Sutton, and Skegness. This was particularly noticeable in the area immediately north of Skegness, where Butlin's first holiday camp opened in 1936. In addition to intensive local services, through express coach routes from the East Midlands were provided.

Scunthorpe became the dominant centre for north-west Lincolnshire, in effect filling a gap in market hinterlands. The opening of the road bridge over the Trent at Keadby in 1916 tapped the Isle of Axholme. The market ferries to Hull from points on the Trent and Humber ceased during the 1920s as access to Scunthorpe became more convenient, although bus services were provided to the New

Holland ferry. Scunthorpe was also an exception since it drew in workers from a considerable area. As Chapter 2 has made clear, the growth in population at Scunthorpe was insufficient to serve the steelworks, and by the mid 1930s most villages within a radius of about 15 miles had through journeys to the steelworks for the main shift-changing times (0600, 1400, 2200 hrs.). These extended as far as Grimsby, about 30 miles.[8]

In certain respects, the summer of 1939 marked the maximum extent of the rural bus network, although the peak in trips made did not occur until ten years later. Wartime cuts in minor routes, and evening and Sunday services, were never fully restored, and the area around Spilsby never recovered the very high level of frequency offered: it was also to suffer closure of the Spilsby–Firsby rail service in that year. However, other kinds of traffic which were to become important in later years, notably schoolchildren, were at that stage relatively minor. Most village schools remained, and secondary education was less widespread than now. Nonetheless, it was realized that children were being required to travel distances too far to walk. Some used public bus services and trains; others were carried on special contract services. Lindsey County Council began the operation of its own school bus fleet in the 1930s. In October 1938, the local education authority provided bicycles for children living more than three miles from St Mary's School, Cowbit.

MUNICIPAL TRANSPORT 1914–1939

As Neil Wright has recorded,[9] electric trams were introduced in Grimsby and Cleethorpes by the Great Grimsby Street Tramways Company in 1901, and in Lincoln by the Corporation in 1906. Traffic grew rapidly in the first decade, as trams provided the first local motorized transport. The Grimsby and Cleethorpes system had been extended to serve People's Park at Welholme Road in 1902 and a short distance along the sea front at Cleethorpes in 1906, but no extensions occurred thereafter.

Between Grimsby and Cleethorpes a basic five-minute service was provided, serving the major corridor of development from the oldest area around the Old Market Place in Grimsby, past the docks and through to the sea front at Cleethorpes. Several types of traffic – to work, shops, and leisure – were thus concentrated on a single route, giving a good density of traffic throughout the day. Despite low fares (a maximum of 1d within Grimsby), the system was profitable, declaring a dividend of 6 per cent in 1906, later rising to 9 per cent.[10]

The Great Central Railway also carried substantial local traffic between the two towns – the only case of intensive local rail passenger
traffic in the county. Although faster, the trains lost much traffic to
the more frequent and accessible trams and toward the end of 1903
a fare war developed. The GCR introduced a 6d zone ticket giving a
person unlimited travel for a week, later replaced by 6d bundles of
twelve single tickets, which were still on issue in 1938, then priced
1s 3d.

Improved communications were related to the growth of Cleethorpes as a residential area for Grimsby, as well as a resort. By 1901
Grimsby had a population of 63,000 and Cleethorpes 12,500. By 1921
Grimsby's had grown by 25 per cent to 82,000 but that of Cleethorpes
by over 100 per cent to 28,000.

An unusual extension of the urban transport system was the
Grimsby and Immingham Electric Railway, opened on 15 May 1912,
and extended to Immingham Lock Gates on 17 November 1913. At
the Grimsby end it terminated just west of the Alexandra Dock,
providing a local service within the West Marsh district where it ran
as a street tramway: proposals were made to connect it with the rest
of the tram system, but never effected.[11] The route was operated by
the Great Central, forming one of the few examples of an 'interurban'
electric tramway in Britain. Apart from linking the inhabitants of Immingham (where a small town grew inland of the dock) with Grimsby,
a major function of the line throughout its life was to carry workers
from Grimsby to Immingham Docks, a role which grew greatly after
the second world war as new industries were established along the
Humber bank.

The street tramways in Grimsby and Cleethorpes were unusual in
that they remained for long in private company ownership, whereas
most systems, like Lincoln, were electrified under municipal control.
Tram traffic increased rapidly during the first world war, reaching a
peak of 15 million trips in 1921, two and a half times above the level
of 1903. However, mileage run by the tramcars had risen only 14 per
cent. Every car was pressed into service, but serious overcrowding occurred. Grimsby Corporation retained powers to purchase the
tramway. On 3 February 1921 a town poll was held, with 3,698 voting
in favour of municipalization and only 2,155 against. In August 1921
the Corporation received an Act empowering it to work tramways,
trolleybuses, and motorbuses. From 6 April 1925 the Corporation took
over the operation of tramways within the borough, together with 22
of the company's tramcars. Some 16 cars were purchased from the
Sunderland and District company to augment the fleet. A depot was

erected in Victoria Street North, and J. C. Whiteley from South Shields was appointed manager.

The high cost of tramways deterred their extension to serve other parts of the town. Attempts by other local bus and charabanc operators to run services competing with the tramway were rejected in 1914 and 1920 by Grimsby Corporation, in its role as regulator of services. However, other operators introduced services from local villages, and these began to carry traffic within the town from areas not served by the tramway, notably Scartho Road and Laceby Road, south of the old centre.

The poor condition of the tram route from Riby Square along Freeman Street led to early trolleybus replacement by Grimsby Corporation in October 1926, the service being extended along Hainton Avenue to Weelsby Road. Motor bus services were introduced, the first from Old Clee to Riby Square on 20 November 1927. The second followed on 3 June 1928, replacing the Old Market–Welholme Road tramway. The tramway within Grimsby was thus reduced to the main line from Old Market to the boundary with Cleethorpes, operated jointly with the company as a through service.

Further bus services were introduced, serving the Nunsthorpe and Scartho areas south of the town and passengers along the route to Cleethorpes via Weelsby Road. By 1930 a fleet of 21 single-decker motor buses had been built up, serving six routes. The first double-decker was delivered in that year, and by 1939 some 21 were owned. For the year 1928–9, the corporation trams carried 8.5 million passengers, the trolleybuses 3.2 million, and motorbuses 3.35 million.

In 1927 Grimsby obtained an Act to incorporate the parishes of Scartho and Little Coates to the south and west of the town, in which much new housing was rapidly being built. Its population thus rose to 92,000, a level which it maintained for many years thereafter. However, the municipal bus service did not expand immediately to match this, as the council had agreed with local independent operators not to extend its own services beyond the old boundary for five years. When this period ended in July 1932 a dispute began with the operators – Provincial and Ada Motor Services. Takeover was effected in June 1934, when Corporation motor bus services were extended to the villages of Humberston and Waltham.[12] Provincial's bus operations were then reduced to hire work and a sea front route in Cleethorpes.

Cleethorpes UDC began its own bus services in 1930, with routes to Humberston and joint operation on the route to Grimsby via Weelsby Road. From 18 July 1936 the Urban District, which became a municipal borough in the following year, took over the remaining local operations of the Great Grimsby Street Tramways Co. and Provincial Tramways, with 22 cars and the depot and power station. The Grimsby portion of the main tram route was converted to trolleybus operation from 22 November 1936. The Cleethorpes part of the tramway continued to run until 31 March 1937, when it too was replaced by trolleybuses, and a through service resumed. Along Cleethorpes sea front the trolleys were extended to the Bathing Pool, then the limit of development.

A joint Grimsby and Cleethorpes transport undertaking was suggested in 1936 – a logical move in view of the common area served – but did not become a reality for twenty years. By the end of the 1930s a modern transport network served both towns. On the Grimsby system, total patronage by all modes had risen from 11.7 million in 1925–26 to 19.7 million in 1936–37. Although losses were incurred in some years, operation was generally profitable.

In Lincoln a fairly extensive tramway network was authorized under an Act of 1900, but only the line along the High Street to Bracebridge, incorporating the rebuilt horse tramway, ever operated. This featured the somewhat unusual Griffith-Bedell system of surface contact studs in place of overhead wires. From time to time plans were produced to give the uphill district a public service. These even included a proposal in 1909 for a funicular railway on a 1 in 5 gradient up Steep Hill to Castle Square. In March 1913 an offer from the British Automobile Traction company to run a bus service in the city was received, followed by one from the Provincial Tramways Co. in September. In January 1914 heads of agreement were reached with the National Steam Car Company, but the company had to withdraw from negotiations in August.

As in Grimsby, patronage of the trams rose rapidly during the first world war – by about 30 per cent between 1915 and 1918 – and revenue was further increased by a 50 per cent fares rise in July 1917. With these extra funds, it was possible to convert from the surface contact system to overhead supply in 1919.[13] Further offers from bus operators were received in 1920, but by this time it was clear that the Corporation was determined to run its own service under powers in the Lincoln Corporation Act of 1915. Eleven single-deck Dennis buses were purchased, fitted with bodies by the Lincolnshire Automobile Co. at Louth. On 30 November 1920 bus service no.1 began, serving the Burton Road area in the north of the city. This was followed in 1921 by services to West Parade and Monks Road. Thus housing in the north of the city was now served. New development was occurring in the St Giles area, north-east of the Cathedral, and service here began in March 1921 (see below, Chapter 8, p. 204).

Bus operations grew steadily during the 1920s. By 1926 as many passengers were carried on buses as trams, and services south of the city centre were established. In December 1927 the first Leyland 'Titan' double-decker was delivered, and successfully driven through the Stonebow at the north end of the High Street. The last tram made its journey on 3 March 1929, and thereafter an all-bus fleet was operated. However, growth in the 1930s was much less rapid than in Grimsby and Cleethorpes,[14] as the city was not empowered by the Act of 1915 to run outside its boundary.

RAILWAYS

The railway grouping of 1923 had little immediate effect on the county. The Great Central and Great Northern both became part of the London & North Eastern Railway (LNER). There was little overlap, save for duplication of services (passenger and fish) from Grimsby to London, the GC services to Marylebone via Lincoln being withdrawn in favour of the GN route to Kings Cross via Boston in 1924. The London, Midland and Scottish Railway (LMSR) also had a role in the county, taking over the interests of the Midland Railway between Nottingham and Lincoln, and becoming joint owners with the LNER of the Midland & Great Northern Line through Bourne, Spalding and Kings Lynn. Investment on the GN routes remained fairly low, apart from some improvements to the east coast main line through Grantham and the rebuilding of Skegness station with additional sidings for seasonal traffic in 1936.

The continued growth of the iron and steel industry at Scunthorpe stimulated important developments in the north of the county. In 1928 a new marshalling yard was opened as well as a new station in Frodingham to replace the former site. Iron-ore reserves in the immediate vicinity of the town became inadequate, and regional movements from other reserves in the limestone hills developed. The earliest were those around Claxby (closed in 1885), Honington, Lincoln and Caythorpe.[15] The most substantial were those in the Saxby area, initially opened out by the construction of the M&GN route in 1894. In 1912 a branch line was authorized from the GN east coast main line at Highdyke, near Grantham, serving open-cast mines around Colsterworth. This route was in operation by 1916 and was extended during the 1920s and 1930s as new mines were opened in the area to serve the Appleby–Frodingham works at Scunthorpe. By the late 1930s an output of up to 700,000 tons a year was being produced compared with 400,000 in the previous decade.[16] A basic service of two trains per day conveyed the ore to Scunthorpe, initially via the main line and Doncaster, but from 1932 they were rerouted via Lincoln and Barnetby to reduce congestion on the main line.

This traffic flow remained important until the 1970s, when the Highdyke area mines were abandoned in favour of higher grade imported ore. A similar flow took place from Holton-le-Moor, on the Barnetby–Lincoln line, where ore from the chalk ridge was conveyed to sidings by aerial ropeway.

In 1925 the LNER revived a scheme for a Blyton and Scunthorpe line, linking with the Gainsborough–Barnetby route, powers for which had been held by a subsidiary company of that name which was incorporated within the LNER in 1923. An Act was finally obtained in 1929, but the line, essentially a blocking move to any invasion of north Lincolnshire, was never built, following the LNER/LMSR working agreement of 1934. Had it been constructed, it would have formed a useful route for the Highdyke iron ore traffic.

Fish traffic remained important – some eight complete trains per day were despatched from Grimsby in 1923 – and rose by some 10,000 tons per year between 1922 and 1928. In 1934 the LNER completed the construction of No. 3 Fish Dock, which became the main base for the deep-sea fleet.

In 1926 the LNER completed improvement works at New Holland Pier for the Hull ferry service, followed in 1934 by two new ferries, the *Wingfield Castle* and *Tattershall Castle*. Although providing easier access for motor vehicles, they followed the traditional pattern in being coal-fired paddle steamers, the shallow draught of the Humber at this point not permitting screw vessels. They were joined by the similar *Lincoln Castle* in 1940, and these three ships then maintained the ferry service until the late 1970s. A curious move by the LNER was the resumption of the Gainsborough–Hull service for a period in the 1920s. The vessel used is thought to have been the *Dundie Dermont* of 1895, acquired from the North British Steam Packet Co. in 1928. The rebuilt Victoria Pier at Hull was opened in 1937, in which year the last market boats ran to the city. Thereafter the only link was the New Holland ferry, to which a network of feeder bus services had developed during the 1920s. Employment generated by the railways at New Holland declined as the railway laundry closed in 1931, followed by the locomotive works and tarpaulin repair shop by 1939.

Following the schemes for railway tunnels beneath the Humber in the 1880s and again in 1908, Hull Corporation promoted a Bill in the 1930 session for a road bridge of cantilever spans between Barton and Hessle. This fell victim to the recession, but anticipated closely the site eventually chosen for the suspension bridge finally opened in June 1981.

Immingham, opened shortly before the first world war, played a major role as a coal export port, the function for which it was primarily designed. In 1929, some 2.75 million tons were exported. Passenger cruises, principally to the Norwegian coast, were also developed by the Orient Line, to which through specials were operated from Marylebone and Manchester by the LNER until 1939. The Tor Line used it for its Dutch and Swedish passenger services in the 1960s and early 1970s.

Local passenger services received some new equipment in the form of steam 'rail motors', built by Claytons of Lincoln, and also by Sentinel. For example, a service using a Sentinel railcar was introduced between Grimsby and North Thoresby in 1928, and they were also used on the New Holland–Immingham service. However, their performance was generally poor, and services reverted to locomotive-hauled operation until the arrival of diesel multiple units in the 1950s.

Bus competition began to divert traffic from the railways as early as the 1920s. The first service to close to passengers was the North Lindsey Light Railway from Scunthorpe to Whitton and Winteringham on 13 July 1925 (even in 1922 the passenger service had declined to one train per day in each direction) the line remaining principally as a link to Lysaght's steelworks (later RTB). It was followed by the Bourne–Sleaford route from 22 September 1930, and the Isle of Axholme lines from 15 July 1933. The Spilsby–Firsby branch closed to passengers on 11 September 1939.

Short distance traffic on remaining lines was also hit by road competition. Between 1936 and 1938 alone, passenger journeys originating at Boston, Horncastle, and Spilsby fell by 11 per cent. By 1938 only 64,000 out of a total of 294,000 tons of freight entering the port of Boston did so by rail.[17] However, growth in agricultural traffic came to the railways as well as the roads from the creation of refineries to process sugar beet, grown under state subsidy, at Brigg, Bardney, and Spalding.

WORLD WAR II

The initial impact of the second world war was to cause substantial curtailment of services, notably long-distance express coaches, leaving rail as the major interurban carrier. Rationing of fuel and cessation of new car production reduced private motoring to a very low level. Demand in the seaside resorts was severely reduced. The seafront 'runabout' service at Cleethorpes ceased for good, and four relatively new trolleybuses became surplus to requirements, being sold to Nottingham.

Some restrictions on public passenger transport became more severe as conditions worsened. Fuel shortages and the blackout resulted in severe cuts to evening and Sunday services. In Grimsby and Cleethorpes, bus services parelleling the trolleybus routes were cut back so as to concentrate demand on electric traction. Bombing, which mainly affected Grimsby, caused further disruption and loss of vehicles.

Apart from the seaside, however, passenger demand grew strongly as full employment returned, and many additional movements were made by members of the forces. Numerous RAF stations grew rapidly, as recounted in the next chapter, providing additional demand for local bus services, and for long-distance travel from the nearest railhead. At Grantham station, for example, 420,000 tickets were sold and collected in 1938, but 990,000 in 1944.[18] Passengers carried on the buses of Lincoln City Transport, whose pre-war traffic had been depressed by high levels of unemployment in the city, rose from 9.7 million in 1939 to 16.3 million in 1945. Grimsby's bus and trolleybus traffic rose from 17.6 million passengers in 1939–40, to 28.0 million in 1944–45. Enterprise and Silver Dawn suffered considerable staff shortages, because of the priority given to the steel industry, and it employed women drivers as well as conductors.

Pressure on bus operators was relieved as deliveries of new utility vehicles began in 1942. These included a substantially higher proportion of double-deckers than in pre-war fleet intakes, augmenting passenger capacity. Greater cooperation between operators could have helped, but even under wartime conditions negotiations between Lincoln City Transport and the Road Car company failed to achieve any result.

An invasion rumour at one stage caused two army officers to request the LNER District Superintendent at Lincoln to take precautions prescribed under such circumstances, which would have included destruction of bridges. On checking the position with LNER control he found no truth in the rumour and took no action, but nonetheless the alarm spread over a wide area before it could be scotched.[18]

Immingham and Grimsby docks were requisitioned by the Admiralty. In 1942–44 Immingham was used for American arrivals, and subsequently marshalling of Mulberry piers for the Normandy landings.

RESHAPING OF THE RAILWAYS

The 1945 Labour government pursued a policy of nationalization through the Transport Act 1947, leading to the formation of British Railways under the British Transport Commission, from 1 January 1948. The former LNER lines and the Midland and Great Northern route in the south of the county passed to the Eastern Region; the former LMS line to Lincoln was allocated to the London Midland Region. Also placed under the BTC were the railway-owned docks at Grimsby and Immingham, the Humber ferry services, and the Lincolnshire Road Car Company, which was nationalized as part of the BAT–Tilling group, along with the railways. The names were changed, but little change in the pattern of operations was evident initially.

However, the basic weakness of the rural branch lines, hit by bus competition from the 1920s, remained, and closure resumed. The Bourne–Essendine line closed to passengers from 18 January 1951, followed by the Louth–Bardney line on 5 November of that year. Louth ceased to be a junction from 4 December 1960 when the last train left for Mablethorpe. A major closure was that of the Midland and Great Northern line through south Lincolnshire on 28 February 1959. The branch from Essendine to Stamford saw its last passenger train later that year, on 13 June. The last remnant of local passenger services over the Lancashire, Derbyshire, and East Coast line between Shirebrook North and Lincoln ceased on 17 September 1955. From 2 November 1959 the line from Sykes Junction across the Trent at Torksey was closed: Lincoln–Sheffield trains were diverted via Gainsborough, although the section from Sykes Junction as far as the river was subsequently reopened for freight, to serve a new oil terminal.

Many lines remained open for freight, and few widespread complete closures took place until the 1960s. However, parts of the North Lindsey line (reduced mainly to a steelworks feeder) went in 1951 and 1961; and the last part of the Louth–Bardney line ceased to carry freight in 1960. The Spilsby line closed to freight traffic in 1958, and the Billingborough–Sleaford section of the Bourne–Sleaford route in 1956. On closure of the M&GN to passengers, the sections west of Bourne and east of Sutton Bridge were also closed to all traffic.

However, a fairly extensive rail network still remained in 1962, most lines closed having been the minor GNR branches originally built by local companies. Passenger traffic had often gone many years before to more convenient local bus services. Little specific change to bus services was needed, although Horncastle–Woodhall buses were diverted to terminate in the station yard at Woodhall Junction on the closure of the Horncastle branch in 1954.

Remaining passenger services were modernized through the introduction of diesel multiple-unit trains from 1955, under the modernization plan of that year. By September 1957 most local passenger services in the county were worked in this form, except for some longer-distance services and many seasonal operations. The diesel multiple units were based at Lincoln depot. Following further closures in the early 1960s, this became one of only three motive power depots in the county, the others at Immingham and Scunthorpe concentrating on freight locomotives.

Subsequent developments arising from the modernization plan included the rebuilding of Cleethorpes station in 1961, and the underpass at Retford in 1965. This enabled the Sheffield–Retford–Lincoln/Grimsby services to pass under the East Coast main line, removing a congested flat crossing. However, the similar flat crossing of the Lincoln–Nottingham route and the main line just north of Newark still remains.

In addition to complete closure of lines to passenger services, other routes experienced closure of intermediate local stations in an effort to speed up services between major centres: for example, on the Peterborough–Grantham section of the East Coast main line in 1957, and many points on the Grimsby–Peterborough line in 1961. This route-by-route approach, however, led to curious results. Large villages such as Kirton-in-Holland lost their rail services entirely, while minor stations on other routes remain open to this day – such as Havenhouse, on the Skegness line, whiich lies some distance from the nearest significant village.

The worsening financial position of the railways, transferred from the British Transport Commission to the newly-formed British Railways Board from January 1963, resulted in the appearance of the 'Reshaping Plan' of Dr Richard Beeching in March of that year. The report envisaged closure to passengers of the Grimsby–Peterborough line with its branches to Skegness, Mablethorpe, and Lincoln, the New Holland network, and perhaps most surprising, the Lincoln–Nottingham route. Many small passenger stations and freight depots were to close entirely, while some uneconomic traffics, such as certain freight flows and highly seasonal seaside traffic, were to be abandoned. Shortly after the report appeared, previously approved closures between Boston and Woodhall Junction, and Immingham Dock and Goxhill took place, the last trains running on 15 June 1963. A replacement Boston–Lincoln service via Sleaford was provided.

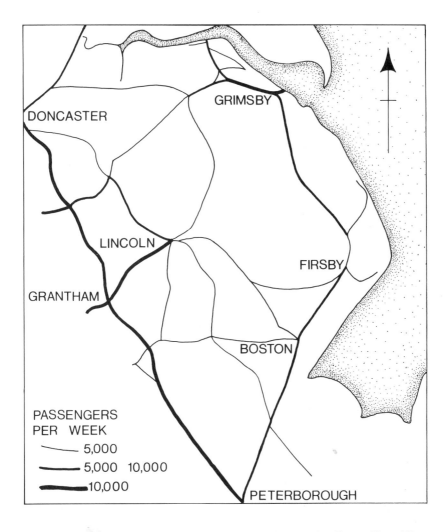

Fig. 5.4 Passenger flows on railways in Lincolnshire, at April 1962. Dotted lines denote fewer than 5,000 passengers per week, light solid lines between 5,000 and 10,000, and heavier solid lines over 10,000. The dominance of the east coast main line is clear, with the only flows over 10,000 per week within the county being between Lincoln and Nottingham; and Cleethorpes, Grimsby, and Habrough. Other important flows were those along the East Lincolnshire line (Grimsby to Peterborough), Lincoln to Sheffield, and the spur to the New Holland ferry. Source: Vol. 1 of the *Reshaping Report*, also known as the 'Beeching Report', British Railways Board 1963. Note that the use of April data was criticized at the time, since the role of lines with substantial seasonal traffic – such as that to Skegness – would be understated.

The Lincolnshire rail network by 1963 included few minor branch lines as such, but consisted mainly of interurban links between sizeable towns. As the map for passenger traffic (Fig. 5.4) shows, only the Lincoln–Nottingham, Grimsby–Habrough–Hull, Lincoln–Sheffield and Grimsby–Peterborough flows accounted for over 5,000 passengers per week. At first sight it seemed surprising that all these routes (apart from Lincoln–Sheffield) were to be axed, but this was explained by the freight traffic flows, which are heaviest in the west of the county. However, the extraordinary proposal to eliminate the Lincoln–Nottingham route was never satisfactorily explained: indeed, in the second part of the reshaping plan the route was selected as part of the network for development.

The second part of the plan, published in February 1965, also advocated Grimsby–Scunthorpe–Doncaster, and Grimsby–Lincoln as major routes for development, a decision which clearly accorded with the distribution of population and industry in the county. By building a new curve at Newark between the Lincoln–Nottingham route and East Coast main line, use of the Grimsby–Lincoln–Newark route for London as well as Midlands traffic became possible. Accordingly, the Lincoln–Honington Junction line was closed on 30 October 1966, the Lincoln–Grantham service being replaced by a Lincoln–Newark Northgate service to connect with main line services to London.

The closure proposals were vigorously opposed by local councils and other bodies – notably the East Lincolnshire Railway Protection Association – which presented evidence to the hearings in 1963 and 1964 of the Transport Users' Consultative Committee for the East Midlands. In both cases, the TUCC concluded that extensive hardship would be caused by the closure, and saw no means of alleviating it: indeed, very few alternative plans for bus services were produced at that time.

BR subsequently formulated alternative proposals, including a bus service from Cleethorpes to the New Holland ferry, and a scheme for east Lincolnshire in which the important seasonal link from Nottingham to Skegness via Grantham and Boston would be retained, but the other sections would still close. Repeat TUCC hearings were held in January 1967 (for the New Holland services) and May 1968 (east Lincolnshire), with the same conclusions as before.

In June 1969 the Minister of Transport, Mr Richard Marsh, announced a reprieve for the Cleethorpes–New Holland, and New Holland–Barton services, although the Immingham Dock–Ulceby–Grimsby service which had been introduced on closure of the Grimsby–Immingham tramway in 1961 (see below) ceased from October 1969. However, Marsh's successor, Fred Mulley, subsequently gave consent to the east Lincolnshire closure plans. These came into effect with the last London–Grimsby train via the East Lincolnshire line on Sunday 4 October 1970. The Grimsby–Firsby, Boston–Spalding–Peterborough, Firsby–Lincoln and Willoughby–Mablethorpe lines then ceased to carry passengers. Freight traffic remained for a few years more on the Grimsby–Louth section, subsequently acquired by a preservation group (although no services have commenced).

Grimsby–London services were diverted via Lincoln, which thus gained a through London link. In the south of the county, a basic Nottingham–Grantham–Boston–Skegness service provided the main link. While providing quite well for major seasonal flows, the resultant routing to London via Grantham was very slow and indirect compared with the former route south from Boston.

Much of the traditional wagonload freight movement was also abandoned as uneconomic during the 1960s and early 1970s, resulting in traffics such as Grimsby fish, cattle, and most agricultural produce no longer using rail. Branches which had remained open for freight after closure to passengers generally closed totally, except where bulk traffic was handled.

Since 1970, Lincolnshire and South Humberside railways have generally experienced a more positive pattern of change. No further significant closures have taken place – indeed, the Spalding–Peterborough line was reopened to passenger service on 7 June 1971 with support from Holland County Council and Spalding District Council. At first, only a very limited morning and evening service was provided, but in recent years this has been augmented to an all-day service at a similar level to that before 1970, carrying through services to Lincoln and Doncaster, following the closure of the thinly used section of the Great Northern and Great Eastern 'Joint Line' between Spalding and March in 1985. This has been the only passenger closure since 1970.

On the opening of the Humber Bridge on June 1981, the Cleethorpes–New Holland, and New Holland–Barton services were combined to form a Cleethorpes–Barton service (with a new station at New Holland town), interchange being offered at Barton with the Scunthorpe–Hull bus service over the bridge. Sunday services on the New Holland line were retained with support from Humberside County Council from 1976, which assists in the marketing of the current rail and bus connecting services as 'Humberlink'. Several routes have been partly converted to single-track working to reduce costs, notably Gainsborough–Brigg, Boston–Skegness and Grimsby–Cleethorpes.

Lincolnshire County Council supported the reconstruction and reopening of stations at Metheringham and Ruskington on the Sleaford–Lincoln line in the 1975, the former with bus-feeder services. After many years debate, the two stations in Lincoln were rationalized from 11 May 1985, when a connecting curve was built between the Nottingham line and the old 'goods avoiding line' south of the city, which permitted Lincoln–Newark–Nottingham services to run into Central Station, and St Marks Station was closed. The first new diesel units since the modernization plan of the 1950s, the Sprinter type, entered service on the Lincoln–Nottingham–Derby and Crewe–Nottingham–Grantham–Skegness services in 1986. However, the level of service on the Grimsby–Brigg–Gainsborough route has declined in favour of the Grimsby–Scunthorpe–Doncaster–Sheffield service (closure of the former is now proposed).

The Cleethorpes–London service has been converted to High Speed Train operation (one service each way daily), although speeds north of Newark remain low. The intensive HST service on the main line has brought substantial improvements to services from Grantham, and also shortened the journey time from Lincoln via Newark to London. Electrification of this main line will bring further changes.

BUSES AFTER 1945

The immediate postwar period saw further growth in bus traffic as full employment continued, while car ownership and use remained severely restricted by rationing. Seaside traffic grew rapidly as normal bus services, and also express coach operations, were restored from the summer of 1946. Delays in delivery of new vehicles was in many cases a restraint on the growth in traffic which could be handled. A higher proportion of double-deckers in new deliveries – Lincolnshire Road Car had operated a mere handful before the war – also helped to increase capacity (Fig. 5.5). However, scheduled service frequencies did not always rise with the extra traffic, and in parts of east Lincolnshire and the Enterprise & Silver Dawn network around Scunthorpe wartime cuts were never fully restored, additional traffic being handled by larger vehicles and duplication at peak times rather than by raising the basic service frequency.

New urban services developed to serve housing estates, both as an extension to existing urban networks in Grimsby, Louth and Scunthorpe, and in the form of largely new services in towns such as Boston and Grantham, where substantial areas of housing were for the first time located beyond normal walking distance from the town centres.

Fig. 5.5 A Lincolnshire Road Car Leyland TD5 on the Skegness–Boston service. Delivered in 1938, this was one of the few double-deckers operated by the company pre-war, but such vehicles were purchased on a large scale in later years to cater more efficiently for peak traffic. Over the indicator blind is the single light, which in pre-war days was the distinctive company symbol. Source: P. R. White collection.

The Lincolnshire Road Car Company came under state ownership in the form of the British Transport Commission from 1 January 1948, coincident with nationalization of the railways. While compulsory nationalization of bus services never extended beyond this, many operators feared such a move, and began negotiations voluntarily for sale to the BTC. Enterprise & Silver Dawn, renamed Enterprise (Scunthorpe) Passenger Services Ltd. in 1948, was taken over by the BTC from 1 March 1950 and immediately incorporated into the Lincolnshire Road Car Co. as the northern area of that company. However, for many years it functioned largely as a separate unit, with former Enterprise Managing Director Arthur Drury as area manager until 1962. The other substantial operator to be taken over by LRCC was Wright of Louth, also in 1950, with his rural network in east Lincolnshire, and some suburban routes into Lincoln. Three smaller operators were also acquired in 1950.

Figure 5.6 shows the extent of LRCC's network in 1950 – the maximum extent of its operations – including services acquired from Enterprise and Wright. Incorporation of the Enterprise fleet of 150, along with the other acquisitions, brought the total fleet to 538. Milage operated per annum had increased from 10 million in 1939 to 13 million in 1949, and 17 million following acquisitions in 1950. However, by 1963 it had fallen to 15 million. Passenger totals peaked

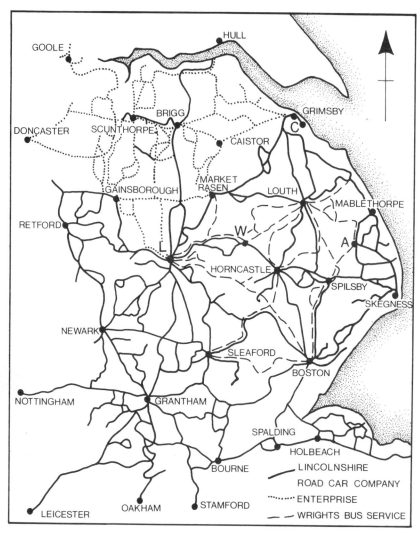

Fig. 5.6 Operating areas of the major bus companies in 1950, at the time of Enterprise and Wrights being taken over by the Lincolnshire Road Car Co. The solid lines are those worked by Road Car in its own right, hatched lines for Wrights, and dotted for Enterprise. Note that other smaller independents continued to operate, and fill some of the apparent 'gaps' on the map shown.
L = Lincoln, W = Wragby, A = Alford, and C = Cleethorpes.
Source: P. R. White.

in 1950 at 53 million, but fell to 40 million in 1959. Route milage increased from 2,200 to 4,800 as a result of the 1950 takeovers: by 1963 this had fallen to 4,500.

A similar peak in operations was seen in the municipal sector. Lincoln's all-time high was 19.8 million passengers in 1952 – corresponding to 300 journeys per head of population.[14] Grimsby peaked at 34.4 million in 1949. However, deficits were already being recorded by the major public operators in the late 1940s, as costs of wages, fuel, and new vehicles rose faster than traffic revenue. The first fares increases for many years became necessary around 1950 and continued thereafter because of higher costs and reduced traffic resulting from greater car ownership and use.

In 1955 Grimsby Corporation Transport replaced its Riby Square–Hainton Avenue trolleybus route by motorbuses, the last trolleys running on 2 October. One-man operation was introduced through conversion of some old single-deckers. These were used, *inter alia*, on a service replacing the street tramway section of the Grimsby and Immingham Electric Railway, over which the last car ran on 30 June 1956. GCT also ordered a batch of new vehicles for one-man operation, received in 1956. This approach was followed by its successor, Grimsby–Cleethorpes Transport, which placed large numbers of similar vehicles in service during its early years.

Cleethorpes Corporation Transport likewise suffered financial losses, and introduced its first one-man buses in 1954. These financial pressures gave a spur to amalgamation discussions, and from 1 January 1957 the Grimsby and Cleethorpes Joint Transport Committee came into being, controlled by a committee of councillors from both authories. Immediate savings were effected through the closure of the Cleethorpes depot and concentration of all activity on the Grimsby base. Under General Manager John Rostron, an energetic programme of efficiency improvement and network restructuring began. One-man single-deck operation was rapidly extended to cover the lower-density routes (one man double-deck operation not being legalized until 1967).

From 28 September 1959, the all-day service on the Grimsby and Immingham tramway – still operated by British Railways – ceased, being replaced by a joint bus service with Lincolnshire Road Car (no.45), between Immingham Docks, Grimsby and Cleethorpes. This marked the start of joint LRCC/GCT operation, subsequently extended to the new service for the Willows Estate, which began in 1967, The tramway finally closed on 1 July 1961, additional peak services to the Humber Bank factories being provided by GCT and other operators.

The remaining trolleybus route last ran on 4 June 1960. Bus routes terminating in Grimsby were extended through to Cleethorpes to give extensive new links, in common with other network changes since

Fig. 5.7 A Lindsey County Council Bedford school bus at Sturton-by-Stow in 1947. The County began operating its own buses in the 1930s and expanded the fleet substantially after the second world war as secondary education grew and village schools were closed. Source: P. R. White collection; original, Sharpe of 181 Wragby Road, Lincoln.

inception of the undertaking, a process which would have been much more difficult had the two boroughs remained in control of separate operations. Economies were also made through judicious purchase of second-hand vehicles. A high level of patronage, financially viable operations, and low fares were successfully maintained during the 1960s, small losses in some years being offset by surpluses in others. Minibus operation was introduced in 1959 to serve the Humberston Fitties area, since covered by full-size vehicles.

However, from the late 1960s, a less progressive policy was followed. The growth in one-man operation slowed down, and the previously less innovative Lincoln City undertaking became the first to achieve complete one-man operation in the early 1970s. The rate of passenger decline accelerated, and not until the early 1980s were complete one-person operation attained and more positive marketing policies introduced.

Rural bus services throughout the county experienced some expansion in the early postwar period, mainly through the addition of morning peak journeys suitable for those working in major towns. As the demand for traditional agricultural labour declined, the journey-to-work market expanded. At the same time, rising car ownership from the early 1950s hit the traditional evening and weekend demand for rural bus services. Evening and Sunday services began their rapid decline which today has resulted in their elimination on all but the busiest routes.

However, daytime facilities have generally remained, even where introduced in recent years. For example, a morning peak journey from Caistor to Grimsby was not introduced until the late 1960s, yet this remains in operation with a limited shopping service, despite the elimination of evening and Sunday services some years ago. The decline of the cinema has been a further factor in the latter process.

Peak demand for bus services also increased as a result of the provisions of the Education Act 1944 which, as well as expanding the scope of secondary education, required local education authorities to provide free transport where children lived above certain distances from school (two miles up to the age of eight; three miles above this age). The additional demand was catered for by an expansion of Lindsey County Council's own school bus fleet, the placing of contracts with bus and coach operators (mostly in the independent sector), and in some cases, placing children on regular public services, with season tickets purchased on their behalf by the local education authority. Further expansion of demand for school buses came from the closure of village schools, requiring even the youngest children to travel by bus (Fig. 5.7).

This expansion of contract work helped the independent operators in particular to compensate for the loss of public demand on the scheduled network from the early 1950s. Market day and Saturday shopping services could be maintained at low marginal cost by using buses or coaches required for school contract services at Monday to Friday peaks. However, little was done in Lincolnshire, especially in Lindsey, to coordinate the school buses and other public services. Many villages were reduced to a low level of public service, while school buses continued to pass through but were not able to carry other types of passenger.

In common with some other large operators in Britain, the Lincolnshire Road Car Company had extended through the takeover of small operators in the 1930s and 1950s to a greater extent than was otherwise warranted. Some services might have been more efficiently run in the hands of such small concerns. By the late 1950s, LRCC was already experiencing some difficulty in maintaining rural operations, and in 1958 began a policy of handing over services to local operators by agreement. For example, the outstation at Bourne was closed in 1961, the Bourne–Sleaford route being jointly operated with

Delaine of Bourne, reputed to be the first joint working agreement between an independent company and a BTC company. Many services from Horncastle depot were handed over to small companies in 1960, although no takers were found for the Horncastle–Louth route, which instead suffered a severe cut, for that period, from a daily service to two days per week. This process of transfer of rural services to local companies has gathered pace in recent years, culminating with the loss of substantial parts of the remaining network in 1986, under the system of competitive tendering introduced under the Transport Act 1985.

An early attempt at innovation in rural transport was made in 1964, when an experimental service from Donington-on-Bain to Louth was started, following the initiatives of the Jack Committee on rural bus services in 1961. However, it was poorly managed and attracted little use. Subsequently, greater success was found through the development of a 'social car' scheme for volunteer lift-giving, and a post-bus service based on Louth. However, even in 1987 the vast majority of scheduled public passenger transport services are provided by full-size, conventional buses, this type of vehicle being required to meet peak demands for school traffic.

County councils played little role in rural public transport, except through school bus provision, until the Transport Act of 1968, when powers were introduced permitting them (and district councils) to support 'rural' (undefined) bus services, on a 50/50 basis with central government. Accordingly, requests were made by Lincolnshire Road Car, and subsequently by some independent companies, for support for specific services to the then three county councils. Holland and Kesteven provided some assistance, but Lindsey was reluctant to do so. While this was understandable in so far as the services in question could have been operated more efficiently (for example, at higher speeds), this also reflected the county's willingness to accept a very low standard of mobility for rural dwellers without access to cars. Subsequently, the formation of the new county council in 1974 led to a more consistent approach to bus service support, and also rail-based schemes, such as the reopening of Metheringham and Ruskington stations (see above). However, the overall level of support was generally low, and while most parts of the county retain some sort of bus service, frequencies are generally poor.

SOME CONCLUDING OBSERVATIONS

Little of the story of public passenger transport in this chapter has been unique to Lincolnshire. The general pattern is typical of most

low-density rural counties: a possibly overextended rail system at the
start of the period, followed by rapid growth of bus services in the
1920s to give a maximum extent of the rural network in 1939.
Patronage peaked in the late 1940s with most network growth subsequently concentrated in urban areas to serve new housing.
Railways were reshaped in the 1960s, often drastically, to match new
demand patterns. From the early 1970s, a more positive approach
was adopted to the remaining rail services, and local authorities were
also able to use their powers to assist bus operations. However, rising
car ownership continued to affect demand. Even by 1966, as the
sample census of that year showed, cars accounted for the majority of
motorized journeys to work – clearly predominating in the rural areas.
However, in much of the county, pedal cycle and walking comprised
the majority of trips, rather than mechanized transport – suggesting
that change from the early part of the century described at the beginning of this chapter was not perhaps so great as one might imagine.

However, not all the changes were inevitable, and a more positive
approach could often have been adopted. For example, systematic
coordination between the Lincolnshire Road Car Company and the
municipal bus operators could have provided much better bus services
to the newer suburbs and adjoining villages of the larger towns
without additional resources being required. Not until 1980 were Lincolnshire Road Car buses able to pick up passengers for local travel
within the city of Lincoln, for example. The licensing system may have
ossified patterns, discouraging both coordination and direct competition. Perhaps under the 1985 Act matters will be brought to a head.
Already, at the time of writing, strong competition exists between
Road Car and the municipal operations around Grimsby and Lincoln,
but the market is unlikely to sustain both at their present levels.

In the rural area, more could have been done to coordinate school
and public bus service provision although greater efforts have been
made since 1985. More attention should have been paid to good
quality interurban links, as well as purely local connections to the
nearest town. East Lincolnshire in particular suffered badly from rail
closures. Following the end of most rail services in October 1970, only
piecemeal bus links were added, with no attempt to strengthen the
main links lost through rail closure, such as Grimsby–Louth–Boston,
on which limited-stop services could have been easily introduced.
However, the purpose of local history is to record facts, not speculate
on what might have been, however tempting that may be to the
author.

Bibliographical note

Much of the material in the chapter has been drawn from primary sources. This is particularly true of the bus industry, for which timetables, newspaper reports, local authority minutes and direct interview with operators provided much of this data, rather than other published work. Much of the basic research in this chapter was completed in the late 1960s and early 1970s, when it was still possible to interview pioneer operators in their retirement. A few articles from the technical press of this time also amplified statistical evidence.

Railway and tramway history is somewhat better documented, as the references to this considerable range of recently published work show. Although much of this is material of an 'enthusiast' nature rather than dealing with economic and social questions, the basic chronology of events is easily established.

The assistance of local authority officers in providing access to records, and that of bus operators, is much appreciated. Also of great value was the timetable collection held by the Omnibus Society in London. A good deal of the basic work was carried out with Alan Tye, with whom I have coedited the *Lincolnshire and Humberside Transport Review* since its inception in 1963 (whose columns thus record directly events towards the end of the period covered in this chapter).

Notes to Chapter 5

1. N. R. Wright, *Lincolnshire towns and industry*, Lincoln, 1982. (This book includes a map of the rail system in 1914, p. 130.)
2. G. Dow, *The Alford and Sutton Tramway*, 2nd edition, published by the author, 1984.
3. N. R. Wright, *op. cit.*, p. 249.
4. *ibid.*, pp. 173 and 199.
5. C. H. Grinling, *The history of the Great Northern Railway*, London, new ed. 1966. Late nineteenth-centry figures appear on pp. 397, 418, 425, 431, 437, 441, 445, 449.
6. G. Dow, *Great Central*, Ian Allan Ltd., Surrey 1965. See vol. 2, pp. 249 and 350 (appendix); Vol. 3, p. 350.
7. A. J. Baker, *'The Delaine' of Bourne*, Delaine Coaches Ltd., Bourne, 1983.
8. P. R. White, *A history of bus and coach services in north-west Lincolnshire*, Omnibus Society, London, 1983.
9. N. R. Wright, *op. cit.*, pp. 249–51.
10. J. H. Price, 'Great Grimsby Street tramways', part 2, in *Tramway Review* (Light Rail Transit Association, London), 1984, vol. 15, p. 236.
11. J. H. Price, *op. cit.*, part 5, vol. 16, p. 70.

12. P. R. White, 'Scartho and the motor bus', *Omnibus Magazine* (Omnibus Society, London), October 1969, pp. 187–90.
13. D. H. Yarnell, 'The tramways of the City of Lincoln', *Tramway Review* 1971, issue no. 65.
14. P. R. White, *Passenger transport in Lincoln*, Omnibus Society, London, 1974.
15. N. R. Wright, *op. cit.*, pp. 169–71.
16. D. Jackson and D. Russell, *The Great Central in LNER days*, Ian Allan Ltd, Surrey, p. 107.
17. F. A. Molyneux, 'Geographical aspects of the development of Boston', unpublished MA thesis, University of Nottingham, 1968.
18. N. Crump, *By rail to victory* (the story of the LNER in wartime), LNER, London.

CHAPTER 6

THE IMPACT OF THE ROYAL AIR FORCE

by Barry Holliss

Abstract *In order to avoid repeating what has already been written by Halpenny, Hancock, Blake et al., about aerodromes and the operations conducted from them, this chapter focuses attention on the impact of the RAF on the county itself. In particular, the relationships between service personnel and the local population and between aerodrome construction and the local economy are explored. Prominence is given to the role of Lincolnshire railways in the movement of RAF personnel, whose population at one time during the 1939–45 war reached a figure equivalent to the population of the whole of Grimsby, Lincolnshire's biggest town.*

LOCATION AND LAND USE

The main impact on the county came, as may be expected, in the second world war. Prior to this Lincolnshire had only been used by the RAF to a limited degree, since after the first World War and the demilitarization of Germany it was considered unthinkable that that country could once again be our enemy. In fact, for a time, the defence planners considered that France could be the main threat to the country, and the airfield building programme was therefore centred in Kent and Sussex. For England in 1939 this was indeed lucky, since the German forces, having swept through the Low Countries and France, based most of their bomber fleets in France, closest to the 'White Cliffs'.

During the first world war the county was in the main a haven for fragile aircraft and fledgling pilots, as several flying training schools were located here, as were some Home Defence squadrons to combat Zeppelin raids. It was also the base for the anti-submarine patrols on the lookout for raiders in the North Sea. Flying-boats and airships were used, working out of the Royal Naval Air Service station at Killingholme (see Chapter 7, p. 169). Cranwell was a major RNAS

Fig.6.1 The Fitters' School at the West Camp, Cranwell, c. 1920, illustrates the vast scale of RAF operations in Lincolnshire. Source: E. Croft postcard collection.

training section, using aircraft and airships, a place so large in 1916 that it had to have its own spur from the main railway at Sleaford (Figs. 6.1 and 6.2). By 1918 it was busy enough to have two Manning & Wardle locomotives assigned for duty on the branch. The line continued in use until 1957, using a diesel locomotive; then the line was taken up and the station made into the main guardroom.[1]

Even bomber aircraft were light enough not to need hard-surfaced runways, so all 1914–18 airfields were grass surfaced. An airfield of 1914 was typically a grass square with 2,000-foot sides. A large number of hangars was required to accommodate the aircraft as they were mainly of wood and canvas and susceptible to weather damage. Up to seven hangars, meant only for use during the war but many of which were still standing in 1939, of brick or wood, 180 by 100 feet, plus a further dozen canvas ones, could well be seen. Living accommodation for the officers and men, if they were lucky, was in wooden huts. The unlucky ones lived under canvas.[2]

With the dramatic run-down of the armed forces in 1919 nearly 75 per cent of all airfields were shut. A considerable local infrastructure had grown up with these sites. The resident population had furnished provisions, transport, some accommodation, certainly a lot of beer in the hostelries, and no doubt a great deal of comfort provided by the local girls. The removal of a source of income was greatly felt.

Fig. 6.2 A train leaving RAF College Cranwell station on 28 May 1953, with personnel travelling to London for duties at the Coronation of HM Queen Elizabeth II. The line was built between 1916 and 1919, during which period temporary track was used for carrying building materials and supplies onto the airfield. Passenger services were run on a regular basis from at least 1919 until 1927, when competition from buses brought them to an end. However, passenger trains like this one continued to run on an occasional basis for the movement of large parties. Trains with as many as 13 coaches, weighing over 400 tons, could be hauled over the branch line which joined the main railway system at Sleaford. Source: RAF College, Cranwell; caption based on sources given in note 1, p. 154.

Peace, disarmament, and appeasement were the order of the day until the early 1930s when it was realized that Germany was re-arming. The Royal Air Force was allowed to expand, and a number of expansion-scheme airfields was built or developed in Lincolnshire. Notable amongst these were Waddington, Scampton, Digby, Hemswell, Manby, and Kirton-in-Lindsey.

These stations were quite attractive. Buildings were of brick and of a standard neo-classical design, as approved by the Royal Fine Arts Commission. The Society for the Preservation of Rural England was also asked for its views. Each station looked like any other, so that it was possible for an officer or man who was transferred to assimilate himself with ease. Standardization also had the benefit of keeping costs down for the fittings, which could be interchangeable and bought in bulk.Barrack blocks were two-storey buildings, as were married quarters for officers and men. Large and well-equipped messes were

Table 6.1 *Airfields in use in 1918*

Name	O.S. Ref.	Acres	Role
Bracebridge Heath	121.985673	123	Aircraft Acceptance Park
Braceby	130.015355	38	Emergency Landing Ground
Buckminster	130.893235	125	Aircraft Acceptance Park
Bucknall	121.170690	32	Emergency Landing Ground
Cockthorne	121.070875	56	Emergency Landing Ground
Cranwell	130.025515	3000	Naval Training
Cuxwold	113.177008	80	Emergency Landing Ground
Digby	121.042570	440	Operational
Elsham	112.042135	750	Operational
Freiston	131.385405	90	Naval Training
Gosberton	131.240310	55	Emergency Landing Ground
Greenland Top	113.180115	112	Operational
Grimsthorpe	130.015215	---	Emergency Landing Ground
Habrough	113.148130	---	Headquarters
Harlaxton	130.902325	380	Training
Hemswell	112.941908	150	Training
Immingham	113.183140	26	Naval Kite Balloon Station
Kelstern	113.246909	90	Emergency Landing Ground
Killingholme	113.166203	140	Naval
Kirton in Lindsey	112.945025	120	Operational
Leadenham	121.960520	86	Operational
Lincoln (Handley Page)	121.996702	---	Manufacturers
Lincoln (West Common)	121.960720	---	Manufacturers
Market Deeping	142.130100	75	Emergency Landing Ground
Moorby	122.290644	82	Emergency Landing Ground
New Holland	112.080230	85	Emergency Landing Ground
North Coates (Fitties)	113.372028	500	Operational
Scampton	121.965798	900	Operational
Skegness	122.564656	---	Naval
South Carlton	121.965762	200	Training
Spitalgate	130.935342	---	Training
Swinstead	130.015230	64	Emergency Landing Ground
Tydd St Mary	131.455185	125	Operational
Waddington	121.982360	250	Training
Wellingore	121.988545	300	Naval
Willoughby Hills	131.355455	25	Emergency Landing Ground
Winterton	112.920190	55	Emergency Landing Ground

Source: works cited in footnotes 1, 3.

provided for all ranks, whilst the aircraft hangars were neatly sited and screened by trees wherever possible. Construction of airfields was leisurely and the buildings could be well finished. When war came, however, rush was the order of the day, with utility the watchword.

There was no real problem in obtaining the land for a new airfield, since it was compulsorily purchased. A swift takeover was, however, not the end to the problems of building an airfield. Many contractors said they could do the job, quoted the price, were told to get on with it, and then found that most of their best men were engaged on other jobs. Non-skilled men were most probably in the army, or excused through ill-health or by being too old. However, those local men who were fit enough found that this work provided a secure, if not too comfortable a job, for up to a year. The increased load on the contractor also meant that he was short of vehicles. New ones were going to the forces so that any sort of locally owned vehicle not already requisitioned could be hired out at a reasonable price. Most of the wartime airfields had buildings classified as temporary: Nissen huts and Maycrete (poured concrete) buildings were the main personnel accommodation, but hangars (described as temporary) were made of brick and metal. Certain buildings such as gymnasia, watch-offices, latrineblocks, guardhouses and air-raid shelters were more often than not brick-built. It is a credit to the builders that the brick and concrete buildings have stayed up on disused sites – perhaps because they are so well built.

By 1942 a standard hard-surfaced airfield had three runways, one 2,000 yards long, the others 1,400 yards, each at approximately a 60 degree axis to the other. All were 50 yards wide and could be surfaced in concrete, tarmac, or a mixture. The site covered an average of just over 600 acres (compared with 92 acres in 1914 and the 385-acre average of 1918). To complete the runways and taxiways, usually three times as long as the three runways combined, 175,000 cubic yards of concrete and 32,000 square yards of tarmac were needed. Under the site ran 50 miles of pipes and conduit with immeasurable miles of wiring.[3]

The introduction of so many airfields into the county brought many problems. First there was the sterilization of so much farmland. Airfields by their nature must be built on reasonably flat land, well drained and of a suitable composition. There could not be any major woodland or urban use requiring clearance. Among the more notable flying hazards was Dunston Pillar, situated on the A15 south of Lincoln, close to RAF Waddington and RAF Digby and Coleby Grange. Originally built in 1751 as a land lighthouse to guide travellers over the heath, it stood 92 feet high. The precaution was taken to remove the upper part of the Pillar, so that the top was then on a level with nearby trees. The statue of George III which had been erected in 1810 to commemorate his golden jubilee, replacing the lantern made redundant by the enclosure of the heath,[4] was removed and after various vicissitudes now stands in the Castle grounds at Lincoln.

Communications also had to be reasonable, not only for the movement of personnel and equipment, but also during the construction

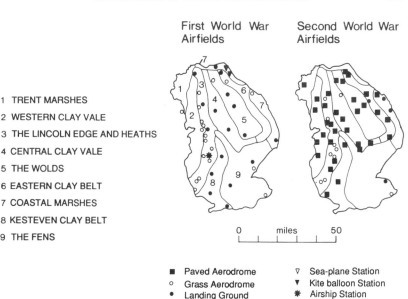

First World War
Airfields

Second World War
Airfields

1 TRENT MARSHES

2 WESTERN CLAY VALE

3 THE LINCOLN EDGE AND HEATHS

4 CENTRAL CLAY VALE

5 THE WOLDS

6 EASTERN CLAY BELT

7 COASTAL MARSHES

8 KESTEVEN CLAY BELT

9 THE FENS

0   miles   50

■ Paved Aerodrome   ▽ Sea-plane Station
○ Grass Aerodrome   ▼ Kite balloon Station
• Landing Ground   ✳ Airship Station

Fig. 6.3   Lincolnshire airfield locations. Source: R. Blake.

or reconstruction phases. It is reckoned that very few airfields in the county were built more than 3km (just under two miles) from both an 'A' class road and a railway.[5] The distribution of airfields over different geological and soil areas is shown in Fig. 6.3 with a notable absence in the Fens, and a concentration on the limestone uplands.

Table 6.2 shows the acreage of land enclosed by airfields in Lincolnshire at the end of 1945. It shows only airfields, and excludes land taken up by such as decoy sites (dummy airfields), starfish sites (dummy fire sites), ranges (AA, bombing, gunnery, musketry), marine-craft units, maintenance units (air parks, bomb stores, workshops), radio relay stations, radar sites, headquarters units, RAF Regiment depots, and hospitals, all of which took up valuable land and laid an additional burden on communications and the existing facilities of the area.

LOCAL INVOLVEMENT

Stations had a considerable emotional impact on Lincolnshire people, as men stationed in them did not lead a segregated life. It is true that most stations had the camp cinema, recreation rooms, gymnasium, NAAFI, and messes but many of the men (and women) decided that life off site was better than on it, and went into the nearest town and village, especially to the pubs and cinemas. They also built up the

Table 6.2 *Land use by airfields on 31 December 1945*

Name	O.S. Ref	Acreage	Use
Bardney	121.140712	680	Operational
Barkston Heath	130.970415	c 680	USAAF
Binbrook	113.189959	c 680	Operational
Blyton	112.863900	690	Operational
Bottesford	819415	part in Leics	Operational
Caistor	112.086021	310	Operational
Cammeringham	121.965839	650	Operational
Coleby Grange	121.005605	400	Operational
Coningsby	122.225635	c 650	Operational
Cranwell	130.025515	3000	Training
Digby	121.042570	440	Operational
Donna Nook	113.425979	335	Operational and range
Dunholme Lodge	121.995784	715	Operational
East Kirkby	122.342618	855	Operational
Elsham Wolds	112.042135	50	Operational
Faldingworth	112.037849	720	Operational
Fiskerton	121.045730	630	Operational
Folkingham	130.049301	c 630	USAAF
Fulbeck	121.900510	670	Operational
Goxhill	113.115218	500	USAAF
Grimsby	113.279025	c 650	Operational
Harlaxton	130.902325	380	Training
Hemswell	112.941908	750	Operational
Hibaldstow	112.083009	450	Operational
Kelstern	113.262922	900	Operational
Kirmington	112.095103	575	Operational
Kirton in Lindsey	112.945972	422	Operational
Ludford Magna	113.208179	579	Operational
Manby	122.385866	580	Training
Metheringham	121.105610	650	Operational
North Coates	113.372028	500	Operational
North Killingholme	113.131169	740	Operational
North Witham	130.946225	742	USAAF
Sandtoft	112.750075	700	Operational
Scampton	121.965798	900	Operational
Skellingthorpe	121.925688	650	Operational
Spilsby	122.450645	635	Operational
Spitalgate	130.935342	c 500	Training
Strubby	122.450810	700	Operational
Sturgate	121.879878	790	Operational
Sutton Bridge	131.476194	320	Training
Swinderby	121.873615	c 400	Operational
Waddington	121.982360	c 800	Operational
Wellingore	121.988545	300	Training
Wickenby	121.088803	670	Operational
Woodhall Spa	122.204610	700	Operational

Source: Willis and Holliss, as footnote 3.

congregations at local churches; they joined in the social life of the village and, of course, took an interest in the opposite sex.

Aircraft crashes might occur near the stations as a result of flying accidents and many damaged aircraft did not quite 'make it' home to base, some being destroyed on their own airfield at the very end of a perilous flight.[6] Some 360 Lancasters actually crashed in Lincolnshire. Many of the dead taken from crashed aircraft, or men who died in the hospitals, were buried in the village church-yards and the local population could not help noticing the burial party's slow-marching to and quick-marching back from the funeral. When married officers managed to find a billet near the station it was not uncommon for their wives to live with them, and many of the latter were comforted in their sorrow by the village when their men failed to return home. Of course many local families had sons and daughters serving in the forces and any loss incurred by the squadrons at the station would bring home to parents realization of the dangers which their offspring were facing.

At the outset, the attitude of the local population to the arrival of over 2,000 men and a couple of hundred women in their parish was one of distrust and jealousy. The situation threatened the community which had grown up over the centuries with an approximate balance between the sexes, local men marrying local girls. Many of the men drafted into the area were single, and with a 10 : 1 ratio of RAF men to WAAF women it was not unexpected that they would look towards the nearest settlement for companionship. Those young, and not so young, men who lived in the area viewed the competition with disdain and mistrust, and it was not unknown for a married man away with the forces to be very concerned about the fidelity of his wife when he knew that an RAF or USAAF unit was stationed nearby. On the other hand, the RAF were generally made welcome, though the WAAFs were not unnaturally looked upon as competition by the local girls.[7]

Each RAF station normally had two favourite pubs, one for the officers and the other for other ranks. If there was an army camp nearby the soldiers frequented separate houses, and it was a foolish man, a drunk one, or a brave provost officer who entered a pub or cafe frequented by another service. Not surprisingly there was little love lost between the services. The only exception to this rule was where a pub was close to a railway station, where all services met and bemoaned their draft 'chit'. Fist fights were difficult in full uniform, with kitbag and rifle.

When an airman, or even an officer had had too much to drink, the usual excuse was that he was letting off steam, or had finished his tour of duty. Unfortunately the local police did not always see things this way and one man, 'Bluey' Freeman, was court-martialled on 21st April 1943 for being drunk and being arrested in Grimsby. Another man, an Australian, was brought up before Newark magistrates for poaching and said, 'My father was deported to Australia for poaching, and I hope you will give me the same sentence.' This man spoke for many Australians who served with Royal Australian Air Force squadrons in Lincolnshire and who thought the countryside terrible and the weather worse. Another Australian commented, 'If they cut the balloon cables, this bloody place will sink.'

Whilst many public houses became renowned for their liveliness (for example, the Marquis of Granby at Binbrook, and the Horse and Jockey at Waddington) other more unusual places were chosen for special celebrations. The aircrew of 460 Squadron held a party on the pier at Cleethorpes for the ground staff and almost a thousand attended. As the night grew older and the party rowdier one intrepid 'type' decided to dive off the end of the pier and go for a moonlight swim. The only trouble was that the tide was out!

High spirits were a release from the tensions of combat. Crews had to complete a tour of 30 operational sorties before they were rested by being posted to a training unit or another theatre of operations less busy or unsafe. Less than one in three of these men succeeded in completing their tours.

With over 35 operational airfields in the county, each with one or two or three bomber squadrons of twenty aircraft, the noise level when an operation was being mounted can be imagined. (The editor once counted over 100 bombers in the sky within a few moments, as they circled to gain height before setting off for a raid). This noise not only affected the residents, but also the airmen who were not on duty. It was, therefore, usual to place their living quarters away from the activity and where possible in a fold in the ground so as to minimize the nuisance. The dispersal of sites around the airfields was not only for humanitarian reasons. It lessened the possible damage which arose from enemy attacks and the effect of aircraft crashing on the field with full bomb loads, something which happened quite often. There was also the danger of aircraft blowing up whilst being loaded. Waddington village was the unfortunate recipient of the bomb load of a Luftwaffe aircraft which missed its target. A landmine fell on and demolished the church and severely damaged the rest of the settlement.[8] At East Kirkby a Lancaster bomber of 57 Squadron blew up on its dispersal site, killing three people and destroying four other aircraft.[9]

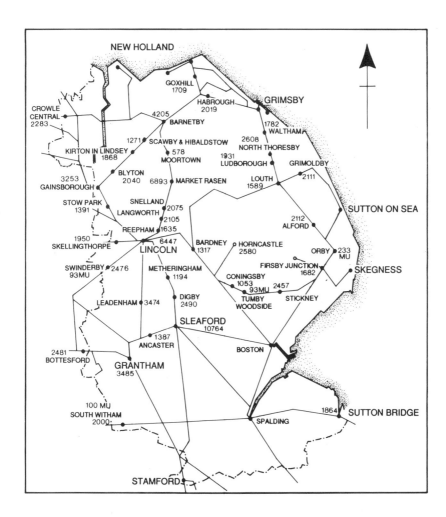

Fig. 6.4   Lincolnshire railways showing maximum potential loadings of RAF passengers. Source: B. R. Holliss.

LOGISTICS

To maintain the aircraft, the stations and the war effort, considerable manpower and equipment were needed. In all, over 90,000 men and women were located at flying stations in the county. To get them there and to send them away on leave and to other duties was a considerable operation. Whereas the army moved its troops around in road convoys, the RAF preferred to use the railway. The county had a number of railway lines radiating from Lincoln, Grantham, Spalding, Boston,

Table 6.3   *Use of rail stations by RAF/WAAF personnel*

Railway station	RAF stations served[2]	[3]Personnel
Alford Town	Strubby	2,112
Ancaster	Barkston Heath	1,387
Bardney	Bardney	1,317
Blankney & Metheringham	Metheringham	1,194
Barnetby	Elsham Wolds	2,561
	Kirmington	1,194
Blyton	Blyton	2,040
Bottesford[1]	Bottesford	[1]2,481
Coningsby	Woodhall Spa	1,053
Crowle Central	Sandtoft	2,283
Digby	Digby	22,490
Firsby Junction	Spilsby	1,682
Gainsborough	Hemswell	2,282
	Sturgate	971
Goxhill	Goxhill	1,709
Grantham	Folkingham	1,298
	Harlaxton	236
	Spitalgate	1951
Grimoldby	Manby	2,111
Habrough	North Killingholme	2,019
Kirton in Lindsey	Kirton in Lindsey	1,868
Langworth	Dunholme Lodge	2103
Leadenham	Fulbeck	2,835
	Wellingore	639
Louth	Donna Nook	1,589
Lincoln	Coleby Grange	1384
	Scampton	2,588
	Waddington	2,475
Ludborough	Kelstern	1,931
Market Rasen	Binbrook	2,397
	Faldingworth	2,238
	Ludford Magna	2,258
Moortown	Caistor	578
North Thoresby	North Coates	2,608
Reepham	Fiskerton	1,636
Scawby and Hibaldstow	Hibaldstow	1,271
Skellingthorpe	Skellingthorpe	1,950
Sleaford	Cranwell	10,764
South Witham	North Witham	2,000
Stickney	East Kirkby	2,457
Stow Park	Cammeringham	1,391
Sutton Bridge	Sutton Bridge	1,864
Swinderby	Swinderby	2,476
Waltham	Grimsby	1,782

Notes

1 Bottesford Station is in Leicestershire as is part of Bottesford airfield. However, part is also in Lincolnshire, hence its inclusion in this table.

2 The railway stations of the same name as the airfield were not necessarily the closest

3 The establishment figures are as at 31 December 1944.

Louth, and Barnetby, heavily used for the transport of personnel, stores, and munitions, and laying a considerable strain on an overloaded system (Fig. 6.4). Table 6.3 shows the number of RAF/WAAF personnel who might have used an individual station when moving to or from nearby airfields. These figures do not take into account personnel at other RAF installations such as Nocton Hall Hospital, Belton Park training depot, other training establishments, and radar sites such as Stenigot.

Tables 6.4–6.6 show the potential loadings which would have occurred if all RAF personnel located at airfields on particular routes had been in transit at the same time. For example, at Lincoln 6,447 personnel could potentially have converged on the stations by road, while another 51,304 could have passed through by rail, necessitating a change of train in all cases. The branch lines involved had, in peacetime, as few as three trains on weekdays, with less, if any, on Sundays. Operated with old stock, and often comprising less than four carriages of non-corridor compartments, the conditions for passengers were less than satisfactory. Other lines were better served, but even they also could become packed with servicemen, kitbags, and rifles. Of course, this possible mass-movement of RAF personnel never occurred, but the figures indicate the size of the overall problem in relation to the regular small number used by local inhabitants who in peace time would only have shared a train with a few others.

Table 6.4 *Loading on Lincoln station*

Route	Frequency	Loading
Lincoln (as destination)	More than 7 a day	6,447
Lincoln–Grimsby	5 a day	19,510
Lincoln–Gainsborough	More than 7 a day	4,644
Lincoln–Chesterfield	3 trains a day	1,950
Lincoln–Boston	More than 7 a day	1,317
Lincoln–Sleaford	More than 7 a day	14,448
Lincoln–Grantham	7 trains a day	6,959
Lincoln–Nottingham	More than 7 a day	2,476
		57,751

When looking at the possible loading figures it could be that some locals might well think this maximum to have happened as they were unaccustomed to the crush and sight of so many people on the station. Barnetby in the north of the county was a junction of three lines and

had a possible loading of 36,449 persons as shown in Table 6.5. Firsby
Junction can well be described as being in the middle of nowhere. The
village of Firsby was a mile to the south of the station which had only
a few houses and an inn nearby. It was, however, the junction of four
lines. Table 6.6 shows the potential loading on this station.

Table 6.5 *Loading on Barnetby station*

Barnetby (as destination)	4,205
via Gainsborough and Grimsby	10,451
Barnetby–Doncaster	2,283
via Lincoln and Grimsby	19,510
	36,449

Sleaford was the potential destination for over 10,000 persons going
to the flying training school at Cranwell, which in 1944 also housed
a radio school and ground-trade training units. A single track railway
existed from Sleaford to Cranwell, but it was purely military; no station is indicated in either Bradshaw[10] or Connollys[11] and it is not
shown on the 1939 Ordnance Survey map. (See also Chapter 5, p. 119
for tickets issued and used at Grantham; and p. 135–6 above, this
chapter and Fig. 6.2 for Cranwell railway).

Table 6.6 *Loading on Firsby Junction*

Firsby Junction (as destination)	1,682
Firsby and Woodhead Junction	3,492
via Boston and Grimsby	10,092
Willoughby, Sutton and Louth Branch	2,222
	17,307

As each Lancaster bomber could carry an offensive load of 14,000
lbs (6.25 tons) and in certain cases 22,000 lbs (9.82 tons), an enormous
stockpile of bombs had to be held in the county, split between airfield
and bomb-storage area. On the airfields the bomb dump was well
away from the rest of the airfield in an area which on plan looked like
a racetrack. Storage areas, were located very close to the railway, as
that was the best way of delivering the ordnance, which was taken by
road to the airfields as required. The four Lincolnshire sites were at
Orby, Swinderby, Tumby Woodside, and South Witham (Fig. 6.4).
     At Orby the storage area was in the railway yard and nearby lanes.
This was a satellite of Market Stainton and No. 233 Maintenance

Unit. The MU headquarters was not near a railway and the munitions were stored along roadside verges and in roadside woods. Although these woods have since been cleared, the many ramps across the roadside ditch can still be seen. This MU also had a satellite at Wragby. The site at Tumby Woodside was in the railway yard and was a satellite of Swinderby, which had opened as 93 MU on 23 August 1939 in the fields by the side of Swinderby railway station. This location was renamed Norton Disney when Swinderby airfield opened. It had another satellite storage site at Fox Covert, probably the wood of that name in the western part of Norton Disney parish. South Witham site (No. 100 MU) opened on 27 March 1942 and closed about 1950, having at one time satellite roadside storage sites at Stretton, Stretton Road, and Moor Lane, most of these in Rutland. With all the building work, ranges, bomb dumps, and other military installations in the county, travel, already difficult, was to be made worse.

Construction of an airfield involved closing a number of roads (see later for detail) but in certain circumstances this was not possible. Where main roads ran past sites, or where no alternative routes could be provided, it was then necessary to control the use of the road. This was either for security or safety, such as when aircraft dispersals or bomb dumps were sited across a road.

Main roads presented a security problem, since it would have been easy for persons with malicious intent to get a good view or easy access by travelling along the highway. This was not so easy in those locations away from main routes, as the only persons who would normally be on the road would have been local inhabitants, soon known to sentries. When such a main road caused a security problem the local inhabitants were once more inconvenienced, as identification was demanded at either end of the road, and delays occurred whilst vehicles were stopped for this purpose. This was in addition to the many road barriers erected in case of invasion.

Another problem arose when the local population, used to walking on footpaths from one village to another, found that a runway had been laid across it. Many of the older ones were not amused, and continued under cover of darkness to exercise their rights.

A detailed examination of the current Ordnance Survey maps and a comparison of these with the 1939 military edition will show the number of roads closed or diverted. Figure 6.5 illustrates this for RAF Waddington, and indicates by broken lines a network of roads in use before 1939.

The B1178, which formerly ran in a straight east–west line from Waddington to East Mere, is the main permanent diversion. In the

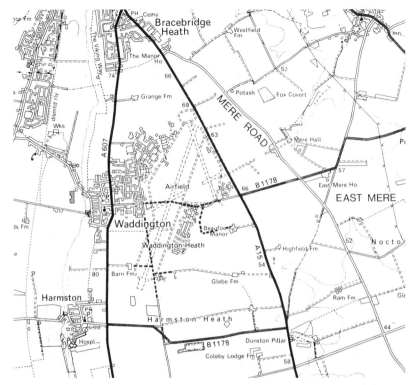

Fig. 6.5   Waddington airfield, showing road closures caused by flying activities. Sources: B. R. Holliss and Ordnance Survey; reproduced from the Ordnance Survey map, with the permission of the Controller of Her Majesty's Stationery Office, Crown copyright reserved.

1950s, in the early days of jet bombers, the A15 traffic was diverted eastwards by Mere Road and the B1178, but traffic lights were later erected underneath the flight path, still in use in 1987.

Although an airfield was a closed community, personnel and buildings were widely distributed throughout the area, as the plan of Metheringham airfield (Fig. 6.6) illustrates. Some of the living quarters were nearly three quarters of a mile from the administration area and up to two miles from the other extremities of the field. Not only did this mean considerable movement of personnel and transport of equipment through and around the village of Martin, but it also placed a burden on the road surface and system.

In many cases both the airfield and dispersal sites have been demolished and the whole area returned to agriculture, but in other cases farmers, contractors, and others have found the temporary buildings of use as farm outbuildings and stores. Sometimes the water

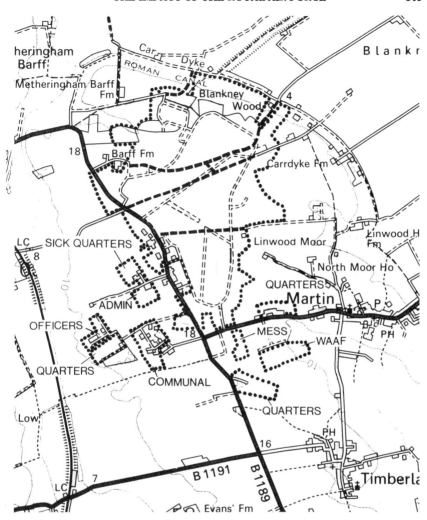

Fig. 6.6   Metheringham airfield, showing location of RAF building. Sources: B. R. Holliss and Ordnance Survey; reproduced from the Ordnance Survey map, with the permission of the Controller of Her Majesty's Stationery Office, Crown copyright reserved.

tower and sewage works built for the airfield have been kept and used for the local area. In a number of places one can still see concrete tracks leading off roads into nowhere, or one may come across a building in woods, ivy clad, and windowless, for which no particular reason can be immediately ascertained.

Table 6.7 *State of second world war airfields in 1980s*

Site	Use of runway	Use of buildings	Use of hangars
Bardney	Dug up	Road haulage	Warehousing
		Intensive poultry	Crop spraying a/c
Barkston Heath*	RAF	Demolished	Warehousing
Binbrook*	RAF	RAF	RAF
Blyton	Kart-racing		
Bottesford		Demolished	Commercial storage
Caistor	Intensive poultry	Farm stores	Barns
Cammeringham		Retained	Farmer
			Haulage contractor
Coleby Grange			Farming
Coningsby*	RAF	RAF	RAF
Cranwell*	RAF	RAF	RAF
Digby*	RAF	RAF (Signals)	RAF
Donna Nook*	RAF	RAF (Range)	RAF
Dunholme Lodge	Reduced in width	formerly school	
East Kirkby	Crop spraying	Museum (aviation)	Storage
	Storage		
	Gliding		
Elsham Wolds	Now crossed by approach to Humber Bridge		
Faldingworth	See text		
Fiskerton	See text	R.O.C. HQ	
Folkingham	Storage	Demolished	
Fulbeck	Occasional motor sport		Storage
Goxhill	See text		
Grimsby	Car storage		
Harlaxton	Open cast iron ore mine		
Hemswell	Motor sport	Indust & comm site	EEC Intervention
Hibaldstow	Sunday market		Removed
	Lincs police training		

Of these airfields built for the first world war, in the expansion period and for the second world war, what of their present state?

The end of the second world war saw many airfields close down in a short space of time. Even though they were not wanted, the sites were retained under 'Care and Maintenance' and sometimes used for various other purposes.[12] For example, Faldingworth has a particularly interesting history. Closed for flying in 1948 it was placed in Care and Maintenance until 1957 when it was made a secure store for nuclear weapons. The south-west part had bunkers, watch towers, searchlight posts, barbed-wire entanglements, concrete walls, and a no-man's land, all under a 24-hour armed police guard. This was not

Table 6.7 (cont) *State of second world war airfields in 1980s*

Site	Use of runway	Use of buildings	Use of hangars
Kelstern		Hay store	
Kirmington	Humberside airport		
Kirton in Lindsey	Army—as Rapier Barracks		
Ludford Magna	Broken up		
Manby	E. Lindsey D.C.	Grain stores	
Metheringham	Public road	Microlight training	
North Coates*	RAF	RAF	RAF
North Killingholme	Indust. estate	Indust. estate	Warehouses
	Intensive poultry		
North Witham	Forestry Commission		Store
Sandtoft	Light aircraft	Museum (trolley-bus)	As buildings
Scampton*	RAF	RAF	RAF
Skellingthorpe	Housing, school		
Spilsby	Poultry		Industry
	County highways depot		
	Motor sport		
Spitalgate	Army—Prince William of Gloucester barracks		
Strubby	Helicopters		EEC Intervention
Sturgate	Civil flying		
Sutton Bridge*	Potato Marketing Bd	RAF	
Swinderby*	RAF	RAF	RAF
Waddington*	RAF	RAF	RAF
Wellingore			
Wickenby	Civil use		Hangar Store
Woodhall Spa*	RAF	RAF	RAF

* = still in use

Source: works cited in footnotes 1, 3.

marked on any Ordnance Survey map of the time. A domestic site was built in 1959, which was refurbished in 1980 to make offices for a company testing cannon shells (British Manufacturing and Research Co.). The nuclear site is now used for the storage of non-nuclear explosives in bulk. In 1972–3 the Officers' Mess area was used for the temporary housing of Ugandan Asians, and later placed on the market. The married quarters were sold, creating a new village.

Fiskerton was used in 1947 by the Ministry of Health to accommodate homeless families, the hutted camp being used for this purpose. Goxhill was also used for this purpose and later for the storage of Home Office emergency-use vehicles, such as 'Green Goddess' fire engines. The rundown of the RAF brought problems to two sections of the community. Landowners who had had their fields taken were hoping to recover them, for they had only been paid a basic level of compensation, not in one lump sum, but in instalments. Spilsby airfield was first sold off at public auction in 1962, only two years after the previous landowners had received their final compensation instalment. The new owners took over any buildings and concrete areas still extant without any financial help towards removing them so that the land would be returned to cultivation. The farmers however, often made use of the well-built buildings and sold off the runways for use as hardcore for the new motorways. The other section affected by the run-down were local persons employed on the sites.

The closure of RAF Manby on 31st March 1974 caused considerable hardship in an area that had become dependent on the station for a great part of its way of life.[13] The situation had been made more difficult with the increase of the civilian workforce over the previous two decades because of the removal of conscription and cost-cutting exercises. After closure, the married quarters were used to house personnel from Binbrook, whilst part of the domestic site was purchased by East Lindsey District Council for its headquarters at a price of £100,000. The area bought included the parade ground and Tedder Hall, the previous home of the College of Air Warfare. In 1978 the former motor transport site and machine gun ranges were bought by Lincolnshire County Council for use as a highways depot. In the same year the five C type hangars were upgraded, re-roofed and repainted to become EEC grain-intervention stores. These projects did alleviate some of the unemployment, but not to any great extent. The remaining areas of the airfield were put up for sale at various times after 1978 and in July 1980 the bulk of the site, including the runways, was bought by Mr Paul Toynton for £415,000. For this price he acquired 280 acres at nearly £1,500 per acre, but also included in the price were two control towers. It is hoped that the imposing officers' mess will be converted into a home for retired servicemen.

The county has had to readjust from the time when 1.5 per cent of its land surface was in use by the RAF, with something like 90,000 RAF personnel, to a time when there are only seven operational airfields and a number of non-flying stations. Even these latter establishments have been reduced, including the hospital at Nocton Hall (1985). Binbrook closed in 1988, thus creating problems similar to those experienced at Manby.

Despite the reduction in the facilities required by the RAF, it still has an effect on the county. Perhaps the most significant is the noise and environmental hazard. Even small jets make considerable noise, whilst living under the flightpath of a Tornado aircraft can be intolerable. The pattern of noise varies from station to station, and it is surprising to realize that whereas airfields such as Coningsby inflict intense noise, this is often of short duration, whereas the environs of

Cranwell have to suffer continual noise at lower levels. At Scampton there is a restriction that no building over 150 feet in height may be erected within a two mile radius, this ban being extended for a further two miles from the end of the runway in a wedge shape. In the first three-quarters of a mile of this wedge the building height is limited to 50 feet. This restricts industrial development, as does the further restriction within a 7 mile radius on any development likely to generate refuse or sewage, or which would attract bird life and thereby raise the possibility of birds striking aircraft with disastrous results.

The airfields and air force locations also bring problems of employment, economics, housing, and schooling. These problems have been comprehensively discussed in Barber's article on the socio-economic impact of the RAF in Lincolnshire.

Bibliographical note

For the average person interested in this subject there is little to find which goes beyond the usual squadron histories when browsing through normal bookshop shelves.

The books mentioned in the bibliography are one-offs and not part of a series. Willis and Holliss provided a microcosm of each airfield at 1st December 1944, S. Finn's *Lincolnshire air war* provides snippets about the County but concentrates on aircraft accidents. The two books which deal with the County and aviation, Terry Hancock's *Bomber county* and Ron Blake *et al.*'s *The airfields of Lincolnshire* consider each site and are an excellent introduction to the subject of the impact of the RAF.

Interested persons could well examine carefully Ordnance Survey maps, both 7th edition and Metric, to establish for themselves the siting and evident land use of each site. Comparison between the first and the second will reveal the reduction in use which happened in the intervening years. Examination of the Military version against the 7th edition will show the effects on the countryside from the beginning of the Second World War to the end.

It is when the reader gets into the realms of dedicated researchers and preservationists that new facts may come to life. The Airfield Research Group is notable in the recording of airfield histories whilst a number of airfield control towers and other buildings have been restored by preservation and memorial groups.

The best collections of material are however in government hands. The Property Services Agency has aerial maps of airfields, as does Keele University. The Air Historical Branch of the Ministry of

Defence has an outstanding collection of documentation as has the Royal Air Force Museum. The Public Record Office at Kew also has a large stock of archive material, but it has to be said that whereas the former organisations are willing to advise readers where information may be found one has to know what is required when visiting the PRO.

Notes to Chapter 6

1. T. N. Hancock, *Bomber county. A history of the Royal Air Force in Lincolnshire,* Lincolnshire Library Service 1978, p. 5. See also T. N. Hancock, *Bomber County 2,* Lincolnshire Library Service, 1985. A.H.C., 'The little-used branch line: the Cranwell and Sleaford Railway of yesterday and today', *Journal of the Royal Air Force College,* November 1953, pp. 171–77; *Great Northern Railway Society Newletter,* undated extracts kept on file in the library at RAF College, Cranwell.

2. *Bomber county,* 1978, p. 15.

3. D. Willis and B. Holliss, *Military airfields in the British Isles,* Enthusiasts Publications, 1987. A little-known point about aerodrome construction is that from the mid 1930s, barges belonging to E. Bisby of Thorne were used in the transport of Canadian timber into Brayford Pool, Lincoln, from whence it was despatched to airfields under construction (M. Taylor, 'The Fossdyke navigation', *Lincolnshire Life,* November 1986, p. 24).

4. *White's Directory of Lincolnshire,* 1856, p. 356.

5. R. Blake, M. Hodgson and B. Taylor, *The airfields of Lincolnshire since 1912,* Midland Counties Publications, 1984, p. 206.

6. *ibid.,* p. 206.

7. *Bomber county,* p. 87.

8. S. Finn, *Lincolnshire air war 1939–1945, Book Two* (Control Column via Brayford Press), Lincoln 1983, p. 52.

9. *Airfields of Lincolnshire,* p. 75.

10. *Bradshaw's railway guide and timetable 1938,* repr. London 1969.

11. *British Railways pre-grouping atlas and gazetteer,* W. Philip Connolly, Ian Allen Ltd, 1976.

12. C. Barber, 'The socio-economic impact of the RAF in Lincolnshire,' *Trent Geographer,* No. 2, 1981, Trent Polytechnic.

13. B. Barrymore Halpenny, *Action stations 2,* Patrick Stephens, 1981.

CHAPTER 7

THE CHANGING COASTLINE

by David N. Robinson

Abstract *The chapter opens with a description of new commercial developments on the coast in the early part of the century and continues with a discussion of sea defences. Part of this story leads into an account of the important Sandhills Act of 1932. Despite efforts to guard against the sea's onslaught, the storm-surge of 1953 had disastrous effects. In contrast, the coast south of Gibraltar Point has been the subject of reclamation schemes, rather than defence. Defence against possible German attacks during two world wars is then discussed, followed by the happier subject of the holiday industry. The final section describes the creation of nature reserves, among them Gibraltar Point.*

Small-scale maps show the Lincolnshire coast as a blunted peninsula with a smooth outline, but this masks a paradox. Between Mablethorpe and Skegness sandhills, now reinforced with concrete walls, defend the lowlying Lincolnshire Marsh, while to the north and south thousands of acres of saltmarsh have been reclaimed from the sea. At the opening of the century sand-dunes were an adequate sea defence from Donna Nook to Gibraltar Point, with clay banks along the Humber and round the Wash. Only at Cleethorpes was there a clay cliff, and this had been landscaped and fronted with a promenade in the 1880s. However, beyond Brighton Street the houses along Sea Bank Road on a low clay cliff were in danger of being washed away. Under the 1902 Cleethorpes Improvement Act four acres of foreshore were reclaimed by a massive sea wall 2,000 feet long and 18 feet high containing 15,000 tons of concrete. Although the incomplete wall was breached by the sea in two places in January 1905, the area between the wall and the cliff was filled with 135,000 tons of shore sand and the Kingsway Gardens and promenade were laid out by 1906. Lady Henderson, wife of the Chairman of the Great Central Railway Company, cut the ribbon to open this new addition to the resort on 12 July 1906, having earlier in the day cut the first sod for Immingham Dock. The Boy with the Leaking Boot statue which stood in the Kingsway

Gardens (later removed to the Town Hall away from vandals) was presented in 1915 by John Carlbom, the Swedish Consul; the original is in Hasselbacken in Sweden.[1]

South beyond the Kingsway, the Council purchased 36 acres of seafront from Sidney Sussex College, Cambridge in 1902, and a seawall was erected in 1912; a further 230 acres were bought from the Marquis of Lincolnshire in 1921. Here the Bathing Pool was laid out in 1925, the Boating Lake in 1928, and the sea defences completed by building the Marine Embankment enclosing 120 acres of the Buck Beck marshes to the dunes at Humberston Fitties in 1928–30. All amenity development was behind the sea defences: the Olympia sports stadium (reopened as the Winter Gardens in 1946), caravans at the southern end, and the 'Wonderland' amusements on the North Promenade. There before the first world war was the spidery Warwick's Tower with spiral lift and revolving observation platform, Hancock's Palace of Pleasure, the Arab Village, a tortuous Fairy river, a bicycle railway, swings and roundabouts, a water chute into the sea, helter-skelter, the Twopenny Switchback built on the beach, the Joy Wheel and the Figure Eight railway.[2]

Skegness on the other hand was gaining land from the sea almost from the inception of the resort. The purpose of the sea wall of 1878 was not to keep out the sea but to carry the promenades, it being the Earl of Scarbrough's responsibility as landowner to provide roads and services to encourage builders to buy plots or lease them at a low rent. The northern limit of the planned town was Scarbrough Avenue, and the town north of that was not developed until the 1920s, by T. L. Kirk, a Nottingham solicitor, and J. H. Canning. In the edge of the scrubbed covered sandhills – 'The Jungle' – was George Burrows's Chalet Theatre, and on the new foreshore beyond North Parade was the Figure Eight railway built by Thompson's Patent Gravity Switchback Railway Company in 1908 (dismantled 1970). In a sandy hollow of the foreshore dunes off North Parade, Fred Clements established his concert party reputation from 1904. With the exception of the war years, 1914–18, they stayed there until 1930 in what became known as Happy Valley; two years later the Sun Castle or Solarium was built there. Accreting dunes in front of the Grand Parade had been enclosed by the Earl of Scarbrough in the late 1880s to make the formal Marine Gardens. The foreshore beyond was of parallel sandy ridges and wet, sometimes muddy, runnels or swatches. In summer, local children dug sand bridges or laid planks across the swatches, charging trippers for using them.

In December 1921, Skegness Council Surveyor R. H. Jenkins presented his master plan for the development of the accreted

Fig. 7.1 The first dodgem cars in Britain, at Skegness. Shortly after opening his large amusement park at Skegness in 1929, Billy Butlin introduced the Canadian dodgems to Britain, advertising them in typical flamboyant style by driving one with a lioness in the car. Source: David N. Robinson Collection.

LET BUTLIN DRIVE YOUR
BLUES AWAY

foreshore which had been purchased from the Earl of Scarbrough for a modest £15,590. The plan showed a boating lake, bathing pool, putting and bowling greens, tennis courts, refreshment rooms, formal gardens, and shelters. The boating lake was opened in 1924, and was extended two years later. The old Marine Gardens were transformed into bowling greens, tennis courts and an artificial rock garden, and the open-air 'Wonder Pool of the East Coast' was opened on Whit Monday 1928, followed the next year by the Orchestral Piazza (later the Embassy Centre). Also in 1929 Billy Butlin opened a large amusement park south of the pier, where he introduced the Canadian dodgems to Britain (including water dodgems) and the seaside zoo (Fig. 7.1). The dunes north and south of the town were excellent for golf links, established at Seacroft in 1898–99 and the North Shore course in 1911, and hotels sprang up along the front including the Seacroft Hydro in 1908–09. Later came the National Deposit Friendly Society's Convalescent Home on North Parade (1927; it became the Town Hall in 1964) and the Derbyshire Miners' & Friendly Societies' Convalescent Home at Winthorpe (1928). The still accreting foreshore at Skegness enabled development of amenities even further from the original parades with the construction of The Bracings in the 1950s.[3]

By contrast again the coastline changed in the tidal Humber with the building of the country's only twentieth-century port at Immingham, and a dock extension at Grimsby. The increased draught and

size of shipping required the construction of a deeper dock; the
Humber Commercial Dock Company was formed and an Act of
Parliament in 1901 authorized a new dock adjacent to the existing
docks at Grimsby. Before committing itself to financial support, the
Great Central Railway Company sought the advice of Sir John Wolfe
Barry who confirmed earlier findings (of 1873) that Immingham was
the most suitable site, where the deep water channel is closest to the
south bank, and a new Act was obtained in 1904. However, financial
negotiations with the Earl of Yarborough, owner of the land on which
the dock was to be built, dragged on to within two years of its opening
(Fig. 7.2).

Construction by contractors Price Wills & Reeves began in 1906
under their manager and agent Robert Holloway, five of whose six
sons and two of whose brothers were under-managers, supervisors,
and engineers on the site. It involved 160 miles of dock railways, over
a hundred boilers in steam daily for five years in locomotives, excavators, continuous bucket diggers, cranes, pumps, and portable
engines, quarrying stone at Brocklesby, building seven hydraulic coal
hoists, and finally pumping 360 million gallons of water from the
Humber into the new dock. The finished dock of 50 acres, with an
entrance lock 1,000 feet by 90 feet, accepting vessels up to 34 feet
draught, was opened by King George V accompanied by Queen Mary
on 22 July 1912. Commercial development was slow until after the

Fig 7.2 Immingham Dock, 1912. The Great Central Railway produced a series of
postcards of paintings for the opening of the dock in 1912. This one shows the dock
offices (right), a heavy cargo crane unloading pig iron, the timber pound, and the north
coaling jetty in the Humber (left background). Source: David N. Robinson Collection.

second world war, but in the 1920s and 1930s the eastern of the two jetties into the Humber was used by Blue Star and Orient liners for summer cruises to the Norwegian fjords.[4]

With the growth of the fishing industry in the inter-war years, increased dock capacity was required at Grimsby. The construction of the 40 acre No. 3 Fish Dock in 1930–34 involved excavation in the estuary to create the North Wall and land on which coaling jetties, new repair slipways, and graving docks could be built. The two lock pits were also widened to 35 feet and 45 feet, the lifeboat station there having been moved to Spurn Head in 1907 because of inability to launch at all states of the tide.[5]

SEA DEFENCES

The central part of the Lincolnshire coast has been open to scouring by the sea since the thirteenth century, and there is constant longshore movement of beach material southwards from Donna Nook to Gibraltar Point. In order to try to slow down this movement and to maintain good beach levels, wooden groynes (or breakwaters) had been built from the 1860s at Trusthorpe and between Chapel St Leonards and Ingoldmells. Angled slightly south of normal to the coastline, they were lines of king posts with planking stringers, and supports on the south side. Early this century further groynes were built at Sandilands (then Sutton le Marsh), and all were regularly maintained. They were the responsibility of first the Commissioners of Sewers and from 1937 the Alford Drainage Board. The Commissioners were also responsible for the outfalls of rivers, streams and drains (or grifts). Originally draining through gaps in the dunes, they had been controlled with gowts (or gotes) – wooden doors pointing seaward which opened at low tide to let out land water and would be closed by a rising tide. At Mablethorpe, Sandilands, Anderby, Chapel St Leonards and Ingoldmells reservoir basins were constructed behind the gowts to avoid inland flooding if there had been heavy rain before a high tide; outfalls were tunnelled through the dunes and covered by breakwater structures across part of the beach. The basin at Mablethorpe was also utilized as a swimming pool, where 'professor' Hobson Bocock gave lessons in the 1920s. Natural gravity land drainage became increasingly less effective, and after the second world war pumping stations were built at Anderby Creek (1946) and Chapel St Leonards (1948); and by the 1970s every outfall from Mablethorpe to Skegness was pumped.[6]

With the continuing rise of sea level the sandhills had inevitably been breached during storm surges in previous centuries. The method of repair employed by the Commissioners was to fill the gap with a bank made of clay, usually dug from clays exposed on the foreshore, and then to encourage a covering dune by brushwood 'hedges' or kidding set on the seaward side of the bank to trap wind-blown sand. The costs of the work in the Lindsey coastal parishes were met by assessing 'acresilver', a rate calculated on the number of acres owned. When work on a drainage outfall was required, or there was a serious emergency due to damage to sea banks, inland parishes also had to pay a levy. Maintenance of the sandhills was vital; at Ingoldmells for example there had been constant fines for cutting 'sines' (marram grass) which bound together the sand of the protecting dunes.

Undoubtedly a major attraction of the Lincolnshire coast was the expanse of golden sand backed by well-vegetated sand dunes 50 feet high in many places. The sands at Skegness were used for car races both before and after the first world war, but it was the quietness of the 'picturesque' sandhills that were eulogized in 1908 as the setting at Huttoft for Woldsea – A Garden Village by the Sea. The Huttoft Town Planning Syndicate produced a scheme for a 1,100 acre township with a two-mile sea front from Anderby Creek to Sandilands. In the years up to 1914 the titled, well-to-do and about-to-retire colonials came to inspect the site, look at the plans of thatched cottages and stockbroker Tudor villages, and went away again. The coast there remained in its natural state.[7]

At Mablethorpe the owners of adjacent 'inlands' claimed they automatically owned the sandhills and beach above high water mark. They let some parts to the Urban District Council who re-let to amusement caterers at increasing rents as more trippers came. In 1912 the owners decided to let direct to the caterers. Alarmed at the loss of income, the Council obtained an Act of Parliament in 1914 by which it acquired ownership of the sandhills. In one of the ensuing disputes over title before the Court of Appeal in 1918 it was adjudged that owners of adjacent lands did not have an automatic right to ownership of the sandhills, but that possessory title could be acquired as a result of exercising acts of ownership over a period of at least twelve years.

The effect of that judgment was to encourage 'inlanders' elsewhere to enclose and build on the dunes. Bungalows, shacks, caravans and old bus bodies and railway carriages appeared wherever a track gave access to the sandhills and seashore. Chapel St Leonards was transformed from three farms and an inn to a flourishing seaside-orientated centre within five years; houses were built on top of the dunes at Anderby Creek and bungalows in the dunes at Soldiers Hole; 'camps' appeared at Ingoldmells and Bohemia (the latter by 1921), together with the Trusville Holiday Camp of caravans at Trusthorpe.

Fig. 7.3 An Osocosy family bungalow, set in the sandhills at Bohemia near Sutton on Sea in 1923. The corrugated iron bungalows were only 15 feet in diameter, with bedroom and living room. Source: David N. Robinson Collection.

Bohemia, established by E. du Soleil Tupper, was a collection of circular corrugated iron huts ('rusty pork pies') on top of the dunes near Sutton on Sea. The huts were fifteen feet in diameter, double lined with stained wood floor, and let furnished with electric light, water supply, oil stoves, linen, crockery and cutlery – all that was required for 'the very ideal of a Gipsy holiday life'. The rents paid for the round 'Osocosy' huts for two persons ranged from 15s a week (October to March) to £2 12s 6d (August). However, the earth closets and poor drainage of developments such as Bohemia were regarded as an acute health hazard by the County Medical Officer of Health (Fig. 7.3).

More squatters enclosing the sandhills and erecting 'eyesores and abominations' brought to a head the question of traditional public access through the dunes to the beach. Triggered by the specific case of a hotel car park on unenclosed land at Sutton on Sea, Lindsey County Council began an investigation of the whole question of ownership rights of the sandhills in 1927. The result was the promotion of a Parliamentary Bill in 1930 to grant powers to preserve all the sandhills and beaches from Donna Nook to Gibraltar Point as open spaces and to regulate future development. At Bohemia £4,750 was paid in compensation for disturbance, a compromise reached with petitioners at Skegness, and the far-sighted Bill was given Royal Assent in July

1932. By 1937, 17 controlled areas had been designated, 48 new huts were on the controlled sandhills at Mablethorpe and Sutton, and 30 at Anderby Creek, Chapel St Leonards, and Ingoldmells. About 500 acres of land were purchased from about 130 owners for over £35,000, and the camp sites at Huttoft and Ingoldmells were acquired and caravans evicted. The Act had been effective in stopping undesirable development.[8] (See also Chapter 8, pp. 199–200.)

The increasing number of holiday-takers in the twentieth century brought a new sea-defence problem: trampling of the dunes, leaving areas bare of vegetation, particularly on the seaward side, and hence more vulnerable to wave attack. Two short sections of vertical sea wall had been built in the nineteenth century, at Mablethorpe Convalescent Home in 1871 (rebuilt by Alford Drainage Board in 1952) and for the promenade at Sutton in 1885. In the early years of this century sloping wooden plank defences and a timber promenade were constructed round the outfall basin promontories at Mablethorpe (1907) and Ingoldmells, with similar structures in the 1920s just north of the Convalescent Home, at Trusthorpe near Bohemia, and simple timber piling between Sutton and Sandilands and at Chapel St Leonards. At the former outfall promontory of Chapel Point was an experimental form of sea defence. This was of oak posts driven into a clay toe to the dunes, with between them a basketwork of ash poles – a simple but effective method of absorbing wave energy, which lasted for around 40 years until replaced by steel-piled concrete defences in the 1940s. The timber work at Mablethorpe was replaced in 1925–26 by concrete stepwork using unemployed miners funded by government grants under the Ministry of Employment. Unfortunately the stepwork was only laid on baulks of clay in the sand and not reinforced, and did well to survive nearly 30 years. Other sections of concrete stepwork replaced much but not all of the timber work in the 1920s, 1930s, and 1940s at Trusthorpe, Sutton, Sandilands, Chapel St Leonards, and Ingoldmells.[9]

THE STORM-SURGE OF 1953

The motley collection of sea defences existing in 1952 – sandhills, wooden walls, poor quality wartime concrete, slabs of concrete on sand and isolated steel-piled concrete walls – were inadequate in both strength and height to withstand the storm surge on the night of 31 January 1953 (Fig. 7.4). The human consequences of the multiple breaching of the sea defences – 41 dead, total evacuation of Mablethorpe and Sutton, and flooding of 20,000 acres of land – were greater than any previous catastrophe of similar magnitude because of the growth of holiday resorts and retirement homes.

Fig. 7.4 Mablethorpe, after the storm-surge of 31 January 1953. The sea completely destroyed the sea wall and sand dunes 400 yards south of Mablethorpe pullover, washing sand into the streets and flooding the town to a depth of five feet (Source: David N. Robinson Collection)

As the afternoon tide rose on 31 January, the pounding waves moved closer, their massive undertow scouring sand from the narrow beaches and then clawing it from the sandhills. Sea walls were pounded and began to crumble, but still the tide rose until waves crashed against the dunes behind the walls or washed over the top and began to erode the landward slope of the defence. At 5.25 p.m. the defences gave way completely at Sandilands: the sea blasted a quarter-mile wide breach in the timber-piled dunes – the notorious Acre Gap – spreading a huge fan of sand over the fields behind, and the tide flowed unimpeded through the gap. Over the next two hours the sea pounded ten more major breaches in the defences between Mablethorpe and Ingoldmells, and wrecked the promenades at Mablethorpe and Sutton. One of the key breaches in the promenade at Mablethorpe was just north of the Convalescent Home. This gave way at 7.10 p.m. and the sea, as at Bohemia and Sutton, drove masses of sand and water into the streets. An estimated 860,000 tons of sand were washed into Mablethorpe, and there was up to eight feet of sand in the streets and round the houses in Sutton.

Between Sandilands and Chapel Point the dune-covered earth seabank largely disappeared along many stretches, and there were major breaches at Sea Bank Farm, Elder Cottage, and Chapel Six Marshes. Those who had ignored the Biblical injunction and built their holiday homes atop the dunes at Anderby Creek found the front rooms hanging precariously over the beach. The steel-piled defences at Chapel Point held, but the promenade and dunes behind were heavily battered. At Trunch Lane near Chapel the narrow trampled dunes were breached along a 600-yard section. The patched-up step-work north of Ingoldmells Point, known as 'Ingoldmells Mess', suffered badly and there were breaches at the Point itself. The sandhills gave way in front of Butlin's Holiday Camp, which was flooded to a depth of six feet.

At Skegness beach chalets were carried away; the well laid-out gardens disappeared under salt water for the first time in their seventy years' existence, the amusement park was flooded, and the north-west corner of the pier was extensively damaged. The town was saved by the wide foreshore and the original promenade wall. The eastern dunes at Gibraltar Point were cut back to reveal wartime beach defences. As the surge swept in to the dead-end of the Wash, the tide rose by more than six feet above the predicted level at Boston, and clay sea banks were breached or overtopped in the Welland and Nene estuaries.

North of Mablethorpe towards Donna Nook the beach widens, backed by dunes and reclamation banks, but even here there were many minor breaches, and one major breach at Sea Lane, Saltfleet. As the tide turned into the Humber from Donna Nook, it was constricted by the funnel shape of the estuary; banks were overtopped, thousands of acres of reclaimed lands were inundated and RAF North Coates was evacuated. At Cleethorpes sand was washed into the bathing pool and amusement facilities became a tangle of wreckage, particularly between the pier and Wonderland. In Suggitt's Bay the sea blasted through the railway embankment, flooding nearly 1,000 homes. Holes were torn in the piers at the entrance to Grimsby docks. Between there and Killingholme Haven the Humber bank was reduced in height by three feet and there were many minor breaches with flooding of factories; Immingham power station was put out of action, and two ships in dry dock were capsized.

A total of 34 miles of sea defences had been destroyed or very severely damaged. There was a fortnight before the next high spring tide in which to win the 'battle of the breaches'. Under appalling weather conditions of rain, wind, and snow 4,000 troops and workmen erected sandbag walls across the worst breaches. From the Humber to the Wash contractors were given instructions to bring in all the draglines, dumpers, piledrivers, bulldozers, and other heavy equipment they could gather and work day and night. Two thousand lorries made two or three journeys daily transporting Scunthorpe slag, chalk,

and other stone from as far afield as Derbyshire and Northamptonshire, pouring 25,000 tons of material into the breaches every 24
hours. The Acre Gap alone swallowed 40,000 tons of Scunthorpe slag,
brought by rail to Sutton, with a continuous line of lorries operating
for four days.

The contractors worked on into the spring, rebuilding clay banks
from Saltfleet to Cleethorpes, along the Humber bank and in the
Wash, using material excavated from borrow pits in the fronting
saltmarshes, repairing eroded dunes with brushwood kidding, and
along the exposed holiday coast building new solid defences with in-
terlocking steel piles driven firmly into the foreshore clays and
concrete or grouted stone walls topped by a curved wave wall. By the
end of March the bill had reached £4.5 million, on top of which there
would be repair of the approach roads fractured by the abnormal
weight and volume of traffic.[10]

The post-flood reconstruction work included the erection of some
250 new groynes, including a few experimental low and rounded
'Dutch' groynes covered in bitumen at Winthorpe. The number and
length of the wooden groynes appeared to be no more effective than
the smaller number earlier in the century, and by the 1970s many
were in urgent need of repair. The rebuilt defences gave a continuous

Fig. 7.5 Humberston Fitties in the early 1970s. In the foreground is Cleethorpes
caravan park, centre the Humberston Fitties camp of bungalows and caravans, with
the outfall of Tetney Haven beyond. Source: M. F. Wood.

armoured skin to the coastline from Mablethorpe to the northern end of Skegness, but by the 1970s further work was necessary to repair deteriorating older concrete stepwork and to raise the height to prevent overtopping by greater surges. One of these, on 12 January 1978, removed two sections from Britain's fourth longest pier at Skegness. Pieces of timber decking and a cast-iron armrest from the seating were found the next day three miles south at the end of the spit at Gibraltar Point. The pier was never rebuilt and the isolated seaward pierhead theatre was finally taken down.

To call Humberston parish's coastline Fitties is a misnomer, despite the common use of the term, since 'fitties' is a Norse word for foreshore saltings (Fig. 7.5). Most of these had been enclosed by Anthony's Bank in 1795, and within 40 years sand-dunes had formed against it. The dunes were occupied by the army in the first world war at the south-east end of the boom to the Haile Sand fort, from which there was an anti-submarine chain with steel netting to the Bull Sand fort on a sandbank in the middle of the Humber estuary, with a second chain to Spurn Point. After the war the ex-army huts were supplemented by other makeshift holiday homes, and the Humberston Fitties Campers' Association was formed in 1925. Unfortunately the dunes were not included in the pioneer Sandhills Act of 1932. By 1947 there were about 60 huts and bungalows, and 240 more were erected in the next nine years and the dunes were in a degraded state from the effects of visitor trampling. The outer dunes were severely cliffed and at one point breached in the 1953 storm-surge, after which brushwood kidding, fencing, and marram grass planting were undertaken, along with some conifer planting. The then Grimsby Rural District Council, as the landowner, prepared a new layout and a drainage scheme for the camp, and in 1958 introduced 1,300 caravans on 120 acres of land behind the dunes which the Council had reclaimed in 1941. This increased trampling pressures on the dunes, and the remedial measures were inadequate to combat increased scour by wave action. In the 1940s the meandering outfall of Tetney Haven reached low-water mark south of the Haile Sand fort, but the swinging meanders moved the outfall north, flowing through the boom, which was removed in 1965–66. The effect of this movement was to give deeper water progressively nearer the dunes and thus increase the wave action. Following the half-hearted attempts to deal with the erosion of the dunes, an £18,000 gabions wall was built in 1962–64. However, the next two winters' tides revealed a serious defect as sand was scoured from the beach and the filling of slag slipped out of the steel mesh basket onto the beach. Erection of groynes had little beneficial effect, and the amenity value of the foreshore was almost

Fig. 7.6 Some of the first Borstal boys at North Sea Camp beginning the work of constructing a reclamation bank in the 1930s. Source: North Sea Camp.

completely lost.[11]

RECLAMATION OF SALTMARSH

Reclamation schemes have been mostly located in the Wash, since apart from the small enclosure at Humberston, the only other saltmarsh reclamation in north-east Lincolnshire was of part of Tetney Outmarsh, between Tetney Haven and North Coates Point, the first in the area for nearly 130 years. The 200-acre scheme had first been proposed in 1947, but was not achieved until 1974–75. The dry summers of 1975 and 1976 allowed underdraining earlier than the usual five-year waiting period.[12]

The Wash coast has seen much more reclamation activity, which led in the 1970s to concern for conservation, the Wash having been designated a Grade 1* Site of Special Scientific Interest under the National Parks and Access to the Countryside Act of 1949. To the east of the Nene, successive reclamations were made at Wingland in 1910, 1917, 1951 and 1974 totalling some 2,000 acres; and on the west the little embayment of Boatmere Creek was enclosed in 1978. West of the Holbeach Air Firing Range (in use from 1926–27) reclamations were made at Holbeach and Moulton in 1949–50 and 1956. The boys at the Borstal North Sea Camp (later H.M. Detention Centre) near Freiston began reclamation work by hand in 1936, using narrow-gauge railway lines and tubs to move the marsh clay they dug to the bank site. The first stage was completed in 1942, with later enclosures in 1955, 1965, and finally in 1979 to complete the 970-acre project which became the Camp farm (Fig. 7.6).[13] Meanwhile private enterprise had reclaimed similar narrow strips of saltmarsh at Wrangle (1960) and Butterwick (1972).

Along the Friskney–Wainfleet frontage, two zones of reclamation have been possible where saltmarsh developed in the shelter of Gibraltar Point. A small enclosure in 1919–20, still using hand methods (where the seaward side of the bank was turfed by unemployed men), was followed in 1948–49 by a 1,400 acre reclamation by a consortium of frontagers. This required approval by the Air Ministry as it involved moving the bombing range (established in 1938) and by the War Department, the Ministries of Agriculture and Fisheries, Transport, and Works, and agreement with the Duchy of Lancaster over creeks below high water mark of ordinary tides within the marsh, before presentation of plans to the East Lincolnshire Joint Town and Country Planning Committee. Dragline excavators were used to build the 10,000-yards long enclosure bank, excavating material from borrow-pits in the saltmarsh seaward of the bank. The total cost was £49,850 or about £35 per acre, at a time when adjoining land was worth £80 an acre. Most of the reclaimed land was grazed at first, some of it for sixteen years before the first crop was taken.[14] By 1966, when 120 acres alongside Wainfleet Haven were reclaimed, costs had risen to £224 per acre. The last major reclamation was again by a consortium and entailed moving the Wainfleet Air Weapons Range even further out across the foreshore.[15] This long narrow strip along the Friskney–Wainfleet frontage was enclosed in 1976–78, despite being breached in the January 1978 storm-surge. The narrowness of these reclamations clearly demonstrates the greatly decreased width achieved compared with those of the seventeenth century.

Between the wars there was a spate of schemes which would have completely changed the Lincolnshire shore of the Wash, including the Dynamatic Electrical Company of 1928 for harnessing tidal power, and the hastily hatched Dutch engineer's plan of 1937 for a barrier from Wrangle to Snettisham in Norfolk, draining works on river outfalls, and the creation of polders.[16] The most grandiose plan was that of 1929–30 for a straight 15-mile long Wash Speedway between high and low water marks from Gibraltar Point to Clay Hole at the mouth of the Witham. A 20-feet high bank of two lines of sandbags with silt pumped between would protect 10,277 acres of foreshore with the 200-yards wide racetrack surfaced with non-skid 'carpo', a 12-mile TT track, 6-mile motor boat speedway, aerodrome, stadium for dirt track, greyhound, pony, and trotting racing, golf course, sand yachting course, restaurants, hotels, an amusement park, a grandstand four miles long and parking for 50,000 cars. At the five-hour Board of Trade Inquiry into the application of the Automobile Racing Association, supported by Earl Howe, Sir Alan Cobham, and Sir Malcolm Campbell, it was confidently asserted that there were no known constructional difficulties 'of a technical character'. However, shortage of capital and opposition from frontagers protecting grazing rights and the traditional access to the foreshore for shrimping and cockling quickly killed off the scheme.[17]

In the 1960s attention focused on the Wash for its potential for storing fresh water. In 1965 the 'Binnie Report' proposed a barrage with locks and sluices to cut off about half the area of the Wash, high-level freshwater storage reservoirs, and use of fly ash to assist in large scale reclamation. Hard on its heels came architect Harry Teggin's fantasy of a city of 750,000 people on reclaimed sand and silt banks, with deep water docks in the Lynn and Boston Deeps, polders and water storage reservoirs, and an airport at Wainfleet, all with road and rail links.[18] The only tangible sign of the Water Resources Board's ensuing feasibility study into water storage was the 300-yard diameter circular trial bank, completed in the 1970s on Westmark Sand on the east side of the Nene outfall just beyond the Lincolnshire county boundary.[19]

THE COAST IN WARTIME

In the wars, the coastline had to be defended against the possibility of enemy landings and attacks, but between 1914 and 1918 it was on only a limited war footing. Concrete pillboxes and machine gun posts were built at key points on the dunes, and forts were built at the entrance to the Humber to protect shipping (at a cost of £2.5 million, but not completed until 1918, too late to be of any use).[20] There was a Kite Balloon Base at Immingham Dock, where the Admiral East Coast had his headquarters, and a seaplane base at Killingholme with a timber slipway for launching into the river, used for a short time by the US Naval Air Service, and which had the largest hangar (800 feet by 220 feet) ever built in the county. As part of the Humber defence system a Night Landing Ground was established late in 1916 near the sea bank at North Coates Fitties, and was in use by 33 Squadron until the end of enemy raids in 1918, when it became home to 404 Flight of 248 Squadron flying anti-submarine patrols over coastal convoys. For a short time in 1914 anti-Zeppelin patrols flew from a field on Burgh Road, Skegness, while a flying training airfield was established at Freiston from 1916, with some aircraft also used for anti-Zeppelin duties.[21]

Fig. 7.7
'The Jolly Fisherman',
by John Hassall.

This famous painting of the jolly
fisherman was adapted as an
advertising poster for Skegness
in 1908. Source: David N. Robinson Collection.

During the second world war the whole of the coast was taken over
by the armed services. Coastal fortifications included six-inch gun
batteries at Grimsby, Mablethorpe, Winthorpe, Gibraltar Point, and
Freiston Shore where both the emplacements and batteries still
remain. A considerable number of rectangular and hexagonal concrete pillboxes, some camouflaged as sheep pens or pig styes, were
built into the dunes or on top of the sea wall at strategic points. Heavy
ordnance positions north of Theddlethorpe were of brick with a reinforced concrete roof, and lines of four-feet cube concrete blocks were
laid down for anti-tank defence at Gibraltar Point, Saltfleetby, and
Donna Nook. On the open beach was a continuous framework of iron
poles and barbed wire, not all cleared away after the war where they
became incorporated into the dunes.[22]

Part of the US Army Transportation Corps – a detachment of the
12th Major Port – was stationed at Immingham Dock,[23] Butlin's
Holiday Camp became *HMS Royal Arthur,* and RAF North Coates
was taken over by Coastal Command to attack enemy shipping. A
decoy airfield and relief landing site was built at Donna Nook, where
the sands had been a bombing and gunnery range since 1926–27 with
three bombing and ten gunnery targets. Gibraltar Point was used for
army training with a rifle range using moving targets towed along a
narrow gauge railway, Ingoldmells had a bomb and gunnery range,
and there was a battle training school at Anderby Creek.[24]

GROWTH OF HOLIDAY MAKING

The holiday industry has played a prominent role in the economy of the coast, and has made the county known to many Midlanders and others. The numbers of excursionists to Edwardian Skegness rose steadily from 226,880 in 1902 to 321,260 in 1907. In February 1908 the Great Northern Railway purchased for £12 from artist John Hassall an oil painting of a smiling, pipe-smoking fisherman bounding along a sandy beach. The words 'Skegness is so Bracing' were added for a poster, which everyone has seen somewhere, to advertise trips from King's Cross for 3s return (Fig. 7.7). Numbers increased to 356,400 in 1910, and in 1913 the total number of passengers arriving at Skegness exceeded three-quarters of a million. In the eight weeks up to 4 August 1914 the figure was 407,000. It was never the same again, even though the waves on the shore became those of the North Sea rather than the German Ocean. On the other hand the remote resort of Freiston Shore on the coast of the Wash near Boston, with its two large hotels (Plummers and Marine) and described in the first half of the nineteenth century as 'the Brighton of the middle classes in Lincolnshire', together with the equally remote 'Lido' on the Welland beyond the Hare and Hounds at Moulton Seas End and the marshy fringe of the Wash at Gedney Drove End, continued to attract visitors, particularly at weekends, into the 1930s.[25]

By the 1920s and 1930s, cars and motorcycles were competing with the train as a means of getting to the seaside. On the record Whit Monday 1930, 70–80,000 people came to Skegness in 31 excursion trains, and up to 10,000 in charabancs, cars and motorcycles, some arriving before many resident visitors had finished breakfast, at peak rates of 1,200 an hour on the Burgh Road and 850 an hour on the Wainfleet Road. Over 10,000 people went to the Bathing Pool (only a quarter to bathe) and all 130 boats on the Boating Lake were let by 10 a.m.[26] A new era in seaside holidays began when the Butlin Luxury Holiday Camp at Ingoldmells opened in Spring 1936. Representing an investment of £100,000 and a test of judgment, its motto was 'Our true intent is all for your delight.' The former farmland on which it was built lies between the Roman Bank and the sandhills, the strengthening of which created a large hole which Butlin turned into a boating lake. A water supply was obtained by boring 80 feet through the marine silts and boulder clay into the underlying chalk. One day when Butlin was travelling from Skegness to his amusement park at Mablethorpe, the site had appealed to him, because of its road access and proximity to the beach.[27]

The Great Northern Railway also had a 3s return from King's Cross

to Mablethorpe, which attracted 96,000 people in 1906, including
5,400 trippers on the August Bank Holiday Monday. When D. H.
Lawrence returned to the 'flat dree coast' in 1926, he found
Mablethorpe 'rather nice, a quite common seaside place, not very big,
with great sweeping sands that take the light, and little people that
somehow get lost in the light, and green sandhills'. Inter-war excursion traffic reached a peak of 166,000 in 1936; by this time Butlin's
amusement park was on the levelled dunes where Mrs Benson's
seaside pavilion of 1884 had been, but an attempt in 1930 to build a
swimming pool over the tidal basin of the drain outfall had been unsuccessful. Excursion traffic never recovered after the second world
war; there were 136,000 passengers in 1959 but the following year
the Louth-Mablethorpe line closed, and numbers dwindled to 6,500
to Mablethorpe and 12,500 to Sutton in 1963. Seven years later the
towns lost their remaining rail link.[28]

At Cleethorpes it was the Manchester, Sheffield and Lincolnshire
Railway which brought in the excursionists, from Sheffield at 6s
return first class or 3s in 'covered carriages', and from Retford and
Gainsborough at 5s and 2s 6d (Fig. 7.8). Although the concert hall at
the end of the pier was destroyed by fire on 6 July 1903, it did not
deter the railway company from buying the pier the following year.
The hall was replaced with a cafe and shops, and a new pavilion complete with stage and dance floor was built part way along the pier in

Fig. 7.8 Edwardian day trippers crowd the north promenade at Cleethorpes. This
photograph is taken from the pier, with the clock tower of the railway station in the
background, centre left. Source: David N. Robinson Collection.

1905. Here were Alf Wilson's White Star Pierrots and The Imperials, and later (1911) Ellison's Entertainers, while Miss Nellie Dyson's Jolly Mascots had a stage on the beach. The installation of heating later allowed its use in winter, and with an extension to seat 600 the pavilion provided regular concerts; after 1923 there were celebrity concerts on Sundays only, although it had become the home of the highly acclaimed Cleethorpes Music Festival from 1909.

In 1935 the pier was purchased from the London and North Eastern Railway (as it had become) by the local authority under the Cleethorpes Urban District Council Act of 1928, and three years later the entrance was altered to give access from the promenade (instead of from the cliff gardens). As an anti-invasion precaution the authorities breached the pier deliberately in 1940, only to find after the war that the estimated £26,000 for putting it into good repair was prohibitive, and the seaward section was demolished leaving a rump of 335 feet. Two hundred tons of timbers went to rebuild Leicester City's football grandstand and most of the remaining materials went into the construction of Wonderland on the North Promenade.[29]

The Skegness Steamboat Company had been running paddle steamer trips from Skegness pierhead, round the Wash and to Hunstanton, from the 1880s, and other steamers brought trippers from the Wash ports. In the late 1920s the North Sea Steamship Company operated a triangular Skegness–King's Lynn–Hunstanton service, and in 1929 as many as 7,000 people were landed on the pier from pleasure boats. As sand accreted on the foreshore the depth of water became insufficient for pier landings and passengers were transferred to small boats from the beach. The pier suffered a disaster on 21 March 1919 when the motor schooner Europa dragged its anchor in a gale and the tide swept the stern under the pier midway between the two sets of shelters. The continued battering demolished 150 feet of the pier; a temporary gangway was erected, but it was twenty years before the break was finally repaired.

When the pier entrance was altered in 1936–37 the original balustraded ramps were demolished, and a new entrance in 'Odeon' style was erected with cafe and shops incorporated. During the first world war the pier had remained open, to reduced business, but during the second world war it was occupied by the RAF at the pier head and the Navy at the entrance, with the Army between. In 1946 a steel and glazed frame was erected over the concrete framework which had replaced the original ironwork between the entrance and the beach steps (installed 1929–30). This became a penny arcade and provided much of the pier's income. When the pier had been in financial difficulties in 1914, Lord Scarbrough bought the remaining

Fig. 7.9 Beach concert party at Mablethorpe. From 1906, Jack Clements produced concert parties in the summer on a small temporary stage on the beach at Mablethorpe, with daily performances at 11.30 a.m., 2.45 p.m., and 6 p.m., or if wet in the Victoria Gardens (Source: David N. Robinson Collection)

shares; he sold the pier to a syndicate of four local businessmen in 1964. The entrance was altered again in 1971: the flight of gracious steps leading to the deck was removed and the building brought down to ground level—a characterless mass of glass and concrete with an amusement arcade, prize bingo, and luxury variety bar.

The building at Skegness pier head was variously the Concert Hall, the Saloon, the Pavilion and the Pier Theatre as the auditorium was extended to incorporate open deck. The Band of the 16th Lancers played there in 1911, and in the decade before the first world war Surtees Corne's Orchestra gave daily concerts on the Deck, and there was 'refined variety entertainment' in the Saloon. In the 1920s there was Contri Tait providing music and Will Gardner's Skegness Entertainers, the Pier Confetti Fete, and the Masked Carnival. In the post-war era there was the popular Jan Remsden Trio and nineteen seasons of Ted Dwyer's 'Follies on Parade'. Other attractions have been roller skating and diving off the end of the pier – in the 1920s by the one-armed Daredevil Leslie.[30]

Following the success with his entertainers at Happy Valley north of the pier during the day, Fred Clements built a stage with canvas roof over the audience on the lawn of Hildred's Hotel for evening shows. In 1906 his brother Jack extended the idea to Mablethorpe with a stage for concert parties and deckchairs on the beach just south of the pullover, and evening shows in the Victoria Pavilion Theatre (later a cinema and bombed in 1943) (Fig. 7.9). At Skegness in 1931

Fred Clements opened the Arcadia Theatre on Drummond Road for evening shows, and showed electric pictures at the Lawn. Later he built the Tower Picture House, designed as a theatre with dressing rooms, where his Christmas pantomimes were prepared for other parts of the country. Avril Angers was a dancer with the Clements Royal Entertainers in 1934 when Kay Kendall went to watch her father in the show, and Elizabeth Allen first had the urge to go on the stage when watching Arcadia shows.[31]

On the coastline between the main resorts the 1932 Sandhills Act enabled the County Council to control the demand for camping and caravanning facilities in the post-war years. The number of static caravans between Cleethorpes and Skegness rose from 4,200 in 1950 to 11,000 in 1959, 18,600 in 1969, and peaked at around 21,000 in 1974 (8 per cent of the United Kingdom), with over a third at Ingoldmells, often dubbed 'caravan city'. To these can be added over 2,500 chalets at Humberston, Mablethorpe, and Sutton, 3,000 at Butlins (including 1,700 for self-catering), and 500 at the Derbyshire Miners' Club Holiday Camp. These figures are a clear indication of the post-war shift to self-catering accommodation, including the conversion of guest houses and small hotels to flats.

In the 1970s the coast from Skegness to Mablethorpe had 120,000 bed spaces available, of which 90 per cent were in caravans and chalets. At the beginning of the century virtually all accommodation was in boarding and lodging houses except for the few hotels. In Skegness lodging accommodation was concentrated on Lumley Road and the seafront; by 1964 Lumley Road had been converted to shopping and the dominant area for boarding houses and small hotels was the seafront, particularly on Grand and South Parades, mostly properties built in the first decade of the century and between the wars. However, the town still had some 300 bed and breakfast establishments in the 1970s. The main catchment areas of the resorts were essentially established even before the railways, that is South Yorkshire for Cleethorpes and the East Midlands for Skegness and Mablethorpe. They have not changed.[32]

NATURE RESERVES

As early as 1907 it had been suggested that 'the physical geography of the Lincolnshire sandhills might usefully be taught in the schools of Lincolnshire and the Midlands', and later the 'longest strip of sandhills in Great Britain' were described by the Council for the Preservation of Rural England as 'sanctuaries of nature', but nature reserves on the coast are mainly an achievement of the post–1945 period. By the 1970s, 45 miles of the coastline were afforded some form of protection for their scientific status and natural beauty, fourteen miles of which were nature reserves largely established through the work of the Lincolnshire and South Humberside Trust for Nature Conservation.[33]

On the Saltfleetby–Theddlethorpe coastline the dune system, including the area of unique maritime fen at Rimac (named after a Baltic ship wrecked there), was divided into grazing units by banks with watering ponds dug in hollows in the ancient dunes. By the 1920s the grazing enclosures had been abandoned, and in summer 1928 a firm of estate agents from Long Eaton in Derbyshire started to lay out Rimac-on-Sea with 188 plots for huts and bungalows. Within three years 40 huts had been erected 'of varying degrees of ugliness'. Further development was thwarted by the compulsory purchase by the Air Ministry in 1932 of the dunes and marsh of the whole of the Saltfleetby–Theddlethorpe coastline to establish an extension to the Donna Nook bombing and firing range. The purchase also included the foreshore above high water mark of ordinary tides – surveyed in 1905 and already an arbitrary line without real meaning. In 1956 the then Lincolnshire Naturalists' Trust was able to establish a nature reserve where Rimac-on-Sea would have been; in 1968 the Nature Conservancy Council purchased most of the rest of the land from the Ministry of Defence and the whole 1,100 acres was declared a National Nature Reserve. The construction of the Viking Gas Terminal in Theddlethorpe parish just inland of the dunes in 1970–72 involved cutting a pipeline trench through the dunes at the southern tip of the reserve. Use of the bombing range ceased in 1973, with final removal in 1976 when that at Donna Nook was reactivated.[34]

Six and a half miles of coastline from Saltfleet Haven to Somercotes Haven and including Donna Nook, covering some 2,400 acres of dunes, strip saltings, and foreshore, achieved nature reserve status in 1978, managed by the Trust mainly by agreement with the Ministry of Defence. Immediately to the north, Grainthorpe Fitties was designated a Site of Special Scientific Interest in 1968, and at Tetney-North Coates the Royal Society for the Protection of Birds leased a 2,500 acre reserve of marsh and dune foreshore. Some of the oldest Wash saltmarshes at Frampton and Kirton were established as nature reserves by the Trust and the RSPB. The broader concepts of coastal conservation stemming from the Sandhills Act were developed by Lindsey County Council in 1966 to apply outside the main holiday concentrations of Skegness–Ingoldmells, Chapel St Leonards, Anderby Creek and Sandilands–Mablethorpe by providing suitable opportunities for the day visitor to enjoy infomal recreation, while at the same time conserving the natural features of the coastline.[35]

At the beginning of the century there was a small community at Gibraltar Point, with the Coastguard Station, families at Sykes or Tennyson Farm and at Gibraltar House, formerly the Ship Inn and built across the Wainfleet St Mary and Croft parish boundary. There was also a large family in 'Noah's Ark', originally a pilot vessel hauled out of Wainfleet Haven onto the marsh, but shortly to be broken up and burnt. By the 1920s two sailing barges used for bringing gravel from Heacham in Norfolk to Skegness and for carrying grain, were moored in the Haven; the eastern dune line had reached its limit and in 1922 a storm beach was thrown up from the end across the southern edge of the saltmarsh. Then some distance from the sea, the Coastguard Station was abandoned in 1925.

Land at Gibraltar Point in the parish of Croft had been sold off in 1923 from the extensive Tyrwhitt-Drake estates to Mr J. Giles and Mr G. E. Hyams of Skegness; they proposed to develop a garden city where a rifle range had been set up near the eastern dunes. In 1930 just over 200 acres of sandhills and saltings were bought from Giles and Hyams by MacLean Estates to develop the Tennyson Glen estate of 800 houses, with promenade, concert pavilion and formal gardens. Only three show houses were built on Aylmer Avenue before the company went into liquidation in 1934, and Lindsey County Council purchased the land for £12,000, with borrowing sanctioned by the Ministry of Health because of extraction of sand from the dunes. Gibraltar Point had been saved from development, but little could be done until after the war, although in 1939 the Lincolnshire Naturalists' Union had suggested that a bird observatory be established there. Gibraltar House was demolished in 1939; after Sykes Farm was derequisitioned by the army it was partially burnt down in 1947.

In 1948 the Lincolnshire Naturalists' Trust (later the Lincolnshire & South Humberside Trust for Nature Conservation) was formed; through the drive and initiative of its honorary secretary A. E. (Ted) Smith, then University of Nottingham Resident Tutor for South Lindsey, Lindsey County Council quickly agreed to the establishment of a nature reserve. Later an area of dunes and foreshore owned by Skegness Urban District Council was added. In 1952 the County Council designated their part of the reserve as the first Local Nature Reserve in England and Wales under the National Parks and Access to the Countryside Act of 1949.

From its inception as a nature reserve, the value of Gibraltar Point for education and research was stressed. An old army building in the east dunes became the bird observatory in 1949, which, with 'Fred's Place' (a former single-decker Nottingham bus brought there in the late 1930s) and a former gun emplacement, provided accommodation for zoology, botany, and geography students from Nottingham University until 1958. In that year the County Council acquired the old coastguard station (two extensions had been built in the 1930s when it was used as a holiday home) and leased it to the Trust as a field research station. Laboratories and dormitory accommodation were added in 1964 for residential field teaching for Lincolnshire and other schools, for adult courses run by the University of Nottingham Department of Adult Education, and for use by amateur naturalists.

A small display and information centre was built on the main car park in the early 1960s. By the 1970s the number of visitors to the reserve (including Prince Charles on 14 July 1971) had built up to 200,000 a year, and in 1974 the County Council, with grant-aid from the Countryside Commission and the Carnegie UK Trust, built the Visitor Centre with an exhibition and sales area; a freshwater mere, complete with viewing hide, was also created.

With its dynamic complex of sand-dunes, saltmarshes, sandy beaches and mud flats, Gibraltar Point was recognized for its international scientific status by designation as a National Nature Reserve. The successful protection of this part of the Lincolnshire coast and the conservation of its fragile and diverse habitats and their rare plants and animals, while at the same time ensuring that the large numbers of visitors do not damage what they came to enjoy – including a programme of education at different levels – was a pioneer example of successful collaboration between a local authority and a voluntary body.[36]

Bibliographical note

The bulk of the material for this chapter is derived from the author's *Book of the Lincolnshire seaside*. This very full illustrated book sets out the physical history of the coastline, the battle against coastal erosion, and the saltmarsh reclamations since the sixteenth century. Chapters dealing with the growth of the holiday industry are 'The day of the tripper', 'Beside the seaside', 'Piers and Pierrots', and 'Conserving the coastline'; the latter also reviews the establishment of coastal nature reserves. Other relevant chapters are 'The great storm surge of 1953' and 'What shall we do with the Wash?' (for reclamations as well as the abortive schemes of the 1930s and 1960s). The book has a more extensive bibliography than that listed below, except for publications after 1981 – principally Ekberg's *The book of Cleethorpes* and Kime's *The book of Skegness*. Both have full bibliographies.

The basic problem for the changing coastline has been, and will continue to be, the rising sea level. This requires heightening, improvement, and maintenance of sea defences, and the increasing pump drainage of low-lying land in the Outmarsh and the Fens. Source material here is in the annual and internal reports of the Lincolnshire River Division of Anglian Water, and publications of Drainage Boards (including J. R. Elkington (ed.), *Louth Drainage Board: 1938–1988*, Manby, 1989).

Notes to Chapter 7

1. C. Ekberg, *The book of Cleethorpes*, Buckingham, 1986, p. 74.
2. D. N. Robinson, *The book of the Lincolnshire seaside*, Buckingham, 1981, ch. 7.
3. *Lincolnshire seaside, ibid.*, chs. 7 and 8; W. Kime, *The book of Skegness*, Buckingham, 1986, ch. 9.
4. A. R. Tailby, *Immingham: The story of a village*, Immingham, 1970, ch. 9; E. Hollowday, 'The Hollowday family and the building of Immingham Dock', *Lincolnshire Life*, 27, 4, 1987, pp. 22–7.
5. D. N. Robinson, 'No. 3 Fish Dock, Grimsby', *Lincolnshire Life*, 24, 4, 1984, p. 22.
6. J. R. Elkington (ed.),*Alford Drainage Board: 50 Years*, Manby, 1987 (booklet).
7. *The Lincolnshire seaside*, ch. 8.
8. J. Sheail, The Impact of Recreation on the Coast: The Lindsey County Council (Sandhills) Act 1932, *Landscape Planning*, 4, 1977, pp. 53–72; *The Lincolnshire seaside*, ch. 13.
9. J. R. Elkington (ed.), *Alford Drainage Board: 50 Years*.
10. F. A. Barnes & C. A. M. King, 'The Lincolnshire coastline and the 1953 storm flood', *Geography*, XXXVII, 3, 1953, pp. 141–60; Lincolnshire River Board Report, 1953; D. N. Robinson, 'The failure of the coastal defences of East Lincolnshire', *Survey*, 3, 2, 1953, pp. 37–44; D. N. Robinson, 'The sea defences of Lincolnshire', *Lincolnshire Poacher*, 1, 4, 1953, pp. 29–32; D. N. Robinson, 'The great storm flood of 1953', *Lincolnshire Life*, 12, 11, 1973, pp. 40–3; *The Lincolnshire seaside*, ch. 11; F. H. Tomes, 'Damage and remedial measures on the Lincolnshire coast', Conference on North Sea floods, 31 January/1 February 1953, Inst. Civil Engineers, 1954, pp. 212–22.
11. D. N. Robinson, 'Humberston Fitties holiday camp: a brief on sea defence and condition of the foreshore', prepared for Grimsby RDC, 1972.
12. D. N. Robinson, 'Coastal evolution in north-east Lincolnshire', *E. Midland Geog.*, vol. 5, pts 1 and 2, pp. 62, 70, 1970; 'Reclamation from the sea in Lincolnshire', *MAFF: ADAS Annual Report*, 1980, pp. 55–7.
13. J. W. Hanson, 'North Sea camp', *Lincolnshire Life*, 25, 8, 1985, pp. 26–27.
14. G. E. E. Buchner, *A reclamation near Wainfleet, Lincolnshire*. Institute of Civil Engineers, Maritime and Waterways Paper No. 12, London, 1949.
15. K. Sanders, 'RAF Wainfleet Air Weapons Range', *Lincolnshire Life*, 27,

6, 1987, p. 26.

16. W. E. Doran, 'The Wash', *Geographical Magazine*, 1965, pp. 885–97.

17. *The Lincolnshire seaside*, ch. 12.

18. H. Teggin, 'Britain's Europort: The real treasure in the Wash', *Architects Journal*, 15, 1969, pp. 142–98.

19. Central Water Planning Unit, *The Wash water storage scheme: report on the feasibility study*, 1976; Hydraulics Research Station, *The Wash storage: a historical review*, Report DE26, Wallingford, 1975; Water Resources Board, *The Wash: estuary storage, report on the desk study*, 1970; F. White, *A basin full of water*, Kings Lynn, 1968.

20. C. Ekberg, *The book of Cleethorpes*, 1986, p. 97.

21. R. N. E. Blake, M. Hodgson, & W. J. Taylor, *The airfields of Lincolnshire since 1912*, Leicester, 1984.

22. UK Fortifications Club, 'World War Two defences of Lincolnshire', unpub. report, 1979.

23. P. Jaeck, 'A Yank at Immingham', *Lincolnshire Life*, 27, 4, 1987, pp. 28–9.

24. Blake *et al, op. cit.,* 1984.

25. R. E. Pearson, 'The Lincolnshire coast holiday region', unpub. MA thesis, University of Nottingham, 1965; *The Lincolnshire seaside*, ch. 8.

26. *The Lincolnshire seaside*, ch. 8.

27. R. North, *The Butlin story*, London, 1962, ch. 4.

28. *The Lincolnshire seaside*, ch. 8.

29. Ekberg, *op. cit.,* chs. 7 and 10; *The Lincolnshire seaside*, ch. 9.

30. S. D. J. Hannam and D. N. Robinson, 'The end of the Pier?', *Lincolnshire Life*, 18, 11, 1979, pp. 18–24; W. Kime, *The book of Skegness*, 1986, ch. 4; *The Lincolnshire seaside*, ch. 9.

31. D. N. Robinson, 'The Clements story', *Lincolnshire Life*, 15, 7, 1975, pp. 32–36.

32. Lincolnshire C. C., *Development on the coast: subject plan,* Lincoln, 1981; Lindsey C. C., *The Lindsey coast: a policy for holiday development*, 1973, *The Lindsey coast: access and car parking*, 1974.

33. A. E. Smith, *Nature conservation in Lincolnshire*, Lincoln, 1969 (booklet).

34. D. N. Robinson, 'The Saltfleetby–Theddlethorpe coastline', *Transactions Lincolnshire Naturalists' Union*, XXI, 1, 1984, pp. 1–12.

35. Lindsey C. C., *The Lindsey coast: a policy for conservation*, 1971; D. N. Robinson, 'The north-east coast of Lincolnshire: a study in coastal evolution', unpub. M.Sc. thesis, Univ. Nottingham, 1956; 'Coastal evolution in north-east Lincolnshire', *E. Midland Geog.*, vol. 5, pts 1 and 2, 1970, pp. 62–70.

36. D. N. Robinson, 'Gibraltar Point Nature Reserve', *Lincolnshire Life*, 9, 6, 1969, pp. 48–51; *The Lincolnshire seaside*, ch. 13; A. E. Smith, *op. cit.,* 1969; R. B. Wilkinson, 'Notes on Old Gibraltar Point', unpub. notes, 1987.

CHAPTER 8

THE EARLY DAYS OF PLANNING

by Sally Scott

Abstract *This chapter, more than any other in the book, concentrates on the first half of the century. The 1947 Act ushered in a new era in planning which has continued with relatively minor adjustments down to the time of writing. What happened before 1947 was spasmodic by comparison, and related only to the main urban areas and the difficulties caused by development pressure on the central parts of the coastline. Nevertheless, an apprenticeship was served which came to fruition after 1947, including the appointment of some of the pioneers to full time posts in planning. The close relationship between planning, politics and housing is explored, a theme reappearing in the next chapter.*

After establishing the institutional context, both nationally and locally, three main strands are considered: first, involvement in statutory planning through the preparation of town planning schemes and membership of Joint Planning Committees: second, the Lindsey County Council (Sandhills) Act of 1932 which represents a pioneering attempt to manage development outside the current planning legislation; and third, the question of housing, in terms of the local response to the principles of the Garden City Movement with which planning was strongly associated.

INSTITUTIONAL CONTEXT

A comprehensive system of physical planning for England and Wales was established by the 1947 Town and Country Planning Act which made it mandatory to prepare development plans for all areas and to control most forms of development by requiring developers to apply for planning permission. The system had evolved from 1909 through a series of Acts that allowed local authorities to prepare town planning schemes for restricted areas and to exercise some control over development within them. The area covered by plans gradually increased in size and number but did not include all land until 1947, whereas a form of development control had been extended to all land in 1943.

The degree to which local authorities participated in pre-1947 planning varied greatly, not least because most of the early Acts were enabling rather than obligatory. Much has been written about the period from 1947 to the present day and only general works on planning history have covered the earlier period. Local material exists to illustrate how different parts of the large rural county of Lincolnshire responded to ideas and legislation in the period before universal mandatory planning. This chapter, therefore, is concerned with the period up to 1947 to fill in some details of the early picture at the local leval.

The institutional context of planning at the national level is associated with the health and sanitary reforms which were introduced to combat the often appalling housing conditions associated with nineteenth-century industrialization and urbanization. Thus the first planning legislation was appended to a Housing Act, and responsibility for the 1909 Housing, Town Planning Etc Act (sic) lay with the Local Government Board whose main function had been to supervise the national sanitary administrative system established by the 1875 Public Health Act. The association between housing, town planning, and health continued when a Ministry of Health was created in 1919 and took over planning functions. The first Minister of Health was Christopher Addison (a Lincolnshire man by birth and upbringing), and both the 1919 Act and some of the earliest of the country's council houses that were built under its provisions came to be known by his name (Fig. 8.1a).

In 1925 the Town and Country Planning Act consolidated town planning law and separated it from housing, but planning remained under the remit of the Ministry of Health. During the second world war it was realized that positive action and consistent policies would be needed to cope with post-war reconstruction on a national basis. In recognition of these needs a separate Ministry of Town and Country Planning was set up in 1943, which remained operative until 1951.

Local planning activity was subject to central bureaucratic procedures and checks. Under the 1909 Act, Local Planning Authorities (LPAs) had to seek authorization to prepare a scheme. The 1919 Act repealed this provision but it was reintroduced in the Town and Country Planning Act of 1932. Under the terms of all planning Acts, schemes had to be submitted to the Minister at both preliminary and draft stages, when they were subject to open-ended consultations before being amended, approved or rejected. Inspectors, appointed by

Figs. 8.1a and 8.1b Early council houses. 8.1a (above): One of the four pairs of semi-detached council houses built by East Elloe Rural District Council on the A17 near Fleet in 1920, under the Addison Act (1919 Housing, Town Planning etc. Act) Note the complicated roof pattern. Tiles and windows have been replaced and porches added **8.1b**(below): One of two pairs of semi-detached houses built by the same District Council in 1923, with less elaborate design than the earlier ones shown in Fig. 8.1a, under subsequent legislation with more economical provisions. Source: Mrs S. Scott (1988).

government, held local public inquiries at preliminary and draft stages and reported to the Minister on any objections or representations.

An embryonic form of development control created by the 1919 Act was strengthened in 1932 and came to fruition in the 1943 Town and Country Planning (Interim Development) Act. There was a right of appeal against a local refusal of a development permit and there could be a public inquiry after which the Minister considered his Inspector's report before making the final decision.

Other powers included those to make regulations and orders under the terms of the various Acts and to issue guidelines. The 1935 Restriction of Ribbon Development Act added another bureaucratic complication, giving independent powers to local highway authorities and to the Ministry of Transport in relation to new roads, including those that formed part of the proposals in planning schemes.

Until 1947 the responsibility for implementing planning at the local level lay with county boroughs and both urban and rural districts, which thus formed the LPAs. From 1919 Joint Planning Committees could be formed by neighbouring LPAs, usually to prepare regional plans, but they had no executive powers unless the constituent authorities delegated their powers to the committee. A Local Government Act of 1929 gave an official planning role to county councils for the first time by entitling them to be represented on Joint Planning Committees (JPCs) and by allowing any LPA to delegate its powers to the county council. The 1947 Act made county councils and county borough councils the main planning authorities and this remained the case until 1974 when a two-tier system of districts and counties was created.

Planning, as with other council services, was organized through committees of elected councillors advised by departments of paid staff or by outside consultants. Councils could create new committees or add planning to the functions of existing ones. Locally, Lincoln, Grimsby, and Cleethorpes were the first to act, in 1913. Some early committees survived while others faded away and were reconstituted in another form. A second phase followed the 1919 Act as more authorities decided to prepare schemes.

The word 'planning' in a committee title did not necessarily mean that the council intended to act. In some cases a particular councillor or pressure group was eager to use the new legislation. If such a councillor was in a powerful position then action was more likely, as Hartley showed in his study of housing policy in four Lincolnshire towns.[1] Thus, in Scunthorpe Councillors Read and Quibell wanted to promote the preparation of a town plan along garden city lines under the 1909 Act. D. J. K. Quibell pursued this approach until, like some other Labour candidates, he was unsuccessful in the 1919 local elections. The issue was then taken up by James Henderson who used his position as chairman of the Housing Committee to push ahead with both a housing and a planning scheme under the 1919 Act, despite little enthusiasm from fellow councillors. In Lincoln, positive action was more assured once Clement Newsum engineered a committee reorganization with himself as chairman of the Housing and Town Planning Committee in 1919. Continuing pressure from a well-organized Public Welfare Committee, a voluntary group led by the Dean of Lincoln, Dr T. P. Fry, and from the Lincoln Trades and Labour Council also provided a stimulus.

Lindsey was the first of the three county councils to enter the fray when a planning sub-committee was appointed in February 1933 as part of the Highways Committee to be responsibe for any matters arising out of Lincoln's planning scheme. Matters relating to the Sandhills were the separate responsibility of a Sandhills sub-committee which reported back to the General Purposes Committee. Lindsey was also the chief motivator behind the creation of the East Lindsey Advisory JPC in the mid 1930s. Between 1943 and 1945 all the LPAs became constituent authorities of one of the five JPCs then set up in the geographical county, namely East Lincolnshire, North Lincolnshire, Lincoln and District, Kesteven and Holland. All the county councils had to establish full county planning committees when the 1947 Act came into force.

For councils wishing to prepare schemes, lack of staff with any planning education or experience was a problem in the early days. The Town Planning Institute was formed in 1913 and sought to establish planning as a separate discipline, but in the inter-war years most Members and Associated Members who took the Institute's examinations had an initial qualification in one of the other three land-based professions of civil or municipal engineering, architecture, or surveying. They continued to dominate the profession after the war. Robert L. Stirling, for example, began his career as an articled pupil to Lincoln's City Engineer in 1924; his interest in planning grew when he went to work for Southport and after returning to Lincoln as Chief Assistant Engineer in 1933 he embarked on a planning qualification, taking the finals of the Town Planning Institute in 1942 before becoming planning officer to the Lincoln and District JPC in 1944 and then to the Lindsey County Council in 1947. He recalls that between the wars the City Engineer acted as a general factotum, dealing with roads, sewerage, parks, refuse, bye-laws, council housing and all other building construction. Planning was simply added to these functions in Lincoln as in most other LPAs.[2]

STATUTORY PLANNING

Statutory planning began with town planning schemes under the 1909 Act, which was permissive only. It allowed LPAs to ensure 'proper sanitary conditions, amenity and convenience' in areas of new development only, by zoning land for different uses, controlling the number of buildings per acre, allocating areas of open space and setting out the road framework. Joint schemes were not permitted, but LPAs could prepare plans for areas outside their administrative boundaries. This feature provoked fears about possible boundary extensions in adjoining councils and was exploited to those ends by some LPAs. In fact, improvements in transport allowed outward suburban growth and thus made many areas just outside the current boundaries ripe for development schemes. Nationally the Local Government Board approved 172 resolutions to prepare schemes, but only 13 were actually completed in the ten years the Act was in force. The outbreak of the first world war put a brake on planning activity, as in Lincoln.

First phase

Lincoln was considering schemes for two areas. The first was the 1,235 acre Boultham Park Estate then situated in Branston Rural District, bought by a syndicate in 1913 primarily for residential development. Both Branston and Lincoln vied for the right to prepare a scheme to ensure high standards. Lincoln was quite open about its intention to apply for the incorporation of this and other areas to the west and south, and felt that this made them the proper planning authority. Eventually it was agreed that Branston would officially submit a scheme prepared with the help of Mr McBrair, the City Engineer and Surveyor. Only seven months later both councils insisted that any scheme was solely the responsibility of the other and the matter foundered. Lincoln's expansion plans were delayed and negotiations proved difficult with the syndicate.[3] The sheer size of the project may also have been an inhibiting factor.

The second site lay to the north, near the Lincoln School along Wragby Road and was within the city boundary. A scheme was approved in principle in December 1913 that involved the purchase of about 60 acres to provide 900 homes. The site was over a mile from the nearest foundry but the corporation felt proposals for a cheap omnibus service would overcome this obstacle. An application was made to the Local Government Board for a loan to buy the land. At the subsequent public inquiry in May 1914, differing opinions on both housing and planning and private versus municipal enterprise were expressed. The Town Clerk, Mr W. Bagshaw, stated that '...if private enterprise did not meet the need then he thought the Corporation was satisfied that it was their duty to provide the houses themselves, and he might say that it was with considerable reluctance that the council decided to embark on a scheme of that sort'. Mr Arthur Taylor, the city's first socialist councillor and later Labour MP for Lincoln, spoke on behalf of the Lincoln Trades and Labour Council that had long campaigned for more working-class housing and had collected 600 signatures in favour of the council's proposals. There was a counter-petition with 366 signatories made up of local builders and the more important property owners and ratepayers. They did not object in principle to 'something' being done, the inquiry heard, but they wanted an adjournment until a full scheme had been prepared and costed. Their view that a scheme would cause the rates to rise was not supported by the inspector. The most Mr McBrair would say about details was that '...the land would be developed more or less on the lines of a garden city.'[4] Eric Scorer, subsequently Lindsey County Council's first full-time clerk, appeared on behalf of the Boultham Park syndicate: he was not actively opposed to the proposals, but pointed out that his clients had suitable land for workmens' dwellings and had built 200 houses in eighteen months.[5]

In August 1914 the sanction to borrow came through, but in the meantime the council had been considering other land to the north which they felt would be opened up to private development by their own housing scheme. They resolved to include this additional 140 acres in the planning scheme to ensure lower densities, more open space and a better road layout than the usual private development might give. At the end of July, George Peplar, later chief planner at the Ministry of Health, took the local inquiry into the council's application to prepare a scheme.[6] However, growing preoccupation with the war effort led to the matter being dropped before official approval came through, but the original 65 acres were bought and formed part of the city's first council housing area after the war.

Lincoln showed itself willing to control private enterprise and to initiate municipal development according to the new standards for residential areas. Its decision on municipal enterprise was taken reluctantly but indicated some local consensus on the moral necessity to provide more, better, and reasonably priced houses for rent. This represented a considerable change from the corporation's previous reluctance to make public improvements to the city: a new water supply was provided only after a hundred deaths from typhoid in 1905, for example.[7] Although the Boultham scheme was a nonstarter, it seems likely that the city would have proceeded with the smaller Wragby Road planning and housing schemes had the war not intervened: it had always been intended to have an overall layout, but for building to proceed in stages.

Other LPAs which flirted with the early use of planning powers were Grimsby and Cleethorpes but, as already hinted, they were at least partly interested because of their respective boundary aspirations and fears. The same consideration played some part in Scunthorpe. It was 1919 before five adjacent settlements amalgamated as Scunthorpe and Frodingham Urban District Council; the promotion of a scheme by Scunthorpe alone between 1911 and 1913 was viewed with suspicion by the other authorities. As we have seen, nothing came of the idea at the time but the promotion of a garden town at Scunthorpe persisted and today signs on the main roads into the town still proclaim 'Scunthorpe: The Industrial Garden Town'.

Second phase

The second Housing, Town Planning Etc Act of 1919 reemphasized the importance of improving residential standards through planning schemes and municipal housing. It became mandatory for all LPAs with a population over 20,000 to prepare a planning scheme by 1926, although this time limit was later extended several times. In practice it was urban authorities which commonly took the initiative; as neither Holland nor Kesteven had any towns of this size no schemes were prepared. In Lindsey four towns exceeded this population, namely Grimsby, Lincoln, Cleethorpes, and Scunthorpe, and all carried out their obligation to prepare schemes. Size was not the only criterion, and the growing seaside towns of Skegness and Mablethorpe, with very much smaller populations, also took action under the Act. The contrast between activity in Lindsey and the other two counties is very marked, but not surprising when the distribution of population and industry is taken into account, with pressure for development very much skewed to the north, as Chapter 2 has already shown.

Many schemes begun under the 1919 Act or the consolidating Act of 1925 were finally approved under the provisions of the 1932 Act, as in the cases of Mablethorpe, Scunthorpe, Cleethorpes, and Grimsby's Area 1 scheme. Others, like Skegness, Lincoln, and Grimsby's Areas 2 and 3 schemes never received final approval by the Minister although they were used for development control purposes.

Lincoln

Lincoln again considered a scheme after the war but a formal resolution was not passed until 1923. This time proposals involved all the open land in the city, plus 5,235 acres in Branston Rural District to the south and 1,785 acres in Welton Rural District to the north. Other land in the north was withdrawn after discussions with Lord Monson's agent.[8]

The city appointed an architect as assistant to the surveyor in 1920, specifically to work on the Wragby Road housing scheme, choosing Alfred Hill, ARIBA, from 40 applicants. He also had an interest in planning and by the time he left in 1924 had become an Associate Member of the Town Planning Institute. His duties were extended and in 1923 and early 1924 he was largely responsible for preparing the initial planning scheme, with the help of a temporary town planning assistant, Harry Hill, who also worked on Mablethorpe's scheme in the 1930s.[9]

More than 5,000 acres were allocated for residential development in the plan area, mostly at an average gross density of 12 dwellings to the acre. West and South Commons were the major areas of open space and land was zoned for industrial use. Several stretches of new road were indicated, either to open up new areas or to link with the existing network to create through routes. The most contentious proposal was for a ring road sweeping eastwards around the city from the junction of Doddington and Newark roads in the south-west, up the cliff edge and across the Witham to join Wragby Road near Bunkers Hill before curving around to link with the Gainsborough Road at Bishops Bridge.[10]

The Minister insisted that the Branston and Welton RDCs should administer the scheme in their areas, but they prevaricated, fearing heavy expenditure on roadworks and possible liability for compensation. LPAs were liable to pay for loss of development value and were thus reluctant to refuse interim development permits. Lindsey viewed the rural districts' attitude with concern, feeling that '...it will give the Corporation grounds for a further extension of their boundaries'. In 1932 they still felt the rural districts were playing into Lincoln's hands '...by not discharging their duty. If Town Planning is a good thing in the County then some authority in the County ought to pay what is required.'[11] From 1933 progress waited on consultations both locally and centrally over the line of the ring road, its width and cost. Protracted discussions did not resolve the differences and when the final draft was deposited in the summer of 1939 both Kesteven and Lindsey lodged formal objections. History repeated itself when the outbreak of war again stopped work. However, in 1943 a Reconstruction Committee, chaired by J. W. F. (later Sir Francis) Hill and aided by academics from Nottingham University together with R. Stirling and other City Engineer's staff, began comprehensive surveys of existing conditions as a basis for a post-war development plan. A Civic Survey and Housing Exhibition was held in September 1944 at the Usher Gallery to illustrate their findings.[12]

Most of the pre-war scheme's road proposals were modified or abandoned after the war but an eastern by-pass was not finally rejected until 1979. Much residential development 'jumped' the scheme's boundaries into nearby villages.

Scunthorpe

Scunthorpe and Frodingham Urban District Council was the only Lindsey LPA to employ private consultants. The internationally prestigious firm of Patrick Abercrombie and T. H. Johnson was engaged in 1920 to prepare a scheme along garden city lines. They produced an outline plan for the whole town and an equally large area outside its boundaries in March 1921. Momentum was lost when difficulties arose over areas of responsibility, the length of time the firm took to proceed further, and payment for work done. In January 1927 the firm agreed to finish work but asked the council to pay more than the agreed fees to cover extra work. Despite some acrimony, Professor Abercrombie offered his services as an expert advisor whenever needed.

The consultants' plan was by far the most sophisticated of the Lindsey schemes. It sought to link the fragmented pattern of development that had arisen from the origins of the urban district as five separate villages by establishing an overall road network that emphasized north–south links both by boosting two existing routes and building a third on the western edge of proposed development. Large-scale residential areas were proposed for Brumby and Frodingham to span the gap between Scunthorpe and Ashby. Housing areas were to have neighbourhood centres where residents would be served by local shops and other amenities within half a mile of their homes. The average density was to be ten dwellings per acre and never more than twenty inside the borough boundary. The plan provided for a system of parks and amenity areas in the form of a continuous belt of open space along the western escarpment, with playing fields and parks throughout the town, and a number of well-treed boulevard type roads. A civic centre site was reserved between Laneham Street and Station Road: the architectural treatment was to take the form of a semi-circle set around with public and business buildings and with a new railway station to the south.[13]

Final approval was given by the Minister of Health in March 1939, after many consultations, delays, and modifications. In the early 1930s the Humber Bridge Bill referred to on pages 116-17 was the cause of some delay. After its deferment other road proposals and the question of financial liability for them once again held up progress. The letters that passed between the parties shows how there was a vicious circle of waiting for comments on comments.[14] The scheme as finally approved was in many ways a watered-down version of the consultants' vision. Land in the existing central shopping area was excluded, the strict zoning proposals for industrial areas were modified and the amount of open space was much reduced, all on the recommendation of the Minister of Health, who in the latter case feared that the open space allocations were beyond the financial capacity of the council. The idea of neighbourhood centres was also dropped, only to be resurrected in the first post-war planning report. Some modifications resulted from the building of the A18 trunk road in 1933 which the consultants had not anticipated.

Low-density residential development on a large scale did take place between Scunthorpe and Ashby in the inter-war period but, apart from the Redbourn Village Society scheme in the Cottage Beck Road area, much of it was repetitive and almost solely composed of the 'ubiquitous semi' in the view of R. L. Stirling. As in Lincoln, many homes for commuters were built in villages within travelling distance despite the very large allocations for housing within the scheme's boundaries.

Grimsby and Cleethorpes
Grimsby showed some desultory interest in a scheme before the first world war as part of its strategy for boundary extensions but did not seriously enter the field until 1920 when several resolutions were passed to prepare schemes for different areas. Area 1 involved 2,040 acres in the Old Clee, Weelsby and Waltham district, of which 583 acres were in the borough and the rest in Grimsby Rural District. This was the most contentious of the schemes because it involved land adjacent to Cleethorpes in which both towns had an interest. The initial proposals were ready in June 1926 but it was September 1932 before the public inquiry on the preliminary statement was held. At the inquiry the representative of the Sleight estate objected to part of his client's land being zoned as private open space and asked if the Corporation was willing to compensate the owners for loss of development value. The Town Clerk, Mr J. W. Jackson, offered to rezone the land for building, a vivid illustration of LPAs' fears about compensation liability: his offer was accepted on the spot! Final approval was given by the Minister in 1938 after some further modifications, the most important being the rescheduling of Weelsby Park from private open space to residential, at 12 houses to the acre.[15] Several of the major road proposals were never effected, such as an extension of Hainton

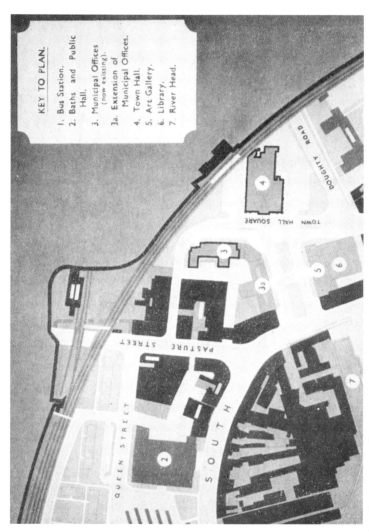

Fig. 8.2 Plan for suggested post-1944 city centre in Grimsby. In 1944 it was possible to consider what should be done in planning terms when the war was over, and it was particularly urgent in places like Grimsby which had suffered from bombing. This is a photo of a plan for the Town Hall area to become a civic centre, seen at the Grimsby Tomorrow Exhibition. Compare with Fig. 8.6. Source: Lincoln Central Library, from pamphlet in the Pye Collection.

Avenue to Peaks Farm West, nor were all the residential allocations developed, including the Weelsby Park area mentioned above, which it appears was rescheduled to prevent claims for compensation.

Areas 2 and 3 were treated as one and involved most of the undeveloped land in the south and west, bounded by the River Freshney on the west and the borough boundary on the south. Very large areas were allocated for housing, at densities that ranged from eight to 26 houses per acre: the large amount of land zoned at the higher densities of 16 and 20 to the acre was unusual for this era of planning and reflected a local attitude that the usual 12 density was only suitable for 'middle class' areas.[16] Several new roads were indicated to open up new areas for development:[17] one such was Cambridge Road/Ely Road which was eventually built on more or less the same lines as the scheme indicated. Others were never constructed, for example, one to link Yarborough and Cromwell Roads to open up the area to industrial development. Most of the land zoned for housing has been developed for residential use, unlike the two areas zoned for industry. Areas 2 and 3 were not formally approved, although the draft scheme did reach the Minister in December 1937.

In the same month the council decided to prepare scheme number four, to cover the existing built-up area.[18] The outbreak of war halted efforts for a while but, like Lincoln, Grimsby's Special Reconstruction Committee held an exhibition in 1944 to show their ideas for 'Grimsby Tomorrow'. A special exhibition plan of area 4 indicated current land uses, some new proposals and a central area redevelopment zone of 70 acres bounded by the Dock Estate, the railway, and Victoria Street. A model showed details of the redevelopment, including the proposed Civic Centre in the town hall area.[19] (See Fig. 8.2.)

Cleethorpes included all the unbuilt land within its boundary and a large area outside when it resolved to prepare the first scheme in February 1919. The Minister of Health excluded two areas, including Old Clee which lay in Grimsby and which was included in its scheme the following year. A second scheme for an area to the north was initiated in March 1924: in June the two schemes were merged.

The plans involved 24 road proposals. Those which were subsequently implemented included widening Humberston Road, building a new road to link it with Taylors Lane, and extending Brereton Avenue southwards from Lestrange Street. A new boulevard along the southern shore to cater for holidaymakers rather than heavy traffic was never built although it remained in the scheme. Residential densities were planned at between eight and twenty dwellings per acre, but the emphasis was on the higher densities and as time went on there was pressure to accept more of the higher density development.[20]

The scheme nearly obtained final approval early in 1933 but the deadline of 31 March 1933 could not be met, so the whole scheme had to be redrafted under the terms of the 1932 Act. Cleethorpes and Grimsby were supposed to liaise with one another over their respective schemes, not least because their road proposals met at their mutual boundaries. The long-established rivalry and Grimsby's desire to incorporate Cleethorpes made liaison difficult and at the last public enquiry in December 1936 the Inspector complained that the two authorities should have reached agreement before the enquiry was held.[21] As with other schemes, the long delays between the various stages meant that ideas and standards, for example on roundabouts and dual carriageways, kept changing and this protracted the consultation procedures further. Final approval came in 1938.[22]

Mablethorpe

The three seaside resorts of Mablethorpe, Trusthorpe, and Sutton all lay within the boundaries of Mablethorpe and Sutton Urban District Council, the smallest of the LPAs to act in Lincolnshire with a resident population of only 2,852 in 1921. The visitor population to the urban district, however, rose from 70,000 to 129,000 between 1921 and 1926 according to the town's surveyor, Mr Maugham, with visitors arriving by train and road. This level of increase and the possible consequences in terms of development led the council, spurred on by Lindsey County Council, to make a resolution to prepare a scheme in April 1926. The aim was to control future development and to rectify existing deficiencies. The first proposals added 41 miles to the existing 26-mile road network and included a north–south route for through traffic west of the railway, a new direct road link between the three settlements east of the railway, and improvements to the existing tortuous route. Residential development in between the three settlements was planned at the low density of ten buildings to the acre west of the railway and eight to the acre between the railway and the shore where boarding houses were expected. Other provisions included 13 areas of open space, a swimming pool, two aviation grounds, and a new station, civic centre, and municipal offices at Trusthorpe to make it the administrative as well as the geographical centre of the urban district. The Inspector at the scheme's first public inquiry in 1927 commented sharply on the council's lack of planning expertise. He had to point out that it was obligatory to fix building lines on new roads, that the foreshore was Crown property and neither it nor land for new municipal offices could be shown on the plan as open space, and that in relation to roads '...there is no need to fill up the map with unnecessary detail'.[23]

Very protracted and sometimes acrimonious consultations followed over the question of new road lines and building lines on existing roads between the Mablethorpe LPA, Lindsey, the Ministry of Transport, and the Ministry of Health. Each tended to blame the others. The Ministry of Transport refused to divert a grant for improving the existing Mablethorpe to Sutton road to the building of a new road as in the scheme. At the public inquiry into an amended scheme in February 1931 the county council had still further road amendments to suggest. Consultations resumed, further changes were made, and final approval was given by the Minister in September 1938.[24] Many of the original proposals came to nothing, for example no new railway station was built, Trusthorpe did not become the administrative focus, and the coast road remains tortuous.

Skegness

Unlike Mablethorpe, Skegness was a planned holiday town from the start. The principal landowner, Lord Scarbrough, realized the potential for growth and commissioned a plan which was ready in 1875. By 1905 the area between Scarbrough Avenue and Lumley Road was built largely in accord with the plan. Scarbrough spent large amounts on roads and amenities like pleasure gardens and the pier, often as the largest shareholder in separate companies.[25] In addition to its function as a resort, Skegness also expanded its resident population, mainly by inward migration of retired people between 1901 and 1939, from 2,520 to 10,240.[26]

The council first resolved to prepare a scheme in 1921 to provide for a future population of 40,000 to 50,000: a semi-circular road around the town and a 1,000 acre belt of parkland were envisaged. In August 1923 the council wrote to the county council to explain that '...due to the attitude of the principal landowner in the Urban District of Skegness, namely Lord Scarbrough, not being favourable towards any scheme, the council have passed a resolution not to proceed with same'. Over the next few years the county countered Lord Scarbrough's objections with the argument that road traffic was increasing rapidly, unplanned building would prejudice road improvements, voluntary agreements with landowners would not be legally binding and, finally, that the Committee of Inquiry into the town's proposals for boundary extensions had recommended the preparation of a scheme.[27]

In February 1927 Skegness again embarked on a scheme and 14 months later the preliminary proposals were outlined at a public inquiry. The newspaper report was headlined 'Big Scheme of Town Planning, A Seven Mile Ring Road'. In fact the road plans were less dramatic than they sounded; they consisted mainly of relatively short stretches of new road to link with existing or improved roads. For example, Burgh Road was to be improved and to be linked to the town centre via Grosvenor Road and a new section to the Roman Bank: this proposal was completed and the new link called Lincoln Road. Other suggestions came to nothing, such as the southern section of the so-called outer ring road. Residential densities varied from ten to the acre in the east, 12 in the centre to only one in the outer, agricultural zone. The ultimate population of the town was still seen as 40,000 to 50,000, but the basis for this seems to have been purely subjective. The elevations of new buildings on High Street were to be Jacobean in style, to help make it more attractive. Shops were expressly excluded from sections of Drummond Road, the Parades, and the North Shore Estate.[28]

Four years later the preliminary scheme was approved by the Minister after consultations about roads and the likely effect of the Lindsey Sandhills Act. Further amendments were made to ensure conformity with the regional coastal plan prepared first by Abercrombie and then by the East Lindsey JPC, both of which are discussed in later sections. Inevitably, endless negotiations ensued concerning standard road widths and building lines. Although Skegness adopted the draft scheme in 1939 it never received formal ministerial approval even after the East Lincolnshire JPC took over responsibility for it in 1943.

Planning progress between the wars

Throughout this period the Ministry of Health was urging LPAs to prepare schemes and to proceed more quickly. The evidence from Lindsey shows that some councils were willing to take advantage of the opportunities the new legislation offered to control development to ensure higher standards, and to allocate land for future use. All six schemes encountered very long delays essentially owing to overlapping responsibilities for roads between local authorities themselves and the Ministry of Transport, worries about liability for compensation, and the lengthy bureaucratic procedures and consultations emanating from the Ministry of Health itself.

As we have seen, the Lindsey schemes varied in their scope, degree of sophistication and the extent to which they were implemented. As elsewhere, they were fragmentary in character in that only a few schemes were prepared in relation to the number of LPAs. They did not include existing development and did not relate to surrounding areas because legislation was not geared to truly comprehensive planning. Schemes allocated areas of primary land use related to a road framework but they were not based on clearly defined objectives or forecasts, nor did they indicate the time-scale involved: they appeared to represent a finite plan.

On the positive side, many sensible proposals were made and sites allocated and reserved by development control. Undesirable forms of development were avoided through the mechanism of zoning separate areas for different and incompatible uses. Lower residential densities were a very important feature of all the schemes and standards of development were raised generally. Although actual development could deteriorate into low density suburban sprawl unless careful attention was paid to the design and layout, this has to be measured against the legacy of overcrowded, insanitary slums of the early Victorian period and the high-density monotony of post-1875 bye-law terraced housing. The measures of the day could not prevent development from leapfrogging the boundaries of schemes to peripheral areas or to villages within daily travelling distance. The only way to try to plan comprehensively for a wider area was through regional plans prepared by Joint Planning Committees, which are considered next.

Joint planning committees
Nationally a number of JPCs were formed in the 1920s and 1930s to prepare regional plans, but the only local one was the East Lindsey Advisory JPC, created in the mid 1930s to prepare a scheme for the coastal hinterland. The area stretched south of Cleethorpes to the Wash and was under increased pressure for holiday development following the restrictions placed on the immediate coastal zone by the Sandhills Act (see below pp. 200-1). Louth and Spilsby Rural Districts and Alford Urban District were constituent authorities in the JPC whose fourth member was Lindsey County Council: the clerk to the committee was Eric Scorer, chief proponent of the Sandhills Act. Abercrombie and Kelly were engaged, who had already prepared a number of regional schemes, and they presented their plan in 1936. They recommended zoning large areas of open space to act as breaks in what they saw as inevitable coastal ribbon development; building a new road for through traffic with access roads leading off the coast, and a system of granting interim development permits valid for only three months to many holiday-related applications.[29] Later in 1936 the committee reconstituted itself under the terms of the 1932 Act and dropped the word advisory from its title, but membership remained the same. The committee decided to use the Abercrombie report as the basis for a scheme to be prepared by its newly appointed

planning officer, Mr S. E. Brearly. The outbreak of war restricted work on the draft scheme and in 1941 the office at Alford was closed down and work stopped altogether.

The Town and Country Planning (Interim Development) Act of 1943 made all land subject to interim development control. The local response was to establish five JPCs, involving all the LPAs, in Lincolnshire which gave many of them their first experience in planning. East Lincolnshire and North Lincolnshire JPCs were set up in 1943 while Kesteven and the Lincoln and District JPCs followed in 1944. Holland established its JPC in 1943 and advertised for a planning officer in late 1943, early 1944.[30] All the JPCs appointed a qualified planning officer and engaged a small staff that typically included one or more town planning assistants, surveying assistants, draughtsmen, and clerical officers. The Ministry of Town and Country Planning issued circulars and guidelines that emphasized the need for basic surveys and population studies to provide a proper basis for assessing and planning for future needs, a lesson learned from the inter-war period. The JPCs produced much survey material, but updating the often very out-of-date Ordnance Survey maps took up valuable time, as Brian Bell's last report as Kesteven JPC's planning officer laments.[31]

It was common for applications for approval of plans under the local bye-laws to be treated as applications for development permits: these were considered by the JPC which then forwarded recommendations to the LPA who issued the decision. The fact that not all LPAs provided any feedback on whether or not they had taken the advice was a problem for the East Lincolnshire JPC. Publicity was given in order to alert people to the need for permission to carry out even minor forms of development. One hundred plans a week were dealt with at the Brigg office of the North Lincolnshire JPC in 1946 and this inevitably meant less time for other work since at that time the entire establishment consisted of the planning officer, A. R. Head, and four others.[32] The volume of applications in Kesteven, on the other hand, was only 143 in the first 15 months.[33]

None of the committees had reached a very advanced stage of scheme preparation by the time that the 1947 Act came into force on 1 July 1948, although some preparatory work was done. For example, Robert Stirling had presented a report on the future urban development area for Lincoln[34] and Mr H. I. Newton, planning officer to East Lincs. JPC, had recommended a number of modifications to the draft scheme for the coastal hinterland. Out-of-date basic maps, staff shortages and, in some cases, the volume of development control work, all contributed to the lack of progress. Another reason was the divided allegiances of the authorities. Those with draft or operative schemes could not see the point of joining together, while others had particular rivalries with other local authorities. Grantham and Cleethorpes only joined the Kesteven and North Lincolnshire committees respectively after the threat of a Ministerial order.

At the Kesteven JPCs last meeting Mr Bell, who went on to be the first, and only, county planning officer for Kesteven, reported that, 'Our efforts have been unspectacular and our achievements devoid of popular distinction, but we bequeath to our successors first a substantial and valuable mass of basic information, methodically recorded, and second a tradition of co-operation between the county district councils and the county council.'[35] Mr Stirling gave a report on the establishment of the Lindsey county planning department which he was to head at one of the last meetings of the Lincoln and District JPC. He noted that the three operative schemes of Cleethorpes, Mablethorpe, and Scunthorpe would cease to be effective under the new Act but that they would be useful, with modifications, for development control purposes pending the 'development plan', the new term for schemes. He further noted other work done in the county, but concluded that much basic map work remained to be done before real planning could begin. The new staff structure was to be nine staff at headquarters in Lincoln and 21 others shared between three area offices at Lincoln, Louth, and Brigg.[36] Mr R. N. Whiston, planning officer of Holland JPC, also went on to be the planning officer of Holland county planning department: his recommendations were accepted that the county should prepare the development plan and that development control should be in the hands of two area sub-committees at Boston and Spalding.[37]

THE SANDHILLS ACT

In addition to statutory planning, Lindsey County Council also initiated some unique planning measures in the coastal zone by means of a privately sponsored Act of Parliament.

The Lindsey County Council (Sandhills) Act of 1932 brought in another form of development control by introducing a system of licences in the Lindsey coastal zone (see also Chapter 7, pp. 159-62). The sandhills covered an area some 40 kilometres in length from north to south and up to 500 metres in width and represented the longest such area still in a natural state in Great Britain. Increasing pressure for holiday development, and consequent sporadic building in the form of bungalows and shacks of all shapes, sizes, and materials came with the growth of private motor traffic (Fig. 8.7). More sections of the sandhills were enclosed which reduced public access while the uncontrolled development posed a health hazard, prejudiced the future provision of amenities, and added to future infrastructure costs. Under the terms of the Act, the county was enabled to designate controlled areas where it could prohibit or remove buildings and enclosures through a system of licences: it could also zone areas for different land uses and acquire land by compulsory purchase for five years after the Act came into force. The county's Sandhills sub-committee dealt with the designation and licencing procedures. By 1937, 17 areas had been designated and although the council was at first reluctant to purchase land it came round to the view of its clerk, Eric Scorer, and bought as much land as possible before the power of compulsory purchase ceased in 1937. Another effect of the Act was to take any designated sandhills area out of the scope of town planning schemes.

According to Sheail, the county council, spurred on by its clerk, promoted the private Act because the machinery of statutory planning was too slow for the urgency of the problems faced in the sandhills: the inter-war experience of planning schemes certainly bears this out. He points out that the scope of planning schemes was wider than the situation required as the county did not intend to produce a full-scale plan for the whole area, which would have needed all the LPAs in the affected area to delegate their planning powers to it.[38] Another factor may have been that the effectiveness of interim development control was too unsure in view of the fact that developers could ignore it and hope for the best. Even more important was the fact that refusal of a licence did not incur liability for compensation, as could refusal of interim development permission. The Sandhills Act thus enabled the county to act quickly and effectively and to gain wide practical experience in managing competing land-uses that gave it an advantage over the other Lincolnshire counties when counties became the overall planning authority after 1947.

HOUSING

Finally, some consideration of housing is required because it was so intimately associated with the growth of planning ideas and legislation. A brief look at some local housing built in the 1920s illustrates how these early ideas were translated into the fabric of our towns. Three examples of housing carefully designed by architects in tune with the garden city approach serve to show some common features on both the private and public sectors.

Early planning was very strongly influenced by the garden city and suburb movement. The ideas of Ebenezer Howard, founder of the garden city concept, found practical expression in the two new towns of

Letchworth and Welwyn Garden City before and immediately after the first world war. Elsewhere, garden city ideas and standards were translated into garden suburbs in a number of towns.

Swanpool Garden Suburb in Lincoln represents the most important attempt by private enterprise to build a self-contained community on garden suburb lines. In December 1917 Mr Culpin, representing the Garden City and Town Planning Association gave a lecture on housing in Lincoln which aroused the interest of Colonel J. S. Ruston, one of Ruston and Hornsby's directors. He bought 25 acres of the Boultham Hall estate, formed the Swanpool Co-operative Housing Society and engaged A. J. Thompson, an architect well known for his work with Raymond Unwin in Letchworth and elsewhere. More land was bought and in March 1919 a further public meeting was held to promote a much more ambitious scheme involving some 2,000 houses in a development to be called Swanpool Garden Suburb. The audience was invited to invest in shares through the Swanpool Public Utility Society that could attract government subsidies. All the tenants were to be shareholders with a minimum £5 stake which was very low compared with the usual £200 to £450 minimum elsewhere. The Society would build and own properties, and manage all its affairs through a committee of working men and employers or other 'representative gentlemen'.[39]

Figure 8.3 illustrates the comprehensive and ambitious layout. A Central Avenue linking Swanpool itself with a Central Square formed the main axis, with gently curving avenues, cul-de-sacs and quadrangles leading off it. Full provision was made for a variety of open spaces and for recreational, social, and educational facilities. There was even to be a power station to provide central heating and hot water, a proposal that anticipated Lincoln's first district-heating system by some 50 years. Swanpool was the subject of two articles in the *Architects Journal*[40] and was one of sixteen locations illustrated and discussed in a contemporary book on housing.[41]

Drainage proved a difficulty, but the immediate reasons for abandoning the scheme seem to have been financial setbacks and employment problems in the city's engineering firms. The Society had had to buy the full 340 acres so as to have a complete scheme of development to attract the subsidies, but the government loan of 75 per cent was only payable after work had been completed on specified small stages of purchase and construction. The take-up of shares was low and it proved impossible to raise a loan. The city council refused to take the scheme over and in 1922 the undeveloped land was sold to Colonel Ruston and ownership of the land already developed passed to Swanpool Garden Suburb Ltd in 1925. The shaded area on Figure

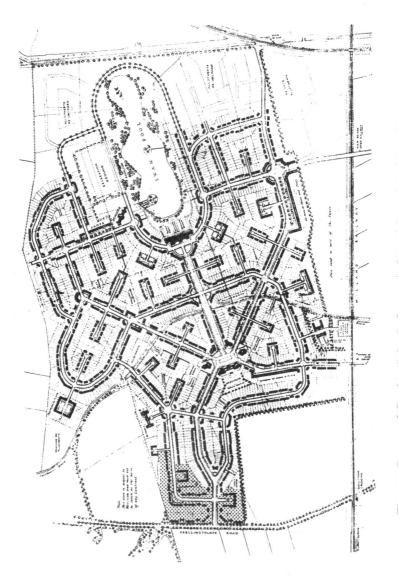

Fig. 8.3   Swanpool Garden Suburb. Source: *Architects' Journal*, 16 July 1919.

8.3 shows the 113 houses actually built which were gradually sold off to the sitting tenants. In 1945 there were still 57 tenanted houses, including all those in Westwood Close; number 10 was finally sold to a Mr Booth, insurance inspector for £685 in 1947. In 1948 the house fetched £750 and by 1950 the price was £1,700.[42] The present owner moved there in 1959 and recalls that the long-established residents formed a close-knit community, living as a kind of village, cut off to some extent from Lincoln by distance and enjoying village activities such as Guy Fawkes bonfires provided by the local farmer.

Residents were proud of their houses which have a variety of spacious and interesting internal plans belied by the external unity of the rendered, mainly terraced blocks (Fig. 8.4). The houses have steep, hipped roofs and great care was taken with the fenestration and the detailing of doors and chimneys. Hartsholme Drive, as far as Westwood Drive, is narrow and curving with mature trees that overhang the road and provide a taste of the leafy garden suburb that was intended. The houses of Westwood Close are grouped around a grassed square that used to be well cared for but is in 1987 a somewhat bald parking lot. Unsympathetic changes have occurred to some of the houses, despite extra development control powers taken by the

Fig. 8.4 Swanpool Garden Suburb, Lincoln. Note the complicated roof design which was echoed in Addison Act houses (Fig. 8.1a). Source: C. H. James and F. R. Yerbury, *Small Houses in the Community,* 1924.

city council in the past: in 1986, Swanpool was designated a Conservation Area in recognition of its architectural and historic importance.

In the public sector, the garden suburb influence is seen most clearly in housing built, or under contract, under the Addison Act in the short period before July 1922, when financial aid was withdrawn. The council houses and estates of subsequent housing acts are generally more monotonous in design and layout, with lower space standards and less attention paid to landscaping. Hartley shows that Lincoln and Scunthorpe responded very positively to the opportunities provided by the housing element of the Addison Act whereas Cleethorpes and Grimsby were reluctantly persuaded by central government to use the Act, building 136 and 224 Addison houses respectively.[43]

The layout of the St Giles estate in Lincoln and the 234 Addison Act houses built there are good examples of the era. The land had been bought for the 1914 housing and planning schemes. In fact, the Ministry of Munitions built the first 200 houses on the site on land

Fig. 8.5 St Giles Estate, Lincoln View from St Giles parish church, Lincoln, when under construction, May 1935, showing the plain style of the council houses on this estate, their large gardens, and the social provision represented by the two schools and Methodist church. The further school was for infants, located opposite the Methodist church in Addison Drive (named after the 18th century essayist, not the Minister of Health!) The junior school is out of sight to the left, while in the foreground is St Giles Secondary Modern School, in Lamb Gardens, the plan of which incorporates an open quadrangle, in keeping with the current vogue. Source: *Lincolnshire Echo*.

fronting Wragby Road which was bought from the council: the houses were sold to a property company and then to the sitting tenants. The estate layout and the first council houses were essentially the work of Alfred Hill, already mentioned in relation to the inter-war planning scheme. Like Swanpool, the design follows the garden suburb approach with its softly geometrical road network that incorporates cul-de-sacs, quadrangles, and a circus. A large site was reserved at the centre for schools and the school grounds now form the major open space (Figs. 8.5 and 2.4). Grass verges and trees were an important part of the layout and small areas of amenity open space, as in Ruskin Square and The Oval, form an integral part of the design with houses grouped around them. The Addison houses now lie between the Ministry of Munitions houses and the rest of the estate which was built in stages under a number of housing acts. The Addison houses are distinguishable by having larger plots than many later houses, by the use of small terraced blocks interspersed with semi-detached houses and the unifying use of rendering. In 1936 a church (St Giles) was built, largely from the materials of the early Georgian St Peter at Arches, which had stood in the High Street. The estate today retains its coherent overall design and the intimacy of the best of the groupings of houses, but other areas have deteriorated physically. There are still many trees and some leafy open spaces, but others have been lost. The area suffers generally from a lack of parking spaces and garages that is exacerbated by narrow roads, and by being dissected by Ruskin Avenue and Outer Circle Road: they were conceived as part of a ring-road system north of the city long before modern traffic levels and solutions were envisaged.

The final example is in Scunthorpe. As with the planning scheme, consultants were employed to design the first council housing estate at Crosby to the north of the town. The first architect was Segar Owen but he was quickly replaced by the architectural firm of Brocklesby and Marchment.[44] J. S. Brocklesby was an arts and crafts style of architect who was already working on council housing at Merton in Surrey. Scunthorpe were pleased with the speed with which Brocklesby proceeded, not realizing that he was using plans first prepared for Merton.[45] He designed the layout of the Henderson Avenue section of the now much larger Crosby estate, and most of the 518 houses built or under contract before the Addison Act subsidy was withdrawn. The main axis of Brocklesby's plan is Henderson Avenue and a loose grid of roads leads from it. The large circus feature called The Circle, part way along Henderson Avenue, now forms a large green set with trees, but the plan of 1920 in the borough museum suggests that it was originally intended that a large building would form a focal point on the site of the green.[46] As in the previous examples, the housing units are semi-detached pairs and small terraced blocks which are sometimes grouped around small open spaces. Rendering is again used and unifies the scheme, but house designs, facades, and decorations vary. Only a few of the original patterned windows and wrought iron gates to the passageways now remain, but the wide verges and trees have survived. The Crosby Improvement Scheme of 1969 sought to relieve the problems caused by modern traffic and parking needs but this has not been entirely successful visually. Nevertheless, the substantial houses and garden suburb approach of Brocklesby's part of the estate compare very favourably with the later area to the west and the Buckingham Street development to the east.

PLANNING AFTER 1945

There was hostility to planning from the start from those who saw it as interference in property rights and the free market. In the early years planning was of interest to only a few in the county but those few were persistent. Eric Scorer's name is prominent both as the main architect of the Sandhills Act and in his active promotion of planning schemes by LPAs wherever he saw pressure for development. Even he, however, could not see the need for comprehensive planning. Herbert Copeland, a later clerk to Lindsey, recounted how '...leaning on a farm gate and gazing over Lindsey's broad green acres, Eric Scorer had remarked, "after all, Copeland, what is there to plan?"'[47]

The general climate of opinion became more favourable during the second world war as post-war reconstruction became inevitable. Under the 1947 Town and Country Planning Act Holland, Kesteven, and Lindsey county councils, together with Lincoln and Grimsby county borough councils, became the LPAs, although some powers could be delegated to county districts.

LPAs were required to submit comprehensive development plans for their areas by July 1951, but the deadline was extended. Surveys of existing conditions and projections of future growth and land-use needs provided the background information on which plans were based and were published as reports. The county plan provided a framework of broad land-uses and communications and indicated the areas where more detailed plans would be required, such as town centre redevelopment areas. The 1947 procedures remained in force until 1968 when a new Town and Country Planning Act introduced changes in response to a period of reassessment in the mid 1960s. The changes involved the introduction of more flexible overall plans called structure plans to take the form of a written statement supported by diagrammatic illustrations and three different types of local plans.

Structure planning in Lincolnshire came after local government reorganization in 1974.

The main features of post-war planning as far as the public is concerned have been high-rise flats, the redevelopment of town centres and the building of new roads, often requiring the destruction of existing buildings and the inherited pattern of streets. This destruction fuelled a growing concern for the preservation and conservation of first individual buildings and then groups of buildings. Conservation of the countryside and coast became more important public issues as pressure for housing and recreation gathered momentum after the war.

In a relatively remote, rural county like Lincolnshire with much high grade agricultural land, especially in the south, much emphasis was inevitably placed on using the 1947 Act's powers to prevent development. Holland's 1951 report of survey made clear that the priority was to safeguard the area from any development that might injure local farming prosperity. Large areas were zoned as 'white land' where the policy was that existing land uses should, for the most part, remain undisturbed. Holland carried out its statutory duties and the county development plan was approved in 1954 and more detailed town maps for Boston and Spalding followed later. It was not until the early 1970s, however, that a wider range of policies were produced. Holland had, for example, no explicit rural settlement policy until 1970, whereas most counties had adopted variations of key settlement policies much earlier.[48]

The 1967 Civic Amenities Act introduced the idea of conserving and enhancing areas of special character and value rather than just

Fig. 8.6 Model of Gainsborough town centre, early 1950s. Gainsborough, like Grimsby (Fig 8.2), suffered heavily from German bombing, so redevelopment was an urgent post-war task. When Lindsey County Council prepared the statutory Town Map in 1952, it was used as the basis for this model to illustrate town centre redevelopment. Source: Lincoln Central Library.

Fig. 8.7 Bohemia: shanties on the Sandhills. a general postcard view. Source: D. N. Robinson Postcard Collection.

individual buildings. Kesteven designated the whole of Stamford within the lines of its medieval walls as the country's first conservation area in 1968, thanks to the particular interest of Dr K. R. Fennell, the deputy county planning officer. Kesteven's county development plan was approved in 1954 and town maps for the Lincoln Fringe, Sleaford, and Grantham followed in the 1960s. Other policies related to rural development and conservation on a county or district basis.

The county development plan for Lindsey was approved in 1955, as was the first town map for Scunthorpe. Town maps for other urban areas followed and town centre schemes for Scunthorpe and Gainsborough (see Fig. 8.6). Lindsey found much to plan on the industrializing south bank of the Humber where the possibility of a new city was investigated by central government in the 1960s. There was great pressure for development on the coast to which the county responded with a series of policies on holiday development, conservation, and carparking and access. Many other surveys and policies were produced on matters such as industry, and settlement and recreation in the countryside. Gainsborough was the only local authority in the administrative county to go ahead with an arrangment with the Greater London Council under the Town Development Act, 1952. The agreement was made in 1967 and ceased to be effective in the mid 1970s; by that time 23 firms had established themselves in Gainsborough under the scheme, and 150 families had moved up from London. The scheme was thus of limited success in relieving congestion in the capital and improving employment in Gainsborough, but the 810 jobs helped reduce the effects of overall job losses in the town in the period.

The successes and failures of planning in Lincolnshire remain to be analysed more fully, but in some ways the pattern of the early years continued up to local government reorganization. Since then the situation has changed. Planning functions were split between the new Lincolnshire county council and the district councils. Planning still flourishes in some of the districts, but in 1984/5 the county council employed fewer staff and had lower net expenditure per head than any other English shire county.

Bibliographical note

Local reference libraries, county archive offices, local planning departments, and the journals and libraries of professional associations are the main sources for material relating to planning in Lincolnshire.

Reference libraries usually hold standard general works on planning plus a wide variety of local information which may include contemporary newspaper articles, information on planners and local government councillors, copies of planning documents and council minutes and reports. The same sort of material may also be deposited in archive offices.

Local planning departments hold current planning material and some keep their own archives or can pinpoint where relevant data is kept: they may know of former planning officials who could provide oral evidence. The central source for statutory plans and policies is now the Department of the Environment.

The *Journal of the Royal Town Planning Institute* and the *Town Planning Review* contain many valuable articles on planning at the national and local level. The libraries of the professional institutes have indexes of information held.

Notes to Chapter 8

1. Owen A. Hartley, 'A housing policy in four Lincolnshire towns 1919–59', unpublished Oxford D.Phil. thesis, 1969, copy in LAO. See also Chapter 9, pp. 235–9.
2. R. L. Stirling, 'Memoirs of planning in Lincoln and district up to 1947', transcript in LAO and Lincoln Central Reference Library.
3. Boultham Hall Estate papers on town planning, 1913, in LAO.
4. *Lincoln Leader*, 30 May 1914
5. *Lincolnshire Chronicle*, 29 May 1914
6. *Lincoln Leader*, 29 July 1914

7. C. Bray, K. Grantham, and A. Wright, *The enemy in our midst: the story of Lincoln's typhoid epidemic 1905*, Lincoln, 1987.

8. LAO LCC Parcels 1783, Lincoln Town Planning Schemes 1923–50.

9. LAO. Lincoln, Minutes of Housing and Various Committees 1914–20 (L1/1/21/3) and Minutes of the Housing and Town Planning Committee (L1/1/35/1–4).

10. Lincoln Draft Town Planning Scheme, scale 1 : 2500, nd but post-1935, held in Lincoln City Planning Department.

11. Letters dated 12/11/26 and 19/9/32 in LCC Parcels 1783 LAO.

12. Stirling, *op. cit.*; see also pamphlet on City of Lincoln Civic Survey and Housing Exhibition in Lincoln Central Reference Library.

13. Scunthorpe and Frodingham UDC, Town Planning Committee Book, June 1920 to December 1929 in the Borough Solicitor's strong room, Civic Centre; see also P. Abercrombie and T. Johnson, Outline Plan of Road Scheme, 1922, scale 6 inches to 1 mile in Scunthorpe Borough Museum. See also M. E. Armstrong (ed.,) *An industrial island: a history of Scunthorpe*, Scunthorpe 1981, especially Chapter 12.

14. LCC Parcels 1640, Scunthorpe Town Planning Scheme 1931–1947 LAO.

15. *Grimsby Evening Telegraph*, 12/9/33 and 13/9/33; and Grimsby Area Number One Planning Scheme Maps dated June 1926 and May 1938 in South Humberside Area Record Office (SHARO) and Grimsby Area Number One Planning Scheme Written Statement, 1938, in Grimsby Central Reference Library.

16. Hartley, *op. cit.*

17. Grimsby Areas Number Two and Three Planning Scheme maps dated 1937 and 1939 in SHARO.

18. Grimsby Town Council Minute Book 1937–38 in Grimsby Central Reference Library.

19. *Grimsby tomorrow*, pamphlet in Pye Collection in Lincoln Central Library.

20. *Grimsby Evening Telegraph*, 26 July 1932.

21. *ibid.*, 8 December 1936.

22. Information in this section is from 53/D/768 and Box 51/A1 SHARO: detailed scheme plans are also listed but cannot be found to date.

23. *The Standard*, 14 May 1927 in LCC. Parcels 1640, Town Planning Schemes including Mablethorpe and Sutton 1925–43 in LAO.

24. Correspondence, LCC Parcels 1640 in LAO.

25. R. Gurnham, 'The creation of Skegness as a resort town', in *Lincolnshire Hist & Archaeology*, vol. 7, 1972.

26. Skegness and Ingoldmells Town Map, Report of Survey, Lindsey Planning Department. nd ?1955, Lincoln Central Reference Library.

27. LAO LCC Parcels 1641, Skegness Planning Scheme 1921–43.

28. *Louth Standard*, April 1928, cutting in LCC Parcels 1641.

29. Report by P. Abercrombie and S. A. Kelly accompanying Regional Planning Scheme, 1936, LCC Parcels 1389/1390/1391 in LAO.

30. Memo dated 5 January 1944 in file on East Lincolnshire JPC in LCC Parcel 1779, LAO.

31. Kesteven County Council Minute Books, 1942–48, LAO.
32. East Lincolnshire JPC Minutes in LCC Parcel 1782, LAO.
33. Kesteven County Council Minute Books, 1942–48, LAO.
34. Lincoln and District JPC, report on the Urban Development Area for Lincoln and Neighbourhood, in Lincoln City Planning Department.
35. Kesteven C.C. Minute Book, report dated 28 June 1948 in LAO.
36. Lincoln and District JPC, report dated 27 January 1948 in LCC Parcel 1779 in LAO.
37. Holland County Council Minute Books, Volume 1947–48, LAO.
38. John Sheail, 'The impact of recreation on the coast: The Lindsey County Council (Sandhills) Act 1932', in *Landscape Planning 4* (1977), 53–72.
39. Reported in *Lincolnshire Chronicle*, 'Somewhere to live', p. 7, 1 March 1919
40. *Architects Journal*, 16 July 1919 amd 24 May 1922
41. C. H. James and F. R. Yerbury, *Small houses in the community*, 1924.
42. Information from the deeds of the present owner.
43. Hartley, *op. cit.*
44. Scunthorpe and Frodingham UDC, Housing Committee Minute Book, 1919 and 1920 entries, in Borough Solicitor's strong room, Civic Centre.
45. C. Spencer and G. Wilson, *Elbow room: the story of John Sydney Brocklesby, Arts and Crafts Architect*, chapter 8.
46. Brocklesby and Marchment, Crosby Housing Scheme for Scunthorpe and Frodingham UDC, 1920, scale 1 : 1,250 plan. NB the plan says it was prepared for P. Abercrombie but there is no indication in any other source that this was the case; but see Armstrong, *Industrial island*, pp. 138–9, who favours Abercrombie.
47. Stirling, *op. cit.*
48. Review of Rural Settlement Policies 1954–1980 prepared for the Directorate of Rural Affairs, Department of the Environment, by Marten & Voorhees Associates, 1980

CHAPTER 9

POLITICS 1885–1974

by Owen Hartley

Abstract *This chapter raises issues about the nature and content of political life at the local level, and, although factual material is limited in scope, it is based on wide reading in Lincolnshire newspapers as well as in general political theory. The relationship between national and local politics is debated in such a way that the empirical examples of planning (Chapter 8) and education (Chapter 10) are seen in a wider perspective. The chapter contains a summary of Lincolnshire representation in Parliament from 1885 at which date Olney's detailed account finishes. However, the main concern is with the politics of local councils. What sort of people became councillors, did they attempt to be democratic in their political lives, how did party politics affect their actions, what were relationships like between councils and within councils? Housing is used as a brief case study. Finally, attention is paid to Lincolnshire itself as a political concept.*

THE NATIONAL AND THE LOCAL IN POLITICS

Every writer on local politics seeks to balance the claim that they were determined within a national framework against the claim that national politics constitutes the sum of local political activity in all parts of the country. This essay emphasizes the former approach. Richard Olney has already clearly shown the interconnections between national and local politics in the nineteenth century, and in the twentieth century they did not diminish.

The arguments rest on two observations, one about local people and the other on local politics. The first observation is that the characteristic local political figures of 1900, a local shopkeeper, a solicitor, a doctor, a cleric, and a local manufacturer or industrialist or farmer, are not often now to be found. The reasons adduced for this observation are that there has been a decline in local control of local business (as shown in Chapter 4), and the professional classes are more concerned with professional standing than with local affairs. People of middle social rank, on this view, no longer have strong local interests;

their worlds are national, even international, in the context of their personal careers and interests.

The second observation is that national perspectives dominate, therefore local policies are difficult to sustain. This holds true of economic organizations, where Lincolnshire units are outposts of a larger corporate empire, local government, where the common phrase about the position of education in the 1944 Education Act, 'a national service, locally administered', has become true of all services, and, most crucially, in the very political entities that guide politics, the political parties, where national party policies overcome local scruples (e.g. for Lincoln Conservatives in housing, for Scunthorpe Labour, in comprehensive schools).

These two observations, however, do not show a predominance of the national over the local. It is true that middling sorts of people no longer seek public political office. The Lincoln butcher who recommended his candidature at a local election before 1914 on the grounds that 'Lincoln needs a butcher' was, rather inelegantly, taking the view that professional standing led to civic duties. This view would now be rare, but the new councillors, manual workers, public sector employees, teachers, are neither deficient in public spirit nor, more importantly, are they less ready to identify with the local situation.

As for local policies, they have always been difficult to sustain in a national context. Consider the Lincolnshire coastal towns: created by nationally oriented railways, they declined when factors largely out of their control changed: the location of fish stocks for Grimsby, the new preferences of the mass holiday market for Cleethorpes, Mablethorpe, and Skegness. In local government service, local authorities have as much resisted their introduction (e.g. Lincoln health before the 1904–5 typhoid outbreak) as welcomed national legislation. Political parties moreover have very little capacity to coerce local parties into doing what is wanted of them; discussion and persuasion are simply more effective.

The conclusion is that the local and the national perspectives are inextricably linked, the local always being subject to the greater national changes with little inherent capacity to resist them, but not thereby being reduced to irrelevance or impotence.

The rest of this essay assumes this point. In the next section the theme of 'democracy' is considered in both its national and local aspects. There follows both a discussion of the formal limitations of public politics which were created by national legislation but found local variation, and the informal limitations of parties and groups which had similar national networks. From this we turn to the specific style and content of Lincolnshire politics, in its internal affairs and in the politics of Lincolnshire itself.

DEMOCRACY AT WORK IN LOCAL POLITICS

The most obvious fact affecting both national and local politics over the period 1885–1974 was the increase in the numbers of enfranchised voters – the 1884 Representation of People Act doubled from one third to two-thirds the adult male electors as a proportion of the total population. The 1918 Act was much more far reaching: virtually all male adults and most women over 30 years of age became voters, an increase which in many constituencies tripled the number of voters. The 1928 Equal Franchise Act enfranchised women on the same basis as men – they promptly became a majority of the total electorate. The 1948 Representation of People Act ended plural voting in Parliamentary elections, and the 1969 Act virtually ended it in local elections while reducing the voting age to 18. Thus, over the period, electoral power shifted from a relatively small group of men to a very large electorate containing more women than men. The consequences of this change however were very slow to unfold.

The most readily analysed effect of the increase in the number of voters was on the political parties which sought to woo the newly enfranchised. The Liberals and Conservatives both seemed able to exploit the change of 1884, but after 1918 the Liberals were unable to beat either the Labour Party or the Conservatives to win either local or national political office on their own. At the national level Liberal support enabled Labour Governments to come to office in 1924 and 1929, but in Lincolnshire, as elsewhere, Liberals founded alliances with the Conservatives either informally, or through a system of 'Independent' candidates, or even in a formal anti-Labour alliance e.g. the Grimsby Municipal Group 1949–53. The decline of the Liberals was not of course merely a consequence of failing to win over a large new electorate, but it was a clear element in their problem.

The liberals, however, succeeded elsewhere. The liberal view about the nature of politics persisted in assumptions that were reasonable before 1884, but were slowly found to be impractical in a 'democratic' world. The key liberal assumption was that parties and party representatives were in simple daily contact with electors, but it was increasingly difficult for representatives to feel that they knew their public in any simple fashion as a consequence of day by day living. The extraordinary respect in Lincoln accorded to Councillor Fordham (1922–47) was because, as an insurance agent in the ward for which he was a representative, he could actually know his voters. It was difficult even in rural areas to have face-to-face acquaintance with even a fraction of the electorate, and as local authorities and electoral divisions grew in size and population during the century, the relationship of the councillor to the electorate became more obviously a matter of rhetoric rather than reality.

Equally disconcerting for the liberal view was the realization that 'the public' was widely differentiated and, as numbers increased, so did the differentiation. There was no arrival on the political scene of a united 'working class' with broadly similar tastes and interests, nor was it opposed by a middle or upper class with equal internal coherence. Again, the language of rhetoric either about 'the public' or its major components was observably at odds with reality. The issues that politicians wrestled with were deeply divisive as much within as between parties, and decisions on a majority basis were hard to achieve. The simplest evidence for this is the very revealing and varied preferences that were sometimes elicited from local people about the council housing they preferred. Not surprisingly such surveys were few and a more standard product than that preferred was actually supplied.

Finally, although representatives could conceive themelves, when they met together, as collective guardians of the public good, they were always uneasily aware that the decisions they took were not to be readily exposed to public scrutiny. Politicians turned naturally to the argument that 'if you don't like what's being done, use your vote', but, when pressed, would admit that knowing what was being done in the first place was often very well hidden. Minutes of the meetings were rarely available, the local press had a 'sensible' relationship with the politicans, and if, with secrecy, suspicions of foul conduct might flourish, that possibility was preferable to the harder reality of having to fight every issue out in public as well as in the more private political world.

To acknowledge that for the whole of this period politicians worked with constitutional practices and a language of democracy, of which they could not make much sense, is very important. It explains the steady cynicism about politicians and politics and precludes any observer from saying what Lincolnshire people believed about anything, and may explain the low turnout at local elections. The politicians rested their careers and prospects of happiness on making adequate guesses on what might be acceptable and uncontentious policies, but both they and their publics were wary of what democracy might eventually entail.

Fig. 9.1 Sir Berkeley Sheffield (1876–1946), with his speakers in Brigg at the 1907 by-election, in which he broke a Liberal representation almost continuous since 1885. This was at least partly due to the resignation of Mr H. J. Reckitt of Hull who had been involved in a scandalous divorce. Sir Berkeley sat for Brigg 1907–10 and 1922–29 and lived in the constituency at Normanby Park, a seat leased from the Sheffields by Scunthorpe Borough Council in 1964 as a leisure facility. He was the borough's Charter Mayor in 1936. See also Fig. 4.6. Source: Scunthorpe Central Library; caption, Armstrong, *An Industrial Island*, pp. 77, 153–4, 213.

CONSTITUENCY POLITICS

We now turn to two institutional frameworks within which Lincolnshire politics were conducted, the Parliamentary constituencies and the local government authorities. Much of Lincolnshire politics was inevitably about controlling these institutions, getting preferred candidates elected to them and monitoring their behaviour.

The history of Lincolnshire Parliamentary elections divides into three periods following reconstructions of the constituencies by national legislation: 1885–1918, 1918–83, and since 1983 (see Fig. 9.13 and Appendix, Table 6). In 1884 and 1918 the electorate was substantially increased as a proportion of the total population. In addition, it should be noted that that population was itself increasing, yet in 1918 and again in 1983 the county was allotted small numbers of seats. Therefore, it became increasingly difficult for candidates to keep in contact with the electorate despite changes in transport and communications. The overwhelming temper and preference of Lincolnshire voters in Parliamentary elections was for local persons

Fig. 9.2 The opening of the Iron and Steel Club at Scunthorpe in 1927, a working men's club with Labour affiliations. David Quibell (1879–1962) is second from the left on the second seated row from the camera. He was MP for the Brigg Division which included Scunthorpe, 1929–31 and 1935–45, and was created Lord Quibell in 1945. He was the first person to be made Freeman of the Borough of Scunthorpe (1948) and was the Coronation Mayor in 1953. Source: Scunthorpe Central Library; caption, Armstrong, *Industrial Island*, pp. 153, 158, 213.

sharing their prejudices and peculiarities. Long service in a constituency combined with a distaste for national office might help forge a bond of affection of similar strength to local knowledge and presence. The Lincolnshire electorate was however not always offered what it preferred. A majority of Lincolnshire constituencies have had a moment when local preferences made nonsense of any attempt to fix constituency politics into a rigid party or determinist mould. Thus:

Grimsby – the joyous political career of Sir George Doughty, 1895–1914, who changed political allegiance in 1898 but held the seat for all but a few months in 1910.

Grantham – the career of W. D. Kendall, an Independent, elected in a by-election in 1942 beating a national candidate, Air Marshal Longmore. Kendall went on to defeat both Labour and Conservatives in 1945.

Lincoln – Dick Taverne, who as sitting but resigned member, won a by-election against official Labour and Conservative opposition as

'Democratic Labour' in 1973 and again in the first 1974 general election.
Holland with Boston – W. S. Royce as the first Labour MP in Lincolnshire 1918–24 and a strong 'Liberal' tradition thereafter..
Brigg – the extraordinarily similar political views of two local men: Sir Berkeley Sheffield 1907–10, 1922–9 (Conservative) and D. J. K. Quibell 1929–31, 1935–45 (Labour) (later Lord Quibell) (see Figs. 9.1 and 9.2).
Louth – the election of Mrs Wintringham in 1921–4 to succeed her Liberal husband (Fig. 9.8).

The mention of Louth also brings up the point about locally well-loved, long-serving, but decidedly 'independent' MPs who did not concern themselves over much with national party views: Sir Cyril Osborne in Louth 1945–69, Lord Willoughby de Eresby, Stamford 1933– 50, H. F. C. Crookshank, Gainsborough 1924–56, Commander Maitland, Horncastle 1945–66. These were men of their own substance and never party hacks: and partially commended themselves to their constitutencies on precisely these grounds originally. The relationship of an MP to a constituency is a complex matter, especially since, with democracy, personal links with even a fraction of the electorate were so difficult to sustain. But MPs like these were able to sustain the interest of the party faithful in politics and sometimes gave the sprawling electorates a sense of being united. Crookshank at Gainsborough seems to have been peculiarly skilled in giving his consitutents the impression that 'Gainsborough' was a reality and not just a mere collection of voters in approximate geographical propinquity, numbering sufficient to compose a parliamentary constituency, as elsewhere in the county outside Grimsby and Lincoln.

Even when they were not local, or long serving and liked, MPs in Lincolnshire seem to have spent unusual amounts of time defending themselves, their parties, or governments, from what were clearly perceived to be hostile critics in the constituency. Their newspaper reports and speeches are not relaxed accounts of effective stewardship, but recitals of efforts made; and, with the greatest pleasure, differences with government of one's own party are especially featured whenever these occur. Being a Lincolnshire MP was not ordinarily a sleepy matter.

In this it was quite different from constituency politics as such. Between elections the constituency parties slumbered, the electoral victors were moved more by worries about their MP than about party controversy. At elections there was an increasing tendency towards ritualism and formality. Electioneering was undertaken; but with

large, often scattered electorates, and after 1918 comfortable
majorities for the winning parties, there was neither necessity on the
part of national parties nor the technique necessary to bring Lincolnshire constituencies to life. Before 1918 most Lincolnshire seats
were capable of switching from one party to another, often with tiny
majorities (usually less than 40 in Grantham) and the sense prevailed
that elections in Lincolnshire mattered for national parties. But between elections, the constituency parties slipped into quietude, even
though the structure of politics was changing around them. The
labour movement had deep roots in the agricultural areas – the first
Lincolnshire Liberal-Labour candidate stood for Horncastle in 1885
and the first Lincolnshire Labour MP was in Holland with Boston in
1918. The party organizations were remiss in not attending to the
phenomenon; both Liberals and Conservatives failed in rural as in
urban areas to channel such views towards themselves. Equally,
Labour failed to cultivate its rural connections; towards the end of the
period it had lost Lincoln and the constituency based on Scunthorpe,
through contituency neglect, to the Conservatives (see Appendix,
Table 6). The very instruments of mass democratic control, the political parties, seemed less capable of sustaining themselves over time
than might be imagined.

LOCAL AUTHORITIES

Although parliamentary politics have their significance, the major
factors in Lincolnshire politcs are local authorities, and the major
point about them is their numbers and rate of survival. By 1900 there
was a remarkable proliferation of elected local authorities created
substantially by recent legislation. The three county councils,
Lindsey, Kesteven, and Holland were created in 1888 with Lincoln
and later Grimsby as county boroughs, and a network of urban and
rural districts with parish councils in 1894, superimposed on an existing structure of school boards and poor law unions with a scattering
of special commissions and other nominated bodies. By 1974 this
proliferation had been much reduced. The details of these changes
can be seen in Table 1 of the Appendix, but it is worth noting two very
different administrative processes which led to the simplification. The
first was national pressure, culminating in the 1974 Local Government Act which reshaped Lincolnshire into two counties, and the
other a local process of adjustment and adaptation of which the major
instances are the County Reviews of the 1930s, which not only
reduced the numbers of authorities, but also advanced some in rank,
notably Cleethorpes and Scunthorpe.

The spirit which animated these changes was fuelled by diverse thoughts. There was the mystical belief held by academic observers and professional administrators that larger size equalled greater efficiency and which was the public argument offered for every change. It was often supported by politicians eager to overcome the obstacles to power by changing the ground rules, or those eager to promote the virtue of their district by expansion. It was acceptable to a public which never quite saw in local government a method of fulfilling a democratic control of their lives. As voters, the public were unenthusiastic and, while knowledge of local politics was often substantial, it was hard to believe that it was controllable. The respectable classes among the public found it easy to equate the local with the petty, absurd, or possibly corrupt.

Thus the central institution for politics in Lincolnshire was not accepted with very much enthusiasm, either by those inside its workings or those it was meant to serve. In Lincolnshire, local politics held no place of honour. Yet in at least two respects this view was misplaced. In so far as it can be investigated at all, the evidence does not point to the virtues of size, and indeed there were some indicators that small authorities might have been more capable of delivery of what the public wanted. Secondly, local authorities were quite responsive to public opinion, because politicians had very stong incentives not to annoy or arouse their electors.

Consider first the case of the size of authorities. It is something of a shock to face the fact that smaller local authorities are better, but there are parallels in other services. In 1920 the police force of Louth consisted of a Chief Constable and ten others. A Royal Commission on the police thought this absurd, yet that force maintained a permanent night foot patrol in Louth, which a force twice the size in a Louth division 40 years later could not do. Abolishing Louth's Police Force may possibly have benefited policemen, but it is not clear whether the Louth public would have been happy at the outcome. Specialist police skills now, as then, come from elsewhere, but the local police are no longer 'local'.

It is equally easy to lose sight of the the the fact that, in terms of what local authorities were actually doing, smaller units became more desirable as the years passed. The services dominating local government provision in the twentieth century have been education by the counties and county boroughs, with some grudging powers to districts at times, and housing by the county boroughs and urban and rural districts. Neither had been on the list of major local government functions in 1900 – education was added in 1902, and housing was effectively compulsory after 1919, but rarely considered before that time. There are at least as many arguments in favour of smallness in both services as a criterion for organization for the public benefit as of size for the benefit of the service providers. The inability of the local government structure to adapt to the size of areas best able to deliver services links naturally back to our opening point, the failure to translate formal 'democracy' into practical terms. The debate over local government in the late 1980s has again raised these issues publicly.

It is somewhat harder to show that politicians were sensitive to local feelings because the best evidence is of a negative sort. Thus, the extraordinary reluctance of Cleethorpes and Grimsby to have local authority housing after 1919, even to clear 'slums', is capable of being interpreted as a consequence of the absence of any significant voices to urge the contrary policy and a contentment with the existing situation (especially by the Labour representatives of the rate-paying and adequately housed skilled workers). Given the picture of politicians avoiding risks in order to sustain their careers, the absence of criticism will be taken by them as indicative of public content, and in the absence of any better evidence, by the outside observer too. Responding positively to local preferences by doing things is somewhat harder to demonstrate, especially since most of the things to be done were being encouraged by national parties or governments anyway. Despite its negative character, the evidence does point to local authorities being more sensitive to local sentiments than the public were ordinarily aware of.

What may have killed enthusiasm about local authority politics was the high level of additional conflict, not stemming from service provision, that such politics invariably exhibited. Conflict, with its connotations of a disruption in ordinary relationships, was never popular with many people. It might be acceptable, even necessary in politics, if it were devoted in the end to decisions about clear public good, but many conflicts in local government were both structural, between local authorities, and internal to the local authorities themselves. Simply to list these conflicts is also to identify the confusion and complexity of local politics:

(a) County borough and municipal borough *versus* county council, e.g. about land extensions for housing (as shown in Chapter 8), or powers (especially in education), or just a feeling that neither side understood what the other was about.

(b) A feeling of mutual distrust between urban and rural districts. However, since the offices of many rural districts were actually located within an urban district, there was a sentimental feeling in the population about 'their' town.

(c) Rural districts *versus* parishes, a conflict underexplored everywhere, but which observation indicates is closely paralleled in feelings and substance to

(d) Districts *versus* county council. In this area Lindsey seems to have been notoriously inept, while Kesteven was notably successful.

(e) And the special case of Cleethorpes *versus* Grimsby. Both were ever aware that the simple reformers' logic would put them together and tried to find ways of avoiding such an outcome (especially when Grimsby became Labour controlled, a position thought impossible to sustain if Cleethorpes was included).

(f) Councillor–official – without a clear political-administrative distinction, the relationship between councillors and officials employed by the Council was one that had to be negotiated afresh with every appointment. Councillors claimed democracy and power on their side, officials claimed expertise, professionalism, and ultimately, the dedication of their time, as their basis for control. Determined councillors still directed in detail – Matthew Larmour, Housing Committee chairman in Grimsby, actually went in each morning to the offices to consider the correspondence himself. In rural areas, officials made decisions and hoped that the explosions of indignation from councillors had insufficient force to change policies. Every authority differed in this respect, and establishing what local customs and practices were is a necessary, though time-consuming, aspect of research.

(g) Inter-committee and inter-departmental conflicts. Given the tradition of each senior official having a committee to service (or *vice versa* of each committee having a senior official to supervise) it is equally significant to observe that inter-departmental and inter-committee conflicts were quite normal: education, detested by everyone because of its insatiable demands for resources, housing and health in rivalry, parks and cemeteries struggling for recognition. Mechanisms exisited for general committees, such as Finance and General Purposes or Policy and Resources, but their efficiency was always doubtful, and the mechanisms of the party caucus were equally unlikely to generate mutual goodwill.

(h) Personal conflicts. Politicians need to be tough and ambitious, but local government gave little recognition of what they should aim at: to know quite well when they had 'arrived'. In boroughs the mayorality became such a symbol so that men of undoubted shrewdness became sentimental about their mayoral year and thought it the high spot of their public careers. The counties and districts had nothing similar, because the chairmanship of the council was barely ceremonial enough, and, inevitably, games of 'one-up-manship' were common.

We have described local authorities as the major institutions for politics in Lincolnshire, but have indicated that they were not in a very strong sense 'popular' institutions and often encompassed quite other sorts of politics than 'public debate between parties about policies'. Indeed, policy was, for most of the twentieth century in Lincolnshire, much the least relevant element at stake in local politics. Since in effect, no one knew what a successful policy would look like, it could never be identified, except perhaps that buildings, council houses, or new municipal offices for preference, did appear to have a physical presence that indicated at least some success.

PARTY AND INDEPENDENCE

A complete picture of politics in Lincolnshire cannot neglect some consideration of those elements which gave life and dynamism to the formal institutions. These elements are the political groups, primarily political parties, who contested elections, the organized interest groups and the network of affiliations that every local councillor possessed. 'Party' is generally accepted as a necessary constituent of democratic representative government. This point was, however, for much of the period actually denied by many seeking office in Lincolnshire, who claimed to be independent of party politics. Before 1914 this was a very rare claim indeed, except by those engaged in moving from one party to another, usually through Liberal Unionism on questions of national significance (Ireland and Tariff Reform). The national party affiliations of virtually all candidates were known or discoverable before 1914, though many said that such an affiliation was for national political purposes and was not very relevant locally.

In this they were making a point that political parties as such were organized on a constituency basis and not a local government one. Parties in local government units had to be specially created, even when, as in Grimsby and Lincoln, the constituency and the local government area coincided and had a separate existence from the constituency party. This was especially the case if the core of the local government party became the councillors who were elected.

Independency, then, had before 1914 a sense of being a willingness to regard local issues as different in kind and quality from those of national politics, so that, for example, liberals, who in national politics would scorn socialist plans for national public controls of industries, would accept the municipal socialism of a local authority running transport facilities or gas or electricity undertakings as good for the locality – and be joined by local conservatives taking the same view.

Fig. 9.3 Distribution of Acham's Dole, Grimsby 1914. The occasions of local politics have often included charitable causes. Here we see the distribution of Acham's Dole on the steps of Grimsby Town Hall in 1914. Holding the loaf is Councillor W. Beels, with Councillors W. E. Fletcher and J. Barker to his left. The uniformed figure is the Mayor's Officer. Source: Grimsby Central Library; caption: Boswell and Storey, *Grimsby As It Was*, Vol. I.

After 1914, however, Independence as a label began to mean cover for liberals and conservatives uniting to combat the Labour party. The independent label required no one to declare whether he or she was, in national politics, either Liberal or Conservative (and it is now often difficult to discover what they actually were), and it did enable those who had a genuine dislike of party politics to serve their communities with honour. In this, however, they were mistaken. In order to make local authorities work, some effective organization is needed and those who insisted on personal independence could never become part of the ruling group. Such a ruling group also found that it needed in practice to operate as a political party.

After 1948, when the Conservative Party decided to discourage independency in local government and to get its supporters to stand under a real party label, independency began to decline. This was assisted by the natural aging process whereby existing independents retired and failed to recruit their replacements. Thus, by the end of the period, party was again a substantial public element in the working of local authorities, in the way they had remained for constituency politics.

The functions of parties were to recruit candidates, create an election-fighting organization, have some policies for the candidates and voters to aspire to fulfil, and to organize the business of the representative bodies to which they were elected. For constituencies, there was no shortage of candidates offering themselves to the parties (but too few were local candidates) and the organization of business for the elected MP was a national matter. On policies, constituency parties contented themselves remarkably with broad national policies, with, in manifestoes, the barest mention of local economic concerns such as agriculture, fishing, and steel. The constituency parties as observed above were not especially efficient on the mechanics of fighting and winning elections. In comparison with the parties at the local government level they appear mildly ineffectual.

Even at local authority level, the only local party that fulfilled all requirements was the Scunthorpe Labour Party 1945–74. The Labour Party was usually able to put together candidates, policies, and an election-fighting organization: it usually fell down on the mechanics of party group meetings before council and committee meetings and in sustaining party block voting after such meetings. Other parties, Liberal, Conservative, or Independent, invariably had greater difficulty with recruitment and policy and again could rarely keep their representatives voting together on a consistent basis. The habit persisted of regarding parties as essentially national in character and that an independent view was always possible in local affairs. The consequence was that it is impossible to analyse Lincolnshire local authority politics in classic national party fashion.

The cause of this is that while national parties make much of their differences of principle and were either in or out of office, the differences of principle at the local level were often muted and, since councillors bore collective responsibility, the national language of politics often appeared exaggerated. The standard local riposte to a speech filled with national party rhetoric was on the lines of, 'Will it help Mrs Smith?' Moreover, the parties were much more obviously coalitions of individuals, each with a geographical concern, a particular set of friends, acquaintances, and interests. These could easily outweigh any party differences. Councillors from Scunthorpe or Cleethorpes on Lindsey County Council were invariably more loyal to each other, irrespective of party affiliations, because they perceived themselves as representing their area in quarters which ignored them. The same is true at different local government levels.

These views of councillors go some way towards explaining the comparative ineffectiveness of organized interests in Lincolnshire in influencing local politics, especially when compared to their national counterparts in national politics over the same period. The churches, trades unions, local companies, and voluntary organizations were rarely able to insist on their point of view being taken into account. Grimsby was before about 1885 a company town, obedient to the broad wishes of the railways, but after that date the railway influence was negligible; Scunthorpe, which might have seemed a likely company town, has had a long history of disregarding the iron and steel industry leadership on every issue.

Organized interests sometimes got a hearing because the local authority needed their services – teachers for education, doctors for health, builders for housing – but the technique of local authorities was to turn all such groups into supplicants for favours and to make decisions on any case 'on its merits'. Even so, it is still puzzling that the National Farmers' Union, with a vigorous branch structure and a legendary capacity during this period to get national government to accede to its wishes, was not inclined in rural Lincolnshire to become a political force.

We cannot neglect party and interest as elements in Lincolnshire politics, but frequently we find it suggested that the groups councillors belonged to are more significant. Everywhere in Lincolnshire there is a local folklore, very rarely breaking into print, about who really runs a place. The simplest example is the belief in Lincoln that there is a 'Cathedral set' of those living at the top of the hill who really run Lincoln. Other variants of geographical area of the socially notable and wealthy are, in particular, church connections, a Masonic lodge, a connection of cousins, the organizers of an agricultural show, but there is virtually no evidence to support any of these views.

THE STYLE OF POLITICS

This section looks at the local politicians as people, with their personal characteristics, the style of local politics or what was the characteristic way of conducting business, and finally, the content of politics – what it was the politicians fought about.

Politicians might claim to be ordinary people, but they very plainly were not. Indeed the discrepancy was often marked; not a single fisherman was a councillor in Grimsby after 1885. Councillors were largely male, middle-aged, and better educated than average, with jobs that permitted afternoon or evening meetings and, if committee chairmanships were involved, considerable time away from the job itself. The demands on time and energy were considerable and not surprisingly there was quite a high turnover amongst professional people in the ranks of councillors. Parish councils were less demanding than county councils and rural less than urban authorities, but at every level politicians had to be well organized to cope. Moreover, once a politician, also perhaps a JP, and certainly if one stayed for

Fig. 9.4 Sir Francis (J. W. F.) Hill at a ceremony held on 23 March 1974 to mark the gift of his coin collection to the City of Lincoln. On the left is Basil Arnold, City Sheriff, the hidden figure wearing the mayoral chain is Councillor Peter Archer, JP; behind Sir Francis is Councillor J. W. D. Gardiner, Chairman of the Libraries, Museum and Art Gallery Committee, and the lady behind the cabinet of coins is Alderman Mrs Mary Sookias. Sir Francis gave a lifetime of service to his city, as a solicitor, politician, and historian. He was a member of the City Council 1932–74, Mayor 1945–46, and was made a Freeman in 1961. He unsuccessfully contested Peterborough for the Liberals in 1929 and Lincoln for the Conservatives in 1950. His work in local government affairs extended far and wide, as chairman of the Association of Municipal Corporations 1957–66, President of the European Conference of Local Authorities (in Strasbourg) 1966–68, and President of the International Union of Local Authorities (at The Hague), 1967–71. He had a long association with the University of Nottingham, starting in 1937 as the Lincoln representative on the Council of the University College, and culminating in his installation as Chancellor in 1972. Source: *Lincolnshire Echo*, caption: F. T. Baker, *Lincolnshire Echo* 28 October 1972 and Municipal Mutual Insurance Ltd., Press Release August 1974 (Sir Francis was chairman of this company, which provided £150,000 for the establishment of the Francis Hill Chair of Local Government at the University of Nottingham).

long enough, a committee chairmanship, the mayoralty or chairmanship, and sundry other offices were available to those prominent in local affairs.

Exactly when the first woman councillor was elected in Lincolnshire is unknown. Lady Guardians did exist before 1918, since some were ratepayers in their own right and therefore eligible. But from a handful in the 1920s there developed a substantial body of women councillors by the 1970s, and especially at parish level. The demands of a political career were not reduced for women, and it is by no means clear whether they had anything special to contribute to politics except their symbolic presence. The Women's Institute movement was training country women to conduct business in meetings, just as the trades union movement had trained men. It would be interesting to know how many women councillors had come from that sphere. Nor is it possible to tell who was was the lowest status of person to be elected to a Lincolnshire authority. There is no case known of a person who was a garbage collector at the time of election (examples elsewhere do exist), but given high social mobility in Lincolnshire, it was possible for formerly poor people after 1918 to become councillors. Years of formal education do not of themselves make politicians, but notably longer periods in formal education were common among councillors.

But such personal characteristics were less significant than others: the ability to read minutes, to listen for long periods, to make decisive interventions into discussions, to be clear headed, not to lose one's temper, and if possible, to be able to draft formal notes or resolutions – such were the hallmarks of the effective councillor or politician and, by admittedly subjective evaluation, only about half of those who were politicians had in fact the necessary skills. People drifted away from politics as not being for them: those with the skills developed a lifetime career devoted to politics. It was the greatest enjoyment they had and, for many, the only thing in which they could use their real talents, so uninspiring were their ordinary occupations.

The skills brought to the task by leading figures were considerable. Some would have been successful at whatever they attempted in life. Sir Francis Hill in Lincoln, given the lowly Chairmanship of Parks, Cemeteries, and Allotments at the beginning of his career, managed to get his name in the local press weekly for some new innovation in what everyone else dismissed as an impossible role (Fig. 9.4). Alec Moore in Scunthorpe always wrote out his speeches and gave a copy to the local press, thus ensuring that his views were reported. Frank Broddle of Cleethorpes knew to the minute the Grimsby evening paper deadlines and timed his speeches to obtain the headlines and ensure that opponents replies were the dead news that might not get printed the next day. Their skills would not have disgraced Baldwin or the young Harold Wilson among British Prime Ministers. The organizational brilliance of a Larmour (Grimsby), Pittwood (Scunthorpe), or Snook (Lincoln) was conceivably wasted on local government; they deserved a bigger canvas, but interestingly all explicitly chose to devote their skills to a locality.

Fig. 9.5 George Deer in the robes of the Mayor of Lincoln 1933–34. A native of Grimsby, in his early twenties just before the first world war he became a trade union official in Lincoln. In 1945 George Deer defeated Sir Walter Liddall to become Labour MP for Lincoln, having recently served a year as Sheriff. He moved seats to Newark in 1950, thereby avoiding a clash with Frank Hill in the parliamentary election of that date, and served for nearly 20 years in parliament. He was an important campaigner for traffic improvements in Lincoln, and his work eventually bore fruit in 1958 with the opening of the Pelham Bridge over the main railway junction. Perhaps more notably he was much exercised in the 1920s by the plight of the poor and the unemployed, and there was an occasion when he hired a couple of circus elephants to lead a demonstration of the unemployed, intended to impress the Board of Guardians. Everything was decorous until the elephants decided to trample across the grounds of the Workhouse (off Burton Road, since demolished) and reared up on their hind legs to peer into the room where the Board was meeting. Not only did George Deer rebuff the Chairman's words that 'There isn't a man of weight and standing among the lot of you,' he also persuaded the Guardians to grant extra relief to help with the winter weather. Source: Lincoln Central Library; caption: Fred Morton, *Lincolnshire Echo,* 31 October 1985.

Fig. 9.6

The Hon. Francis McLaren (1886–1917) was the Liberal MP for Spalding 1910–17. As the second son of the first Baron Aberconway he was a member of an intensely political family. His grandfather, Duncan Mc-Laren, came from humble origins on the west coast of Scotland, leaving school at 12, and went to work in the retail sector in Edinburgh. He became a member of the City Council and Lord Provost, before being elected as an MP for Edinburgh in the 1860s. He was a radical and married Priscilla Bright, sister of another well-known radical, John Bright. Their son Charles, father of Henry and Francis, also became a Liberal MP, and Stafford was one of the constituencies he represented. Charles married Laura, daughter of Henry Pochin, a wealthy chemist and businessman, who bought the Bodnant estate near Conway, Denbighshire.

Francis McLaren was educated at Eton and Balliol College, Oxford, where he took a second in history in 1909. While a student he showed an interest in Liberal politics, especially economic questions, and spoke occasionally in the Union 'in a clear, charming style'. On going down, he became a member of the Inns of Court, but was elected MP for Spalding in 1910 at the age of 23, the youngest MP in the House. His elder brother Henry was also elected as a Liberal. Francis was a 'rather dashing figure', and seems to have been popular with everyone, so much so that on his marriage in 1911 no less than 2,100 constituents travelled from Spalding in five special trains to Bodnant for the occasion. He was Parliamentary Secretary to Mr Lewis Harcourt, 1910–15, while Commissioner of Works, and later Secretary of State for the Colonies.

In September 1914 McLaren joined the RNVR, becoming a Lieutenant, later acting Lieut. Commander, and was in the RN Armoured Car Squadron serving with distinction in Belgium and Gallipoli. He was then in Egypt with the armoured cars, but transferred to the Royal Flying Corps. After a long illness he was posted to Montrose for further training, during which he was killed in a flying accident, when his aircraft dived into the sea (20 August 1917).

Mr Asquith paid tribute to Francis McLaren in the House of Commons: 'One of the youngest and most loved of our members, who was cut off in a youth of radiant promise, still untarnished by disappointment, a man with clear and firm convictions, a faithful and loyal friend, for whom those who knew him best knew how much there was in the coming years to be hoped for.' Truly a worthy representative of the 'lost generation'. Photo by courtesy of Mrs Nancy McLaren. Caption based on *Who was Who 1916–1928*; *Debrett's Illustrated Peerage and Baronetage*, 1985; *Balliol College War Memorial Book 1914–19*, vol. II; and information from Mr Kenneth Carlisle, MP for Lincoln, a grand-nephew of Francis McLaren.

Fig. 9.7 Sir Archibald Weigall (1874–1952) was Unionist MP for the Horncastle Division 1911-20 and the photo shows him electioneering at Coningsby. Captain Weigall served in South Africa in 1902, but retired from the Army and was land agent to the Earl of Londesborough at Blankney when he married in 1910. During the first world war he became a Lieutenant Colonel and Inspector of the Quarter Master General's Services in Northern Command. He was also on several government committees managing food, salvage, and surplus government property. He had interests in agricultural education, having been a Gold Medallist himself at the Royal Agricultural College. Lt .Col. Weigall was knighted in 1920 and was Governor of South Australia 1920–22. On his return to England, he and Lady Grace Weigall continued to live at Petwood, a house she had built at Woodhall Spa in 1905. Here the Weigalls held a string of vast parties and historical pageants. As heiress to the Maple furniture fortune, Lady Weigall had other houses in London and Ascot, to which they retired in 1933, when Petwood was turned into a hotel, serving as Officers' Mess for the 617 'Dambuster' Squadron 1943–45. Source: D. N. Robinson; caption: *Who Was Who*, Vol. V, 1951–60, p. 1149 and D. N. Robinson, *The Book of Horncastle and Woodhall Spa*, Buckingham 1983, pp. 132-3.

We ought sensibly to pause briefly and consider the 'permanent' politicians, the professional staff employed by local authorities in Lincolnshire. It is difficult to judge professional competence; some, who liked living in Lincolnshire, were clearly very able, but there were a large number whose competence was merely adequate. Sir Harold Banwell, the most successful of them (town clerk of Lincoln, county clerk of Kesteven, secretary of the Association of Municipal Corporations, and in retirement, leader of the Conservatives on Lincoln

Fig. 9.8 Mrs Margaret Wintringham (1879–1955), Liberal MP for Louth 1921–24, the first British born woman MP to take her seat (Lady Astor, first woman MP was an American). Margaret Longbottom was educated at Keighley Girls' Grammar School and at Bedford College, London, becoming a Grimsby headmistress before her marriage in 1903 to Tom Wintringham of Little Grimsby Hall, near Louth. The Wintringhams were keen Liberals and busy in public life. Margaret was a VAD at Louth Auxiliary Hospital during the first world war, Chairman of the Women's War Agricultural Committee, which was concerned with food supplies, President of the Louth Women's Liberal Association and a JP for Lindsey. At the by-election of June 1920, Tom became MP for Louth, but died of a heart attack in the House of Commons in August 1921, and Margaret won the ensuing by-election. She increased the majority in 1923, but was defeated in October 1924. She contested Louth again in 1929 and Aylesbury in November 1935, both unsuccessfully, but became President of the Women's National Liberal Federation. From 1933 to 1945 Mrs Wintringham represented Caistor on the Lindsey County Council and this picture is taken from the County Council group photo of 1933. Source: Panora Ltd., caption *Who's Who of British MPs*, Vol. III, 1919–45, ed. Stenton and Lees (Harvester Press) p. 388, *Obituaries from the Times 1951–60* (Newspaper Archive Developments Ltd.) 11 March 1955 and H. A. Wickstead, *Lincolnshire, Lindsey*, 1984, p.54.

Council) was given to the view that the Lincolnshire range of competence and incompetence was one of the widest in the country. As politicians, however, few had much skill. Even in Grimsby, where the privileges of office were considerable (the Borough Engineer could have the path from home to church cleared by his department on a snowy Sunday), there were few instances of professional power exceeding the normal negotiable limits. The most effective professionals indeed were to be found teamed with the most dynamic politicians in a nearly unstoppable combination, as Banwell did in fact combine with Sir Francis Hill.

Quite how we can characterize the differences between different localities in their local style, even when such differences are quite clear, has perplexed most observers. The essence of the matter is in the local rules of the game, which when established are difficult for individuals to override, and which when acquired in early youth are almost impossible for individuals to break. The cases of the irascible George Deer (see Fig. 9.5), whose early political life was in Grimsby but whose political career was in Lincoln, where he was never quite accepted (and was, characteristically, denied the freedom of the city he desperately wanted) and Charles Franklin, who came as a gentle and thoughtful figure from Lincoln to Grimsby and never had the impact his skills deserved in their rough politics, indicate how the rules worked.

Whether Lincolnshire has a distinct style seems possible. At present it is a matter of anecdote, but to one who has lived long in Yorkshire, the characteristic Lincolnshire style is in actually getting things done rather than talking about them. Another outsider to make this kind of observation was Hedley Warr, headmaster of Louth Grammar School (see below Chapter 10, p. 271).

What did Lincolnshire politicians actually disagree about? Three broad fields can be discerned:

(a) Is the activity part of our job or not? Local government is capable of developing a service once it is agreed that it should be provided, but such agreement takes time and energy to establish. The extent to which housing, education, sanitary controls, planning controls, are desirable have all been fought over. At the constituency level, much of the disagreement is whether or not the public has a relevant part to play in the activity, especially in economic affairs.

(b) How is the activity to be financed? This is a question both of the overall cost of the activity and of the time span required to make financial arrangements. Not getting deeper into debt vies with the actual present cost of a project as grounds for viewing any project with suspicion. At all levels of local politics, such considerations were always present, even when there seemed to be government funds or a buoyant rate-income present. To arrive at judgments on such matters was never an easy task; with the best will in the world, colleagues in the same party or faction could find themselves in disagreement.

Figs. 9.9 and 9.10 Ceremonial occasions in Boston, 1910. These two photos were taken on the same spot in front of Boston Assembly Rooms. **Fig. 9.9** (above) shows a Mayor's Sunday about 1910, with the procession on its way to St Botolph's Church (the Stump). The top-hatted man with mace is Burfoot Trevitt, the last Town Crier and Corporation Messenger. Mayoral processions helped to give a political identity to the boroughs which no County Council or Rural District Council can claim to have matched. **Fig. 9.10** (facing) shows another ostensibly political event, long reduced to ceremonial – the proclamation of a new sovereign, in this case George V (1910). The photo is a still from a cine film presented in 1910 to Boston Borough Council by a Mr Lawrence. Sources: 9.9, Lincoln Central Library, caption; G. S. Bagley. 9.10, Boston Borough Council and Lincolnshire and Humberside Film Archive, caption; P. Ryde.

(c) Who gets what? The problem of who was to get the resources available from political action, or how they were to be distributed, perplexed everyone. It was easy to think in terms of one's own group and interests, but most issues involved making judgments between two or more other groups. There was a developed sense of fairness which could be applied as a general rule, but there were no grounds for working out inter-personal claims to limited resources except arbitrary rules (e.g. in allocating council housing, grammar school places) and even fewer for those claims of location, as to where the cemetery or old persons' home might be most advantageously put. Politicians and officials struggled to make sense of a world where not everyone could have what they wanted and where there were too few sensible principles to determine choices.

Fig. 9.10

THE POLITICS OF HOUSING

So far the analysis offered has been in very general terms. To illustrate politics in action, we may take as examples the responses of Cleethorpes, Grimsby, Lincoln, and Scunthorpe to central government requirements, after both world wars, for local authorities to build houses for letting.

The first general point is the independence of local authorities: though central government wanted certain kinds of results and worked very hard to get them, local authorities could prevaricate and fix their own priorities. The second general point is that the responses of local authorities were in each case very much in line with what had happened *before* the war. It has become traditional in twentieth century British history to attribute to the impact of war the cause of major changes. Each case, however, needs to be demonstrated, and it is very doubtful if large administrative organizations ever do anything after a war other than attempt to resume business as usual. War accelerates or exaggerates change in technology and attitudes, but the results only slowly emerge in administrative and political action.

Thus, when central government wished to encourage local authority homebuilding in 1919 and associated such housing with town planning, of the four Lincolnshire authorities only Lincoln was enthusiastic and Scunthorpe interested. Why? In Lincoln, by 1914, two years of intense debate and discussion had led to proposals, halted only by the advent of war (see above, Chapter 8, p. 207). The arguments as to whether the task was a proper one for local authorities, how much it would cost, and to whom the building contracts should go and the houses be let had all been ventilated. In Scunthorpe, there had been some pre-war interest in town planning, but housing had to be considered seriously during the war as the expansion of the iron and steelworks drew in a wider population.

When new problems come before local authorities, most councillors are inclined to avoid risks. Only a few will take chances. By 1914, in Lincoln the skilled political leadership of the Liberal Newsum had outmanoeuvred both Labour and Conservative councillors by going further and faster than they had recommended in the housing scheme. The result was that by 1919 there was all-party agreement on Lincoln's response to government initiative. In Scunthorpe, Quibell and the Labour party might have done something similar, had the area been amalgamated earlier than 1919, but it was left to Henderson to fight the local economists and sustain a housebuilding programme. In Cleethorpes, Wilkinson sought to move obdurate colleagues, despite his own doubts. In Grimsby, Johnson, a Liberal, attempted to build his own and his party's fortunes in a Conservative dominated council by supporting a housing scheme.

In each case, besides the personal politics involved, there was a dynamic element of bargaining between authorities, especially using the town planning elements of the 1919 scheme. Grimsby and Cleethorpes were obviously keen to use the legislation to advance or deny Grimsby's claim on Cleethorpes; Lincoln used housing as a lever for incorporating Bracebridge UDC; and in the area to become Scunthorpe, the existing authorities manoeuvred to use the legislation for their own advantage.

The outcome of the combination of government pressure and local politics was very varied, in part because the national policy took insufficient account of the shortages of manpower and building materials. Cleethorpes was bullied into building by the threat of the government itself building, and then did a minimal scheme with some proficiency. Elsewhere, national pressure led to grand local schemes that had no prospect whatever of success as local authorities coped with what became a major failure of the 1918–22 coalition government. The process broke each of the local politicians involved with housing: Parker in Lincoln fled to the comparative calm of the Watch Committee, having seen Lincoln's high hopes comprehensively

Fig. 9.11 Alderman and Mrs Roberts, parents of Mrs Margaret Thatcher, when Mayor and Mayoress of Grantham, 1946. Alfred Roberts was born in Northampton-shire, one of seven children. He left school at 12, but despite this achieved a better education through the use of library books. He was a lifelong Methodist, serving as a preacher, and worked in a Grantham grocer's shop until, in 1917, he was able to start his own business in one of the town's poorest areas, selling out in 1959 on retirement. Alfred Roberts was elected to Grantham Borough Council in 1927 as an Independent, but it was suggested that at heart he was a Liberal. He served Grantham for 25 years, nine as an alderman, and for many years he was Chairman of the Finance Committee, a very powerful position. All this came to an abrupt end when, after the 1952 election, Alderman Roberts was outvoted in the aldermanic election, as the Labour party, victorious for the first time, needed a quota of aldermanic seats in proportion to their majority. Many councillors felt that Roberts deserved better treatment, but his own final words to the council were 'No medals, no honours, but an inward sense of satisfaction. May God bless Grantham forever.' He had been Chairman of Grantham's 1937 Coronation Celebrations, and President of the Grantham Rotarians in 1936. After his death on 10 January 1970 at the age of 77 he was described as 'one of the town's very great gentlemen. His fine example of steadfast principles, his service to the town as Councillor, Alderman and Mayor, and his devoted work for the Methodist Church and Circuit, all these will be remembered.' Source: Rt. Hon. Mrs M. Thatcher; caption: M. G. Knapp.

mutilated; Watkinson in Cleethorpes was defeated at the polls; Henderson in Scunthorpe left public life; Johnson in Grimsby went into a state of amicable incompetence for a decade. The political lesson was clear: don't trust big central programmes of action.

In 1945, again, central government with a little more planning, but not much more intelligence, sought large-scale local authority housing projects. Cleethorpes was reluctant to act once again, and the leadership on an Independent and Conservative Council was left to Marklew, a Labour councillor who, as Johnson in Grimsby had been in 1919, could be denied the credit if successful and blamed if, as expected, all fell apart. Marklew in fact did remarkably well, but this did not help his party in local esteem: only himself. Grimsby was more ready to act in 1945 than in 1919, since the Labour group had taken control and saw in housing a possibility of major success, as did Larmour, the Housing Committee Chairman. Larmour also succeeded more than his party. The building was slow and erratic but Larmour took no personal blame and consolidated his stature. In Scunthorpe, the Labour councillor O'Dowd had become Housing Chairman in 1937, so impressed were his Independent and Conservative colleagues. He had more scope after 1945 with a Labour local majority and some considerable success in manipulating the rules of central–local interactions on housing. In Lincoln, so complete was the all-party agreement that the housing chairmanship was left to comparative lightweights to get on with, while politics went on elsewhere.

The real post-war politics of housing was not in whether to build or not, but who was to do the building. Cleethorpes and Scunthorpe both worked out amicable relationships with local builders that also permitted the use of national contractors. But both Grimsby and Lincoln had major power struggles with local builders, which were resolved by both using outside contractors and their own direct labour force and, in Lincoln, dissident local builders. Equally difficult was the allocation of houses. Everywhere local people got preference. Scunthorpe got rid of an unpopular deputy town clerk in 1948 by not allocating a council house to him and councillors' cases proliferated. One Grimsby personality was brought low by appearing to 'fix' his daughter's council house.

The politics of allocation as a final illustration of a general theme also permits one final general point to be made: the absence of effective democracy. At no point in 1919 or afterwards were the public explicitly asked whether they wanted local authority housing or what local policies should be in the types of houses built, the rental levels, or the choice of tenants.

The assumption that lies behind these illustrations is that central and local governments knew best. Their politics were the ones that really mattered.

LINCOLNSHIRE AS A POLITICAL CONCEPT

While politics thrived in Lincolnshire, the concept of 'Lincolnshire' itself evoked little support from those in political office. Support for Lincolnshire existed at a basic popular level and this was exploited by politicians and officials. But they themselves could not make much sense of it. Thus, in 1966, when one of the few symbols of Lincolnshire, the minor counties cricket eleven won the championship, it meant more to an author then living in a mid-western American town than the fact that England won the World Cup the same summer. But I knew when I returned to research in Lincolnshire that Lincoln politicians of learning and wisdom would regard north of Caenby Corner as *terra incognita*, that officials from Cleethorpes travelling to Lincoln felt less enthusiastic about it than going to London.

Part of the difficulty was that there was no single unifying symbol or political institution to which Lincolnshire people could look. The decision in 1888 not to have a single Lincolnshire County Council was barely a decision at all, since everyone assumed that a county of such a size must be divided somehow. The consequence was that no institution spoke for Lincolnshire and every other political institution opted instead for its own salvation or perception of interest.

The process of local government reform in 1958–74 brought much of the ambiguity and the feelings to the surface. The Local Government Boundary Commission 1960–65 considered the awkward position of Stamford and while finding that Stamford council itself preferred to be in a Peterborough-based county, there were contrary popular pressures. The Commission also favoured a union of the three counties of Lincolnshire to form one county, proposing as a first step a Holland–Kesteven merger, but discussion soon showed that the only acceptable change was a north–south division of Lincolnshire, as proposed by the 1947 Boundary Commission. This possibility was more fully explored in evidence to the Royal Commission on Local Government in England 1966–69, when the three counties favoured a single 'Lincolnshire' reluctantly, and their districts divided between keeping everything as it was, having a 'Lincolnshire', and moving towards a Humberside county or northern 'Province' of some kind. The latter was particularly liked in Grimsby and Scunthorpe. The Royal Commission did in fact divide Lincolnshire into a north and south, with the northern section being part of a Humberside. That one of the Commissioners was Sir Francis Hill from Lincoln, who

Fig. 9.12 Mayoral procession in Stamford, 1911. As in Boston (Fig. 9.9) so in Stamford, mayoral processions were popular before 1914. This is one of several such photos taken year by year at the corner of St Mary's and St John's Streets. Behind the Mayor's Officer (with mace) is James Dalton in top hat, robes and chain, the new mayor of 1911, and a solicitor in the town. The bewigged figure on Dalton's left is Charles Atter, Town Clerk, another solicitor. The deputy mayor, George Higgs, a tobacconist, follows on the police constable's right. Source: Lincoln Central Library, caption: J. Smith, Curator, Stamford Museum.

quietly asked many political people their feelings on the matter, gave the proposal real weight.

Thus, the urban areas like Stamford, Scunthorpe, and Grimsby opted for non-Lincolnshire solutions and the more rural parts could not agree on a solution which kept a Lincolnshire intact. The calculations done by the local authorities involved were invariably ones about their own institutional preservation. One of the best parish council submissions to the whole Commission proceedings came from Long Sutton, which had lost its urban status in 1932 in a previous reorganization, and gave a most vigorous defence of its own excellent record.

The outcome of such divided counsels was inevitable: a division into a Lincolnshire and a northern part being South Humberside. What was however surprising to the politicals was the controversy in 1971–73 on the actual reformed system. In the north, there was sustained opposition to Humberside, and in unofficial polls the weight of popular opinion was still for a Lincolnshire. Lincolnshire was not unusual in

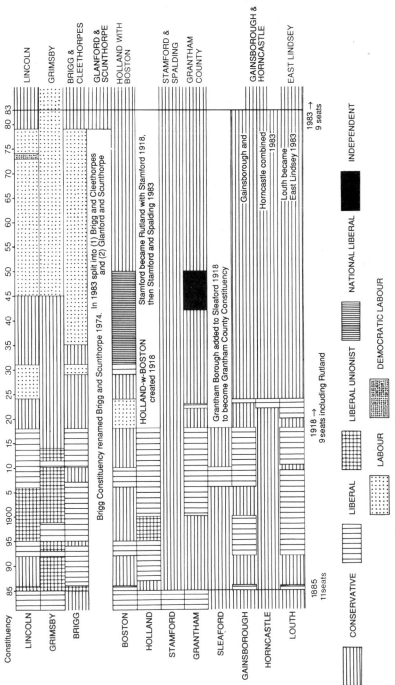

Fig. 9.13 Changes in political control of Lincolnshire constituencies. Drawn by J. Peacock from information supplied by Owen Hartley. See also Appendix, Table 6.

exhibiting a sharp constrast between the views of politicians and officials in the politically sophisticated classes on the one hand and of popular attitudes on the other, but the episode casts an interesting light on both the loyalties of Lincolnshire leaders and the overall performance of their authorities in being able to respond to popular opinions. The absence of any effective democracy in this case ensured that popular wishes were incapable of being translated into political action.

The creation of a divided county still evokes passions of great weight and depth. At the core of these is a popular distaste for Humberside, and a recalculation of the advantages of different arrangements. The harnessing of these feelings to a political campaign is, however, a rather remote possibility. Much more likely is that the politicals will, in any future discussions of local government reorganization, think more seriously of the Lincolnshire solution. That in the end depends on Lincolnshire people caring for it – and finding those symbols of its identity that mean something. Even books like this present volume might have some influence. To speculate on the future of county–regional government in England as it might affect the county, however, is to move from past politics, which might be history, to present politics, which is certainly contentious.

Bibliographical note

This essay is based on two types of documentary primary sources, local newspapers and local authority minute books, supplemented by conversations and interviews with councillors, officials, and some voters. The secondary literature is fragmentary and inevitably concerned with particular places in Lincolnshire over relatively short periods of time and rarely directly focused on politics. On Scunthorpe, for example, there are still only two interpretative essays by me in M. E. Armstrong (ed.), *An industrial island*, 1981 and D. C. D. Pocock's essay on early civic history in the *Appleby-Frodingham News* of 1963 (a company news magazine). 'Politics' can be discerned, and indeed must be discovered, in a wide literature on other subjects like housing, town planning, or education. The section in the chapter above on housing is based on my 'Housing policy in four Lincolnshire towns 1919–59', Oxford D.Phil. thesis, 1969.

For those eager to discover more in detail about the strange world of Lincolnshire politics there is no alternative to an immersion in local newspapers and local authority records, while trying to see whether the generalizations offered in wider studies, based on particular local research, do or do not hold for Lincolnshire; see especially R. Frankenburg, *Communities in Britain* (Penguin, 1966), J. Gyford, *Local politics in Britain* (Croom Helm, 2nd ed., 1984), J. M. Lee, *Social leaders and public persons* (Oxford UP, 1963). In doing so, virtually any clue to the nature of the local situation might prove valuable. Politics is fortunately the 'reading around', for the core is only understood by its action in its periphery.

For the nineteenth century consult R. J. Olney's *Rural society and county government in nineteenth century Lincolnshire,* (History of Lincolnshire, Vol. X, 1979) and *Lincolnshire politics 1832–1885* (Oxford, 1973). The latter contains a complete table of Lincolnshire parliamentary representation for its period.

Two pre-1974 county councils promoted books on their areas, although that on Kesteven, devoting only one chapter to the county council itself, is a very different book from that on Lindsey. The books are: H. A. Wickstead, *Lincolnshire, Lindsey: the story of the County Council 1889–1974* (Lincoln, Lincolnshire and Humberside Arts, 1984) and J. Varley, *The Parts of Kesteven: studies in law and local government* (Sleaford, Kesteven County Council, 1974).

On individual politicians who represented Lincolnshire Divisions in Parliament, or otherwise became distinguished persons, the following reference books are useful: *Obituaries from The Times, Who was Who* (various periods covered in different volumes, by date of death), *Who is Who,* various volumes of *Who's Who of British MPs,* and for Lindsey county councillors there are lists in H. A. Wickstead, *Lincolnshire, Lindsey* (1984).

CHAPTER 10

EDUCATION FOR ALL CHILDREN

by Arthur Wickstead

Abstract *This chapter describes the development of education in Lincolnshire, or rather the growth of the schools for which the five local authorities were responsible. It is not, and could not be, the complete story. It starts in 1903 but only goes to 1974; the story is confined to the schools of the county and makes no attempt to cover further and agricultural education or the full range of responsibilities shouldered by the education authorities after the 1944 Education Act. The story is told by an administrative officer of one of the authorities. The chapter must be read in the context of the other chapters in the book; geography, industrial and agricultural growth, population changes, and local and national politics all contributed to or helped to determine the development of education in the county.*

Photographs can show some obvious changes in pupils and schools over the years from 1900, but can they show anything of the hopes and achievements and disappointments of the many men and women concerned with and for the education of the children of the county? The work of these seventy years can be seen as 'an endeavour to plan and build up a comprehensive system of education, not uniform or rigidly controlled, but placing within the reach of all children the best of which they are capable',[1] a national service but locally administered by the five local education authorities, two county boroughs, Grimsby and Lincoln, and three counties, Holland, Kesteven and Lindsey.

This chapter shows how the elementary and grammar schools of 1900 grew into the primary and secondary schools of today; the period is divided into three by the two major world wars. But within the general picture the chapter emphasizes the main challenges and problems met by the five authorities. They were not rich authorities;

George Philip's Atlas map below. *Bottom centre:* Microscope, with quill pens behind. Bottom right: Exercise book illustrating multiplication. The top question on the right hand page is: What was the cost of three sheep at 3.17s 6 1/2d each? **Source:** Museum of Lincolnshire Life.

Fig. 10.1 The Museum of Lincolnshire Life in Burton Road, Lincoln, contains many exhibits relating to our period. As an example, here is part of the schools section of the museum, showing objects which the better equipped schools might have contained in 1900. *Top left:* The 'School Clock' Face: How to tell the time of day. Prize, one penny. *Middle left:* Exercise book showing land measures. *Top right:* Exercise book, in which the right hand page illustrates the calculation of Compound Interest. Centre: Society of Arts six shillings box of mathematical instruments. *Middle right:* Smith and Dolier's Arithmetical Scales for simplifying sums. In this box the scales are for simple subtraction, i.e. without carrying. The scales were so placed that one 12-digit number is subtracted from the one above, then the child could turn up the answer on a third scale below. *Bottom left:* Jigsaw of the counties of England and Wales, corresponding to

Fig. 10.2 The village school playground at Marshchapel about 1906, with older children at drill. This activity was partly inspired by the militaristic atmosphere of the time, but was also a sensible way of introducing keep-fit exercises, when few schools had a gymnasium or playing field. Source: Lincoln Central Library.

they were hit by industrial and agricultural depressions; the demands of central government pressed hard. But amidst the difficulties, each authority had many elements of good and wholesome progress; there was concern and independent judgment.

From the first they did indeed have problems and challenges. The Balfour Education Act of 1902 placed on them the new major responsibility for all elementary schools, altogether over 600 schools with more than 70,000 children. Then there was the need to give more help to the grammar schools and especially to provide grammar schools for girls. These were immediate tasks in the first twenty years.

Between the wars the legacy of old school buildings (the Black List) plagued county, indeed all, authorities and then came pressure for separate senior schools for all children over 11 (Hadow reorganization).

The Butler Education Act of 1944 raised new hopes, set new standards and asked for new plans. The next thirty years are years of fiercely growing numbers and improving provision in both primary and secondary schools. Yet in some rural areas there was a decline in numbers causing concern for the quality of the very small village school. Grammar schools grew in size and esteem and the new secondary modern schools began to establish their own distinctive reputation. But then, perhaps too soon for the rural authorities, the urgent demand for the rapid reorganization of all secondary schools as comprehensive schools created new problems of planning and provision.

The challenges and problems here sketched out are dealt with in the various sections of the chapter. But who could best tell such a story? Pupil or teacher? Councillor or education officer? Parent or historian? Each would have a particular point of view, a personal estimate of what really mattered. This is a story by an officer of Lindsey County Council for whom pupils and furniture, teachers and buildings, numbers and curriculum alike were all matters of concern over many years.

There can only be space for reference to one or two authorities in relation to each problem. A wide range of sources has been tapped: central government reports and statistical digests; LEA minutes, reports and plans; school histories and log books; personal reminiscences. These only skim the surface and the bibliographical note (page 279-80) suggests where information may be found for further comment and more detailed research.

THE NEW EDUCATION AUTHORITIES TAKE OVER

The new structure of local government established in 1889 has been described in Volume X. Now on 1 April 1903 the five new Local Education Authorities, Grimsby, Lincoln, Holland, Kesteven and Lindsey, five councils acting through their education committees, were established under the Balfour Act of 1902. They were given full responsibility for the Board schools set up from 1870 onwards and partial responsibility for Voluntary elementary schools representing a trend towards bigger and more centralized administration.

The Voluntary schools represented the results of efforts over the last century by such agencies as the Church of England and the Wesleyan Methodist Church. Table 10.1 shows the great achievements of the Anglicans, and that the Wesleyans, as one would expect, had been more vigorous in Lincolnshire than in the country at large; other voluntary agencies and the School Boards had significantly smaller shares of the schools than elsewhere.

The smaller proportion of Board schools in Lincolnshire reflected its generally rural nature and the strong provision by the Church. There were 21 Boards in Holland, 25 in Kesteven and 55 in Lindsey; they mostly administered single schools, in a scattering of villages where the other agencies had failed to provide a school, or one of suitable standing.[2]

Table 10.1 *Responsibility for schools, 1895*

Agency	Lincolnshire Schools		Eng. & Wales Schools	
	No.	%	No.	%
Church of England	449	71.1	11,270	61.6
Wesleyan	26	4.2	501	2.8
Other voluntary bodies	29	4.9	2,078	11.4
School Boards	119	19.2	4,447	24.2

Source: Russell, part 3, p. 11

In the City of Lincoln, no School Board had ever been formed. This was in sharp contrast to Grimsby, where the voluntary agencies had quite failed to meet the demand for school places. The population had doubled during the 1860s and only a quarter of the children were in school in 1870, yet there was no move to establish a School Board until April 1874. The Borough Council only moved because it was then ordered to do so by central government, Alderman Bannister remarking that they had done well to postpone the adoption of the Act for the maximum possible time.[3]

Though sluggish in its start, the Grimsby School Board, with two Anglican and seven Nonconformist members, and later one Roman Catholic, acted with businesslike enthusiasm. A school for 1,000 children, a record in Lincolnshire which stood for many years, was immediately built to a design selected after a national competition. Six other schools followed, so that by 1903 three out of every five pupils were in Board schools, and the 'recognized accommodation' still showed plenty of spare places. Provision included the Higher Grade School in Eleanor Street, an important innovation for senior pupils (see below p. 264).[4]

The first teacher appointed by the Board was a Miss Macqueen from Scotland. At first the Clerk of the Borough acted as Clerk to the Board and an early appointment was that of School Attendance Officer. The School Board had three sources of income: grant from central government based on pupils' attendance and performance, 'school pence' from parents, and a precept on Borough rates. But they made as little call as possible on the rates, and the Grimsby Board established a national reputation in this period of payment-by-results for the high grant they earned from the scholars' performance, at first based on individual testing, then on assessment of whole schools by HM Inspectors. In 1899–1900 Grimsby were outright leaders, 'the grant per scholar being ninepence above the next highest among the County Boroughs'.[5]

The five main councils had already had some experience of secondary education, through a Technical Committee or an Educational Committee, which since 1890 had disbursed a little money from rates and from excise taxes ('whisky money') on technical and secondary education.[6] But this new responsibility for all elementary education was a different matter.

Lindsey Council Council, adopting a West Riding proposal, had protested against 'elementary education being placed directly or indirectly under its control ... any further expenditure on education necessitated by fresh legislation should be met by imperial taxation and not from local sources',[7] a cry which has been echoed down the decades with recognizable modifications.

However, the main concern of the time is now much less familiar, being the problem of spending money on voluntary or sectarian, that is mainly Church of England, schools. Lincoln City did not wish to levy rates for this purpose without the right to appoint a majority of the managers. Throughout the county the nonconformist opposition was fierce, resolution after resolution being passed against 'subsidized sectarian schools'.[8] In Grimsby, a Citizens' League formed in 1903 supported members who refused to pay their rates as a matter of principle. In March 1904 some 60 passive resisters were prosecuted and another 65 later in the year, their goods being distrained and sold to raise the necessary sums. At Kirton Lindsey the Baptist minister went to prison for the same reason.[9]

All authorities delegated most of their new responsibilities to newly appointed Education Committees, which consisted largely of council members with a few non-members co-opted as 'persons of experience in education'. Lindsey knew whom they wanted and did not consult the teachers.

A Lindsey memorandum of 31 December 1902 suggested that higher education, including the grammar schools, would not present much difficulty; the training of teachers was a new obligation of urgent importance; in elementary education there were many problems requiring 'ultimate, but cautious settlement', such as a properly graduated scale of payment for teachers, the 'differentiation of rural from town education ... to develop the faculties of rural children for country life', and the improvement of school buildings.[10]

Before the 1902 Act there were many different School Attendance Authorities each with their own by-laws; in Lindsey alone there were 55 school attendance officers (not all full time) who were to be transferred to the service of the committee. Lindsey County Council was advised to exercise a general control, rather than become 'entangled in the management of individual schools' … 'fairly full discretion should be given to the Managers in matters of detail', such as control of teachers, school timetables (subject to the general direction of the Committee), selection of textbooks, and the supply of furniture within approved estimates.

A first rough estimate of Lindsey's new expenditure was £75,130 for a normal year of which £54,000 was for teachers' salaries; of this £11,530 had to be provided from the rates, at rather less than twopence half-penny in the pound.[11]

The new education authorities found some experienced candidates for the post of education officer. Douglas Chandler, who had become secretary of the large Grimsby School Board in 1891, continued as Secretary for Education in the Borough until 1928. Kesteven and Lindsey both continued the appointments of their Secretaries who had administered the 'whisky money', Hudson Donaldson in Kesteven and Maudson Grant in Lindsey. In Holland, Archibald Alexander Crabtree was appointed Secretary of the Committee at a salary of £175 per annum. In Lincoln, where there had been no School Board and there were especially strong links with the Church, the diocesan inspector of schools, R. C. Minton, having first been offered the post of Inspector by Lindsey, was appointed Secretary in the city. It is to be noted that these men appear to have had no teaching qualifications or experience, and, in the counties, they seldom ventured away from their offices.

RESPONSIBILITY FOR PUBLIC ELEMENTARY SCHOOLS

The LEA would be 'charged with the duty of maintaining and keeping efficient all the public elementary schools within their area which were necessary'. So Maudson Grant in Lindsey reported to his Committee in 1902, but what *was* the condition and *how* efficient were the many schools, Voluntary and Board, for which they became responsible? The managers of each voluntary school were required to complete an enquiry form of 27 sections, as did the Managers of Langton-by-Spilsby C.E. School:

Accommodation for how many pupils: 60.
Name of the School Attendance Officer: Butcher.
Names of teaching staff and annual remuneration: Mrs Bodger, £55 and two monitresses.

Dwelling house for teacher, with rental value: yes, £5.
Use of school building for Sunday School purposes: occasionally.
Details of expenditure on repairs over last three years: £74.
Any requirements by HM Inspector not yet met: none.

and so on.[12]

The managers of the Board schools, now to be fully maintained by the LEAs, also had an enquiry form, with 39 questions, and the managers of Tetney elementary day school reported amongst other matters:

Accommodation for 130 (mixed).
School buildings insured for £700.
Headmaster: A.E. Rainsford, salary £120.
Infants class: Miss Hall, salary £40.
Pupil teacher to be engaged: terms £9 for first year.

The estimated expenditure for 1903 was £239.19s.10d, including £172 for salaries, £11 for books and stationery and £3 for apparatus and furniture. That year HM Inspectors had reported, 'The school is again in a very good state', so on an average of 42 older pupils and 25 infants the Board of Education paid a grant of £67.9s.[13]

Fig. 10.3 Louth Church of England Girls' School, some time before 1914. Note the partition and the coke stove, characteristic schoolroom features of this period; the lace-up boots visible in the front row, the wild rose of the nature lesson on the blackboard. The metal frame desks for four have little or no storage space for books. **Source:** E. Croft postcard collection.

Fig. 10.4 Pinchbeck School 1946, a nice contrast to Fig. 10.3. The desks are still metal framed, but seat only two and have more storage room for books. Real ink is still in use from ink wells let into the level piece of wood at the front of the desk. By this time the girls would all be wearing shoes, but the boy in the right foreground is wearing boots. Top right is the ubiquitous map of the British Empire drawn on a projection which distorts the northern landmasses, including Canada, far beyond their real proportions. Standing in the window is Mr A. J. J. Burton, headmaster. **Source:** courtesy of Mrs D. Edmonds.

Among the records at the Lincolnshire Archives Office are the application forms of teachers appointed to headships of elementary schools in these early years.[14] They could provide the basis of a detailed analysis, but a quick glance has brought to light young women well under the age of 30 appointed as heads of village schools. One went to Wickenby and Snelland School in 1909 aged 21, almost immediately after her two years' course at Lincoln Training College (now Bishop Grosseteste College), with a salary of £70 per annum. There are several instances of men getting headships at the age of 24, and in those days heads played a very full part in the development of village life, because they lived in the villages where they taught, and few country children went to school elsewhere than in their own village. Some schools, however, were not able to attract well-qualified applicants and the small school at Thorganby appointed a Headmistress with only a pass in the preliminary certificate examination.

The Building Regulations for Elementary Schools of 1907 (Command Paper 3571, price 2d) are those under which many Lincolnshire schools were built, although more still were adaptations of existing buildings. A single central hall could be built so that it was readily accessible from the classrooms of each department. Classrooms should not be planned to accommodate more than 50 to 60 children: five rows of long desks or six rows of dual desks were thought to be best. Desks should be slightly inclined, as a flat desk had a tendency to make children stoop. A temperature of from 56 to 60 degrees Fahrenheit should be maintained (Figs. 10.3 and 10.4).

In Grimsby the LEA inherited a fine set of schools from the Board and two-thirds of the children were now in council schools but, although Grimsby was prosperous, little further progress was made. In 1918 HM Inspector commented, 'It is surprising that Grimsby, with its long historic background, which has made such remarkable progress commercially during the last 20 years, should have been content to remain so long in the same educational position as in 1902...intellectually it remains a backwater, which the tide of educational progress never freshens.'[15] Is this apposite metaphor to be taken as an indication that the LEA was simply resting on its late Victorian laurels?

Fig. 10.5 St Faith's School, West Parade area of Lincoln, early in the century. Like school drill (Fig 10.2), dancing was a keep fit activity requiring next to no equipment. The interior of this girls' school, as it was between the wars, is described in the text, p. 255, 261-2.. **Source:** Lincoln Central Library.

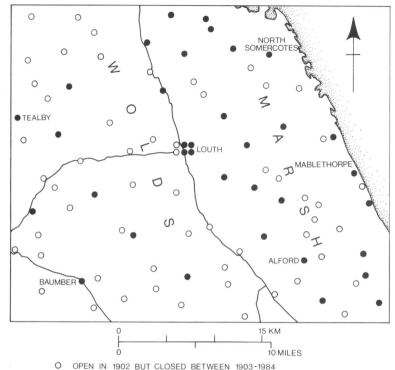

Fig. 10.6 **Primary schools** in Marsh and Wold around Louth in 1902 and 1984. Drawn by Jayne Peacock from data in Board of Education Return 1902 and Lincolnshire County Education Committee 1984.

Three examples are given of how the individual school and the general pattern of schools were always changing as the years went by.

In Lincoln the majority of children were in voluntary schools. The story of the St Faith's Schools shows both the problems and the remarkable number of changes in the nature of schooling. In 1876 a mixed infants' school and a girls' upper school were built on this site in the rapidly growing West Parade area of the city. The infants' school is still (1988) in being as a Church of England (Controlled) School, but in new buildings. The upper school for girls had a boys' department added in 1890 with a separate head. In 1923 this school took senior pupils from other schools. When in 1931 senior schools were built in the city, the two St Faith's departments were reduced to juniors only and in 1935 became one mixed junior school. In 1971 this in turn became a middle school for pupils of eight to twelve.[16] In

1988 St. Faith's is now a junior school again for pupils of seven to eleven. (Fig. 10.5).

The story of the schools in Deeping St James has been well told by C. A. Burchenall and shows how a small community fought through the years for its children and their schools. Tyghe's Schools had started in 1553, a School Board had formed in 1876, there was reorganization in 1889. The Managers wrote in 1906 to the Chairman of the Kesteven Education Committee, 'As so many of our most reasonable recommendations seem to be persistently ignored, we should like to know if the said recommendations have ever been placed before the Education Committee. The Managers feel they should be credited with some knowledge of the requirements of the Schools and at least a modicum of common sense'. There were only two Headmasters from 1889 to 1957; in 1937 the County, in its plans for Hadow reorganization (see p. 265), proposed a central school for seniors at Market Deeping but the war put an end to this. In 1947 the senior year (those aged fourteen and over) were transferred to the HORSA huts (Huts Operation Raising School-Leaving Age) at Bourne and a new secondary modern school was planned for the Deepings area, which finally opened in 1958 to serve nine villages.[17] This is now (1988) a comprehensive school.

The rural area around Louth provides an example of the varied and changing provision in one district with a sizable market-town (population 9,554 in 1921) and in villages of varying size situated on the Wolds and in the Marsh. Figure 10.6 contrasts the many elementary schools, both voluntary and county, in 1902 with the smaller number, renamed primary schools, remaining open in 1984. The closure of rural schools has been a continuous process.

HELP FOR THE GRAMMAR SCHOOLS

For the fortunate few in 1903 there were many ancient grammar schools in the county; the twenty-six 'endowed secondary schools', as they were then officially known, received grants from the Board of Education in London and some help from the LEAs, who were now beginning to be represented on governing bodies (Fig. 10.7A). In the larger towns as at Lincoln and Grantham the boys' grammar schools were in good health, with substantial numbers of pupils, some of them with boarding facilities, a very necessary element in the days before school buses.[18]

A few ancient schools were to fail, largely through the relative decline of their communities, yet they handed on something from their past. Read's School at Corby, founded in 1669, closed in 1908 because

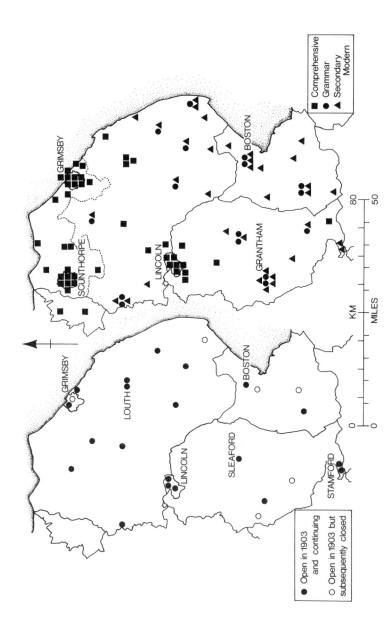

Fig. 10.7 (a) Endowed secondary schools in 1903. Schools closed are identified. No school is indicated at Bourne, whose school was closed in the 19th century and reopened after 1903. **(b) Secondary schools in 1976.** Main towns are indicated. Drawn by J. Peacock from information supplied by A. Wickstead.

of diminishing numbers, but this fine Jacobean building, described by
Pevsner as a 'satisfying composition in a golden brown stone', is now
home to the Arts Centre founded by the late Earl of Ancaster, while
the name of Charles Read has been handed on to the new secondary
modern school opened on the outskirts of the village in 1963.[19]

The Magdalen School at Wainfleet had an even more varied history. Founded by William of Waynflete, Chancellor of England
1456-1460 and formerly Master of Magdalen College, Oxford, the
school had a splendid brick building dating from 1484 which continued in use until 1933, when the Lindsey LEA opened a new mixed
grammar school at Skegness, by now a much bigger centre of population. The original Magdalen School building, having been used as an
army billet in the 1939–45 war, then housed the post-war secondary
modern school, with the help of a few temporary huts. When this
school moved to new buildings in 1966, taking the name with it, the
old school building became the district library.[20]

Also in the smaller market towns of Lindsey, perhaps because of
agricultural depression, endowed grammar schools were having a
hard time, to such an extent that in 1905 a special subcommittee of
the education committee visited all eleven schools in this category. Its
five members were very disappointed. They found a Lindsey total of
491 scholars in accommodation for 890, some apathy on the part of
governors, buildings out of repair or inadequate, no means for teaching practical science, teaching staff inadequate and poorly paid. They
drew attention to the 'singular lack of railway accommodation'. They
recommended a total of £975 in annual grants to the eleven schools
with detailed comments and recommendations for each school. In addition they noted the pressing problem of Scunthorpe, with its rapidly
growing population and suggested a higher elementary school. 'There
is no Secondary School within reach, nor indeed would such a school
be suitable to the requirements of the population, which is almost entirely engaged in the iron industry'. As in the case of rural education,
this demonstrates that another forty years were to pass before education was to be regarded, at least officially, as a means of giving all
pupils reasonably equal opportunities.[21]

The report of HM Inspectors on Queen Elizabeth Grammar School
at Gainsborough (February 1904) adds colour and detail.

The buildings are poor and not well suited for a school ... the whole endowment produces only £39 10s 0d gross ... the boys' lavatory might be greatly
improved if the walls were plastered or tiled ... the equipment for science
teaching is fairly good ... the Headmaster has held his position for 30 years
... a very able teacher ... teaches 29 hours a week ... senior assistant master
is a well qualified and capable teacher ... second assistant teacher ... a good

teacher ... no academic qualification ... salary far too low ... the atmosphere of the school is not strikingly keen and there is no great show of enthusiasm either for work or for play ... questionable whether with so small an endowment and such a site and buildings it can be long maintained.[22]

Numbers had fallen to 40 boys and a private school flourished in the town. In 1905 numbers had risen a little and the Lindsey subcommittee recommended that the annual grant of £100 be increased to £150 so that a third master could be appointed. But the enquiry at Spilsby Grammar School 'drives us to the conclusion that the position is a hopeless one ... we advise that the governors be urged to close the school'. In 1987 the school was still open, though with a new concern about closure.

GRAMMAR SCHOOLS FOR GIRLS

As with the education of ironworkers' children, so with girls; there was no equality in the sphere of grammar school education. In 1900 the only girls' endowed grammar schools were at Stamford and Lincoln, founded in 1873 and 1892 through the redistribution of endowments for boys'schools. At Louth the governors were still stalling on the implementation of the Endowed Schools Act of 1869 until the LEA withdrew their grant of £50, action which produced a scheme for a girls' school in 1902.[23] They were not so successful with the Clee Foundation and in Cleethorpes a girls' grammar school did not open until 1926.

When Miss Masson, the first headmistress, opened Louth Girls' Grammar School in 1903 there were 50 girls in the school, whereas only 37 girls were attending other Lindsey grammar schools. Some of the boys' grammar schools offered places to girls to increase their falling numbers, but these moves were not always welcome. At Brigg the 'rate of decline was accelerated by the admission of girls in 1902'; at Horncastle 'the admission of girls has', thought the Headmaster, 'distinctly lowered the standard of school work'.

The Lindsey sub-committee comforted itself with the knowledge that there were many private schools and ladies' academies, as Kelly's directories confirm, and thought it would be difficult to establish girls' schools. Yet further progress was made before the first world war with the opening of girls' grammar schools at Sleaford and Grantham. In the latter town, Isaac Newton's old school, the King's School, still provided for the boys of the town and its hinterland. Using 'whisky money', the Kesteven LEA had set up the Grantham Institute, which girls could attend, but more action was needed. The county and borough councils set up a joint committee to establish a new secondary grammar school for girls. There was some skirmishing with the

Board of Education, which refused at first to recognize the Institute as a secondary school. But 'in view of the declared intention of the County Council and the Town Council to build a new girls' secondary school on a new site', they recognized a girls' school element in the Institute, requiring the immediate appointment of a principal assistant mistress of good secondary school experience, who would become the headmistress of the new school. Hence the title of the 'Kesteven and Grantham Girls' Grammar School'.[24] A former pupil who became the country's first woman Prime Minister, Margaret Thatcher (née Roberts) opened a major extension to the school in 1986.

PROBLEMS IN ELEMENTARY SCHOOLS BETWEEN THE WARS

The twenty years between the wars were nationally years of both agricultural and industrial depression; it was financially a most difficult time for local authorities. It does, however, represent the transition from the period before 1920 in which only in Grimbsy were a few 'elementary' school pupils educated in a senior school, to the position in 1940 when all LEAs had accepted central government policy that senior schools should be provided for children over the age of eleven. Additionally, there was the deplorable condition of many buildings, a black list of which was drawn up in 1925 by HM Inspectors.

The minutes of a Lindsey Advisory Committee meeting in 1925 show some of the other matters that concerned the LEAs such as teaching methods, the scholarship examination, and new problems like the mid-day meal and the library service, use of slates, and this new thing, the gramophone.

At a meeting of the Advisory Sub-Committee, held at the Offices of the Committee, on Friday, the 13th February, 1925.
Present: Sir Thomas Robinson KBE (Chairman), Alderman W. Grant, The Rev. W. Brown, Mrs M. Borrill, Miss B. Meek, and Messrs. A. Jackson, J. A. Staley, E. Surridge, and W. O. Steele.

1. Supply of Elementary School Materials—The Sub-Committee considered questions relating to Elementary School Supplies and Materials. It was Resolved to recommend as follows:-
(a) That the use of slates be discontinued as soon as possible in all Schools and that rough scribbling paper be used instead.
(b) That the Managers and Head Teachers be authorised to dispose of worn-out books and materials by the best means available, provided that a list of things to be so disposed of or destroyed is first submitted to the Education Office.
(c) That an additional allowance be made for the purchase of needlework materials, the allowance to be at the rate of 1s. 6d. per child taking the subject in each school, this allowance to be in addition to the ordinary allowance

of 4s. per child for books, stationery and other school materials.

2. County Scholarship Scheme—The Sub-Committee considered questions arising on the County Scholarship Scheme. Certain criticisms were made, viz:-

(a) Supervision is not always thoroughly satisfactory.

(b) The two days' examination is too long.

(c) The presentation of all children of the required age group should not be compulsory.

(d) Special cramming for the examination should be debarred.

After full discussion, no definite resolutions were passed, but the Inspector was asked on his visits to Schools to give the Head Teachers to understand that no teacher may set aside a special Scholarship Class.

3. County Library Scheme—The Sub-Committee considered the County Library Scheme, and how far this will meet the need for School Libraries and for books of reference for use of the teachers. It was decided to defer consideration until experience has been gained of the working of the County Library Scheme.

4. Schemes of Work and Time Tables—The Sub-Committee considered the method of preparing and submitting Schemes of Work and Time Tables. It was suggested that a simpler and clearer form of Time Table might be used than that at present supplied. It was resolved that Mr. Twidale be asked to prepare a form of Time Table which he regards as suitable.

5. Methods of Teaching—The Sub-Committee discussed at some length methods of teaching, more especially individual methods such as the Dalton Plan, and the instruction of the older scholars. It was pointed out by Head Teachers that individual methods require more books than can be supplied from the ordinary allowance made by the Committee. It was generally felt that there should be no definite adoption of the Dalton Plan, but that the individual method, more especially among the older children, should be encouraged, and it was explained that in Schools where a special case can be made out, it may be possible to make a grant for the purchase of books somewhat in excess of the ordinary allowance.

6. Organisation of Schools—The Sub-Committee discussed the Board of Education Circular 1350 and the organisation of Schools, more especially the question whether the ordinary division in departments of boys, girls, and infants, is the best plan, or whether the organisation as Junior and Senior Schools with a dividing line at 11 years of age is to be preferred. Considerable difference of opinion was manifested, and it was decided to suggest to the Teachers' organisations that the question should be discussed at some of their meetings, in order that the views of large numbers of those engaged in teaching may be obtained.

7. Board of Education Circular 1340—The Sub-Committee considered Board of Education Circular 1340, by which the Board desire to encourage the retention of children at the Elementary School beyond the age of 14. No resolution was passed.

8. Seating Accommodation for Older Children—The question of suitable seating accommodation for older children was raised, some members of the Sub-Committee expressing the view that for the top class in large Schools containing ex-standard scholars, single locker desks should be provided.

Resolved that the Education Committee be recommended to consider applications for locker desks from schools where there are suitable arrangements for older scholars.

9. Children Remaining on School Premises for Mid-day Meal—The Sub-Committee considered the question of arrangements for the care and supervision of children remaining on the school premises for the mid-day meal. It is well known that in many schools considerable groups of children come from long distances and remain on the premises often without proper care and supervision. The arrangements made at Habrough, Kirton Lindsey and other schools were described, and it was explained that where Managers and Head Teachers can report suitable arrangements, the Committee are prepared to provide the necessary utensils, and, if necessary, to pay for supervision.

10. Method of Payment of Salaries—The subject of the method of payment of salaries in Elementary Schools was introduced, but no definite amendment of the Committee's regulations was suggested.

11. Use of Gramophones—The Sub-Committee discussed the use of gramophones in Schools. The view was expressed that the educational value of this instrument has not yet been sufficiently demonstrated to justify purchase from public funds, but it was thought that in any case where a full scheme for using a gramophone in connection with the school curriculum is prepared, the matter should have consideration by the Committee.

12. School Year—There was discussion on the question whether the Elementary School year should be made to end on the 31st day of July instead of on the 31st of March, as at present. No resolution was passed, but it was suggested that the question is one which might be discussed at the Teachers' Association.

But what was it like in the schools? The St Faith's Schools have already been mentioned and we have a picture of the Infants' School in about 1925, perhaps typical of town schools at this time:

One small room was an office for the Headmistress, where she met parents and welcomed new children, and which was also used for medical examinations when the school nurse came to test our ears, eyes, and teeth, look at our tonsils, and search our hair for nits. Another slightly larger room had a class for the newcomers (or the 'babies'), and the third, a larger room divided by a green curtain held two other classes, each of which could hear what the other class was doing throughout the day. The rooms were high and rather cold in winter when they were heated by large iron stoves fuelled with coke and surrounded by high metal fireguards, where wet socks and pants were often left to dry on a rainy day or if some small person had had 'an accident'. The windows were high up in the wall and nothing of the outside world could be seen but the colour of the sky.

The two younger classes were furnished with tiny chairs and small tables for two, but the 'top' class had long heavy iron-framed desks screwed to the floor. These had wooden seats and tops that were hinged to make it easier for the caretaker to clean. These desks were old, with seats that seemed full of splinters and tops that were so grooved and gnarled that it was difficult to write on them without a hard flat surface. The walls were green, pale green distemper above, and a dark painted dado below. The whole school smelt always of chalk dust, coke fumes, plasticine, and unwashed clothes and bodies .... The school population was very mixed, like the part of the city it served, which included professional families from West Parade and Ashlin Grove, skilled working class families who were in the majority, and the ragged poor from the notorious slum known as 'Waterside', from houseboats on the Brayford Pool, and a few strange families from the brickyards across the West Common.[25]

A view of rural elementary schols can be presented by random quotations from a school log book. Many survive for this period and have yet to be used for systematic studies. This comes from Gedney Dyke School in the fens of Holland.[26]

21 June 1875. Opened this school for first time. 23 this week. Found children very ignorant, not one knows all the letters in the alphabet nor yet one that can make either a letter or a figure.
6 November 1912. Commenced teaching compound multiplication to Standard II.
10 July 1914. This school has been awarded the Rural Infants Challenge Shield having made the highest percentage of attendance for the last year [N.B. The Rural Senior Challenge Shield was also won in 1915].
10 January 1927. J. R. McKnight [the Chief Education Officer] visited the school this morning.
13 September 1937. Four water closets have been fitted for us; central heating installed; school painted inside and out; yard repaired.
29 January 1945. Temperature was only 35 degrees in the Infants Room at 9.30 this morning.

The Reports of HM Inspectors are copied into the log book; in 1927:

The teacher of this little school retires soon after a faithful and useful service of some 20 years. The older children read with fluency and understanding and can express themselves sensibly in writing though their work in this respect is somewhat dilatory .... On the whole the teacher will leave children who have made a good start with the rudiments and who are cheerful and well mannered'.

Were these few years the golden age of the village school? The schoolmaster and schoolmistress, qualified or not, usually lived in the village, and were the respected source of knowledge and wisdom in their community. Pupils were taught the three Rs and might go on nature rambles in a familiar countryside. But many village schools had changed little since 1903: two classrooms in a building dating from the last century, two teachers (probably one, even both unqualified), earth closets at the bottom of the playground, heating from a tortoise stove, a blackboard and easel, a map of the world, an untunable piano, and a timetable approved and signed by HM Inspector were the common scene. Many children had a long walk to school in all weathers; the big boys sat at the back waiting to leave and work on the farms; girls could look forward to little more than staying at home or going into service; holidays were made to coincide with harvests, especially potato-lifting. Few escaped to the local grammar school at ten or eleven.

Meanwhile there was the question of the black list. In 1925 HM Inspectors had drawn up lists of 'worst buildings' in their areas 'as material for practical discussion'. Education committees, and especially managers of voluntary schools, found it hard to meet the standards of accommodation and staffing now set by the Board of Education. At a special meeting of the Kesteven Education Committee the Chief Education Officer pointed out that the necessary improvements could only be achieved either by increasing expenditure or by closing small schools. HMI Quilter informed the meeting that, for example, there were 88 rooms in Kesteven which required partitions, many schools required improved sanitary accommodation, larger and better ventilated cloakrooms, and some a water supply.[27] In July of the same year Holland was facing the same kind of problems, with 21 schools on the black list, one incapable of improvement, the rest only suitable with improvements and/or lower numbers.[28] All authorities were to be haunted for years by this spectre of bad school buildings.

SENIOR ELEMENTARY SCHOOLS — HADOW REORGANIZATION

The Board of Education was urging authorities to reorganize elementary schools but not having much success in rural areas. In 1925 Circular 1350 spoke of a dividing line at eleven and of separate junior and senior schools. Then in 1926 came the Hadow Report on the education of the adolescent; all children should have an appropriate secondary education, but this was at that time interpreted as an extension and development of the existing system of central senior schools under the elementary code. These would be different from, but not inferior to, the grammar schools, which would continue unchanged.

As early as 1923, indeed, Lincoln had started a scheme of reorganization, the Director, R. C. Minton, arguing for proper grading to provide efficient advanced instruction, irrespective of religious denomination. Enquiry and examination would produce three grades of children: those capable of a grammar school course, those for whom instruction in a central school was suitable, and a minority who would be retained in existing schools or who would join a special class.[29] Thus Lincoln started an emphasis on grading which continued for many years. The provision of the central senior schools was the nub of the problem and the city education committee intended an equitable distribution of pupils between four council and five voluntary (essentially Church) schools. This scheme was put into operation, but ten years later the Church could not maintain two of its schools and there was only one Voluntary Aided Church of England Secondary Modern school after 1944 (St Andrew's).

Grimsby had 3,300 children in seven senior schools by 1932, while at the opposite end of the spectrum was Boston with no senior school at that date. Other than the two county boroughs, Boston was the only town then shouldering the responsibility for elementary education. Boston and Grantham had both chosen to adopt these powers under Part III of the 1902 Act, but Grantham had relinquished these in 1920. In this first phase, the state of elementary education in the county area of Holland was much the same as in Boston, only Donington and Crowland having separate schools for senior pupils. Kesteven had senior schools in Bourne and Sleaford, and Lindsey had some six or seven central schools in the towns of Scunthorpe, Cleethorpes and Gainsborough.

Kesteven and Lindsey had many small village schools, more so than Holland, reflecting the pattern of population, but the problem was not only one of size. Managers of village schools also had to be convinced that the new idea of collecting the older children into a separate school was a good plan in itself. They did not like losing the older children from their school, bus journeys were long and the children could not get home for dinner. In many cases managers objected to children being taken away from a Church school to a council school.

This combination of difficulties and objections held up rural reorganisation, and Kesteven had opened no rural central schools by 1940, although plans had been passed in 1939 for the erection of six new schools for seniors. In Holland at this time, there were still only Crowland and Donington with senior central schools, but in Lindsey, in addition to almost complete provision of senior places in Scunthorpe,[30] six rural senior schools had been opened before the outbreak of war and two more had been approved.

The distinctive form of these new, exciting schools can still be discerned within later accretions: an open court surrounded on three sides by classrooms, with a hall on the fourth side (Fig. 8.5). Yet a citizen of Louth criticized the plan for the new Monks Dyke School in the town as 'more like a seaside pavilion than anything hitherto regarded as a school'.[31] Such new schools sold more easily to managers and parents the idea of the central provision of 'elementary' education for children of 11–14. When they saw what others had, they wanted the same in their own area. Moreover, at Alford, which had the first school of this type in Lindsey, the headmaster, Alec Moore, made sure that everyone in the area and further afield knew what was going on, and in particular he provided a hot meal each day at the price of 3d.

GROWTH OF GRAMMAR SCHOOLS

Grammar schools, it will be recalled, had entered the period before the first world war in fitful health, with provision for girls still lacking. The story between the wars is one of gradual but firm growth, as at Bourne, and of new schools such as those at Skegness and Scunthorpe, the 'new towns' of Lindsey, or where there was still a need to provide for girls. New High Schools for girls were opened at Brigg (1919), Spalding, Gainsborough, Lincoln South Park (1920), Boston (1921) and Cleethorpes (1926). At Scunthorpe the new mixed secondary school in Doncaster Road, later renamed the Grammar School, was opened by Lady Astor in 1927, but suffered from competition with the old and more established boys' grammar school in nearby Brigg.[32] In Lincoln, the City School began in 1896 as a Science Day School, using the premises of the forerunner of the Technical College, which stood empty by day. Its numbers went from 24 in 1896 to 153 in 1905 and rose rapidly after the first world war to 370. At the end of the thirties the numbers had risen to 430 and the curriculum had so broadened that when in 1931 the school obtained a governing body separate from the Technical College and the School of Art, it was renamed the City School, and was in effect a boys' grammar school, but with a scientific and technical bias.[33]

Numbers generally had risen; in 1903 the 26 rather struggling schools had few more than a total of 1,000 pupils, mostly boys. By 1920 numbers had risen to over 5,600 of whom more than 2,500 were now girls. There were over 600 boarders. Numbers continued to rise and in 1939 there were about 7,500 pupils in the schools.

More pupils meant more accommodation, which the foundation governors of endowed schools funded with difficulty, yet many schools can show new building of this time. Most grammar schools in Lincolnshire in this period were two-form entry schools, one form of scholarship or free-place pupils, the other of fee-payers.

The Board of Education in London, as their Reports show, and the Education Committees in Lincolnshire were concerned mainly with methods of admission and the scholarship examination, with fees, free places and parental contributions, and with the school certificate examinations. They did not interfere much, if at all, with the running of the schools, which was left to Governors, who left it to the heads.

Fig. 10.8 Pupils of the senior section of Ingham County School in March 1956, on their transfer from this all-age school to Sturton-by-Stow Secondary Modern School. With an age span only a little older than that of the Marshchapel children (Fig. 10.2), the Ingham children seem much more sophisticated, a point especially noticeable in the girls' hair styles. **Source:** *Lincolnshire Echo.*

1944 EDUCATION ACT AND DEVELOPMENT PLANS

Amidst the difficulties of the 1939–45 war came the Butler Education Act of 1944, the basis of the remarkable educational developments of the last thirty years of our period. Under the 'control and direction' of the Minister, the local education authorities were charged with the responsibility of securing adequate provision for the physical, mental, moral, and spiritual development of their pupils in three successive stages – primary, secondary, and further education. Although it did not specify any particular organization, the Act provided for free secondary education for all and for a longer school life. It provided more comprehensively than ever before for handicapped pupils, school dental services, school meals, transport, and grants to pupils and students. There was no limit to the optimism of the architects of the 1944 Act and they drew a blueprint for a continuously expanding range of educational opportunity for everyone from early to later years of life.

Development plans had been prepared before, for example, after the 1918 and 1936 Acts, but none so thoroughly or idealistically as those now required. This is a point where tribute can be paid to chairmen, like Francis Raby of Lindsey, and education officers who spent so much time and effort in preparing their plans in the immediate post-war years when their staffs were not at full strength and an education office was much less populated than it was thirty years later.

In Holland, Sam Newson's job as director was to complement existing grammar schools with a range of secondary modern schools, of which none had been built before the war; each secondary modern school was to have five acres for agriculture and horticulture. (Fig. 10.8 shows senior pupils who would transfer to a new secondary modern school.)

Kesteven's great problem, as we have already seen, was small villages and therefore small primary schools. Under its Director Dr. T. W. P. Golby, 'It was decided that small schools should be retained as primary schools where they could be conducted efficiently and with reasonable economy because of their value to village life as a whole'.[34] When the plan was finally approved in 1951, the astonishing number of 71 out of its 120 primary schools were to be single-class schools for the 5–11 age range. In Lindsey the long struggle to remove senior pupils from every one of the all-age village shools did not end until the opening by the Director, John Birkbeck, of a two-form entry secondary school at North Somercotes in 1964, a small school that immediately created problems for comprehensive reorganization in the Louth area. One of the features of Grimsby, whose Director was Dr P. E. Richardson, was the rapid growth of the borough to the south and west, with a consequent need to keep up with the demand for school places, despite the Ministry's need to see 'children on the ground' before approving plans. In Lincoln (where C. W. Hooton was followed by A. Sutcliffe as Director) there were geographical problems with sites for new schools and difficulties arising out of the voluntary status of several secondary and grammar schools.[35]

Published development plans brought a degree of reason and order to the scene, but they were over-idealistic and had to be altered immediately, under the influence of two problems not foreseen. The government could not keep up with the financial demand made upon it and the numbers of children grew far more rapidly than expected. Raising the school leaving age in 1947 from fourteen to fifteen added an extra age group mostly outside the grammar schools, and this problem was soon followed by the baby-boom of the post-war years, known then as the 'bulge'. This was a flood of about five-years' duration which worked its way up through the school system, but not evenly across the county, since families in new housing estates were families with young children of school age. Peak numbers occurred in primary schools about 1956, in secondary schools in 1961 (see Fig. 2.6). In 1949 there were 96,403 children in the schools of Lincolnshire. By 1974 the total had climbed to 159,576, an increase of 65.5 per cent in 25 years.

GROWTH OF PRIMARY SCHOOLS

Changes in this thirty-year period were great: buildings changed in design and standard; teachers, required in increasing numbers, became more professional and better qualified; children changed as well, better fed, better clothed and more active; teaching methods changed, standards of work improved, despite comments from ill-informed critics. It is difficult to generalize further: at one end of the range there were urban primary schools with 300 children, sometimes in brand new buildings, while in the country could still be found one-teacher schools in decrepit old buildings.

In the sizable towns, new two-form entry infant and two-form entry junior schools were built to cater for the primary age span from five to eleven. A common plan consisted of a central assembly hall, usually doubling as a gymnasium and dining space, with eight large classrooms, two off at each corner. Ancillary rooms such as cloakrooms and staffrooms were better than ever before. Classes in the early post-war years were desperately large but the rooms were light, the school brightly decorated, and playgrounds and playing fields capable of intensive use.

By the sixties, teachers, advisory officers and architects were working together to bring in modifications to create 'groups of teaching spaces'. such as those for private study, or for practical work, and a library.[36] At this time the second bulge in numbers in the primary schools was taking all available money, but by the early seventies it had passed through, and government policy now put a greater emphasis on replacement and major improvement projects. Unfortunately Lincolnshire, where building costs had been relatively modest, suffered significantly from increases in these costs, and a school built in 1974 was not so fortunate as one built even in 1970.

As regards staff in 1944, Lindsey was probably typical of many rural areas in that more than half the teachers in primary schools were 'uncertificated' or 'supplementary', even thirty-eight schools had headteachers who were unqualified: it was unusual to find unqualified staff in secondary schools.[37] The situation was transformed, both in quantity and quality of staff, by the more generous ratios regulated by a quota system, and by the efforts of teacher-training colleges such as the Kesteven College of Education at Stoke Rochford, near Grantham (closed in the late seventies), and Bishop Grosseteste College in Lincoln.

Teaching staff in the village schools were less lonely than in the past, when the parson (especially in Church schools) and the school attendance officer were the only regular visitors and HM Inspector might call once a year. After the war, a growing number of advisory officers visited schools, and chief education officers were now personally known to many teachers. Many courses were run, and by the end of the period teachers' centres and a positive programme of in-service education had brought most teachers into contact with new ideas and good practices. In 1967, the Plowden Report brought many of the new developments together and boldly classified schools according to their success in adopting the accepted philosophy of promoting active learning by children instead of their being passively taught. Were most Lincolnshire schools among those placed in such middle categories as 'good without special distinction', 'a decent school', and 'a school with good and bad features'?[38]

The closure of schools, especially in small villages, was a fact of the whole of the period examined in this chapter, but between 1948 and 1974 the need became more urgent, with 124 closures within the area administered by the new Lincolnshire County Council, and proportionately fewer in south Humberside, owing to its more populous nature. They were distributed as follows: Holland 19; Kesteven 37; Lindsey south of South Humberside 68.[39] Although the development plans had underlined the difficulties of small schools, there had been a declared intention to keep most of them open, as in Kesteven. As the depopulation of small villages and hamlets continued after the 1939-45 war, in some areas numbers were so reduced that closure could no longer await teacher retirements and general consensus; now the education committees faced the problem squarely in the late 1960s, knowing that it was very much a political issue. They set out to establish a new pattern of rural schools suitable for the late twentieth century.[40] (Fig. 10.6 gives a picture in the Louth area.)

In Kesteven, immediate concern was concentrated on the existing one-teacher schools, of which there were now 34, with 21 others on the one/two-teacher borderline. The final sentence of a report submitted in December 1968 said: 'It would seem that the financial saving now possible if all the one-teacher schools were to be closed would be of the order of £37,000 to £48,000 per annum'. Such reports were the subject of wide public disagreement, not least with some of the assumptions underpinning the financial calculations. In the event, Kesteven closed 21 schools immediately, 15 were recommended for closure as soon as arrangements could be made to accommodate the children elsewhere, and decisions on a further 17 were held in abeyance.[41]

In retrospect, this unhappy and protracted business was only the beginning of a long and difficult story which continues, with the difference, however, that there has been a great improvement in the quality and numbers of staff. Indeed, redundancy of teachers has been added to the problems with which the education authorities have had to grapple.

GRAMMAR SCHOOLS AND AUTHORITIES

The story of the grammar schoools after 1944 can usefully be introduced through the recollections of Hedley Warr, who was headmaster of King Edward VI Grammar School, Louth, from 1941 to 1958. A bachelor, he took over both the boarding house and the school; boarders were down to a dozen but the school was rising to 250. He found a timetable in pencil in a mark book, unchanged for some years. At first, he himself taught for 26 periods a week, not now the normal practice of heads in comparable schools. He saw himself as

housemaster, as a teacher, and, if there were time, as a headmaster. The staff was not a strong one; there was a lack of dynamism and most had been at the school a long time; but they were loyal and kind, both to me and their pupils. The boys – and it is they who make a school – were a fine lot; a few clever, most hardworking, polite and gentle; toughs and hooligans conspicuous by their absence. Lincolnshire people do not effervesce; they keep their feet firmly on the ground.[42]

Warr retired in 1958 and by that time the grammar schools, not least his own, had moved firmly into a new phase. All entrants to the school were now selected on merit; numbers rose and forms were overfull; sixth forms grew substantially both in numbers and in the range of subjects. The variety and extent of activities outside the classroom grew and grew.

The development of the grammar schools may be seen in two phases. Up to 1965 most areas were content with their separate grammar and modern schools. There was dissatisfaction where a secondary modern school was below standard in premises or teaching, but there was little vocal criticism on grounds of educational principle. After 1965, the county divided into a comprehensive north and a southern half that defiantly maintained bipartite selective sympathies.

In the total of 35 grammar schools, 18 (the older schools) were voluntary schools and the 1944 Act gave these the choice of independent, direct grant or maintained status. None went independent, putting Lincolnshire in a minority of counties in this respect. Only two schools, Stamford School and Stamford Girls' High School, chose direct grant status, so receiving the bulk of their funds direct from the Ministry of Education, with consequent independence from the LEA. The foundation governors of the 16 other voluntary schools, less well-endowed, had therefore a choice within the maintained system between voluntary aided and voluntary controlled status.

Aided status made the governors responsible for the provision of all new buildings, in return offering greater independence, but only Lincoln School, Christs Hospital Girls High School in Lincoln, and Spalding Grammar School so opted. Apart from King Edward VI Girls' Grammar School in Louth, all other girls' grammar schools were of more recent foundation and were among the 17 County schools. These niceties of status, reflecting the varied historical fortunes of different schools and the growth of population, rather than the educational activities of staffs and pupils, were yet to play a part in the later negotiations on the comprehensive reorganization of secondary education. In Grimsby the old Grammar School, the preserve of the borough freemen, had closed and the pace was set by the two former higher elementary schools, now the Winteringham Grammar Schools, boys and girls.[43]

There was generous provision of grammar school places and, until the post-war bulge in births hit the secondary schools in 1958, there were few areas where 25 per cent, or even more, of an age group were not admitted. For girls, however, owing to the adjustments to 11-plus scores needed because of earlier maturity, competition was apparently stiffer than for boys. Numbers in the grammar schools increased because of large age groups and real growth in sixth forms. These growing sixth form groups were nourished with great devotion and ingenuity: somehow staff found the time and the spare corners, so that in the earlier years two or three sixth formers could be helped in their A level subjects.

In 1960 the numbers in the Brigg and Caistor Grammar Schools and the De Aston School at Market Rasen were carefully examined in the context of future development. With great reluctance the Lindsey Education Committee proposed to the full council that the problem could best be solved by closing Caistor Grammar Schoool, founded in 1630. This proposal produced a memorable protest; on the night before 19 February 1961 when the council were to meet to consider the recommendation, boys and girls from the school marched overnight 25 miles through snow to the county offices in Lincoln. They could surely claim that their petition swayed the Council's decision that morning in their favour.[44]

At North Hykeham, the situation was the reverse of that at Caistor; here a large and expanding suburban population had no secondary grammar or modern school nearer than Sleaford; schools in Lincoln and Newark, though nearer to the childrens' homes, were outside the authority's area. The solution was the building of the Robert Pattinson School as a bilateral school, but when a second school was needed, this became a secondary modern school, and the new school was built as a grammar school. Both became comprehensive schools after 1970, in the second change of policy within a decade.

LINDSEY COUNTY COUNCIL

EDUCATION COMMITTEE

Examination for Junior Scholarships and Exhibitions

MARCH 12th, 1924

ARITHMETIC

Time — 1¾ hours

*Do not attempt more than **eight** questions*

1. Find the total of the following:

tons	cwts.	qrs.	lbs.
62	7	3	2
7	18	1	19
32	13	2	12
4	4	0	21
25	17	3	27

2. Find the least number which when divided by 16, 42, 63, or 72 will leave a remainder of 1.

3. A boy bought a penknife for 2s. 6d. and afterwards exchanged it for 9d. and 210 marbles. How much did he lose supposing the marbles were worth 1d. per dozen?

4. Find the cost of 7 chests of tea each containing 2 qrs. 10 lbs. at £6 2s. 6d. per cwt.

5. How many telegraph poles will be required to support a length of wire 14 miles 3 furlongs 5 chains if the poles are 99 feet apart?

6. A clock loses 5 seconds every 32 minutes. At 10 p.m. on Saturday it is a quarter of an hour fast. When will it be at exactly the right time?

7. If it costs £4 6s. 8d. to feed 13 horses for a week, how much will it cost to feed 3 horses for a year at the same rate?

[Turn over

Fig. 10.9 The first page of the scholarship paper for children in 1924.

Intended at first as a qualifying examination, the process of selection soon became highly competitive even before 1944; the large town junior schools streamed their pupils and vied with each other in the number of scholarships won each year; scholarship winners might pose for special group photographs; in some small country schools a scholarship won was a rare event, to be remembered and recorded in the log book, even on an honours board; there were congratulatory messages in the local press (Fig. 10.9).

The 1944 Act formally set education out into three main stages: primary, secondary, and further; and at the secondary stage it was inevitably selective, in order to match pupils of different aptitude and ability to suitable schools. The authorities took immense pains over their chosen methods of selection for secondary schools. The techniques of balancing actual attainment on a particular day with a child's potential, of assessing the value of coaching and the effects of good and bad schools, queries about age allowance and subjective marking, the value of personal interviews became the subject of academic study and of pragmatic adjustments. Teachers' estimates of pupils' potential had been taken into account in Lincoln as early as 1936. Arthur Sutcliffe and his colleague J. W. Canham produced a method whereby heads' views were quantified, even calibrated, and taken into account.[45] In Lindsey more use was made of teachers' panels, one for each grammar school, to see and then consider the merits of borderline cases. This seemed to be a good method, and it had the merit of creating better relationships between primary and both kinds of secondary schools, which were effective in the wider educational progress of the area.[46]

SECONDARY MODERN SCHOOLS – PARITY OF ESTEEM

We have seen the results of the 1944 Act in terms of selection for grammar school education. But what of those children who were not selected, those who failed the 11-plus examination? As before the 1939-45 War, many living in villages were destined to stay in all-age elementary schools until they reached the leaving age of 15, although for a very few, as for their town counterparts, there might be the prospect of a technical college at 15 or 16. In the first twenty years after the war, the main problems were to find the resources to build the new secondary modern schools, first in expanding urban areas and then in rural areas, and to give all secondary modern schools, wherever they were, parity of esteem with the grammar schools – and authorities differed in their policies, sometimes quite sharply.

Lincoln was distinctive in its policy towards the secondary modern schools. Here, it has been argued, there was positive discrimination against these schools. The 1944 Act stipulated that, in principle, authorities were to provide three types of secondary education: grammar, technical, and modern. In practice rural authorities, along with many county boroughs, provided their technical strand within the walls of secondary modern schools. However, owing to the strong views of Arthur Sutcliffe, previously head of the City School, now chief education officer, not only were there to be no technical schools, even though the distribution of population and school buildings would have allowed this, but also money was spent on technical facilities in the grammar schools. The secondary modern schools were, moreover, starved of the graded posts needed to attract the best staff and did not even know the full extent of their allowances. Consequently, the policy of the education committee was not to provide for external examinations in the secondary modern schools.[47]

The distribution of population, together with the pre-existing pattern of senior schools, gave rise to three broadly contrasting situations in the period 1944-65: older senior schools in the main urban centres, often much in need of improvement; new secondary modern schools in areas of growing urban and suburban population; and small new rural secondary schools to take the senior children from the all-age village schools.

Small secondary modern schools in places such as Billinghay, Stickney, North Somercotes and Crowland can be seen as a continuation of the process of providing education that was understood by and acceptable to parents and managers of village schools. The complete subordination of large areas of countryside to a few major centres, now obviously a more logical policy in terms of later requirements to 'go comprehensive', would probably not have been acceptable in the early post-war period. A new, purpose-built secondary school brought new life and a greater stature to the major villages chosen. The schools provided a friendly and happy atmosphere, though they lacked some stimuli and excitements and could be limited in curriculum. The teachers were not always highly qualified, but they lived in and knew well the places where their pupils lived.

While government policy required the elimination of all-age elementary schools, it also provided money for what was known as 'roofs over heads', the building of new secondary schools in areas of increasing population such as North Hykeham, the greater Grimsby area, and Scunthorpe.

The latter was such an important area of growth that it became the only 'Excepted District' in Lincolnshire. Under the 1944 Act, the Isle of Axholme, Winterton, and Scunthorpe had for a few years a Divisional Executive made up of representatives of the borough council, the rural districts, and the county council. This measure of delegation suited a situation where on average one new school was opened each year throughout the 1950s as new estates filled up rapidly with youthful households. Then in 1961 the borough won still greater delegated powers as an Excepted District. The teachers in Scunthorpe were very active, aimed high and gave a good lead to their colleagues in the rest of Lindsey, but Scunthorpe also took a very fair share of the available county resources. The Borough Education Officer was able to report in 1974 that only 32 per cent of pupils were in schools built before 1939 (this included several built only just before that date), whilst 68 per cent were in post-war schools.

Elsewhere, many children of secondary age were still being taught in National and Board Schools of the Victorian period. The problem of suitable accommodation was probably most severe in the first generation of senior or central schools built in the central areas of the larger towns, such as Elliston Street Boys School, Cleethorpes, Ropery Road School in Gainsborough, and St Andrew's in Lincoln. Laboratories and practical rooms were so poor that some children had to go to other schools for woodwork or housecraft lessons, a strange irony, since their own schools had been originally built to provide a practical education. Some schools were renamed but not refurbished.

Nevertheless the period up to 1965 saw, overall, much progress towards parity of esteem with the grammar schools, or at least a narrowing of the former gaps. This was despite severe shortages of staff in the practical subjects on which secondary schools were intended to place an emphasis. In new schools especially, replete with the latest equipment, new heads and their staffs were able to combine with local enthusiasm and pride to stimulate the work and activities of the school: foreign travel, field work, and school orchestras, dramatic performances, and swimming were no longer the preserve of the grammar schools. The secondary modern schools had been able to move a significant distance towards meeting the increased expectations of children and parents. At the turn of the century about half the girls leaving school had remained at home to help, while 40 per cent had gone into domestic service. Half the boys had gone on to a farm.[49] Now the youth employment service helped pupils, with their new qualifications and livelier attitudes, to go for jobs and careers their parents could not have contemplated.

REORGANIZATION ON COMPREHENSIVE LINES

Before this period of growth and experiment had run its course, the comprehensive argument hit the secondary schools. Indeed, in some authorities, comprehensive reorganization was either complete or well under way before 1965, when the Labour government issued Circular 10/65, stating the 'declared objective to end selection at 11 plus and to eliminate separatism in secondary education', and requiring plans within a year for reorganizing secondary education in all areas on comprehensive lines.

Schools in Grimsby and many in that part of Lindsey to form South Humberside were already reorganized or about to be reorganized on orthodox comprehensive lines, but to the south it was very different. Seven years later, in 1972, the Chief Education Officers of Lincoln, Kesteven, Holland and Lindsey sat down to prepare for the new Lincolnshire and, amongst many other matters, to review the pattern of secondary education. It was indeed varied, if not a hotchpotch. Lincoln was in the process of creating a scheme of middle schools with transfer to comprehensive secondary schools at age 12; Holland though still to be bipartite (grammar and modern) in 1974 was also now committed to a middle school system. Kesteven was bipartite in all centres except for the comprehensive schools at North Hykeham, Branston and, in the south, at the Deepings; Lindsey contributed comprehensive schools around Lincoln and in the northern area; but elsewhere, from Gainsborough to Skegness, the pattern was still that of grammar and modern (see Fig. 10.7b).[50]

Why such variety? In all the five 1944 development plans, only Kesteven had actually included a bilateral school. The emergent variety derives from the complex nature of the county described in this book, from the pattern of population and from political developments. The general growth of education had largely been non-political but Circular 10/65 crystallized the thinking of the councils as had no other educational issue. The strong, apparently permanently Labour council in the borough of Scunthorpe, the alternating control by Labour and Conservative in Lincoln and Grimsby (with Labour in control in 1965) immediately produced firm moves towards comprehensive reorganization, but a consistent policy was difficult to maintain in the wake of Government circulars:

Circular 10/65 Labour: reorganize on comprehensive lines.

Circular 10/70 Conservative: no objection to going comprehensive.

Circular 4/74 Labour: Submit plans for comprehensive schools.

Education Act 1976 Labour: Direct Grant Schools abolished.

Education Act 1979 Conservative: no need to submit plans for comprehensive reorganization.

There had in fact been some movement before 1965. In Grimsby, despite the dominance of the Winteringham Grammar Schools, two large secondary schools had been imaginatively designed and opened as comprehensive schools. In Lincoln a decision was taken to plan a

Fig. 10.10 **The City School, Lincoln,** formerly a grammar school, now a modern comprehensive school, with large expanses of glass and extensive grounds for sport. See text p. 265. Source: Mr. J. Wilde.

large new secondary school as the Yarborough Comprehensive School. In Scunthorpe the Labour-controlled borough education committee had proposed, subject only to the county's final approval, a single sixth form college (16–18) making good use of excellent new school buildings, and six comprehensive schools (11–16). The newly arrived director of education for Lindsey, George Cooke, was faced with difficult problems here (as elsewhere in the county); the borough plan created problems in the rural area which had always looked to Scunthorpe grammar schools, but solutions were found and a plan was submitted to the Department by February 1966. There was also the threat, or hope, of vast expansion on the Humber Bank, even expectation of a new town, in which event the Lindsey Education Committee 'would be prepared from the outset to plan and develop a comprehensive system'.[51]

But three years before the issue of Circular 10/65, an interesting form of reorganization was being considered in the Louth area, the ideas coming from practical cooperation between the schools and not imposed from outside. Yet, in 1963 the Lindsey education committee turned down the Louth Plan, a scheme worked out by the teachers under the leadership of Donald Witney, head of the grammar school, and supported by the governors of all the schools concerned: all children would transfer at age 11 to two high schools (the existing secondary modern schools); three years later parents, with guidance from the schools, could ask, indeed require, that their children should transfer to the upper school (the existing grammar school). When the plan came before the full council in July 1963 the committees's views were reversed after a strong speech by the local councillor, Ralph Bennett, in favour of the governors' scheme, which was then successfully put into operation.[52]

In the south of Lindsey no schemes of comprehensive schools emerged. The pattern of grammar school and smallish modern schools in the rural areas had produced sets of buildings which could not possibly be brought together to make an effective comprehensive school. Equally in Kesteven and Holland no schemes of reorganization were proposed; perhaps some stubborn intention and policy in these decisions were to persist in the new Lincolnshire County Council.

The net result was that in 1974 over 80 per cent of all secondary pupils in the new county of Humberside were in comprehensive schools but in the new Lincolnshire 80 per cent were in grammar and modern schools with only 20 per cent in comprehensive schools. Fourteen years later the pattern remains much the same; pressure for the abolition of selection has somewhat abated but the whole question of secondary education is now, as in primary schools, bedevilled by the drastic fall in school rolls.

Bibliographical note

The material available for reference and research seems overwhelming. The library of the Department of Education and Science is, of course, a main collection on all aspects of education in Britain. The History of Education Society publishes a series of guides to sources in the history of education which includes, for example, no. 6, *Theses and dissertations on the history of education and British government publications concerning education ... 20th century.* There is also a monograph, 'Local history of education in England and Wales: a bibliography', by Peter Cunningham (University of Leeds).

But for Lincolnshire material there does not appear to be any main bibliography, and this note can only sketch out some of the main sources and deposits of records.

Local education authorities

For each authority there are minutes of councils, committees, subcommittees, and special committees; annual and special reports, correspondence, circulars to schools, development plans and plans of schools, legal documents. These are now chiefly deposited in the

Lincolnshire Archives Office (LAO), but material for the authorities now in Humberside may also be in the Grimsby Archive Office.

Schools

Histories have now been published by most of the ancient grammar schools and there is a growing number of accounts of many other schools, both primary and secondary. There is no bibliography, but the Lincoln Central Library has a card index of many.

But for each school there is a wealth of material in the form of log books, registers, and minutes of managers' and governors' meetings, together with reports and publications on special occasions. For schools that have now closed and for many others, the log books and other material will have been deposited in county archive offices.

Academic sources

Reference has been made to theses presented for higher degrees. Of special interest would be the theses presented by teachers in Lincolnshire schools, especially at Hull, Sheffield, Nottingham, and Leicester Universities, because they often took as their topics subjects directly related to the school or area in which they served.

Museums

As an example of the potential, see Fig. 10.1.

Notes to Chapter 10

1. Department of Education and Science, *Annual Report for 1950*.
2. Rex C. Russell, *History of schools and education in Lindsey Lincolnshire 1800–1902* (4 parts 1965, Lindsey County Council), pt. 3, p. 11; Joan Varley, *The Parts of Kesteven*, Kesteven County Council, 1974, p. 114.
3. *Grimsby Observer*, 29 April 1974, supplied by W. P. Knight.
4. W. P. Knight, thesis for M.Ed., 'Development of educational facilities in Grimsby 1871–1902', University of Leeds, 1967.
5. *Grimsby News*, 4 January 1901, from W. P. Knight.
6. Varley, op. cit., p. 114.
7. Lindsey County Council Minutes, 31 January 1903.
8. Russell, *op. cit.*, pt. 4.
9. Knight, *op. cit.* and A. Fisher, *History of education in Kirton Lindsey*, 1981, p. 72.
10. LAO, Lindsey County Council Papers, *Memorandum settled at a meeting of Educational Committee*, 31 Dec. 1902.
11. *ibid.*
12. Enquiry forms in Lindsey Education Committee Office.
13. LAO, S. R. Tetney, 4/1903/2.
14. LAO, Teacher applications Lindsey.
15. Knight, *op. cit.*, quoting PRO ED 53/366D.
16. D. Gowenlock, *St Faith's School*, June 1973. A picture of this school is given on p. 261 by a former pupil.

17. C. R. Burchenall, *The story of education and the schools of Deeping St James, 1957*.

18. Almost every grammar school now boasts a published history, for example: B. L. Deed, *A history of Stamford School*, 1954 and F. Henthorn, *The history of Brigg Grammar School 1919–69*, 1969.

19. D. I. A. Steel, *A Lincolnshire village*, Longman, 1979, chs. 6 and 7.

20. Brenda Parry-Jones, *Magdalen College School, Wainfleet*, Wainfleet Heritage Society, 1984.

21. Lindsey County Council Education Committee, *Report of the Higher Education Sub-Committee on secondary and higher education*, 1905 and M. E. Armstrong (ed.), *An industrial island: a history of Scunthorpe*, Scunthorpe Borough Museum and Art Gallery, 1981, pp. 90–5 and 161–6.

22. Report of HM Inspectors, 1904, copy from daughter of headmaster of the time, the Revd J. R. U. Elliott.

23. Lindsey Educational Committee Minutes 13 Sept. 1901; see also Sheila Fletcher, *Feminists and bureaucrats*, Cambridge UP, 1980, p. 167.

24. Kesteven Education Committee Minutes, 30 Jan. 1907 and later.

25. Private memoir, Miss Joyce Skinner, a former pupil of the school and Principal of Bishop Grosseteste College, Lincoln, 1964–74.

26. LAO, Holland, Gedney Dyke school log books.

27. Kesteven Education Committee, Elementary Sub-Committee Minutes, 13 May 1925.

28. Holland Education Committee, Education Works Sub-Committee Minutes, 7 July and 1 December 1925.

29. LAO, 1/2/23 Memorandum by Chief Education Officer on reorganization of schools, Lincoln City Education Committee, Finance & General Purposes Sub-committee.

30. Armstrong, *op. cit.*, p. 161. and Board of Education List 21, 1938.

31. *Louth Standard*, 4 April 1927, quoted in *Monks Dyke 1929–1979*.

32. Armstrong, *op. cit.*, p. 161.

33. The City School, *Lincoln Jubilee 1896–1946*, pp. 8–18.

34. Kesteven Development Plan; also quoted in address given in 1965 by Dr T. W. P. Golby, 'Twenty-two years of education in Kesteven'.

35. The development plans of all five LEAs are available. See also Board of Education White Paper, *Educational Reconstruction*, Cmd 6458 1943.

36. Lindsey Education Committee, *End of a chapter: Education in Lindsey 1970–74*, 1974.

37. Lindsey Education Committee, Minutes, 24 November 1944.

38. Plowden Report, *Children and their primary schools*, 1967, vol. 1, p. 106.

39. Lincolnshire Education Committee, Report by County Education Officer, 5 December 1978, *Small primary schools in rural areas*.

40. Lindsey Education Committee, Report by Director of Education, January 1970, *Reorganisation of primary education*.

41. P. J. Muskett, 'Village school closures in Kesteven 1949–79', M.Ed. thesis, University of Nottingham, 1979.

42. H. Warr, *Memoirs*, Cheltenham, 1979.

43. E. Gillett, *A history of Grimsby*, Oxford 1970, *passim*.

44. Lindsey County Council Minutes, 19 February 1961.

45. A. Sutcliffe and J. W. Canham, 'Selection without examination', *Education*, 24 June 1955, pp. 1157–8.

46. Lindsey Education Committee, *Report of Working Party on selection for secondary schools*, 1960.

47. E. Byrne, *Planning and educational inequality*, 1974.

48. See Armstrong, *op. cit.* and reports by Borough Education Officer, *Education in Scunthorpe 1961–74*.

49. Board of Education, *Employment on leaving school*, 1898. The figures exclude Grimsby but include the rest of the county.

50. Lincolnshire Education Topic 1.4 *Reorganisation of primary and secondary education* (Local Government Reorganization 1973).

51. Lindsey Education Committee, Memorandum by Director, *Organisation of secondary education*, 1966; Armstrong, *op. cit.*, p. 165.

52. Lindsey County Council Minutes, July 1963 and Memorandum by Director of Education, *Organisation of Secondary Education Oct. 1962*.

CHAPTER 11

CHURCHES AND RELIGIOUS LIFE

by Graham Neville

Abstract *This chapter is about much more than churches (includ-ing chapels) and religious life, for it manages to convey also something about changing lifestyles, and in particular the changes from peace to war, and from war to peace, which occurred twice over in the first half of the century. Indeed the chapter starts with a reference to that almost forgotten war in South Africa. The second section describes church life in peace time in both town and country in the early part of the century, followed by church life in the Great War. The inter-war period was one of structural adjustment, including the Methodist Union of three denominations effected in 1932. The second world war was followed by further development of local ecumenical relations, but the main post-war problem has been one of decline in church-going accom-panied by a serious shortage of clergy.*

The church calendar makes no special provision for the New Year, let alone for a new century. But when Dean Wickham preached his first sermon in the twentieth century, he naturally used the occasion for a little stocktaking of the previous hundred years.

We look back in this city, and see that it has grown in that time from a com-munity of 7,000 persons to one of 50,000. It should make us all ask ourselves whether the community has grown and is growing proportionately in public spirit and corporate life, in the general diffusion of comfort and well-being and self-respect among its citizens, whether in new churches and schools of every grade, in all humanizing appliances and institutions, in everything that can lift the lives and make decent and happy the homes of newcomers, ade-quate provision has been made and is being made for the increase of the population.[1]

He went on to emphasize the need for a sense of corporate respon-sibility in civic and national life at a time of increasing threat to the standards of Christian civilization. For the first time in almost fifty years the nation was engaged in a great war, in South Africa, with all that it meant in suffering and bereavement, while at home social life was marked by the pursuit of pleasure and the adulation of the wealthy. When peace came and was celebrated in the cathedral on 8 June 1902, the Dean rejoiced that war had ended with a negotiated peace and urged the need to use victory for the good of the vanquished. The issues of war and peace were never far from his consciousness. .

The death in 1910 of both Dean Wickham and Bishop King was a turning point in the history of the diocese. But already one of the recurrent themes of church life in the twentieth century had been heard: the theme of war and peace. Edward Lee Hicks, who succeeded as bishop, came to the diocese with a reputation for radical views. During the South African war he had been accused of being a pro-Boer. In the year of his consecration he became President of the Church of England Peace League and continued to hold that office until his death in 1919. In his Primary Visitation Charge, delivered in 1912, he began a survey of the problems confronting Christianity by asking: 'How are we to maintain peace and prevent war between the Christian nations of the West, now that the horrors and wastefulness of war are so much more serious and so much better understood than ever before?'[2]

It is often said that the outbreak of war in 1914 found the churches unprepared. If it was true in Lincolnshire, it was not for lack of prompting from the bishop. The diocese was spared the sight of its chief pastor in the guise of a recruiting officer. Indeed Hicks, though he groped his way to a view of the war which was not pacifist, took a deeply sympathetic interest in the sufferings of conscientious objectors. He housed Belgian refugees in the Palace for some months at the beginning of the war, and later handed it over to be used as a Red Cross Hospital; he went to live in the house of a Priest-Vicar away on military service.

The 1914–18 war affected the organization of the church in ways unknown in previous wars. The parishes were drained of men by conscription, and there were repeated calls for conscription to be extended to include clergy of military age. The Archbishop of Canterbury, Randall Davidson, set his face against any such move and emphasized the two-fold duty of the clergy, as chaplains to the forces and pastors of the civilian population under stress. Bishop Hicks was naturally in agreement with this policy. He was convinced that the clergy should not undertake combatant service, but encouraged them in a variety of forms of national service at home, and accepted the need for many of them to go overseas, without urging them to resign their benefices as some bishops did.[3] The Revd John Michael Stanhope Walker was one of a number of clergy from Lincolnshire who went to France as a chaplain. Within three months he had buried nine hundred men whilst ministering at a casualty clearing station, and his diary records the gruesome context of his work, from which he returned to his country parish, Kettlethorpe, disillusioned and disheartened. Hicks had given support to the war reluctantly. Other prominent churchmen in the diocese took a more militant stance. E. H. Holden wrote to the *Church Times* from Bishop's Hostel, Lincoln, on 23 August 1914 criticizing the complacency of the Football

Fig.11.1 St Peter's Church, Great Limber: the 1914-1918 war memorial corner, with photographs of the dead, still maintained in the 1980s. The popular pictures of 'The White Comrade' and 'The Great Sacrifice' give a religious interpretation to the death of individual soldiers, in contrast to memorials in other countries, where the emphasis is often on patriotic glory. The writings of the Revd G. A. Studdert Kennedy ('Woodbine Willie') popularized this view, especially among non-combatants. Other interpretations are embodied in the wording and symbolism of war memorials erected in churchyards and other public places. The now deserted churchyard at Thorpe-in-the-Fallows declares that the men of 1914–1918 gave their lives for liberty and equal rights (though it carefully records the distinctions of military rank in the names of the dead). A few memorials were put up while the war was still in progress; for example, a cross at Dalderby, erected in 1917 to honour the village from which a larger proportion of men joined up as volunteers than from any other village in England. Source: Graham Neville. Caption: personal observation, *Lincoln Diocesan Magazine*, Diaries of Bishop E. L. Hicks.

Association for beginning the football season as usual, and deploring the attitude of a mother who told her son he need not offer himself for military service because 'If they want him, they'll take him'.[4]

One immediate effect of the outbreak of war was the cancellation of arrangements for the Church Congress, to have been held in Lincoln, because the authorities thought it inadvisable to proceed. A more lasting effect was that large camps were quickly established to accommodate the new armies. Grantham became an important military centre and this inevitably increased the pastoral demands upon the vicar, the Revd W. I. Carr Smith, and the other clergy. The chaplains at Belton Park Camp used the church press to appeal for commendations of churchmen known to have been posted there.[5] At least one local clergyman served in its canteen, and the rector of Fulbeck made munitions in Grantham. Church buildings did not suffer any damage, as they were to do in the second world war, although bombs from a Zeppelin fell close to Scartho Church, as a memorial in the churchyard testifies. But it became more difficult to engage people's interest in their maintenance amid all the other more urgent calls upon their ability to give. For example, the beautiful chapel of St Leonard at the gate of Kirkstead Abbey, which had been too dangerous to use since the 1870s, had been restored and reopened in 1914, but already by the end of that year it was reported that subscriptions had declined.

When at last the war ended every parish turned its attention to commemorating those who had died on active service. Bishop Swayne, newly enthroned in succession to Bishop Hicks, had to remind parishes that memorials in church or churchyard required faculties for their erection, and gave a ruling that the names of living persons must not be included on memorials for the dead. They were of many different forms – an iron chancel screen, a stained glass window or tubular bells, as well as the usual inscribed tablets in church and churchyard crosses outside. They could be impressive and expensive, like the new Chapel of the Resurrection in Great Grimsby parish church, with its roll of over fifteen hundred names. They could be homely and moving, like the rows of little framed photographs of men in uniforms hanging at the back of Great Limber church with coloured pictures of 'The Great Sacrifice' and 'The White Comrade' (Fig 11.1).

THE CHURCHES IN EDWARDIAN LINCOLNSHIRE

To estimate the actual change in church life brought about by the war, we need a base-line from which to measure. Perhaps we find it in the picture of village life in the early years of the century, drawn with loving care and a mixture of realism and romanticism, in the writings of the Revd Richard Lawson Gales, vicar of Gedney 1909–27. The realism is evident in his descriptions of the bitter hardships of working people in the villages. In an essay with the title, 'Why are villages sleepy?', he gives his forthright answer.

The reasons villages are sleepy is because the farm labourers are wretchedly paid, miserably housed, and insufficiently fed. I confess to some impatience in reading in the daily press of a prize won by a farm labourer and his wife at the Lincoln Agricultural Show for bringing up a large family on low wages. People should not be encouraged to do this; they should be incited to demand higher wages. It was not stated what the prize was; possibly a sovereign. It was won by bringing up fifteen children on fifteen shillings a week. Eighteen children were born to the couple, but three of them lie in the churchyard. Of the fifteen living, the youngest is twenty. 'They have never been able to afford a holiday', says the Daily Mirror enthusiastically, 'but still are able to say, "We have nothing to grumble at."' In my own humble opinion, they have a very great deal to grumble at indeed.[6]

This kind-hearted country priest wrote with humble appreciation of 'the brave fight of the cottage woman', whose life is one of incredible monotony and day-long loneliness. In the same vein of realism he described the family feuds which embitter cottage life and invade the apparent calm of the church itself. But he also writes of 'the old objective Christianity, the dwelling on the facts of the Gospels, the deep reverence for the sacraments, the folk-lore of the Middle Ages' as not even yet extinct. In a perceptive discussion of 'The Piety of Simple People' he draws a distinction between the villagers' appreciation of the church's rites of passage and pride in the fabric of their ancient church on the one hand and their lack of interest in societies and training courses on the other. The parson's work is to christen and marry and bury. 'He is apt to be considered a troublesome busybody when urging them to attend meetings and join associations, the objects of which they apprehend but dimly, and the utility of which sometimes appears to them doubtful.' Non-attendance at church is no proof of indifference to what it stands for. They send the old people and the children as representatives to do the highest and fittest work they can perform.

A proper account of the countryman's religion in the early years of the century must include the major contribution made by Methodism in Lincolnshire. The original purpose of Methodist services had been to supplement, rather than to replace, those of the parish church. The vigour of Methodism in the century after Wesley's death had created hundreds of self-sufficient religious societies in the Lincolnshire countryside, but the tradition of complementarity was not wholly lost. R. L. Gales maintained that chapel-goers very seldom raised any difficulty about their children being taught the Catechism by the parson.[7] Canon G. G. Walker has a story dating back to the 1860s of a country vicar who borrowed the Wesleyan choir for a Harvest Festival,[8] and it is unlikely that such cooperation had died out. It was not difficult for individuals to transfer their allegiance from church to chapel and vice versa because the ordinary members of the congregation in either would not have thought in terms of theological principle.

The chapel offered a much more warmly human experience of worship. Indeed, the warmth was more than merely metaphorical. The small buildings, tight-packed with humanity, and deriving additional heat at evening services from the lamps with which they were lit, must have been greatly preferable, for comfort alone, to the draughty parish churches. Generally speaking, heating stoves were not introduced until congregations, and fervour, declined as the twentieth century wore on. Of course, it was not just physical comfort that drew the villagers to the chapels. 'So often', says Gales, 'in the lives of the country poor the softening gleam is Methodist'. The harsh penny-pinching life of the labourer's household could only be redeemed from meanness by a gospel that assured every individual of his or her dignity in the sight of God. Local preachers set the example of simple and direct speech. Tales of their homely teaching abound.

If when ye'r prayin' ye puts things crookedly phra'ased like or says 'em back-end forrards or says Jericho when ye me'ans Jerusalem it doan't matter, the Lord knows what y'er talking about.[9]

There were many older people about in the early years of the century whose grasp of Christian truth was derived from small farmers, shop-keepers and even agricultural labourers who had preached in the village chapels. But there were some signs that the tradition was dying out. Canon Walker refers to a large gathering in a Lincolnshire country town, a year or two before the first world war, at which a speaker reported that in his circuit of twenty-four chapels there was not a single young man coming on as a local preacher. What was going to happen, he asked, when the old men gave up their work?

Underlying these two constituents of village religion there was an even deeper layer, laid down, one might say, in pre-Christian times, but liable to erupt unbidden. Canon Walker tells of residual elements of paganism – belief in witches and spells and spirits – though one of his informants at the turn of the century gave it as his opinion that there were not as many witches as there used to be.[10] Another main constituent of the villager's religion was his unshakable, if ultimately illogical, belief in providence. R. L. Gales says that once when he described the escape of some people from a house struck by lightning as 'a wonder' he was quickly corrected by a man, not notable for his piety, with the words, 'It was a great mercy'.[11] These primitive elements of religion were taken by countrymen into the trenches during the 1914–1918 war – perhaps not belief in witches, but certainly the lucky charms and the fatalism.

The Anglican establishment appeared in the early years of the century to be in good heart. The national picture was of a fairly steady supply of ordinands; in the Lincoln diocese benefices were filled without much difficulty. Most of the clergy were university graduates, with Oxford and Cambridge supplying about half the total. Clergy pay varied greatly. But the unspoken ideal of 'a gentleman in every parish' was largely realized. Non-residence was exceptional and the country clergy with small numbers of parishioners had time to pursue their hobbies and to conduct interested visitors over their churches. Canon Walker, for example, undertook the excavation of the Roman villa in Haceby parish with two other gentlemen.[12] The Revd Hunting Smith Browne Jollye, rector of Stenigot from 1905, presented a remarkable number of confirmation candidates from its population of ninety-six[13] and still had time to serve on local committees and was regarded as the grand old man of the Louth Rural District Council. Under the benign leadership of Bishop King there was an increase in high-church practices without much opposition from parishioners. There was the occasional ultra-Protestant, like the man in Mavis Enderby who denounced the restored churchyard cross as 'that popish thing'.[14] But the general attitude of ordinary churchgoers is probably better represented by the story of a stranger visiting a village church who said to a woman, 'I fear your clergyman is very High Church'. Village woman: 'Well, madam, he do antic a bit'. 'Dear me, what do you do?' 'Well, madam, we love him so much, we antics with him.'[15] Ordinary parishioners were not greatly interested in the niceties of ritual, and were inclined to welcome or reject the ministry of a clergyman for quite different reasons – the warmth of his humanity or his acceptance of their passion for field sports. In the larger towns, however, it was a different matter. Although the law restricted a parishioner's specific rights to his own parish church, it was easy enough to transfer allegiance outside parish boundaries, as far as regular Sunday worship was concerned. Churches like St Swithin's in Lincoln or St Mary's in Stamford developed along partisan lines, with all the advantages of partisanship while party issues were important and all its handicaps when they came to seem unimportant.

The towns of Lincolnshire were moving towards the organized, secularized patterns of thought and action which were to take over from the simplicities of village life as the century proceeded. An interesting example is furnished by the development of Cleethorpes. Frank Baker refers to the dominant influence of Methodism there from 1873 to 1936.[16] The great majority of chairmen of the Urban Board were Methodists or at least of Methodist background, and the energies of Methodists were being directed towards service in local government and philanthropic activities like the management of the Coronation Homes, built in 1902 and 1911. The prayer meetings and the open-air work continued, with processions through the streets and hymn singing led by concertinas. But the urban Methodist community had escaped the grinding poverty and social repression of the countryside. In 1908 the Primitive Methodists could call upon a range of business men to act as Trustees. They included seven fish merchants, two fish buyers, a builder, a provision merchant, two steam-boat owners, a joiner and a painter.[17]

THE EFFECTS OF THE FIRST WORLD WAR

The first great war, unlike the second, divided the nation deeply into two mutually uncomprehending sections, combatants and non- combatants. Among the non-combatants, church life continued in much the same patterns. A new element was introduced in the Church of England by the National Mission of Repentance and Hope. This aimed to recall the nation to religion and to point the way to social reformation after the war. The biography of Bishop Hicks includes an extract from his diary of engagements for July 1916 which shows how some of the activities and organizations carried on alongside the new programme of the National Mission[18]:

July 1	Blesses new vicarage at Gosberton Clough
2	Preaches at Spalding (National Mission = NM)
4–7	Attends Convocation
7	Consecrates churchyard at Gonerby
8–10	Visits West Walshcroft Rural Deanery
12	Diocesan Missionary Festival
14	Visits Sleaford (NM)
15	Confirms at Diocesan Home, Boston; consecrates churchyard at Skirbeck
16	Preaches at Fleet and Gedney (NM)
18–19	Visits Alford and Spilsby (NM)
20	Visits Willingham by Stow
22–24	Visits Horncastle (NM)
25	Addresses Mothers' Union
27–28	Visits Isle of Axholme (NM)

29	Grants institution and licences
30	Preaches at Rowston and in the Cathedral

In spite of his age the bishop had set himself the task of visiting all the five hundred and eighty parishes of the diocese and was still travelling extensively by train, car or carriage to work off a yearly quota of visits, especially for confirmations. The reduction in the number of clergy was reflected in falling numbers of confirmation candidates. During the three years 1911–1913 the average number had been 4,728. In 1914 the number rose to 5,066, but after that there was a progressive decline, as follows:

Table 11.1 *Diocese of Lincoln: confirmation candidates*

	Spring	Summer & Autumn	Total
1915	2,098	1,957	4,055
1916	2,782	1,854	4,636
1917	2,176	1,995	4,171
1918	2,336	1,552	3,888
1919	2,123	1,457	3,580

Source: *Lincoln Diocesan Magazine,* 1920

The erosion of traditional church practice continued on a course set long before 1914.

Those returning from combatant service reacted to their experiences in different ways. Some were totally alienated from religious belief by the futility and irrationality of mass slaughter. Others felt that they had for the first time experienced what it means to live life to the full under the constant threat of death. Amongst these must be reckoned most of the 2,700 men who by November 1918 had sent in their names as potential candidates for ordination. Perhaps the majority returned confused and disheartened, like the Revd J. M. S. Walker. His final verdict was that 'Tommy does not want religion.' But this is only part of the truth revealed by the newsletters he sent home to Lincolnshire. When the battle of the Somme was over very few soldiers came to his regular services or wanted to talk about religion. But at the height of the battle his unremitting rounds among the wounded, with repeated confessions, communions, and blessings, and his quiet moments holding the hands of the suffering and the dying, had been summed up in a different verdict. 'The wounded man is wax. He wants to talk about religion and frequently about his sins.'[19] Back in Kettlethorpe it would not have been difficult to recognize how religion was becoming an occasional rather than a regular feature of the protestant Englishman's life.

The Church of England was perceptibly modified by returning combatants and chaplains and an influx of ordinands of a different type from the generality of pre-war clergy. The changing image of the clergyman is partly indicated in a passage from the reminiscences of Walter Carey, Warden of Lincoln Theological College from 1919 to 1921. By some extraordinary attraction of opposites the fastidiously scholarly bishop who loathed conflict had invited to the college, as its head, the boxing, rugger-playing naval chaplain for whom the Royal Navy was 'the best thing in the world' and the Battle of Jutland a 'high-light'.[20] His influence on the college cannot have been lasting, but while he was in Lincoln his 'principle in trying to manufacture clergy was to make them men first and then clergy'. This involved 'six honest hours of brain-work a day, then plenty of games, an honest religion, and plenty of music and fun'. He made all the students join the golf club – 'so useful later on in life.'[21]

A more significant point, however, is that ordination candidates at the Ordination Test School in the disused gaol at Knutsford knew that money and social class were not the criteria by which they would be selected. Archbishop Davidson had ensured this by his famous pledge that no man approved by the church for ordination should be prevented from training by lack of money. Looking back from the next decade, Bishop Swayne contrasted the position of the pre-war clergy, nearly all possessing some private means and keeping two or three domestic servants, with the post-war situation, in which very few had a private income and many had no domestic help. Extra burdens fell inevitably on clergy wives, whose cheerfulness he recorded with gratitude.[22] The Free Churches and the Roman Catholic Church had never suffered from the same kind of class-based restriction on their recruitment to the full-time ministry. The widening of the social base of the Anglican clergy, added to the experience of comradeship between chaplains of different denominations in wartime conditions, made cooperation in peace-time easier.

The progress of ecumenism, however, was slow. It was noted as exceptional that a united service of thanksgiving was held in Humberston parish church in November 1918, led by the vicar and the Primitive Methodist minister, both of whom lost a son within a period of three months in 1916.[23] Bishop Edward Lee Hicks may have had little theoretical interest in the Free Churches, but he was drawn into collaboration by his fervour for temperance (Fig. 11.2). He had been involved in the work of the 'United Kingdom Alliance for the Total Suppression of the Liquor Traffic' since 1877 and was happy to

Fig.11.2 The Church Army caravan at South Ormsby. In the early years of the century there were two of these at work in Lincolnshire, each with a Church Army Captain as van missioner, and one assistant. Each of them visited twenty or more villages in a season's work. The temperance message was an important part of their work, though it stopped short of teetotalism. The Church Army was more in line with the Church of England Temperance Society, which offered alternative pledges: either 'by God's help, to abstain from all intoxicating liquors, except while a medical order is in force'; or 'by God's help, to abstain from all intoxicating liquors, except at my midday and evening meals'. Bishop E. L. Hicks (1910–1919) was an advocate of teetotalism, and found himself nearer in viewpoint to nonconformists than to the official Anglican position in this respect. Source: W. Hallgarth Collection, Welhome Galleries, Grimsby. Caption: *Lincoln Diocesan Magazine*, Diaries of Bishop E. L. Hicks.

work alongside members of other churches in the support of this cause. Bishop Hicks's attention had first been drawn to it by a village temperance society formed by working men and labourers. In Lincoln diocese he found that a movement had already developed from an original impetus in the village of Heckington, where 112 labourers had taken the pledge in 1906. The correspondence of Bishop King includes evidence that alcoholism was not uncommon among the clergy. An incidental result of the bishop's dedication to temperance was that during the war the provision of recreation huts and chapels for army camps and aerodromes was largely undertaken by the Church of

England Temperance Society rather than the Church Army or the YMCA.[24]

The Wesleyan Methodist Conference met in Lincoln in 1925 and Bishop Swayne was host to eight ministers at the Palace for a fortnight;[25] the Wesleyan president was invited to preach in the cathedral. For Bishop Swayne the point of common interest was not temperance (although he was the president of the diocesan branch of the Church of England Temperance Society) but a shared concern for evangelistic missions. Nevertheless, significant changes in ecumenical relations had to wait until after the next war.

Another delayed effect of war-time experiences in 1914–18 was the encouragement of sacramentalism. In the constant crises of warfare the chaplains found that, almost literally, words failed them. Where words failed, sacraments spoke. At Knutsford the Sunday worship was, without argument, built from the first around a 9.00 a.m. eucharist sung to the music of Merbecke.[26] This foreshadowed the normal pattern of Anglican worship on Sunday mornings as it developed in the middle of the century under the influence of the Parish and People movement. The formation of the Methodist Sacramental Fellowship by 1935 witnesses to the same general tendency in the Free Churches, but it was much less central to their life. Whatever its merits, this movement inevitably tended to devalue the ministry of laymen in corporate worship. In 1918 there were 114 lay readers in the diocese and 592 clergy serving 580 benefices. Ten years later, the number of clergy had dropped to 562 and the number of lay readers had risen to 129. Their combined numbers were quite sufficient to ensure three services every Sunday in every benefice. But as demands for weekly celebrations of Holy Communion increased, it was priests who were needed, not lay leaders of worship.

The period between the wars might have been expected to see some increased interest among churchmen of all denominations in social questions. One of the leading lay churchmen of Lincolnshire, Christopher Turnor, had served on the Archbishop's committee on industrial problems set up in 1916 in connection with the National Mission of Repentance and Hope. An important stage in the drafting of its report took place during a session of several days held at his house in Stoke Rochford. Walter Carey, while Warden of the Theological College, was for a time chairman of the local Labour party.[27] Bishop Swayne in 1920 urged the formation of study circles on social and economic problems and recommended a reading list including books by the Hammonds and R. H. Tawney. In the 1930s the nonconformist conscience was still at work in Methodism, targeting the traditional social enemies – betting, drinking, and the secularization of Sunday. But the District Synod also discussed disarmament and recognized the changing role of women in society by approving 'a New Order of Women's Ministry' in resolutions which treated women as equal but separate.[28] The Synod also passed a resolution in 1935 congratulating the BBC on the high standard of its Sunday programmes, while protesting at the vulgarity of some of the language permitted in broadcasts.

CHURCHES AND CONGREGATIONS BETWEEN THE WARS

The energies of the churches were, however, too easily channelled into their own domestic affairs. The Anglicans were absorbing the impact of the Enabling Act of 1920 which empowered the church to set up parochial church councils and ruri-decanal and diocesan conferences. Diocesan conferences had been meeting under a constitution of 1884, subsequently amended, and ruri-decanal conferences had been set up following a resolution of the diocesan conference in 1906. Now, the new constitution of the diocesan conference increased its size and divided its membership into three 'authorities' – the bishop, the chamber of clergy, and the chamber of laity. One anachronism was removed: the ex-officio membership of the Lord Lieutenant, the High Sheriff, all peers residing in the county, the members of parliament for the county and the boroughs, and the mayor of Lincoln and the mayors of the boroughs. It could no longer be assumed that such office holders were Christians, let alone committed members of the Church of England.

The role of the established church was changing. The Enabling Act had given a degree of freedom in promoting legislation in matters affecting its own life, but within narrow limits; Parliament in 1927 and 1928 rejected proposals for the revision of the Book of Common Prayer approved by the Church Assembly. Bishop Swayne responded by convening a synod of the clergy of Lincoln diocese and inviting them to adopt three affirmations, which had the effect of permitting what Parliament had disallowed and, even more strangely, only what Parliament had disallowed – 'such additions or deviations as are set forth in the Revised Prayer Book as approved in 1928 by the Houses of Convocation and the Church Assembly'. The clergy backed the bishop, and lay members of the diocesan conference subsequently added their support. Parliament had shown itself incompetent to manage the affairs of the established church and the church had edged a little nearer to the status of one denomination among many. As post-war idealism ebbed away and the country sank into a period of economic depression the church in the diocese got on with its own business. When Bishop Nugent Hicks succeeded Bishop Swayne in

1933 he identified three priorities: the reorganization of the Lay Readers Association, provision of churches on new housing estates, and the raising of clerical stipends. These were eminently sensible and practical matters, but they did not match some of the themes which his predecessor had tried to emphasize, such as the need for church people to support the League of Nations and for Sunday School teachers to spend as much time teaching about peace as about overseas missions.

For the Methodists the great age of expansion was over. All the impressive town chapels had been built before the turn of the century. The only town chapels built between 1900 and 1930, according to William Leary,[29] were:

Gainsborough	Shakespeare Street (Primitive)	1904
	Ropery Road (Primitive)	1910
Grimsby	Weelsby Road (Wesleyan)	1909
	Wellington Street (Primitive)	1907
	Stortford Mission (Primitive)	1908
Lincoln	Well Lane (Wesleyan)	1902
	Stamp End Mission (Wesleyan)	1903
	Burton Road (Wesleyan)	1904
	West Parade (Wesleyan)	1907
	Monks Road (Wesleyan)	1914
	Portland Street (Free Methodists)	1904
Louth	Riverhead Mission (Wesleyan)	1925
Scunthorpe	Frodingham Road (Primitive)	1908

Only one of these was built after 1918, and only one was put up by one of the smaller Methodist connections. The evidence of Cleethorpes shows that the social conscience of the Methodist community had begun to divert energies away from purely religious or connexional outlets to more secular matters.

At such a time it was only to be expected that the cause of unity would prosper. Ever since 1918 Wesleyans, Primitives, and the United Methodists had been working for union. There was organized opposition, but eventually a three-stage procedure was approved: acceptance of an Enabling Bill in 1928, a final vote in 1931, and a uniting Conference in 1932. The Methodist Circuits of Lincoln invited the newly-formed Lincoln and Grimsby District to hold its first September Synod 'in their historic city'.[30] Union celebrations were held in the Lincoln Circuit from Sunday 2 October to Wednesday 5 October 1932. Collections taken included those for the equipment and care of local preachers, and for extension work in the new town areas. The question of ministers' stipends was certainly not far from the minds of the proponents of union, who calculated the possible financial savings. The unification of ministries was not too difficult, but there were thorny problems in rationalizing chapels. The Lincoln circuits alone included twenty villages with two (and in one case three) chapels of different traditions. Lincoln itself contained two United, six Primitive, and nine Wesleyan chapels. There were over twenty chapels in Grimsby and Cleethorpes, eight in Boston, seven in Gainsborough, and five in Grantham, and none of the small market towns of Lincolnshire had less than two of the uniting traditions at work in it, with the exception of Bourne, where the diversity of the Free Church tradition was maintained by Baptists and Congregationalists as well as the Salvation Army.

The slow process of chapel closure, enforced by economic realities and declining membership rather than by the desire to initiate a great forward movement in home mission, changed the pattern of Methodist presence in the county. Declining population in the villages led inevitably to closures; in towns, new developments in the suburbs were followed by the abandonment of old chapels in town centres. The net result was a pattern of reorganization which was only in part intentional.

In Lincoln the first decade of the century had seen the building of Wesleyan chapels in West Parade and Burton Road and a temporary iron building in Swallowbeck. A school building in Monks Road was opened in 1914. As the first-fruits of union, a dual-purpose building on the St Giles estate, was opened in 1932. The Free Methodist chapel in Silver Street, once described as 'the gem of the Connexion'[31] (Fig. 11.3), was too close to Wesley Chapel in Clasketgate to survive the union. After the second world war large central buildings struggled on, then two were closed in successive years: Wesley Chapel in 1961 and Hannah Memorial in 1962. In the same period new chapels were built on the Ermine West estate, on the Birchwood estate, and in Monks Road.

The pattern in Grimsby is similar. The main flush of chapel building before 1900 was concentrated in the square mile round the Alexandra Dock. In 1900–10 Methodist interest had reached out to Wellington Street (Primitive) and Weelsby Road (Wesleyan). The former may reflect the affinity, found elsewhere, between the Primitives and the railway community, and the latter is probably a sign of the social respectability which had begun to attach itself to Wesleyanism. In the thirties the Central Hall was built on the site of the old Duncombe Street chapel. Then the central nineteenth-century chapels closed one after another, and the new effort of Methodism

Fig. 11.3 The Silver Street Chapel built by the Free Methodists in 1864. In 1907 they joined nationally with the Methodist New Connexion and the Bible Christians to form the United Free Methodist Church, but this did not affect chapel provision in Lincoln, because the other two denominations were not represented locally; the three chapels in the Silver Street circuit opened in 1904. The Silver Street building was the pride of the connexion, constructed of white bricks, with a front of Mansfield stone, adorned with Corinthian columns. But Methodist union, achieved in 1932, led to its closure in 1940. It became part of the Co-operative Stores for a time, but was later demolished. The other United Free Methodist Chapels in Lincoln have all been closed: Fairfax Street in 1951, Saxon Street in 1957, and Portland Street in 1965. Source: Drawing by E. Vickers (Lincoln Central Library). Caption: W. Leary, *Methodism in the City of Lincoln.*

Fig.11.4 Roman Catholic procession, Spalding, 11 September 1913. Processions in the pre-1950 era were frequently celebratory, rather than concerned to draw attention to a grievance. The photograph is taken in St Thomas's Road, Spalding about 200 yards from the Roman Catholic Church dedicated to the Immaculate Conception and St Norbert in Henrietta Street (built 1876, enlarged 1879 and 1908). Acolytes carry portative lights, and banners follow after. It was the usual practice to process from the church to Ayscoughfee Gardens, where the priest then preached to the assembled crowd. This photo is a still from a 16mm copy of the original 35mm cine film, discovered in the Savoy Cinema, Spalding on its closure in 1974. Source: Lincolnshire and Humberside Film Archive. Caption: P. Ryde and Kelly's *Directory of Lincolnshire, 1922.*

after 1945 went into the Laceby Road site, leaving a rather hollow centre.

The other historical nonconformist churches do not present the same picture. They are too poorly represented in the county to show a changing pattern of distribution. In smaller towns they would not normally have established more than one chapel, unless it were in conscious rivalry. In Lincoln, the Newland Congregational church played a notable part in city life. It attracted immigrant Presbyterian families such as that of Sir Francis Hill, and directors and managers of the city's industries. The turn of the religious tide left congregations in the tradition of independency with no opportunity for so-called rationalization. They either survived or disappeared, but did not amalgamate, at least until the new phase of ecumenism after the second world war.

The development of the Roman Catholic community in Lincolnshire was determined by distinctive social forces. At the beginning of the twentieth century there were three factors influencing the pattern of pastoral provision. First there was the traditional or convert catholicism of a few large landowners with their dependants, such as the Cliffords at Irnham. Secondly there was the seasonal influx of Irish workers for the harvest, some of whom settled permanently (Fig. 11.4). Thirdly there was the settlement of other Irish workers in industrial centres, for such projects as the construction of docks at Grimsby. As the century proceeded the third of these factors became the most important. The urban catholic population expanded rapidly during both the world wars, when workers were encouraged to come from Ireland to take places left vacant by volunteers and conscripts to the armed forces. At one time Cardinal Bourne raised the question of establishing a separate diocese in the county, but this has never been regarded as a practical possibility. The scattered distribution of the catholic population outside the towns has encouraged the establishment of a large number of mass centres.[32] Since the 1939–45 war the presence of catholic servicemen has required chaplaincy provision at the permanent RAF bases. In contrast to the other major Christian denominations the Roman Catholic Church has had to plan for expanding numbers in the present century.

The problems of the Church of England are related to its historic role as 'the church of the nation', committed to the provision of a Christian ministry to every part of the diocese. The decrease of worshippers in any place does not allow it to withdraw its ministry, though population increase elsewhere may be making greater demands upon its resources.

The Grimsby Church Extension Society which Bishop King founded helped to provide new churches before the 1914–18 war. These included St Paul (1908), St Augustine (1912), and St Stephen (1915). In Cleethorpes St Aidan's was consecrated in 1906 and the Christ Church Mission Room in 1911. By 1914 the focus of attention was already turning to the 'Ironstone area'. The parish of St John, Scunthorpe, had been formed out of Frodingham in 1891, and St Lawrence, Frodingham, was enlarged in 1913, both largely due to the generosity of Lord St Oswald. In 1922 the first meeting of the Ironstone Area Church Extension Committee was held and further building projects were launched. In 1924 a new parish church was built for Crosby and the following year St Paul's, Ashby, was built as a daughter church of Bottesford (Fig. 11.5). In the 1930s St Hugh's, Old Brumby, and St Michael's, Crosby, were added. It was a con-

Fig. 11.5 The 'Tin Tabernacle' at Ashby. The closure of redundant churches and chapels in town centres and small villages has been balanced by the need for new places of worship in areas of expanding population (cf Fig. 8.5). The 'Tin Tabernacle', or St Pauls temporary church at Ashby, Scunthorpe, is seen here with the Revd A. V. Chapman and his spring-cleaning volunteers. Originally Ashby was churchless, being a township in the parish of Bottesford. A school-church was erected in 1863, but by 1891 the population had swollen to 1,634 owing to the growth of iron-making, hence the need for the iron church of St Paul's, opened in January 1899 with seating for 400. This building was replaced in 1925 by a permanent structure, under the North Lincolnshire Ironstone Area Church Extension Committee, set up in 1922. Source: Scunthorpe Central Library. Caption: White's *Directory of Lincolnshire, 1892*, Kelly's *Directory of Lincolnshire*, 1922, and Diaries of Bishop E. L. Hicks.

siderable achievement to carry through this programme of expansion, much of it during the economic depression of the inter-war years.

Major restoration of Anglican churches was going on at the same time, including Boston Stump and Louth parish church, but it was the cathedral which called for the greatest effort. Dean Fry raised over £100,000 between 1910 and 1930. When the work was completed, it must have seemed to many that there would be no need for further appeals on such a large scale within a lifetime (Fig. 11.6). That was unfortunately not to be true.

The provision and maintenance of church buildings was a clear challenge to all who cared for the historic churches of Lincolnshire,

Fig. 11.6 Dean Mitchell laying the last stone in the cathedral restoration, 16 August 1932, at the end of more than ten years' work costing £130,000 under the direction of Sir Charles Nicholson (architect) and Sir Francis Fox (engineer). Dean Fry, who had been principally responsible for raising this huge sum, did not live to see the work completed. The figures on the upper level in the picture include the Subdean, Canon J. W. Jeudwine (with beard) and Mr R. S. Godfrey, the Clerk of Works of the cathedral (behind the Dean's right shoulder). Reinforced concrete beams at clerestory level were used to prevent further spreading of the main arches of the central tower and further buckling of the nave walls. This was the first use on a cathedral of the system of drilling holes with jack hammers operated by compressed air. The scaffolding, however, was entirely wooden and covered almost the whole building at some time during the work. Source: Lincoln Central Library. Caption: *Church Times, Lincoln Diocesan Magazine*, and L. Elvin, *Lincoln as it was*, vol. II (Nelson, 1976).

and it called forth a remarkable response. A greater problem, because there is no agreed solution to it, is the problem of adapting the parochial structure to demographic change and the availability of resources. The overall population of the diocese has remained fairly stable, compared with other areas in which there has been rapid urban development. Within that total there has been redistribution involving not only the growth of the urban population, but also a tendency for large villages to grow larger and small villages to become even smaller (Table 11.2).

The composition of village communities has changed with the growth of car ownership and the mechanization of agriculture. Nevertheless the parochial system might have continued with little change into the last quarter of the twentieth century, if other factors had remained constant, such as the minimum stipend considered acceptable and the minimum number of parishioners regarded as justifying a resident clergyman. In 1918 many parochial clergymen who were content to serve very small parishes for stipends of about £200 a year. In the 1980s few would be content to be so underemployed or so underpaid. It is not so much that the diocese has changed its pattern as that patterns of clerical life have changed.

Table 11.2 *Percentage of parishes according to population*

	Under 100	101–250	251–500	501–1000	Over 1000
1918	7.8	27.0	27.8	18.2	19.2
1984	17.3	23.4	19.2	14.3	25.8

Surces: *Lincoln Diocesan Calendar 1918* and *Lincoln Diocesan Directory 1984* (some figures approximate)

In 1918 the combination of parishes had begun; 43 were already held in plurality. But 116 benefices had populations of less than 250, and 11 of these served fewer than 100 persons (if we except a single city-centre church which fulfilled a largely non-parochial ministry) and these were in process of amalgamation with other cures. The factors mentioned above had virtually abolished the figure of the country parson resident in the single parish for which he was responsible. Yet the reduction of the number of clergy available from 655 in 1918 to about 320 in 1984 prevented the increase of town clergy in proportion to the increase of population. At the same time the clergy rejected the stereotype of the leisured gentleman. Their lives were marked by conspicuous activity: more parishioners to minister to, more services to conduct, more activities or societies to organize. In a secular age it was hardly open to them to adopt the other way of justifying their freedom from productive activity – the way of holiness.

The bald figures given above relate to early and late points in a continuous process. Between them a number of adjustments in diocesan policy were made. The first obvious step was to increase the number of pluralities. This policy was made easier by the transition from the age of the railway to the age of the motor car, which brought neighbouring communities together, and the clergy could move more quickly from one church to another on Sundays. The importance of mobility is implicit in a notice included in the diocesan magazine in 1930: 'The Revd E. Graham (Seaton House, Louth) is available to take Sunday Duty. He is a motor-cyclist.'[33] On this evidence it would have been possible to turn back the clock to the bad old days of non-residence when Louth, like other country towns, was described as a rookery, from which the black-coated parsons dispersed on a Sunday into the surrounding countryside.

Any radical rethinking of the Church's strategy would have required strong episcopal initiative. But during the first half of the twentieth century the diocese was unfortunate in its bishops in one respect: they were all either past their prime or afflicted with ill-health. Bishop King was in his seventies when the new century began. Bishop Lee Hicks began his episcopate at the age of sixty-six. His successor, Bishop Swayne, was a comparatively young fifty-seven, but felt his freedom of action severely restricted,[34] presumably by the demands of administration and the sheer size of the diocese. Nugent Hicks had done his best work before coming from the bishopric of Gibraltar to Lincoln at the age of sixty. The next two bishops, Henry Aylmer Skelton (1942–46) and Leslie Owen (1946–47), not only suffered from ill-health but also had to struggle with the problems of war and its aftermath.

THE SECOND WORLD WAR

The second world war affected the details of church practice but not its well-established pattern. Although it was more clearly from the start a total conflict, involving the whole nation, there was not quite the same wholesale removal of men of military age; indeed a lot of servicemen came into the county to man the airfields (Chapter 6, Table 6.3). There was not the same deep division between combatants and non-combatants, for there was warfare in the skies above everybody. Nor were women as restricted in their active participation as they had been twenty-five years earlier. It was easier for the clergy to accept their own role as sustainers of morale on the 'home front', because conscription and the direction of labour had taken the burden of decision away from the individual. Even those who served as chaplains were only allowed to do so on the recommendation of the bishop. In fact, a much higher proportion did so than in the first war. Many of those who stayed in Lincolnshire fulfilled part-time chaplaincy duties, for example with cadet training units, or discovered to their surprise an airfield on their doorsteps. And when the Revd Humphrey Burton, of St James's, Louth, found himself the vicar of a garrison town, he seems to have welcomed the new dimension to parish life which the Grenadier Guards brought in the latter part of the war.[35]

Part of the impact of the war upon parish life, during its phoney period, was through the multiplication of regulations. Bishop Nugent Hicks told the diocese that the county would be a reception area, in spite of the presence of aerodromes and factories;[36] all clergy should undergo anti-gas and first-aid training and obtain permits and armlets to allow them to move about during air-raids. Later in 1939 he emphasized the need to take care of parish documents – a warning none too well heeded, as was shown when a salvage dump at Spilsby yielded up a bundle of papers from the parish of Hagnaby, ranging in date from 1692 to 1864, and three vestry and account books relating to Cumberworth in the early nineteenth century.[37] The problems of blacking out churches led to evensong being transferred to the afternoon in a number of churches. In June 1940 the ringing of church bells was prohibited, except in the event of invasion. The rector of Old Bolingbroke was sent to prison for ringing the church bells on 16 June, but was released and awarded damages when it was shown that the order did not come into force until the 18th of the month.[38] During air-raids on Grimsby three or four nonconformist chapels and the Salvation Army barracks were used as rest centres, and St Barnabas church became a temporary mortuary during a heavy attack in June 1943.[39] The clergy had to be warned that it was a breach of Defence Notices to publish in parish magazines facts about the use of parish halls for military purposes or the units in which parishioners were serving, details of such units in marriage notices, details of air-raids, or even stories from the letters sent home by servicemen.[40]

Press censorship was sometimes honoured more to the letter than in the spirit. In October 1942 the diocesan magazine included the following note: 'Waddington is determined to carry on. The Church has been hard hit, very hard hit, and for one year the Diocesan apportionment was unpaid. That default is to be made good.'[41] This was a fairly direct reference to the destruction of the parish church in the previous year. Two parachute mines had fallen on the village, demolishing the church and nineteen houses. Only one person was killed, but four hundred were made homeless.[42] There was, in fact, very little destruction of church property, in spite of the severe bombing of Grantham and Grimsby and less severe attacks elsewhere. The Methodist chapel in Baggeholme Road, Lincoln, was hit in 1941, but subsequently repaired. Repairs were needed to forty-one Anglican churches, but some of the damage was very slight. The worst effects of the air raids, as far as church buildings were concerned, were in Grimsby, where both the ancient parish church of St James and the twentieth-century All Saints were extensively damaged (Fig. 11.7). Lincolnshire problems were very small, compared with those of some predominantly urban dioceses.

Fig. 11.7 The parish church of St James, Great Grimsby: repair of bomb damage to the north transept, February 1944. One of a series of drawings by A. E. Wade, on permanent exhibition in the church. It had been hit by a bomb on 13 July 1943. A fine modern organ was demolished and all but two of the stained glass windows were destroyed. Sir Charles Nicholson, the architect who had designed the Chapel of the Resurrection in the church as a memorial for those who had fallen in the 1914-1918 war, was appointed architect for the restoration. It was estimated that £20,000 would be required over and above the war damage compensation. The Trawler Owners' Association met the cost of the east window. Source: Mrs A. E. Wade. Caption: *Lincoln Diocesan Magazine.*

Perhaps the most lasting effect of the war on church life was in local ecumenical relations. During the war camps for prisoners of war were set up at Sandtoft and Morton near Bourne. At Horbling services were held for German Lutherans, and later for Ukrainians, mostly Uniats, for whom the liturgy of St John Chrysostom was celebrated in 1947.[43] These experiences may have increased awareness of the world-wide church. Certainly the major English denominations began to view each other in a new way in the second half of the century. In many towns and villages Anglicans and Free Churchmen began to meet regularly in war-time for prayer without regard to denominational barriers. In Boston a congregation numbering 400 met alternately at the parish church and the Methodist church. In Grantham the numbers were about 200 and in Sleaford 100. In Coningsby the Anglican, Methodist, and Baptist ministers conducted prayers once a month, using the three church buildings in turn and drawing a congregation of 80.[44]

ECUMENICAL DEVELOPMENTS AND EDUCATION

This was, no doubt, a basis upon which later ecumenical experiments could be built. But it was essentially a movement among believers; it did not draw in people from outside. Archdeacon Warner in 1939 had other hopes. The black-out was causing difficulties about worship in the evening and he decided to arrange a series of services in the Central Cinema, Lincoln, beginning on Remembrance Sunday. They were interdenominational and unliturgical, and church choirs came to lead the singing. But the experiment did not last. The archdeacon's verdict was: 'Those whom we want to win simply will not come to anything that looks like a church service.'[45] It was a verdict that might be taken to sum up the ecumenical developments of the succeeding decades. An interdenominational crusade was held in Lincoln in 1943, with a procession of witness, open-air meetings, and visits to factories by the Crusaders; but it did not make much of an impact. Later in the war there were ecumenical Religion and Life weeks. In the late 1940s the example of the World Council of Churches (formally inaugurated in 1948) and the British Council of Churches began to give a new shape to church relations at the local level. By 1963 there were local Councils of Churches affiliated to the British Council of Churches in Horncastle, Kirton Lindsey, Lincoln, Skegness, and Spalding, and in the Grimsby area. The impetus towards forming the Lincolnshire Council of Churches derived from an ecumenical conference held at Bishop Grosseteste College in 1966. Close relations between the major Christian denominations led to the subsequent formation of the Sponsoring Body for Lincolnshire and South Humberside. This uninspiring title refers to a highly significant piece of ecclesiastical machinery which has made possible the establishment of official Local Ecumenical Projects. By the 1980s there were a dozen of these, very diverse in character. Most of them involved partnerships of Anglicans and Free Churchmen, but one at least included Roman Catholics.

One of the ironies of ecumenism is that the sphere of education, at one time a denominational battle-field, has become a meeting point of common interests for Christians of different traditions. The development of national policy in education had made increasing demands on voluntary schools with each succeeding piece of legislation, and the 1944 Education Act faced the churches with further demands and decisions. All the surviving Methodist schools accepted Controlled status. The Roman Catholics chose Aided status, with its heavy financial burdens, for all their schools. In the case of Church of England schools, each body of Managers acted independently, and in the event their schools emerged as Controlled and Aided in about the proportion of two to one. More significantly, the Church of England achieved only a small stake in the secondary field, with two Aided (later reduced to one) and five Controlled secondary schools.

As the number of schools outside the control of the churches increased, so churchmen took a closer interest in religious teaching given in council schools. As far back as 1920, the diocesan Board of Education had reported discussions with the local education authorities and nonconformists on the question of religious teaching in the proposed Central Schools.[46] Lindsey had agreed to add the Apostles' Creed to the existing syllabus. Kesteven had not approved this addition, but had agreed (like Lindsey) to allow withdrawal in school time for denominational teaching and to conduct inspections of Religious Education. Holland and Boston had declined to make any changes. The Church of England and the Free Churches participated in the drafting and approval of Agreed Syllabuses after 1944 in accordance with the Act. This practical collaboration and the warmer ecumenical feelings in the period after the second world war helped to make possible some significant developments in the 1960s.

In December 1959 the Free Churches and the Church of England had formed a Central Joint Education Policy Committee, to resolve differences of opinion without the need to lodge formal objections with the Minister. In 1962 the Lincoln Diocesan Director of Education, Canon E. C. Blake, took the initiative in the formation of a local Joint Education Policy Committee, the first permanent ecumenical organization covering the entire county. It pioneered a pattern of joint Anglican/Methodist Controlled schools, encouraged joint courses for school leavers, and brought churchmen and non-conformists into regular contact. In due course the JEPC was absorbed into the Education Committee of the Council of Churches, and the Roman Catholic church accepted membership. So education, which had once been a bone of contention, became an area of fruitful cooperation.

Another significant field of work in which old denominational differences seemed largely irrelevant was that of Industrial Mission. The methods of the Industrial Christian Fellowship founded in 1919 were inclined to seem patronizing and even inconsiderate. During the Lincoln Crusade of 1943 one woman in a factory canteen may have spoken for many when she said she had no objection to religion in its proper place, but she did like to have her meals in peace. The new initiative on lines pioneered by the Sheffield Industrial Mission, led by Canon (later Bishop) E. R. Wickham, was at first concentrated in the so-called Ironstone district. This had opened up new possibilities of understanding between industry and the churches. Bishop Riches appointed the Revd R. W. Dudham (later Archdeacon of Lindsey) to be his whole-time industrial chaplain with a view to similar developments elsewhere in the diocese. There is a veiled reference to tensions between parochial and sector ministries in the bishop's assurance that the scheme would still be based on regular visits of parochial clergy and ministers.[47] The Industrial Mission soon extended its work to Grimsby and Lincoln, and included Free Church ministers in its staff, but the isolation of the industrial areas of the county from each other has made it the more difficult for industrial chaplains to build up a strong corporate identity and to influence the decisions of church bodies in what is still in area, if not in population, a predominantly rural county.

The difficulties of ecumenism are well illustrated by the example of Scunthorpe.[48] An ecumenical Lent Course in 1967, *The People Next Door*, roused enthusiasm and raised hopes of changes – perhaps even the creation of a genuinely free church. But the organizers drew back, realizing that such local unity was, in a wider context, actually divisive. Disillusionment inevitably followed. A local attempt of the Anglican churches in the town to work closely together, as 'The Scunthorpe Group of Parishes', failed, but it had gone on long enough to divert energies away from the ecumenical project.

Two national developments in the field of ecumenical relationships have had little effect in Lincolnshire. The first was negotiations between the Presbyterian and Congregationalist churches which led to the formation of the United Reformed Church in 1972. Neither body was strongly represented in the county. In 1984 there were 18 congregations of the URC in Lincolnshire and South Humberside, but their presence is not sufficiently widespread to alter the ecumenical scene on a large scale. The other national development was the prolonged discussion about reunion between the Church of England and the Methodist Church. Twice the Church of England drew back at the last moment and the two communions were left to work out at local level ways of cooperation short of actual union. A different kind of Christian partnership evolved through the official twinning of the Anglican diocese of Lincoln with the Roman Catholic diocese of Brugge, which has led to the involvement of the Roman Catholic diocese of Nottingham and members of the Free Churches. By the 1980s the main Christian denominations were achieving, locally and nationally, a degree of consensus and cooperation which would have surprised church-goers and chapel-goers in 1900. But as the long-established Christian bodies drew closer together, there was a significant growth of newer religious communities, such as Jehovah Witnesses and charismatic congregations. Because these sectarian groups are more characteristic of urban than of rural life their impact has been limited to a few areas of Lincolnshire and South Humberside. That is even truer of basically immigrant religious groups. Only Scunthorpe, with a substantial Muslim population, approaches the condition of a multi-cultural community.

One other religious body deserves a mention: the Jewish community at Grimsby. Of the many thousands of immigrants from eastern Europe who landed at Grimsby in the half century before 1914, the vast majority went on to Liverpool and the United States, or to larger Yorkshire cities. A few stayed at Grimsby. They managed by 1888 to build a synagogue and became an accepted part of the community. The first of several Jewish mayors was Moses Abraham in 1901. In consequence of declining membership of the synagogue, there has been no resident member of the clergy since 1966.

NEW PATTERNS OF CHURCH LIFE

Over the county as a whole the main post-war problem of the churches was still that of adapting their structures to new patterns of rural life and the shortage of clergy and preachers. The first comprehensive review of diocesan organizations since the nineteenth century was carried out by Bishop Maurice Harland (Fig. 11.8). In an initial statement of policy he said that parishes were becoming less and less self-sufficient and that therefore there must be the planned grouping of parishes, with a strong centre of church life in each area and encouragement of clergy to concentrate on their own particular line in the ministry to serve a group of parishes.[49] The clergy, in November

Fig. 11.8 Rededication of the Royal Air Force chapel in the cathedral, 1949, by Bishop Maurice Harland, supported by Bishop Greaves (suffragan bishop of Grantham 1935–37 and of Grimsby 1937–59). Ever since the 1914–1918 war the RAF presence in the county had been an important element in the pastoral responsibility of the Lincolnshire churches. Chaplaincies were served either by local clergy and ministers or on a full-time basis. The RAF chapel was the last of the three Services Chapels to be dedicated in the north transept of the cathedral. Bishop Harland had himself served as an observer in the Royal Flying Corps and the RAF in the 1914–1918 war. The Holy Communion is celebrated regularly in this chapel by an air force chaplain. Source: Lincoln Central Library.

1947, backed the bishop's proposal to set up a Commission on the Pastoral Reorganisation of the Diocese, and in 1950 the Commission summarized its findings in a popular report with the title *No Secret Plan*. Thirty years afterwards the pattern of pastoral provision in the diocese bore little resemblance to the proposals of 1950, but the bishop undoubtedly succeeded in making clergy and laity open their minds to new ideas.

One of the results of the Commission's work was a meeting at Harrington Hall in 1949, attended by patrons of some of the livings in the neighbourhood, the rural deans of Horncastle and Hill, North and South, and the bishop. Decisions were taken which led to the formation of the South Ormsby group of parishes. The development of this experiment was written up ten years later by the first Rector of the group, A. C. Smith, just before he left the group on his appointment

Fig. 11.9 The parish bus of the South Ormsby group of parishes, about 1958.
The figures in the picture are (from left to right): the Revd B. W. Lowcock (assistant
curate 1957–1962), Deaconess Dorothy Shurlock, the Revd N. G. O'Connor (assistant
curate 1955–1958), and the Revd A. C. Smith (Rector of South Ormsby 1946–1960).
This team took responsibility for fifteen small parishes with twelve churches. The area
covered by the parishes was about 75 square miles, and the population was just over
1,100. The bus used to collect members of the congregation and the choir from the villages and take them to united services at different churches in turn on Sundays as well
as to the Cathedral and churches outside the group on special occasions. The clergy
shared the duty of driving the bus. Average Sunday mileage was 72 and the average
cost was £160 a year. No fares were charged (cf Table 11.3). In the 1950s a Methodist
Travelling Guild was begun in the Horncastle and Alford circuits, using a hired bus to
bring together members of different chapels on a regular basis. Source: A. C. Smith *et
al*, frontispiece, *The South Ormsby Experiment*.

as Archdeacon of Lincoln.[50] The group eventually came to include
twelve parishes, staffed by a rector, two curates, and a deaconess. A
sense of partnership was built up, not only by the group ministry, but
also by practical means such as the production of a magazine and the
purchase and use of a parish bus (Fig. 11.9). An important side-effect
was the provision of a lively setting for the training of clergy who intended to work in the countryside. Other groups were formed. By the
1980s there were no fewer than 26 groups with between five and
twelve parishes in each.

The publication of *The South Ormsby Experiment* showed that it
was considered to be of more than local interest. It looked as if a new
pattern of pastoral care was emerging for the sparsely populated

Table 3   *A week's schedule in the South Ormsby group of parishes*

SOUTH ORMSBY GROUP OF PARISHES					
Sunday in month Parish	3rd May ROGATION SUNDAY	10th May	17th May WHIT SUNDAY	24th May TRINITY SUNDAY	31st May
South Ormsby	8 H. C. 11 M. P.	11 M. P. 6.30 E. P. to Tetford	7.30 H. C. 11 H. C.	8 H. C. 11 M. P.	11 M. P. 6.30 E. P. to Tetford
Driby	3 E. P.		3 E. P.	9 H. C.	3 E. P.
Herrington	6.30 E. P.	11 M. P.	8 H. C. 6 E. P.	11 H. C.	11 M. P.
Brinkhill	11 H. C.	8 H. C. 3 E. P.	8.30 H. C. 3 E. P.	8 H. C. 6.30 E. P.	3 E. P.
Bag Enderby	6.30 H. C.		9 H. C. to Somersby 6.30 E. P.	9 H. C.	6.30 E. P.
Somersby		9 H. C. 6.30 E. P.	9 H. C.	6.30 E. P.	8 H. C.
Tetford	9.30 P. C. 3 S. S. 6.30 E. P.	3 S. S. 6.30 Youth Service Bus	9.30 P. C. 3 S. S. 6.30 E.	3. S. S. 6.30 E. P.	9.30 P. C.; 3 S. S. 6.30 E. P. Civic Sunday
Salmonby		9 H. C.	10 H. C.		8 H. C.
Barforth	3 E. P.		11 H. C.		9 H. C. 3 E. P.
Ruckland		3 E. P.			
Oxcombe			3 E. P.		
Maidenwell & Worlaby				3 E. P.	

areas of the country. But it was a false dawn. It presupposed a team of ministers; but by 1984 only five of the 26 groups had so much as a single assistant for the rector. The decline in the number of clergy had effectively destroyed the hopes which the South Ormsby experiment had raised. If the village congregations were to survive, it would be necessary to adopt other expedients. In the 1980s the diocese pioneered the controversial development of a Local Non-Stipendiary Ministry, with groups of men and women nominated by their parishes for training as ministers, some of whom are chosen to proceed to ordination with a licence limited to their own particular parish.

The Methodist Church, too, had to reassess its strategy. In January 1968 the Revd G. Thackray Eddy, Chairman of the Lincoln and Grimsby Methodist District, writing on 'The Salvation of Rural Methodism' in the *Methodist Recorder*, described the evil results of overtaxing the declining numbers of preachers. Pressure on the ill-equipped to undertake preaching meant that no discipline could be exerted to ensure that exams were taken and further studies pursued. Where the Superintendent had to leave gaps in his Plan, a door was opened to cranks or disgruntled preachers who enjoyed 'freelancing'. The problem must be attacked by centralizing work in the most promising villages, by grouping chapels and holding services on a rota, with the encouragement of 'Travelling Guilds', and by developing ecumenical cooperation.

In spite of the great problems caused by the shortage of clergy, the sparsity of the population and the immense cost of maintaining hundreds of buildings, the churches continued to be an accepted and respected part of Lincolnshire life. Undoubtedly there has been a big decline in church attendance in the twentieth century. Some statistics give an alarming impression. For example, the number of Church of England confirmations in 1900 were 4,350 and in 1945 were 4,211, but have never reached four thousand in any succeeding year, and in the 1980s have been well below two thousand per year. M. G. White, reviewing the state of Methodism in the Lincoln and Grimsby District fifty years after the 1932 reunion, provides the figures in Table 4.[51]

On this evidence, Methodism had a remarkable surge in the fifties and an equally remarkable decline of membership in the seventies. The centralization policy advocated by the Revd G. Thackray Eddy led to the closure of hundreds of chapels. But we need to remember that in 1932 there were over two hundred places with two chapels of different Methodist denominations and nearly 60 with three. In fact 300 chapels could have been declared redundant without losing the Methodist presence from a single community. An interdenominational survey of church membership and attendance in 1979 showed that Lincolnshire compared favourably with its neighbours to west and north, with a 2.7% increase in attendance since 1975.[52]

Table 4 *The Methodist Church, 1932–1982*

Date	Members	Ministers	Places	Local Preachers
1932	23,000	84	670	1,500
1950	18,500	68	550	1,000
1960	21,000	75	565	1,000
1970	17,000	68	418	800
1982	13,247	54	332	—

At the beginning of the century Bishop King did much of his travelling by train and planned his confirmation tours to allow him to spend two nights at a time at each of a number of great country houses, with two confirmations and two dinners, one for the squires and one for the clergy.[53] For all his humane sensitivity he moved in a world divided into the rich and the poor. His successors were able to visit a far greater number of parishes, but stayed in them only briefly – just a meal at the vicarage, a service in church, and then back to Lincoln. Bishop Swayne commented on his enjoyment of these visits to the parsonage, and the way the village women rallied round to stock up the larder for the occasion.[54] Perhaps the bishop had come to be slightly less identified with the gentry and more with the clergy, in the eyes of 'the poor' in the villages. The development of motor transport enabled the bishop to cultivate the trick of ubiquity, even in so large a diocese.

The rest of the clergy became mobile more slowly, the isolation of the parishioners was also progressively broken down. The bicycle was an instrument of liberation, though its contribution to patterns of churchgoing was related less to neighbourliness than to courting or tourism. Already in the 1890s there was a notice in the church porch at Folkingham saying: CYCLISTS WELCOME IN CYCLING DRESS.[55] The church bus in the South Ormsby group of parishes later represented an attempt to exploit mobility to invigorate church life (Fig. 11.9).[56] But in the 1950s it was too late. The other kind of communication was working against it. Why bother to rattle over the roads to get your religion, when you could sit comfortably by the fireside and listen in?

The radio, and later the television, did something to the consciousness of the country-dweller which the petrol engine could not do. It made him, and perhaps even more it made her, a member of a national community. At first it was seen as an ally by the churches. In the 1940s each issue of the diocesan magazine contained details of the religious programmes of the BBC. But when broadcasting escaped from the clutches of John Reith, it seemed to become less friendly to the churches. On Whitsunday 1960 there was a television programme about Lincoln, and the comment in the diocesan magazine focused on the indifference and even antagonism to the widespread influence of the cathedral which people in the streets and in a secular club had expressed.[57] There had always been some people who felt like that. But in the pluralism of the 1960s they got more space on the headlines.

As the community of TV watchers grew to embrace virtually the whole population, the significance of the local church or chapel changed, and it is this change which has altered the meaning of many statistics. If people have continued to attend, it is much less by convention or for entertainment. It need not even be because hymns and sermons and prayers are felt necessary for the inner life, since all these can be offered to the listener and the viewer. It must be chiefly for what men and women and children can find only in the hundreds of church buildings, old and new, which dot the Lincolnshire landscape: the physical reality of the sacraments and the mercy, pity, peace and love which wear a human face.

Bibliographical note

1. There are no published works dealing comprehensively with the churches in Lincolnshire and South Humberside in this period, and general histories of particular towns seldom throw any light on the life and work of the churches, apart from recording the building (or demolition) of churches and chapels. Methodism in particular towns is covered by W. Leary, *Methodism in the Town of Boston* (Boston 1972), W. Leary, *Methodism in the City of Lincoln from its origins in the eighteenth century to the present day* (Lincoln 1969), and F. Baker *The story of Cleethorpes and the contibution of Methodism through two hundred years* (Cleethorpes 1953). A useful record of Methodist buildings is W. Leary's *Temples of his grace, being a record of all Methodist Chapels in Lincolnshire towns* (Chester 1979).

For the Church of England an important source is the *Lincoln Diocesan Magazine*. There are also printed records of the diocesan conferences. These can be supplemented by biographies of bishops (King, E. L. Hicks, Swayne, Nugent Hicks) and a range of reminiscences (R. L. Gales, F. W. Hutchinson, Gilbert George Walker, Walter

Carey, Humphrey Burton). There is a brief history of the Roman Catholic Diocese of Nottingham by G. D. Sweeney: *Centenary Book – A short history of the Diocese of Nottingham* (Newport, Mon., 1950), and the separate issues of the *Nottingham Diocesan Year Book* provide valuable information.

2. National periodicals, such as the *Church Times* and the *Methodist Recorder*, can be combed for information and comment, and files of local papers carry many articles on church life. In the earlier part of the century these included full reports of sermons and addresses.

3. Local libraries (especially the Lincoln Central Library) hold collections of pamphlets, such as popular histories of particular chapels, often prepared for centenaries or other special occasions. These seldom show any critical assessment, for obvious reasons.

4. The Lincolnshire Archives Office holds a considerable quantity of deposited material. In particular, there are minute books of Methodist districts and circuits. For the period 1910–1919 the unpublished diaries of Bishop E. L. Hicks are valuable.

5. There are a few degree theses and unpublished manuscripts which are directly relevant, such as Barry Hinksman, 'Mission and Ministry: ten years' ecumenical work in Scunthorpe' (1980) and W. S. F. Pickering, 'The place of religion in the social structure of two English industrial towns (Rawmarsh and Scunthorpe)', Ph.D. thesis, London 1958.

6. Parish and deanery magazines can be used, with discretion, to throw light on particular areas. A few church guide books carry their history into the present century.

7. The national background of church life in the twentieth century is provided by historical works of a general nature, such as G. S. Spinks, *Religion in Britain since 1900* (London 1952), Roger Lloyd, *The Church of England 1900–1965*, (London 1966), R. E. Davies, A. R. George, and E. G. Rupp, *A History of the Methodist Church in Great Britain*, vol. 3 (London 1978–1983), R. Currie, *Methodism Divided* (London 1968), Alan Wilkinson, *The Church of England and the First World War* (London 1978), D. L. Edwards, *Christian England*, vol.3 (London 1984), and Adrian Hastings, *A History of English Christianity 1920–1985* (London 1986).

Notes to Chapter 11

(LDM = Lincoln Diocesan Magazine)
1. E. C. Wickham, *Words of light and life*, Oxford, 1914, pp. 61–2.
2. E. L. Hicks, Building in troublous times, p. 18, quoted in J. H. Fowler, *The life and letters of Edward Lee Hicks (Bishop of Lincoln 1910–1919)*, London, 1922, p. 191.

3. Fowler, *Edward Lee Hicks*, p. 251.
4. *Church Times*, 23 August 1914, p. 222
5. *Church Times*, 9 October 1914, p. 357.
6. R. L. Gales, *The vanished country folk and other studies in Arcady*, London, 1914, pp. 31–2.
7. R. L. Gales, *Studies in Arcady and other essays from a country parsonage*, Second Series, London, 1912, pp. 27–47.
8. *Tales of a Linconshire antiquary – essays and reminiscences of the late Canon Gilbert George Walker, M.A.*, ed. W. A. Cragg, Sleaford, 1949, p. 14
9. *ibid.* p. 11.
10. *ibid.* p. 10.
11. Gales, *Vanished country folk*, p. 7.
12. *Lincolnshire antiquary*, ed. Cragg, Preface.
13. *LDM*, October 1950, p. 279.
14. J. J. Hissey, *Over Fen and Wold*, London, 1898, p. 304.
15. *Lincolnshire antiquary*, ed. Cragg, p. 10.
16. F. Baker, *The story of Cleethorpes and the contribution of Methodism through two hundred years*, Cleethorpes, 1953, pp. 155–6.
17. *ibid.* p. 161.
18. Fowler, *Edward Lee Hicks*, p. 273.
19. *People at war 1914–1918*, ed. M. Moynihan, Newton Abbott, 1973, p. 70.
20. W. Carey, *Good-bye to my generation*, London, 1951, pp. 40–2.
21. *ibid.* pp. 46–7.
22. W. S. Swayne, *Parson's pleasure*, London, 1934, pp. 268–9.
23. A. E. Kirby, *Humberstone, the story of a village*, 1953, p. 181.
24. Lincoln Diocesan Conference Reports, 1917, p. 20 and 1918, pp. 38, 53.
25. Swayne, *Parson's pleasure*, p. 302.
26. A. Wilkinson, *The Church of England and the first world war*, London, 1978, p. 278.
27. Carey, *Good-bye*, p. 37.
28. LAO, Lincoln and Grimsby Methodist District, Special Synod Minutes 1932-1938.
29. W. Leary, *Temples of His Grace, being a record of all Methodist chapels in Lincolnshire towns*, Chester, 1979.
30. R. Currie, *Methodism Divided, a study in the sociology of ecumenicalism*, London, 1968, pp. 253ff. See also Report of the September Synod in Lincoln, 1932, Lincoln City Library, unbound pamphlet 4678.
31. W. Leary, *Methodism in the city of Lincoln from its origin in the eighteenth century to the present day*, Lincoln, 1969, p. 48.
32. see *Nottingham Diocesan Year Book*, 1983, p. 101.
33. *LDM*, October 1930, p. 143.
34. Swayne, *Parson's pleasure*, p. 287.
35. H. P. W. Burton, *Weavers of webs*, London, 1954, p. 19.
36. *LDM*, July 1939, p. 102.
37. *LDM*, March 1944, p. 267.
38. Burton, *Weavers of webs*, pp. 106-7.
39. M. Smith, *Blitz on Grimsby*, Humberside, 1983, p. 37.

40. *LDM*, December 1939, pp. 189–90

41. *LDM*, October 1942, p. 124.

42. S. Finn, *Lincolnshire air war 1939–1945*, Lincoln, 1973, p. 28.

43. *LDM*, September 1947, p. 211.

44. *LDM*, August 1940, p. 127; September 1940, p. 139.

45. *LDM*, March 1940, pp. 43–4.

46. *LDM*, January 1920, pp. 6–7.

47. Lincoln Diocesan Leaflet, No. 257, January 1958.

48. B. Hinksman, 'Mission and ministry – ten years ecumenical work in Scunthorpe', 1970 (typescript).

49. *LDM*, June 1947, 119.

50. A. C. Smith, *The South Ormsby experiment*, London, 1960.

51. M. G. White, 'Fifty years of re-united Methodism: some aspects of Lincolnshire Methodism 1932–1982', *Journal of the Lincolnshire Methodist History Society*, 3, 9 (1986), pp. 171–80.

52. *Prospects for the eighties, from a census of the churches in 1979*, Bible Society, London, 1980, pp. 76, 82, 86.

53. Lord Elton, *Edward King and our times*, London, 1958, p. 125.

54. Swayne, *Parson's pleasure*, p. 269.

55. Hissey, *Over Fen and Wold*, p. 216.

56. Smith, *South Ormsby experiment*, pp. 37–40.

57. *LDM*, July 1960, p. 109.

CHAPTER 12

CHANGES IN THE QUALITY OF RURAL LIFE: A CASE STUDY OF WELBOURN

by Bill Goodhand

Abstract *In this chapter, three period-pictures are used: Edwardian, inter-war, and post-1950, with short interlinking passages dealing with the two world wars. There has been a fundamental change in the social structure of the village, from one based almost entirely on agriculture and its supporting services to a much more diverse structure including agriculture, defence, other rural employment, and urban employment.*

While local self-sufficiency in terms of services and facilities declined markedly, especially after the inter-war period, the community has remained more stable than has sometimes been supposed, as demonstrated by an analysis of in-migration in 1881 and 1974, and of movements into and out of the village school between 1901 and 1985. Welbourn represents a middle group of villages, between those experiencing continuous population decline, and those expanding rapidly through the building of large housing estates.

Today Welbourn is a village with a population of just under 600, one of a line of settlements spaced at regular intervals along the Lincoln Edge and the A607. About 13 miles from Lincoln and 15 miles from Grantham, the village has had good connections to these towns by rail and bus over much of the twentieth century. A considerable proportion of its buildings are constructed of the traditional local materials of rubble limestone and clay pantiles, which give a sense of continuity, unity, and character. Later additions are mostly infill: privately owned residences, some built in stone, and six groups of local authority houses and old people's bungalows (Fig. 12.1).

THE EDWARDIAN VILLAGE

Before 1914 Welbourn was essentially a farming community in a parish of 3,300 acres stretching from the river Brant in the west

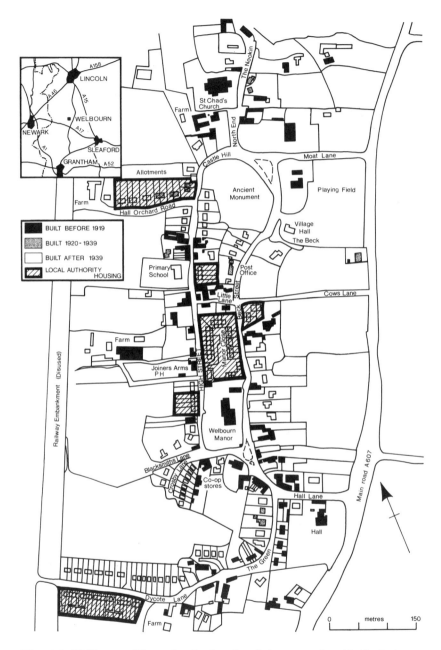

Fig. 12.1 Welbourn village, showing location of places mentioned in the text.
Source: W. E. Goodhand.

across the clay Lowfields up the steep Lincoln Edge and across the Heath as far east as the Ermine Street. The bulk of the population was concentrated in the village, but most of the larger farmsteads were situated outside the village within their holdings. The Heath was, as today, almost entirely an arable area growing cereals and roots, supplemented by sheep farming. On the steep fields of the Edge grassland predominated, while the heavy land of the Lowfields supported mixed farming, including some dairying. Those who served the farming community, such as tradesmen and craftsmen, the parson, and schoolmaster lived in the village.[1]

Table 12.1 *Male occupations in Welbourn, 1881*

Occupational group	No	%
Farmers, cottagers, bailiffs	25	14.4
Agricultural labourers, shepherds, waggoners	96	55.2
Trades/craftsmen	29	16.7
Professions, managers	6	3.4
Railway workers (loco driver, platelayers, lab'r)	4	2.3
General labourers	2	1.1
Miscellaneous (grooms, gamekeepers, gardeners, rat catcher)	12	6.9
Total	174	100.0

Source: Census Enumerator's Book for Welbourn, 1881.

Taken in conjunction with *Kelly's Directory* of 1905, the 1881 population census (the last available census with detailed information) provides an indication of the social structure in Edwardian times. The predominance of agriculture noted in Chapter 2 in the cases of Pinchbeck, Barnetby-le-Wold, and Heckington (Table 2.4) appears again in Welbourn with 70 per cent of the male working population employed on the land. Many of the older children and women were also employed   seasonally on the land. Among the craftsmen were the two blacksmiths, a carpenter, a joiner, and a wheelwright, all of whom spent a large part of their time servicing the farms. The five shops, the inn, the beerhouse, the post office, the three boot and shoemakers, the tailor, the miller, and the coalman served the whole population, but some were also directly related to farming, especially the miller and those shopkeepers who processed local farm products. There were some 25 farm holdings recorded in the 1881 census, with an average size of 180 acres, but the large tenanted farms, over 500 acres, which together employed 53 of the 96 agricultural workers, inevitably dominated the local economy. At the other end of the economic scale were 15 small farmers and cottagers who each farmed less than 50 acres employing only 8 additional workers. However, it was those small-holders who accounted for most of the owner-occupied land in the parish.

Apart from seasonal farm work, employment for women was restricted to domestic service, some of it part-time (44 mainly young women and girls), dressmaking (seven), and presumably helping in the family shop. Eighteen households of the total of 129 contained domestic servants, and seven farmhouses contained living-in male farm servants. In the Edwardian period domestic service was still commonplace, but the number of living-in farm servants had declined from earlier levels.

The death in 1908 of Canon F. A. Leslie Melville acts a benchmark in the life of the village. His obituary said he was noted

for his kindly disposition and promptitude to administer to the wants of his people, he was beloved throughout the parish....The work and good done in the parish by the late Rector, Mrs Melville, and the young ladies cannot be enumerated. The poor and afflicted had in all of them the kindest of friends. In sickness they were simply ministering angels....The calls on the time and on the pocket of the late Rector must have been great. His chief thought was to do what good he could to others, and in a very quiet unostentatious way.... He kept in touch as far as possible with all families in the parish, and when anyone left, or the sons and daughters went out to service, each were reminded of the old home by the receipt of the village almanac every year from the Rector. To his workpeople and those more intimately connected with him, the late Rector was ever kind and generous....His gifts of soup alone have been of the greatest service to hundreds of the poorer class through each successive winter, and many have to thank him for their winter fire.[2]

Melville was one of that fairly rare breed, now extinct: a country parson with substantial private means. Even allowing for the sentimental bias of an obituary, and the fact that not every village parson of the period was cast in the same mould, these tributes reflect an earlier philanthropy of a kind that has all but disappeared. He rebuilt the rectory in 1868, was instrumental in enlarging and improving the school, in restoring the parish church in 1884, and in organizing a night school for young men. A penny bank was opened, a clothing club operated, a working men's club, reading room, and library were established in the school, and his eye for the practical was represented by the pig club. At the Sunday School prize giving the children were offered the choice of warm clothing, calico flannel (for making up girls' underwear), or a book! A garden fete was held at the Rectory, and for parents whose children attended the church Sunday school, there was a tea for mothers at 5 p.m. and a supper for fathers at 7 p.m. Shortly after Melville's death a church meeting room was erected in the village and this provided facilities to play billiards, darts, dominoes and cards encouraging the formation of a young men's club.

In the early part of the century most of the social life revolved around church, chapel, pub, and the Lincoln Co-operative Society Branch, which had been established in 1878. The Co-op ran a bank, a library, held annual knife and fork teas with a speaker, and mounted educational lectures. In fact the Society were confidently laying claim at this time to an important advance in the field of education in rural areas. 'Labourers' children...have had their period of schooling extended by a year because their parents can afford to maintain and keep them from going out to work for that extra time by withdrawing money from their accumulated dividend in the society.[3]

As early as 1895 the Parish Council leased land owned by the Reeve family of Leadenham and ran an allotment scheme, which provided 36 half acre plots. For an annual rent of 16s 9d, labouring men were able to grow vegetables and corn for themselves and their livestock. After the 1914-18 war the Co-operative Society bought the land, but the leases were continued into the thirties. Each year the Parish meeting elected four constables and an overseer of the poor with a grant of £6. During the winter months the village was lit at night by oil lamps, paid for by a rate charge of three halfpence per house and one halfpenny per acre on land.

In the school log books, the highlights of the social calendar were the various feasts and entertainments associated with village institutions, including the school feast which was a forerunner of the modern educational outing. The evening school had an annual social evening which caused the school to close early. The church choir went to Skegness each summer, and the Methodists had a tea or an outing (Fig. 12.7.) The village feast took place in the first week of October; in the previous century this had taken up a whole week, but by 1908 it had been reduced to a Monday and Tuesday. The Sick and Dividing Club had its own feast day and children also went with their parents to similar feasts outside the parish, especially Leadenham, Caythorpe, and Wellingore. On 16 March 1910 the school was closed for an afternoon because of the Hunt steeplechase. On 26 and 28 June 1907 the school closed for the Royal Show, held at Lincoln and attended by King Edward VII. Even a Temperance demonstration, not to mention Canon Melville's funeral, could cause a school closure.

A remarkable example of the effect of Canon Melville's philanthropy is represented in the career of the son of Thomas Robertson, the village tailor and postmaster. While still at school, William Robertson was picked out as a promising boy by the rector, who gave him extra tuition and encouraged him to stay at school beyond the normal leaving age. Robertson worked first in the rector's household, and then progressed to the position of footman at Lord Cardigan's Northamptonshire home at Deene Park. He left Deene Park to join the army, where he rose rapidly, eventually achieving the distinction of being the only man to rise from private soldier through the entire ranks to Field Marshal, becoming Sir William Robertson and Chief of the Imperial War Staff. (Fig 12.2 shows Robertson unveiling the War Memorial.)

Like many larger villages, Welbourn had no resident squire. Canon Melville was the undisputed head of the social hierarchy; a local resident, Miss Bertha Picker, recalls how 'all had to bow and scrape; girls had to curtsey to them [the Melville family] every time we met them'. Similarly, 'men and boys had to touch their caps. We didn't do that

Fig. 12.2 Field Marshall Sir William Robertson, Bart., unveiling the memorial cross in St Chad's churchyard, commemorating the men of Welbourn who had given their lives in the first world war. The photograph was taken in 1920 after the service of dedication conducted by the bishop of Lincoln, Swayne. Is the object top left a close view of the bishop's crook? Sir William was born in the village in 1860 and attended the village school. He enlisted in the army as a trooper in 1877, and remains the only man ever to have risen to the highest position from the very lowest. Source: Welbourn Parish Council.

sort of thing after his death.' As the new rector could not afford to live in the rectory, it was sold to the Bainton family who took over Melville's position as substitute squire. They modernized the house by introducing a piped water supply pumped by a boy from the well, a septic tank, and an acetylene lighting system. Mrs Margaret Clarke, whose father Albert Frith worked for the Baintons as a groom, remembers that they employed a total of eight staff: four female domestic servants, two gardeners and two grooms. One condition of Albert's employment was that his wife did the laundry for the Bainton household. Mr Frith took the laundry hamper by barrow through the village each Monday morning, returning it on a Friday afternoon, by which time Mrs Frith had washed and ironed everything, including stiffened shirts on which she used a glossing iron until they shone like glass.

Because there was no service cottage available, the Friths lived in 'a rat-infested cottage' in the Nookin, which they regarded as distinctly inferior socially to their former tied cottage. The Nookin was a group of about eight cottages at the northern end of the village, one part of which was an old former farmhouse subdivided (Fig. 12.1). The Nookin children are often mentioned in the school log book as suffering a variety of infectious complaints, such as scarlet fever, impetigo, whooping cough, diptheria, chicken pox, and measles. Concern over risk of infection to the village at large often led to all the Nookin children being excluded from school. If an epidemic did take hold, the Sleaford Rural District Council's Medical Officer of Health might close the school, e.g. 31 October to 4 December 1905 for an outbreak of scarlet fever. The Nookin cottages were among those which the Parish Council were to discuss in the 1920s as unfit for habitation.

The burial registers show the high proportion of deaths occurring among the children early in the century: 23 per cent were of persons under 15, and even as late as 1945–54 as many as 10 per cent of those buried in the churchyard were in this age group. The over-75s show a significant increase, from only a third of all burials to two-thirds as expectation of life improved, and the age structure of the community has changed (Table 12.2).

Another feature of village life illuminated by the school records is the tradition for farm workers to change their positions only on 6 April, known as 'flittin' day', as distinct from 'pag-rag day', 14 May, when the single male and female farm servants changed their engagements. In 1909, for example, the headmaster reported at the beginning of the summer term nine new children, 'several of them deplorably backward, who previously lived at very out-of-the-way places.' The numbers of new children at this time of the year varied, but were generally more than ten out of a school roll of between 90 and 100.

Table 12.2 *Average age at death, Welbourn 1901–80*

Period	Deaths		Infants under 1 year		Persons under 30	
	No	Mean age	No	% of all deaths	No	%
1901–10	77	47.8	11	14.2	27	35.0
1911–20	72	55.7	6	8.3	17	23.6
1921–30	49	52.3	8	16.3	14	28.6
1931–40	54	61.9	3	5.5	7	12.9
1941–50	80	60.7	9	11.3	14	17.5
1951–60	63	71.2	2	3.2	3	4.8
1961–70	55	75.4	0		0	
1971–80	46	74.8	1	2.2	1	2.2

Source: Welbourn Church of England Burial Register.

Movements of schoolchildren on this scale call into question the traditional view of the 'stable' village community. Indeed as far back as 1881, as in many Lincolnshire villages, under half of Welbourn's population had been born in the village. The precise figure was 43 per cent, but only 34 per cent of the adults, and the still lower figure of 29 per cent of the female adults were natives of the parish. On the other hand only 11 per cent had come from outside Lincolnshire, and 33 per cent originated from less than ten miles away.

Table 12.3 *Origins of Welbourn schoolchildren, 1901–85*

Origins	1901–15		1921–35		1951–65		1971–85	
	No	%	No	%	No	%	No	%
Welbourn	160	57.3	110	41.9	125	43.6	120	70.6
Within 5 miles	48	17.2	38	14.5	34	11.8	10	5.9
5–10 miles	15	5.4	48	18.3	16	5.6	6	3.5
Rest of rural Lincs	30	10.8	28	10.7	36	12.1	8	4.7
Lincolnshire towns	8	2.9	19	7.3	16	5.6	5	2.9
Out-county	18	6.5	19	7.3	60	20.9	21	12.4
Total	279	100.1	262	100.0	287	100.0	170	100.0

Source: Welbourn Church of England School, Admission Registers.

Turning back again to the school records, Table 12.3 contains a picture of the origins of children at four periods, the first of which spans 1901–15, when 42 per cent of the children entered the school as newcomers to Welbourn. The comparable figure rises in the inter-war period to about 55 per cent, where it stayed until about 1960, after which it falls to a little over 30 per cent, a drop which is only partially explained by the narrowing of the age range within the school. This evidence points to less movement in the population in the 1980s than for the period 1920–60, an interpretation supported by the fact that of the 57 households of 1977 with children aged 5 to 16, 46 (81 per cent) were still resident in the parish in 1987. The decline in demand for farm labour and in the amount of rented accommodation, including tied cottages, appear to be the basic reasons for this greater stability.

However, in terms of the children admitted from outside the parish there have been considerable changes. In particular, the proportions of children coming from outside the county has increased and the distance from which they have come has also increased. Within Lincolnshire too there has been a widening of the circle of origins, but it should be emphasized that the proportion of urban incomers has not changed appreciably among the child-rearing households (Figs. 12.3a, 12.3b, 12.3c, 12.3d). This observation suggests that although an increasing proportion of jobs are now urban-based, there are at least three different types of workers, those who move from afar, those who move from one village to another, and those who remain in their own locality. Such a pattern can be compared to that of Edwardian farm labourers moving at frequent intervals over short distances, including the possibility of returning to Welbourn after a period away. Regular movement on 'flittin' day was so common that men who did this were known as yearly men, and Mrs Dickinson [District Nurse in the early 1930s] recalls that much of their makeshift furniture consisted of tea chests.

This section on the Edwardian period can be concluded by looking at contrasts in life styles within the area, drawn out of two sets of recollections. Mrs Clarke, then Maggie Frith, left school on her 13th birthday in October 1909, going into service at Gartholme Farmhouse, with Mrs Wells, the wife of Fountain Wells the village blacksmith. Her wages were two shillings a week in the first year, which included payment for work on Sundays, and her duties covered all the usual household chores of washing, cleaning, and preparing food. She had a free mid-day meal, but only on a Sunday did she have the privilege of eating with the family. For the rest of the week she got on with her work or waited in the wash house and then ate on her own. Although Mrs Clarke went home each evening to sleep, there was little time or the means, even had she the energy, for pleasure or recreation. A spirited girl, she disliked both the work and the petty

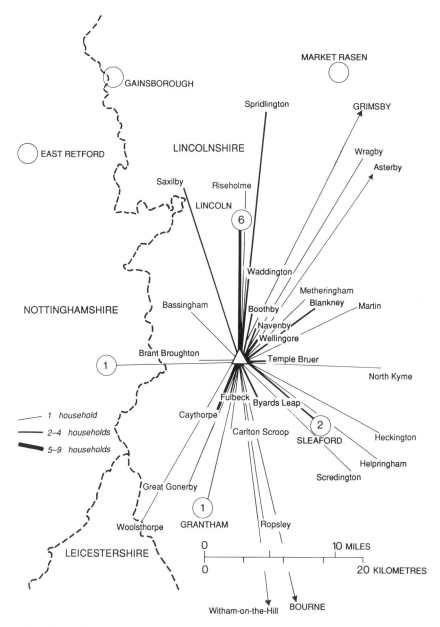

Fig. 12.3a In-migration to Welbourn 1901–15, based on previous place of residence of households with children of school age. Source: data from Welbourn Church of England School. Admission Registers. Map designed by W. E. Goodhand and drawn by J. Peacock.

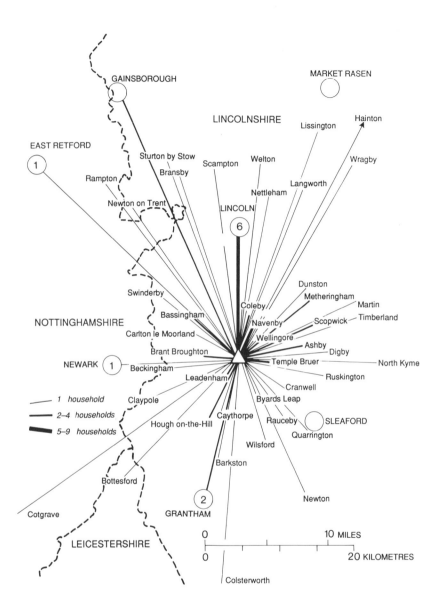

Fig. 12.3b In-migration to Welbourn 1921–35, based on previous place of residence of households with children of school age. Source: data from Welbourn Church of England School. Admission Registers. Map designed by W. E. Goodhand and drawn by J. Peacock.

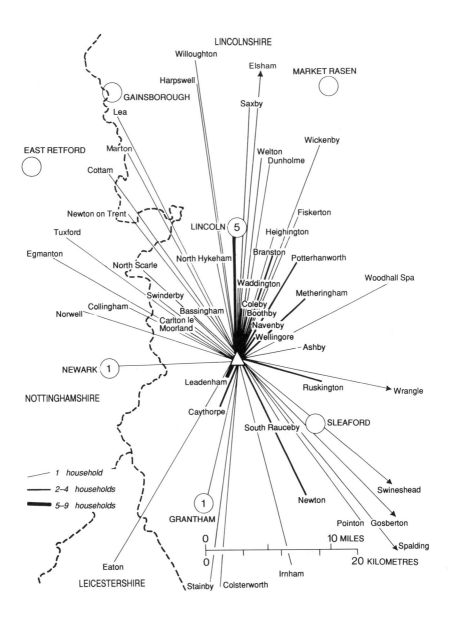

Fig. 12.3c In-migration to Welbourn 1951–65, based on previous place of residence of households with children of school age. Source: data from Welbourn Church of England School. Admission Registers. Map designed by W. E. Goodhand and drawn by J. Peacock.

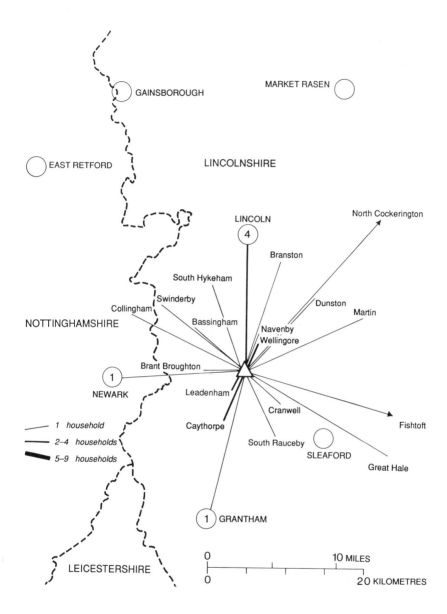

Fig. 12.3d   In-migration to Welbourn 1971–85, based on previous place of residence of households with children of school age; 'school' limited to children of primary school age. Source: data from Welbourn Church of England School. Admission Registers. Map designed by W. E. Goodhand and drawn by J. Peacock.

social barriers, but had to accept that for a young woman in her position 'there was nothing else to do' prior to marriage and the working conditions were 'the same at all the big houses.'[4]

For a young woman from a higher social position life was very different. Mrs Thompson-Close, the daughter of a Derbyshire parson, married a prosperous Leadenham farmer at the turn of the century and after a two weeks' honeymoon in London and Sussex, returned to supervise the domestic servants at Manor Farm. From her diary, her duties appear to have left Mrs Close with ample time for a busy round of social calls, for afternoon tea, or dining out with friends among the leading families of the district. In the summer, flower shows, bazaars, fetes, and tennis or croquet parties featured frequently. There were also regular visits by train to Lincoln, Grantham, and London (only two hours and ten minutes from Grantham), for shopping and attending concerts and the theatre. Hunting, walking, cycling, and driving provided a vigorous outdoor element in this hectic social round. In 1904 the Closes bought the Panhard convertible seen in Fig. 12.4. Apart from taking tea out to men at harvest time, she was very little involved in life on the farm, and the only practical domestic duties mentioned in her diary are embroidery and jam

Fig. 12.4   The Close family, then of Leadenham, in their Panhard car, 1904. This was one of the first privately owned motor vehicles in the area, registered CT 317 by the Kesteven County Council. Mr Close's pose conveys a blend of nonchalance and pride in his new purchase. Source: Mr H. N. Close.

making. At the time of her marriage, Mrs Close was able to purchase a trousseau in Oxford Street costing over £60; Maggie Frith had to live on £5 a year.

WORLD WAR I 1914-18

The Closes' leisured life was shattered by the outbreak of the first world war. The event was not explicitly recorded in the school log book, but the admissions register shows an increase in the numbers of pupils entering and leaving the school, owing to the disturbance to the civilian population caused by the war. Some of the incomers were children of service personnel stationed at Leadenham aerodrome, most of which was on Welbourn Heath, as well as Cranwell. On 26 October 1917 the head stated that 'During the past week four new children have been admitted. The number on roll is affected frequently by the admission and removal of children belonging to parents engaged in military and naval service.' At times the school was used for billeting troops and evening classes had to be stopped due to the fear that the school lights might attract enemy bombing.

On 31 January 1916 Mr Thomas Taylor, the headmaster, recorded that 'Zeppelins visited the village and neighbourhood. The first one appeared about 7.40 p.m. and dropped eight incendiary bombs on the hillside that skirts the village on the east. The skeleton of a bomb weighing 9 lbs was sketched by the boys during a drawing lesson....Its form was very useful for the purpose.'

When King George V visited Cranwell 'Air camp' on 30 July 1916, Mr Taylor was called up as a special constable, and the children were taken by the assistant teachers to join in the welcome to Their Majesties, displaying a portrait of General Sir William Robertson inscribed 'Welbourn – loyal to our King and proud of Sir William Robertson.'

As labour was scarce on the farms, some of the boys were allowed to leave school before the official leaving age, provided they could pass an examination to demonstrate a basic level of academic competence.[5] Other children were given time off school also to help on farms, especially for potato harvest. The school was sometimes closed to allow events to be held in it, such as on 5 and 6 January 1915, when an entertainment was organized by Mrs Fane of Fulbeck Hall and Mrs Bainton of the old rectory in aid of the Red Cross. The village 'Rat and Sparrow Club' provided opportunities for enterprising youths to make a few pence by killing pests which could threaten home-grown food supplies.

Immediately after the war, the school was closed on account of the great influenza epidemic, from 15 November 1918 to 9 December, but attendance was still lower than normal as late as 6 January 1919. Like almost all other villages, Welbourn erected a memorial (in the churchyard) to commemorate the 11 men who were killed in the war, and called on the services of Sir William Robertson to unveil it in 1920 (Fig 12.2).

WELBOURN BETWEEN THE WARS 1919-39

After the war decline set in: although the number of dwellings remained much the same, with 133 in 1911 and 137 in 1931, this disguises a sizable fall in the population from 556 in 1911 to 447 in 1931, average household size falling from 4.18 to 3.26, in line with the general trends noted in Chapter 2. Young families moved out, leaving behind a disproportionate number of older childless couples and widows. This trend is borne out by the experience of the village school, where the numbers of pupils fell from an average of about 90 in the period 1905–14 to 55 in 1930. There was a redundancy of a pupil teacher from the infant room in the 1920s, and the loss of the junior teacher in 1930. Selective out-migration of more enterprising families and declining staff resources in the school probably explain why it had no children leaving for secondary education between 1926 and 1938, compared with an average of two children a year between 1917 and 1924.

After a brief period of wartime prosperity, farming was in a depressed state again, and the continued trend towards labour-saving machinery, especially tractors and self-binders, explains the decline in the numbers of farm workers to 57 full-time workers in 1938. Although some farmers attempted to diversify into such enterprises as poultry and pigs, whose numbers expanded tenfold between 1910 and 1938, their problems can be illustrated by the pigs on one farm which were said to resemble greyhounds, 'being brought up on fresh air and water'. Notably land under permanent pasture increased by 30% in the inter-war period as farmers attempted to cut costs. On the arable side, the introduction of sugar beet offered one of the few prospects for better returns. By 1938 209 acres of beet were being grown and only wheat (338 acres) and barley (382 acres) were more important crops.

Surprisingly, Table 12.4 suggests a relatively stable service sector in the Welbourn area between 1905 and 1937. However, it records the total numbers of enterprises, not the actual workforce involved, and does not indicate any changes in the types of businesses. For example, at Leadenham the blacksmith relied more upon cycle repairs and agricultural engineering, than on shoeing horses. At Wellingore a garage advertised itself as 'motor, agricultural, and electrical engineers, hauliers, contractors, tractors and cultivators', exemplifying the need for diversification. In Welbourn, Arthur J. Wilson, a grocer, ran an omnibus service to Lincoln on Fridays and Saturdays (1922), thus loosening the dependence of his customers on the village shops.[7] Another way of surviving in a locality where trade was declining arose from extending the trading area of the business. George Crosby of Welbourn was a confectioner noted for his Blankney Hunt pork pies, which presumably sold over a large part of north Kesteven. Another Crosby bought up poultry from neighbouring farms, dispatching them from Leadenham station to London hotels. When, in 1922 the Post Office department offered farmers the moderate terms of £4 a year for a shared telephone line it became possible to widen one's customer network at a small extra expense.

Table 12.4 *Numbers of trades/crafts enterprises in Welbourn area, 1905–1937*

Parish	1905	1922	1930	1937
Boothby Graffoe	1	1	1	2
Leadenham	24	21	20	19
Navenby	24	28	29	33
Welbourn	16	16	12	13
Wellingore	26	24	20	20
All five villages	89	90	82	87

Source: Kelly's Directories of Lincolnshire

About 1910 alternative and better paid work for farm labourers was available in the locality with the opening of the ironstone quarry and railway siding at Leadenham, owned in 1922 by the Barnstone Blue Lias Lime Company. The quarry was to close in 1930 as ore extraction by pick and shovel became uneconomic. This prompted the Parish Council on the 20th March 1930 to consider a relief scheme for the local unemployed repairing footpaths in the village which were reported 'to be in a rough state', provided, 'this did not interfere with the necessary work required on farms from May to December'. Fortunately, new construction began at RAF College, Cranwell in the early 1930s providing additional civilian employment which gradually 'put the village back on its feet again'.

When the Lincoln Co-operative Society bought a 350-acre farm in Welbourn in 1915 it extended its influence over the village which had begun in 1878, on the establishment of its first country branch there.

It quickly diversified from grocery and drapery into sales and deliveries around the district of coal, corn, animal feedstuffs, paraffin, and bread baked on the premises. Frederick Bird, who started work at the branch in 1930, recollects that there were then 10 people on the branch staff. In addition, there were six men on the farm, from which milk was retailed direct into the village without being skimmed, and the bulk was taken by motor lorry to the Lincoln dairy. Mr Lawrence Holmes who as a young single man took a job as a milker with Top Farm in 1920, described his situation as, 'one of the best jobs I ever had'. From a weekly wage of 35/- (and a can of milk a day) he could pay his mother £1 for his keep, put 10/- away and still be left with 5/- to spend. New standings for 60 cows were constructed at the Welbourn farm and in 1928 the Society installed a milking machine, steam boiler and sterilizing plant, one of the few local examples of major investment and innovation in agriculture in the depressed inter-war years.[8] The Co-op represented a new departure in rural employment, offering more security and career prospects than had been known before (Fig. 12.5).

Fig. 12.5   The staff of the Welbourn branch of the Lincoln Equitable Co-operative Industrial Society, c. 1910. With a staff of 14 working in the shop, or on the delivery of groceries, meal, paraffin and coal around the district, the branch represented an important source of local employment and a focus for the social life of the village. Notice that it is a completely male staff, a feature of shops changed for ever by the first world war. Source: Miss B. Picker (whose brother is third from the left).

Decline in village population kept the demand for extra housing to low levels, but some new housing was built in an effort to improve amenities. As early as 10 March 1927, the Parish Council were discussing a closure order on cottage properties. In 1910 the Co-operative Society had built two semi-detached cottages near their premises in the High Street, and the Parish Council on 16 March 1926 had discussed the allocation of the first two District Council houses being erected in the village at that time. At five shillings a week, the rents were very high for a farm worker on a pound a week. On 23 March 1936 the Parish Council raised the possibility of more council houses being built for farm workers, and discussed once again the question of closure orders on sub-standard cottage properties.

Mrs E. Dickinson (nee Twell), the district nurse 1930–5, coming from the London docklands, was a keen observer of housing conditions. Many of the cottages were little better than those in London in terms of amenity, but were widely spaced in gardens. Water came from pumps or wells in the garden, or from stand-pipes in the street, some of which are still preserved, supplied from a parochial scheme

Fig. 12.6   Washday for the Hallam household of Chapel Yard, Welbourn in 1937. 'Poshing' the clothes with a dolly peg and 'bucketing' water from a pump or stand-pipe in the street was a strenuous task, especially for the common folk whose jobs dirtied their linen so thoroughly. Mr Hallam's presence suggests that he helped. George and Mary Hallam raised 11 children in this small three-bedroomed cottage, although one daughter was to die of tuberculosis in 1922, aged 16 years. Five of the children later emigrated to the USA, Canada, and Australia. Source: Mrs P. Worsdale.

based on a borehole above the village on the edge of the Heath. In 1922–3 this, together with a mains sewage system, was an early initiative for a rural area. In the house the water was heated in a boiler at the opposite side of the fire to the oven (Fig. 12.6). Sanitation was a privy up the yard, often shared with neighbours. Although a widening range of mains services, including electricity, were available to the village after 1933, only the better-off households could afford the charges. In neighbouring Leadenham, the squire, Captain Reeve actually objected to the village being connected to the electricity mains as he 'thought the poles to be unsightly', despite the fact that a private generator was used to light Leadenham House.[9]

Mrs Dickinson's ordinary families had access to the local doctors in many cases through a club, that at Caythorpe charging five shillings a year per family, which excluded the cost of prescriptions. For those with toothache the doctor would also extract teeth for a charge of one shilling. The seriously ill often had to be nursed at home by their own families assisted by Mrs Dickinson. She recalls one case of pneumonia which she attended almost continuously for 72 hours, wrapping linseed and mustard poultices on the patient's upper abdomen four times a day, while straw was spread on the road outside the house to deaden the noise of passing farm vehicles. Hospital cases went by train or St John's ambulance to Lincoln.

Mrs Dickinson and another nurse were employed by the Navenby and District Nursing Association, extending over six villages, doing their rounds by bicycle. Each household paid a shilling a quarter, which covered everyone for general sickness and free maternity service, the scheme being under the supervision of the Lincoln County Medical Officer. For confinements Nurse Dickinson carried a rubber sheet which went on the feather bed over piles of brown paper and newspaper saved up by the family. The supply of hot water was as problematical as keeping the baby warm. For night deliveries, the oil lamp, or sometimes candles, had to be taken upstairs.

The elderly managed on an old-age pension of ten shillings for a couple, with help from their families. There were no almshouses, but some workers were able to stay on in the tied accommodation they had occupied in their last job. In school, the nurse was responsible for inspecting the children, especially for head lice, but might also draw the attention of the doctors to other problems such as under-nourishment. Many cottage families bought little butcher's meat, relying instead on the pig in their back garden sty.

In the aftermath of the first world war, the Women's Institute was set up in a climate of women's rights which included the extension of the franchise to women over 30. On 18 December 1919, a Parish

Fig. 12.7 Wesleyan Chapel Sunday School annual 'treat'. Pupils, well scrubbed and in their Sunday best, happily pose before setting out on a gaily decorated dray for their annual 'treat' in this case to Lincoln Arboretum, c. 1908. If the young lady with the new bicycle also went, it must have been a hard ride while wearing her long Edwardian skirt. Source: Mrs P. Worsdale.

Meeting was held at the request of the WI to discuss the possibility of building a village hall, and the composition of the committee then set up strongly suggests not only a shortage of good meeting accommodation, but also a desire to have a hall governed in the interests of the whole population, rather than sections of it. As elsewhere, the problem was solved by the purchase of a surplus Army hut, erected on a site just off the Green, bought at a nominal figure and on 9 January 1922, the Parish Council accepted the trusteeship on behalf of the village.

Village activities at this time, some of which took place in the new hall, included the football team which belonged to the Cliff League (Fig 12.8), a women's hockey team (known as the Scarlet Runners), bowls, tennis, cricket, dances, whist drives, the British Legion (meeting at the Joiner's Arms), and girl guides. The Co-op leased land on nominal terms to the football and cricket clubs. They also organized monthly concerts by their Lincoln-based concert party. The tennis club played on a hard court at the Manor, and one of the social highlights of the year was the annual tennis tournament, where the leading families of the locality carried the day. The church choir were

Fig. 12.8   Welbourn football team, who played in the Cliff League in the 1920s, photographed in front of their changing room, officially the Church Room, but usually referred to as the Tin Tabernacle. The football field was loaned to the team by Lincoln Co-operative Society. Second from right in the front row is Mr Thomas Taylor, the village schoolmaster, whose careful recording of school life has helped with the preparation of this chapter. The team's well-worn shirts are in marked contrast to the smart 'strip' worn by the present team who are sponsored by a local building firm. The grim expression on the face of Mr 'Shotty' Wells, the supporter on the right, suggests a poor result or a tough trial ahead. Source: Mrs G. Howard.

very active in this period, and their annual outings included a visit to the Wembley Exhibition, and the Parochial Church Council organized talks by outside speakers. On the 26 March 1926 the W.I. committee were adventurously considering an offer to stage a 'wireless concert' in the Village Hall, using a temporary aerial. By the late 1930s many village homes had a battery operated wireless set, so greatly extending the scope for home-based entertainment.

One of the pre-1914 activities to die out after the war was the holding of evening classes at the village school. Mr Edwin Wilkinson, the village blacksmith, recalls having attended these classes in drawing, arithmetic, and land measurement, but the schoolmaster did not restart them, owing to waning interest and the unruly behaviour of village youth. More attractive, as Fred Bird relates, were cinema and theatre performances in Lincoln, which were only a 1/6d return bus fare away, or if you cycled there, you could afford a fish and chip supper.

The newly formed WI, with an eye to the practical, ran a small library and a clothing club, together with a regular sequence of whist drives and dances and an annual garden fete in aid of local charities, such as, the Lincoln Hospital. The leading WI members also thought it their duty to keep a close check on the standard of social behaviour in the village, as for example, on 23 June 1920 when the Committee resolved, 'not to allow the One Step at future dances', and that, 'the music be stopped in dances if girls were swinging off their legs'. On a more serious note the members were asked, on 7 June 1921, to discuss the question of, 'the harm being done in encouraging girls to be idle by giving unemployment pay'.[10]

WORLD WAR II 1939–1945

Again in the second world war village life can be glimpsed from the school log books, complemented by the Parish Council Minutes. The first hint of the approaching war is a meeting held in the village hall on 22 March 1938 for a discussion on air raid wardens given by the Chief Warden of the Rural District Council, Commander P. Kitwood. Arising out of the meeting was a proposal for the placing of fire hydrants and a supply of hose for the village. The immediate impact on the village of the declaration of war was the arrival on 11 September 1939 of nine evacuees from Leeds with their teacher. This was the first of quite a large number of short visits by small groups of evacuees from various towns, some of them organized officially, others the result of families with Welbourn connections coming away from bomb-damaged homes. Evacuation from the village was also contemplated since 15 Welbourn children were medically examined on 17 July 1940, prior to overseas evacuation, but it is not clear if any actually went.

The war came close to home on the afternoon of 7 March 1941 when a stirrup pump was delivered to the school and 'as we heard bombs dropping somewhere near we spent some time this afternoon under the desks'. The children made a direct contribution to the war effort by working on the land, for example on 13 June 1941 the school closed for a whole week to enable the children to help with sugar beet singling. In the following autumn they spent their nature study lessons gathering blackberries for the village jam centre and on 3 October the school was closed for three weeks for the potato harvest. The next autumn school time was used for gathering rose hips, which were sent away to be be manufactured into rose-hip syrup, an important source of vitamin C.[11]

Various public campaigns were waged to raise money for the war effort, such as on 2 May 1941, when the school closed for a day during War Weapons Week, and on 23 March 1943, when the village set itself the target of raising £2,000 during the Wings for Victory Campaign. The Parish Council Minutes mention that villagers were enrolled as volunteer fire-watchers, using the Mill which overlooks the village as an observation point. Sandbags and stirrup pumps were supplied to all households in 1941.

A number of the men joined the Local Defence Volunteers (known in the area as LDV – Look, Duck, and Vanish), which later became the Home Guard, under the leadership of a local farmer, Austin Pick. Fortunately, the nearest they got to active service was a confrontation with the Leadenham platoon.

Within close distance of Welbourn were RAF stations at Cranwell, Fulbeck, Wellingore, and Coleby Heath, and these were defended by artillery batteries, some of which were in Welbourn parish and the troops were billeted in some of the larger houses. In neighbouring Wellingore there was a Land Army hostel, and on what is now Wellingore picnic site, there was an army camp used later as a prisoner of war camp. The threat of invasion by glider led to the erection of rows of poles to cut down the possibility of safe landing in a flat landscape of large fields. Leadenham Station (in Welbourn parish) played its part in the supplying of RAF stations, as described in Chapter 6, with female porters replacing male staff who had been called up for military service.

Mr Eric Pell, working as a shop assistant from 1943, recalls the subterfuges people used to supplement their rations. Large families registered with several shops in order to qualify several times over for special items off the ration. Poaching played its part, and pig sties were put to good use. Black-market eggs and butter were also available to those 'in the know' and appropriately placed. For the many young, official issues of orange juice and cod liver oil were probably regarded by the recipients to be a mixed blessing!

THE CONTEMPORARY VILLAGE, POST 1945

The war had taken its toll at the school in shortages of materials and staff. On 3 September 1946 the log book records that there was no infants' teacher; the summer holiday cleaning had not been done; the out-offices had not been emptied for a year and the walls had not been lime-washed for two years, while the ash pit had been full for months. When Mr Frank East took up the headship on 28 May 1947 (to stay until his retirement in 1977), the life of the school improved considerably but the chief structural problems remained. Thus the HMI's Report of 1954 describes the school playground as uneven and gritty, the sanitary facilities of the vault type, washing arrangements as consisting of two enamel bowls in an outhouse, water coming from a stand-pipe in the roadway. The school had the use of a nearby pasture for games, and dinners were served in the village hall 600 yards away, after they had been cooked at the Wellingore school kitchen.

Improvements then began to appear, starting with a piped water supply in July 1955, a new playground surface following in January 1956. A canteen was opened in October 1962, and finally in January 1968 the children and staff moved into a new building with two classrooms, hall, cloakrooms, and canteen, with their own playing field.

In April 1937 the number on roll had risen to 59, and stayed about that level until the postwar period when the rise in the birth rate and the recovery of the village population sent the school roll up to the peak of 80 in August 1952, falling soon to about 60 and then to about 40 after the opening of the secondary school.

The parish population level of 447 in 1931 proved to be a low point, since by 1951 it had risen to 521, and between that date and 1981 it has stayed between 500 and 600 (1981 : 579). However, household size has continued to fall and in 1981 it was only 2.54 persons per household, compared with 3.26 in 1931, and not much more than half the 1911 figure.

Declining household size accounts for an increase in the number of houses of 30 per cent between 1951 and 1971 despite a stable population. Pre-war agitation by the parish council for the closure of sub-standard housing began to bear fruit in the 1950s, and 28 dwellings were demolished in the period 1960–75, all but four within the village itself. Policy then changed to conservation of as much as possible of the traditional fabric of the village, and there has been only one further demolition.

Frederick Bird has described one of the houses demolished, which in 1947 he rented for only two shillings a week. The house had brick floors and was extremely damp, and it was not unknown for newts to run across the kitchen floor. The bedrooms were reached by a stepladder and had such low ceilings that the lack of ventilation in summer was overpowering. There was no electricity, water was fetched from a stand-pipe in the street, a copper was used for laundering and baths, and the toilet arrangements were a shared earth closet in the back garden. It is not surprising that Mr Bird's infant daughter developed such severe bronchitis that in January 1951 he was allocated a new council house after the doctor intervened on his behalf.

This council house was one of a group of four in the High Street. In contrast, the 20 family houses built in 1959 in Dycote Lane occupy a more typical council house site on the periphery of the village, lacking pavement access from the rest of the village, but the 29 old people's bungalows are situated on central sites. Apart from a recent development of 20 houses on Dycote Lane, continuing the line of the 1959 council houses private building has taken place only on a limited scale on infill sites. Nevertheless by the 1980s, about half of the households were living in post-1945 accommodation, an average figure for the area (Table 12.5). This modern period also marks a break with the traditional building materials of stone and pantile, with mass-produced bricks and concrete tiles, being used in standardized suburban designs. Despite all this new building, and Local Authority grants to improve other houses, in 1971 there was still a residue of over 10 per cent of the dwellings that lacked one of the basic amenities of hot water, fixed bath, or inside WC. The Nookin area, mentioned above (p. 325) was included in this figure, and while septic tanks had been in use since the 1960s, connection to the sewer was not achieved until 1983.

The occupational structure of the village has undergone radical change since 1881 when about 120 Welbourn men were working on the land, compared with 13 in 1982, or about 8 per cent of the employed population. With the continuing trends of farm mechanization and amalgamation, only eight holdings remain of the 22 recorded in 1950, over 90% of the parish is now under intensive arable cropping, much of it farmed by absent owners and farming companies.[12] Employment in construction accounted for five percent in 1971 and over 23 per cent in 1981, with four building concerns now in the village. Distribution and services employed 70 per cent in 1971 and 57 per cent in 1981.

The parish survey of 1974 revealed that 40 per cent of those in work were employed within the parish; agriculture, light industry, retail trades, education, an old people's home and two airfield maintenance firms provided these opportunities. Sixteen per cent worked within five miles of Welbourn, in, for example, garages and haulage firms. The RAF bases of Cranwell, Waddington, and Digby accounted for 12 per cent. Urban employment was mostly in Lincoln, in which 25 per cent had jobs, particularly heads of households. The decline in the size of the farm work force has been accompanied by a corresponding decline in the numbers of those living in outlying houses, who numbered 63 in 1871, but only 23 in 1975.[13]

The availability of so much relatively local employment suggests that the community may not have been destabilized. Indeed, in 1974, 64 per cent of Welbourn households had been established there for at least ten years, although only a quarter of household heads claimed to have Welbourn origins. Household heads born within ten miles amounted to 29 per cent, while among the other natives of Lincolnshire, 7 per cent had rural origins, and only 10 per cent had been born in Lincoln, a very much smaller proportion than the 26 per cent who came from outside the county. These figures do not support the general view of the outward movement of a local urban population, and lend support to the general impression that rural stability has been enhanced by men remaining as residents in their home localities, although changing their jobs to work outside their parishes, thus counterbalancing 'urban incomers'. (See also above, p. 7.) Perhaps not unexpected is the fact that council house tenants have been the most stable element in the population.[14]

Table 12.5 *Post-war housing in the Welbourn area*

Parish	Nos of dwellings erected 1951–71			Percentage of households living in post–1951 houses	
	Council	Private	Total	1971	est 1978
Boothby Graffoe	4	10	14	24	39
Leadenham	20	25	45	29	34
Navenby	20	137	157	48	55
Welbourn	45	25	70	39	42
Wellingore	52	63	115	50	63

Sources: Kesteven County Council, *Survey of Population and Housing,* and North Kesteven District Council, Rating Records.

One of the results of a relative stability is the accumulation of a substantial number of retired people, with a consequence for changes in the age structure of the community as important as the long-term fall in the birth rate. Table 12.6 shows that the percentage of the population in the age range 0–14 has declined from 37 in 1881 to 25 in 1981, while the proportions in the 65-plus age group have increased from 8 to 18 per cent, even excluding residents in Welbourn Manor Old People's Home. The dramatic rise in the numbers of single-person households helps substantially to account for the fall in the size of the average household noted above.

Welbourn falls into a middle group of villages, between those with a declining population, and those growing rapidly with the building of large housing estates. This was the result of a planning policy in which Wellingore and Navenby were identified as growth villages for the area from *c.* 1950, where 'adequate services can be maintained or provided economically and efficiently'.[15] As Welbourn was seen as not satisfying these criteria, growth has been limited to a long-established curtilage, and in 1977 most of the village became a conservation area following pressure from the Parish Council.

Table 12.6 *Age structure of Welbourn population, 1881 and 1981*

	1881		1981	
Age group	No	%	No	%
0–14	197	37.0	137	25.2
15–65	290	54.5	309	56.8
Over 65	45	8.5	98	18.0
Total	532	100.0	544	100.0
Over 75	12	2.3	37	6.8
Single-person households	7	5.8	45	21.1% of households

Sources: 1881, Census enumerator's book 1881; Census 1981, Small Area Statistics, excluding 33 residents of Welbourn Manor Old People's Home.

As late as 1937 Welbourn still had a baker, blacksmith, shoemaker, carrier, wheelwright, and two butchers, all of whom had gone by 1975, as had one of the two public houses. However, there were three shops in the village at both dates, and mobile services in 1975 included a butcher, fishmonger, greengrocer, baker, bank, and a bi-weekly visit by the library van. The village suffered a major blow in the 1980s, when the Co-op stores closed following previous reductions in service, and in 1987 the remaining shop and post office were amalgamated, so Welbourn now has only the most basic shopping facilities.[16]

The biggest change in education occurred in February 1961 when the opening of the Sir William Robertson Secondary Modern School led to the loss of the senior class of children aged 11–15 from the Welbourn C. of E. Controlled School. The last resident parson left in 1967, and Welbourn became a united benefice with Leadenham. The Methodist Chapel closed in 1973. The railway line closed in 1966, but the basic bus service between Lincoln and Grantham has continued with a much reduced timetable. Even on this well-populated route there are now no evening services, and only a few on Sundays, but there is a basic commuter service. In 1972 a new village hall was erected on a different 4-acre site including a playing field, which is now equipped with a hard tennis court and a children's play area. High levels of car ownership – 77% of all households in 1981 – have maximized participation in a wide range of leisure activities outside the village, such as, golf, walking, swimming, riding and caravanning. Not surprisingly a number of social organizations now draw their membership from several villages, for example, scouts and guides, youth clubs, pre-school play groups, mothers and toddlers, and the Royal British Legion.[17]

One way in which the fundamental change in the village can be gauged is by considering the question of leadership. In the Edwardian period leadership was based on deference, and a pale shadow of this continued to exist in the 1930s, when the Dawson family who lived at the Manor were still distributing groceries and bags of coal to those judged to be in need, and supporting village organizations through their donations. Perhaps it was a sign of the times that the Dawsons were not country gentry or clergy, but owners of a belting factory in Lincoln. Since the second war, the population has become better educated and better off in relative as well as absolute terms. As a consequence, village affairs are settled in a more democratic fashion, with a larger proportion of the population, including many women, taking part in the decision-making processes.

Bibliographical note

Since the subject of rural social history has generated a voluminous literature the following titles must necessarily represent a modest selection of those available. For a general introduction to the topic, V. Bonham-Carter, *The English village*, 1952, traces the recent changes in rural life up to the middle years of the twentieth century. P. Horn, *The changing countryside, Victorian and Edwardian England and Wales*, 1984, provides a comprehensive introduction to rural life in the early years of this century, including World War I; and J. W. Robertson-Scott, *England's green and pleasant land*, revised edition 1949, gives a sharp impression of the depressed state of our countryside in the inter-war period. Similarly H. E. Bates in *Country Life*, 1943, manages to catch the sense of dramatic changes which were imposed on rural areas post-1939 by the war-time emergencies while A. Calder, *The people's war: Britain 1939–1945*, Cape, 1969, gives a convincing overview of the countryside in war-time.

For the post-war years, Paul Jennings: *The living village*, 1972, has produced a very readable anthology of rural life in the 1950s and 1960s based on the village scrap books of local WI groups written for their Golden Jubilee in 1965.

The contemporary rural scene has attracted the attention of many academic observers, but both H. Newby *Green and pleasant land*, 1979, and A. Russell, *The Country Parish*, SPCK, 1986, have produced informative and stimulating accounts of recent social change in rural England.

There are also a number of excellent case studies of the social history of individual parishes covering the first part of the 20th century, in particular, P. Ambrose, *The quiet revolution: social change in a Sussex village 1871–1971*, 1974, and J. Robin, *Elmdon: contrasts and change in a north-west Essex village 1861–1964*, Cambridge, 1980. Of more specific relevance to this volume is the study of Corby Glen by D. J. A. Steel in *A Lincolnshire village*, 1979.

Local history publications are of course very numerous but N. Lyons, *Scotton: aspects of village life*, Scotton WEA, 1980, and D. Edmonds and D. Cox, *My village, Pinchbeck*, Speed Print, 1986, are good examples of this type of 'home-grown' publication. For a more idiosyncratic view of a local community see T. Smallhorn, *Most brute and beastly shire*, Richard Kay Press, 1987, based on the author's experiences as a GP in the Billinghay area after the first world war.

Much relevant data on population, housing and services is readily available within Local Authority planning policy statements and settlement appraisals, as for example, in Lindsey County Council's *Communities in rural Lindsey*, 1973, or North Kesteven District Council/Welbourn Parish Council, *Welbourn village appraisal*, 1979.

Turning to the specific case study of Welbourn, the author was able to draw upon an unpublished village history by M. R. H. Packridge, *Welbourn*, 1938 and Welbourn Parish Council, *The Welbourn story, past, present and future*, 1978, which included a social survey of the village. Of the primary sources available in the parish, the minute books of the Parish Council, the Parochial Church Council, and the Women's Institute were used extensively, as were the Welbourn School Log Books and admission registers. The Church records comprised the registers of baptisms, burials and marriages and the parish magazine. Miscellaneous sources included directories, bus timetables, newspaper reprints, diaries, letters of accounts, and the electoral rolls.

But the most important source has undoubtedly been the oral recollections of many Welbourn residents, past and present. Their memories and views were invariably vivid and frequently humourous, sometimes sobering and always sincere.

Notes to Chapter 12

1. This is a pattern noted in many parts of lowland England, e.g. J. A. Sheppard in D. R. Mills (ed.) *English rural communities: the impact of a specialised economy*, 1973, p. 223, writing of three East Riding parishes in 1851 and 1961.
2. *Lincolnshire Chronicle*, 18 April 1908.

3. Lincoln Cooperative Society: 'A history of Cooperation in Lincoln', c. 1911, p. 87.

4. For information on servants' conditions see J. A. S. Green, 'A survey of domestic service', *Lincolnshire History and Archaeology*, 17 (1982) pp. 65–70.

5. *The Newark Advertiser*, 19 May 1915, reporting on the May Livings, mentioned a shortage of men with more farmers than servants attending. Wages were correspondingly higher with horsemen and waggoners commanding up to £30 for a six month period.

6. Ministry of Agriculture and Fisheries, Agricultural returns, Parish summaries for Welbourn, 1910 and 1938.

7. Mrs F. Howard, who was an assistant at Providence Stores (Wilsons), 1920–34 recalls that the two buses were open-topped charabancs which had to be sheeted over for the return run in the evening.

8. F. Bruckshaw and D. McNab: *A century of achievement: the story of Lincoln Co-operative Society, c.* 1965, pp. 113–115.

9. Mr J. Tithy, whose father was gardener at Leadenham House.

10. For an over-view of social change in the inter war period see P. Horn, *Rural life in England before the first world war,* 1984, J. Stevenson, *Social conditions in Britain between the wars,* 1977.

11. E. Olivier in 'The village at war', *Geographical Magazine*, April 1942, presents an evocative account of how the war changed the lives of the people in a Wiltshire village.

12. Ministry of Agriculture, Fisheries & Food, Agricultural returns, parish summaries for Welbourn, June 1950, 1982, and 1986.

13. Welbourn Parish Council, *The Welbourn story, past, present and future,* 1978.

14. The electoral registers, supported by local knowledge are one of the few means available for assessing population mobility.

15. Kesteven C.C. North Kesteven Rural District Development Policy, 1966. See also G. P. Hirsch (ed.), *Country planning: a re-study,* University of Oxford, 1975, for a detailed planning appraisal of a rural area in Oxfordshire.

16. D. Phillips and A. Williams: *Rural Britain, a social geography,* Blackwell, 1984, provides a comprehensive account of the decline in service provision in rural areas.

17. An interesting insight into village inter-dependence, in terms of social organizations, is given by M. MacGregor, 'The rural culture', *New Society*, 9 March 1972. Further ideas on local social networks are presented in D. White 'The village life', *New Society*, 26 September 1974. For interdependence in commercial services see I. G. Weekley 'Lateral interdependence as an aspect of rural service provision: a Northamptonshire case study, *East Midland Geographer*, vol. 6 (1977), pp. 361–74.

POSTSCRIPT

by Maurice Barley,
General Editor of the Series

The project for a history of the county, planned more than twenty years ago to be completed in 12 volumes on particular periods or themes, is nearing completion. The most difficult volumes have been left until last: one on the county from the end of Roman rule to the Norman Conquest and one on the present century. Since there is little more than a decade left of the twentieth century, a history which stopped in 1900 or 1914 would seem incomplete.

Readers will be aware from personal observation and experience of changes and new developments in recent times; those who have lived through even a few decades will be able to identify themes which have escaped from the formal scheme of this volume. To describe them all is impossible; many can be presented only as events with a date; others may, it is hoped, suggest themselves as questions for which an answer should be sought or as topics for research. For instance, the history of the Women's Institute movement in the county has yet to be written. There is urgent need for a concerted programme of oral recording, which would illuminate many aspects of the county's history.

THE PERFORMING ARTS

One large field of what may be called popular culture which awaits systematic exploration and recording is that of amateur activity in the arts. Its beginnings lie no doubt in late Victorian times. The music festival, dominated by choirs rather than orchestras, has a long history in Yorkshire and it was taken up in 1900 in the north of the county. The form implies of course that there were enough choirs in existence, especially in chapels, ready to compete. Such festivals remained a feature of Lindsey, rather than Kesteven and Holland, owing to the great strength of Methodism there, and the vigour of the Methodist tradition of congregational singing of hymns. It was the only way, especially in rural areas, that young men and women could discover that they had a voice and could learn to read music. Every meeting of a Women's Institute started (and still starts) with singing Parry's setting of Blake's 'Jerusalem'. The Salvation Army played the same role in cities. It had arrived in Lincoln in 1881 and built a new hall in High Street in 1912. It is easier to find evidence of Methodist choirs in Lindsey than in the rest of the county, but Methodism was strong in some fenland villages and engaged in the same cultural activities.

The gentry played a part in setting up festivals at Brigg in 1905 and at Gainsborough in 1911. At Gainsborough it was the Hon. Mrs Sandars of Gate Burton; at Brigg it was Gervase Elwes, himself a distinguished singer, and his wife, Lady Winifrede Elwes. They lived at the manor house, Brigg, and their festival has its place in musical history because the programme included a class for unaccompanied and unpublished songs. It attracted – one supposes by notices in local papers – elderly men who performed songs hitherto unknown, which were recorded by Percy Grainger.[1] One of the songs, 'Brigg Fair', is now well known, thanks to the composer Delius. Folk singing in the county survived long enough for songs to be recorded during the recent revival; the historian must regret that musicologists have not been interested in asking where such songs were customarily performed.[2]

Scunthorpe as a new town had to create its own social life and must have been the liveliest centre of amateur music-making in the county. Its links were with Sheffield and Hull; its doings were reported in Hull newspapers, as were those of Grimsby. It had a choral society from 1881, whose social gatherings were among the chief events of the year, and a philharmonic society from 1911; an operatic society was founded in 1908, to perform Gilbert and Sullivan and Edward German; there was a two-day music festival in 1906. Concerts, including 'cafes chantants' (whatever they were) were given for fun, for good causes such as aid to the unemployed in 1912, or to celebrate a success of the local football team. Concerts usually lost money because the orchestra had to be paid, but losses could be made up by whist drives and socials. One difficulty was that large audiences could be gathered only in a skating rink, where performers and audience froze, or in the market hall unless a new cinema, the Palace Theatre, could be used. If there was a moving spirit in all this, it was Harold Dudley, who became curator of the museum in 1913; he accompanied soloists and directed operas; he had found a wife in musical circles, and Edith Dudley (née Spilman) took leading roles in operas.[3]

The strength of the Methodist choral tradition is strikingly shown in the life of Philip Pape of Barton on Humber, who died in 1982.[4] He was a monumental mason and sculptor, a Methodist local preacher and accomplished tenor soloist; he trained chapel choirs in north Lindsey for fifty years from the 1920s. There was a male voice choir at Brocklesby in the 1930s; male voice choirs competing at the Cleethorpes festival included Pape's Barton quartet and another drawn from the choir of Newland Congregational church, Lincoln.[5] A good choir was in demand to give concerts at country chapels. String bands had given way to organs, and it was usually the organist who trained the choir. The Lincoln Bailgate Methodist choir performed the oratorios 'Olivet to Calvary' and 'The Crucifixion' alternately each Easter.[6]

While chapel choirs performed Stainer, the place for Bach was Lincoln Minster. The prime mover there was Dr G. J. Bennett, organist and choirmaster from 1985 to 1930. In 1896 he formed the Lincoln Musical Society, which joined the Minster choir for concerts. In 1910 Bennett organized a triennial festival which opened with a grand orchestral concert in the Corn Exhange; he conducted the London

Fig. P.1 Empire Day celebrations, Boston c. 1922, photo taken in the centre of the Market Place looking south. The building top right is Boots the Chemists, to the left of which is the 'Five Lamps' gas lamp standard. The procession is coming out of South Street and was probably on its way from South Square to St Botolph's Church (the Stump). Processions of a celebratory nature were a commonplace of the earlier part of the century. Empire Day was 24 May, the birthday of Queen Victoria, and was still observed in some places until well into the inter-war period, with school sports and the like. This photo is a still from a 35 mm film found on the Boston Municipal rubbish dump, producer unknown. The banner probably reads: 'Empire Day Celebrations May 24th C of E School'. After the procession, the film goes on to show sports in Central Park. Source: Don Woolhouse and the Lincolnshire and Humberside Film Archive. Caption: Neil Wright and P. Ryde.

Symphony Orchestra, and distinguished composers – Elgar, Gran-
ville Bantock, Mackenzie, and Walford Davies – conducted their own
works.[7] The festival lasted for two days with 500 performers, including contingents from Notting-ham, Grimsby, and Hull. Presumably
the 1914–18 war put an end to the idea of triennial festivals, but Bennett and his successors, Dr Gordon Slater and Dr Philip Marshall,
maintained the Minster's contribution. Lincoln had of course its
operatic society.

Malcolm Sargent was a Stamford boy and organist at Melton
Mowbray before he became a conductor; he returned to Stamford occasionally to give celebrity concerts. The nearest festivals were those at
Oundle and Uppingham, but the town had a choral society and two
operatic societies, one performing Gilbert and Sullivan, the other
works such as 'Desert Song'. At Grimsby in the 1930s there was a
dramatic society, the Kendal Players, named after Madge Kendal who
had been born there; there was also a madrigal society and what was
probably the earliest youth orchestra in the county. Boston had its
operatic and dramatic societies, as well as a chamber orchestra,
though no dates can be put to them. In 1934 the vicar of St Botolph's,
Canon A. M. Cook, who later became sub-dean of Lincoln cathedral,
formed the Boston Preservation Trust to save Fydell House, which in
the post-war years became a cultural centre, especially strong in
drama.

In the years after 1945, there were arts societies in the towns of
Kesteven and Holland, which encouraged amateur painting; some of
them may have started before 1839, but their origins have yet to be
explored. In the 1960s, the Holland County Council started a rural
music school in Boston, mainly for the benefit of schools, and such
work continued after 1974, when Lincoln's warehouse was adapted
as a music centre.

A pacifist community at Holton Beckering, started in 1939, was
particularly strong in the 1950s; it contributed to amateur music
making, but more especially to drama. Its history deserves to be written.

The place of brass bands in cultural life has yet to be explored. Village friendly societies which were at their strongest in 1900 to 1914,
before Lloyd George's legislation began to have effect, had long formed
bands, which played at anniversaries. In Lincoln in the 1920s, a brass
band could be heard on Sundays, performing in the gay cast-iron
bandstand in the Arboretum. Popular support for musical and
dramatic activities seemed in the inter-war years to be threatened,
first by the cinema and then by 'the wireless'. Grimsby had its Prince
of Wales Theatre and Lincoln the Theatre Royal for   touring

companies; Scunthorpe was visited by Hawkins's Travelling Theatre. Variety theatres were in decline. Lincoln's Empire Theatre of Varieties on Newland (originally built as a Masonic hall, which explains its Gothic design) was one of the first buildings to be taken over for films; elsewhere corn exchanges and friendly society halls were adapted. *Kelly's Directory* for 1930 lists sixty 'cinematograph halls' in the county; they were to be found in every town, large and small, and in some villages. They increased later, until eventually television began to keep their audiences at home.

In the early years of the century there were many villages in which the young men dressed up after Christmas to perform on Plough Monday (the first Monday after Twelfth Night) the traditional plough jag play. It was certainly medieval in origin, though that is not directly proved. It was preserved by oral tradition, which suffered from the effects of the Victorian depression in farming. The conscription of young men for war service in 1914 was the final blow, but it was still possible even in the 1950s to find old men who could recite the words. The idea of recording the plays was one of the many contributions of Mrs E. H. Rudkin to Lincolnshire's cultural heritage. Performances

Fig. P.2 The Burton-upon-Stather (or Burton Stather) Plough Jags, 1907. They are said to have been 'a double gang, who often split up to work a village quickly, gathering together again at the best and likeliest houses'. According to Mrs E. H. Rudkin, there were 'four Hat Men, two Besom Betties, two Niggers, two Hobby Horses, one Doctor, one Soldier, one Lady'. Source: D. N. Robinson Collection.

have sometimes been revived, as for instance by Jack Martin at Barrow in 1953.[8] At a more sophisticated level, the demand between the wars for plays within the compass of small amateur dramatic groups was met by Bernard Gilbert's one-act plays, set in slightly disguised Lincolnshire villages and portraying village characters. How the more lively villages entertained themselves can be seen in old photographs, such as those reproduced in *Barrow Recalled* showing the Britannia Brass Band, Arthur Denby's review (1939) and the village tug-o'-war team (1932) with the row of cups it had won.

One entirely new element in the social and cultural life of villages was the establishment of Women's Institutes. Women had been drawn out of their homes to help in the 1914–18 war effort, working in munitions factories and the land. There were Women's War Agricultural Committees, and in 1917 the Lindsey branches invited a speaker from Canada (Mrs Guest), where Institutes had started, to speak about them. As a result five Institutes were formed in that year, first at Barrow on Humber, followed by Morton, Keadby with Althorpe, Saxilby, and Epworth. Thirteen more were started in 1918 and the Lindsey Federation was formed on 17 January 1919. In Kesteven, there appears to have been an Institute at Carlton Scroop by 1920, and the Federation may have been established in 1922.[9]

ADULT EDUCATION

The development of opportunities for adults to educate themselves has been a striking change of this century. Oxford and Cambridge had from the 1880s sent lecturers to give extension lecture courses in Brigg, Grantham, Grimsby, Lincoln, and Louth. They attracted urban and largely middle class audiences; some were subsidized by Lindsey County Council as training for teachers, but most were arranged by local committees which had to find guarantors to cover the costs.[10] The Lincoln Co-operative Society (founded 1861) had long had an educational and cultural content in its activities; a choir and choral classes, a library and a reading room; it had supported extension lectures provided by Cambridge. The Education Act of 1902 is a landmark, because as well as introducing a coordinated system of national education, it gave education authorities powers to subsidize adult education, powers which were used in the 1920s and onwards.

There is a sharp distinction to be made between villages which increasingly looked back to their past and the county's industrial towns, where working men and women were more concerned with current problems. Admittedly, the great upsurge in the 1870s of spontaneous action by agricultural workers to improve their conditions has its legacy in this century; there were in 1956 over twenty branches formed before 1918 of the National Union of Agricultural Workers.[11] Its predecessor, the Lincolnshire Labour League, had recruited members at Scunthorpe among the labourers who left farming to dig iron ore in green fields, but with time the interests of rural and uban workers diverged.

Trades unions were well established in the county by 1900, with a membership higher than in purely agricultural counties.[12] The years 1909–14 saw labour unrest as serious as at any time in this century. A strike at Scunthorpe in 1909 won recognition of the blast-furnacemen's union (Fig. 4.8), but at the same time ship owners were sending blacklegs by ship to such ports as Hull and Goole, paralysed by seamen's strikes, and Churchill as Home Secretary used troops against strikers. In Lincoln in 1911 soldiers guarded platforms during a rail strike; there were riots and railway offices were set on fire. Food was distributed to strikers' families.[13] Union membership grew rapidly from 1914, and in Lincoln the shop stewards movement was strong. There were trades councils in Grimsby, Lincoln, and Scunthorpe, set up to enable unions locally to speak with one voice, and they had their impact on local politics.

It was in such an atmosphere that a Lincoln branch of the Workers' Educational Association was formed in 1911. Its founding committee included representatives of several unions, and one from the Women's Co-operative Guild. The WEA recruited from nonconformist chapels as well as from unions, men who were more inclined to try to improve their education than to take part in union or political activities. The Lincoln branch was remarkable in that its president was the bishop, Dr E. L. Hicks, and the dean, Dr T. C. Fry, took on the office of treasurer. Both had been appointed by Asquith, the Liberal prime minister.[14] Fry was effectively the founder; he got to know 'downhill' Lincoln by inviting working men to the Deanery on Sunday afternoons to discuss current affairs. This sort of concern was not to everyone's liking; the director of education for the city attended a branch meeting in 1919 to recommend such subjects as astronomy, botany, and geology 'rather than studies of a propaganda nature'. For the next fifty years the branch, inspired by tutors appointed by Oxford (first Helen Stocks, sister of J. L. Stocks, vice-chancellor of Liverpool, and then Alice Cameron) was a focus of concern about social problems. In 1927, when unemployment had become acute, it started a People's Service Club, where men repaired boots and shoes and made or repaired toys and equipment for hospitals and institutions.

The initiative in starting classes in the towns of north Lindsey fell at first to the Yorkshire District of the WEA, based on Sheffield. The first tutorial class in Grimsby was started in 1917 by T. S. Ashton

(1889–1968), then a lecturer at Sheffield and at the beginning of a distinguished career as an economic historian. Classes studied such subjects as the economic history of England in modern times and the structure of modern industry; a WEA branch was formed in 1921. A Scunthorpe branch was set up somewhat later. In 1928 when the university college of Hull was founded, north-east Lindsey, including Grimsby, was allocated to the new college.[15]

One of the roles of organizations is to promote others, though it is usually only by chance that links can be identified. The Rotary movement, started in Chicago in 1905, reached Britain in 1914; the Lincoln club was started in 1922 and no doubt took the movement to other towns. The establishment of a Lincoln Civic Trust in 1954 followed a Rotary Club initiative.

Adult education could flourish only with the backing of a library service. Subscription libraries and those started in mechanics' institutes or by local bodies such as the Spalding Gentlemen's Society (founded 1707) and the Stamford Literary and Scientific Institute (1838) were restricted to members. The landmarks in public library provision are the Act of 1892, which permitted local authorities to provide libraries and to maintain museums, and the Act of 1919 which extended library powers to county councils. From 1879 Andrew Carnegie had begun to give away part of his vast fortune as gifts of libraries to towns and cities all over the English-speaking world. In the United Kingdom 380 buildings are associated with his name; among them are Scunthorpe (1904), Lincoln (1906), and Grantham (1926). Some councils hesitated, as did Grantham for a time, and at Gainsborough one councillor described Carnegie's generosity as blood-money. He was referring to the ruthless way in which Carnegie had built up the largest iron and steel combine in the world.[16] The library in Free School Lane, Lincoln (1914) was one of three buildings there designed by Sir Reginald Blomfield. One other was the water tower north of the castle, built in 1911 to provide the city with pure water from Nottinghamshire after the typhoid epidemic of 1905. The third was the Usher Art Gallery, opened in 1927 following the bequest of a Lincoln jeweller, James Ward Usher, of his collection of watches, porcelain, miniatures, etc. The three county councils adopted the Act in 1924 and 1925, though Kesteven had already used Carnegie money to start a rural service in the Grantham area.[17] Suitable accommodation for branches was identified in villages, and vans soon began to be used for a mobile service.

The 1892 act also covered museums, and the combination of the two was often taken for granted. At Lincoln, the medieval Greyfriars building had in Victorian times housed the library of the mechanics' institute but was vacant in 1906 and so became a museum. At Stamford, the conversion of the elegant market hall in the High Street permitted a museum as well as a library; at Grantham the two were combined in one new building. Lincoln's Roman and medieval heritage provided material for a museum and an active curator, F. T. (Tom) Baker, made it a key centre for promoting interest in archaeology. At Scunthorpe and Grantham a strong impetus came from discoveries made in extracting iron ore, for the overburden from quarrying was removed until the 1930s by men with wheelbarrows, and they had time to see what their spades turned up. The influence of individuals must not be overlooked: Harry Preston, manager of the Grantham waterworks, and at Scunthorpe Harold Dudley, an amateur archaeologist (and musician) who became curator when in 1909 the council was persuaded to set aside a room in the library.

Spalding and Louth did not need to depend on local authority initiatives to develop cultural activities based on a museum. The Gentleman's Society of Spalding is the country's oldest antiquarian society, having been founded in 1709–10 by William Stukeley, whose family seat was Ayscoughfee Hall. It still carries on the antiquarian and literary activites for which it was founded, though its programme of lectures has been widened in recent years. It accumulated an important collection of books and manuscripts, as well as museum objects, housed in a purpose-built museum since 1911. Its membership includes fewer of the county's gentry, but caters for business and the professions, and to an increasing extent for the retired. The Louth Naturalists', Antiquarian, and Literary Society, founded in 1889, moved in 1910 to a purpose-built museum designed by J. J. Cresswell, a Grimsby architect.

LOCAL HISTORY AND ARCHAEOLOGY

The next landmark is the establishment of the Lindsey Rural Community Council in 1927. The prime mover was Eric Scorer, clerk to the county council, and he was advised by Robert Peers, professor of adult education at Nottingham, who had promoted the Nottinghamshire RCC. There was at first no response from Kesteven or Holland. Such Rural Community Councils had as their main objective the development of rural amenities such as village halls and playing fields, but they were also interested in cultural activities such as music. Peers's motive was to create an agent for providing adult education classes in villages. It had been evident that whereas such subjects as economics with some relevance to politics appealed most in cities such as Lincoln, Grimsby, and Scunthorpe, local history was demanded in villages. The university of Sheffield and the colleges of

Hull and Nottingham had agreed (not altogether amiably) on how to divide the county, Sheffield taking Scunthorpe and the Isle of Axholme, Hull the north including Grimsby, and Nottingham the rest. Lincoln and villages round it remained until 1959 an Oxford island.

In 1930 the RCC, led by its redoubtable and yellow-waistcoated director, Major V. North Coates, brought the Lindsey Local History Society into being. There is no need to recount its success, out of which this history of the county emerged, but it is worth while to point out that it became after 1945 a model for other counties when the National Council for Social Service decided to promote local history societies. There is only one other instance of a Lincolnshire organization leading to the founding of a national one. In 1904 a Lincolnshire Farmers' Union was set up, and led to the National Farmers' Union.

Several counties had had from the middle of the nineteenth century societies set up to publish local records. For Lincolnshire, a new era began when in 1910 Canon C. W. Foster, vicar of Timberland, started the Lincoln Record Society. He was also the founder, posthumously, of the Lincolnshire Archives Office, which opened in 1936, a year after his death. A young professor of history at University College, Reading, F. M. (Sir Frank) Stenton, joined the society in 1915 and became a close friend of Foster, a friendship made easier by the fact that Stenton's family home was Southwell, Nottinghamshire, and he and his wife spent vacations there. Stenton persuaded Foster to turn from relatively modern records, compiled in English, such as parish records and wills, to the immense store of medieval diocesan records. That change is also a symptom of the declining influence of the gentry, with their dominant interest in the genealogy of their families. Foster had designated as diocesan archivist, Kathleen Major, daughter of a Fenland farmer, whose B.Litt. thesis had been examined by Stenton in 1931. Foster also drew into the Stenton orbit the young Lincoln solicitor, J. W. F. (Sir Francis) Hill, who had begun to work on the history of the city.[18] The row of volumes of the Record Society, bound distinctively in white vellum, set as high a standard as any local record society, and are indispensable tools for local historians. They make minimal concessions to those who have not learned Latin at school.

Members of village classes in local history found it easier to cope with modern history, but other social changes were widening their vision. The antiquarianism of Victorian parsons and gentry was turning into what can be called archaeology. In 1925 Stenton had drawn Foster's attention to a mound on Loveden Hill in the parish of Hough on the Hill, traditionally the meeting place of the wapentake of Loveden, and suggested an excavation which Foster proceeded to arrange. It was a private affair, with only the local gentry watching the two labourers uncover cremation burials; at the end of the first day Stenton arrived, pronounced that the pottery was Anglo-Saxon and from then directed the excavation – the only time he ever did such a thing.[19] Hitherto, any archaeological material recovered in the county had been found by accident. A few years later a young Cambridge don, Charles W. Phillips, decided to put the county's neglected archaeology on the map, literally, and followed it up by excavating one of the long barrows he had identified on the Wolds.[20] He soon made the acquaintance of Mrs Rudkin, who was for so long the county's greatest asset in discovering its own past, from remotest prehistory to folklore and yesterday's bygones. Her contribution to Lincolnshire culture has been well marked in *A prospect of Lincolnshire.*

An entirely new way of bringing together those interested in local history was the residential summer school, a feature of the adult education movement adopted by the Society. From the 1840s, national and local antiquarian societies had had annual meetings, lasting for several days, to look at monuments of all sorts; some of them still do so, but they were too expensive for the kind of people who attended village classes, and not appropriate for systematic study. The problem in the 1930s was to find accommodation not too hard on the pocket: dormitories at Stamford School, which had a boarding house, and the college at Burgh in the Marsh which had been set up in 1878 for the training of missionaries. There the conditions were truly spartan and no doubt suitable for missionaries, but less attractive even for keen students. After 1945 circumstances changed completely when it became possible to use the Lincoln Training College (now Bishop Grosseteste) and the agricultural colleges at Caythorpe (Kesteven) and Riseholme (Lindsey). Residential courses on archaeology, of which the first was held at Lincoln in 1949, began to provide amateurs with training in the techniques of excavation; another activity in which Lincolnshire, in collaboration with Nottingham University, led the country.

Notes to Postscript

1. R. Pacey in N. Field and A. White, *A prospect of Lincolnshire* (1984), 119–21.
2. P. O'Shaunessey, *More songs from Lincolnshire* (1971).
3. This information about Scunthorpe comes from the manuscript reminiscences of their daughter, Miss Molly Dudley.
4. Isobel Wilson, *Born to blush unseen*, privately printed, n.d., c. 1986.
5. The writer's father was a member of the latter.

6. The writer's grandfather was chapel-keeper there and his daughters naturally sang in the choir.

7. Photograph in L. Elvin, *Lincoln as it was*, II (1976).

8. *Barrow recalled*, Barrow on Humber Civic Society (1988), pl. 34. See also M. W. Barley, 'Plough plays in the East Midlands', *J. Engl. Folk Dance and Song Society* 7 (2) (1953), 68–95.

9. LAO WI/30; 2/WI/1/1, 4. I owe these references to Mr R. W. Ambler.

10. See E. Welch, *The peripatetic university*, 1973.

11. R. C. Russell, *Revolt of the field* (1956); T. W. Beastall, *The agricultural revolution in Lincolnshire* (1978), 232–5.

12. See tables in S. and B. Webb, *History of trade unionism 1660–1920* (1919), appendix V. This edition was printed by the authors for members of the Workers' Educational Association.

13. P. Wardley in M. Elizabeth Armstrong, *An industrial island: a history of Scunthorpe* (1981), 67–74; *Lincolnshire Echo*, 10 August 1987.

14. See *Fancy a man from Pond Street knowing his ABC*, published 1986 by the branch. In a photograph of members in 1911, Dean Fry in the middle row stands between Gordon Key, a familiar figure in Lincoln in the 1920s, and Harry Jex, a boilermaker. Next to Jex is the writer's father.

15. S. Humberside RO, 220 [add.1]. I am indebted to Mr R. W. Ambler and to Drs Jan Crowther and Margaret Noble for this information; Dr Crowther and Dr Noble are to publish a short account of the development of local history in the Hull territory in D. Foster and P. Swan (eds.), *Essays in regional and local history*, forthcoming.

16. T. Kelley, *History of the public libraries in Great Britain 1945–1975* (1977), 115, n. 2.

17. *ibid.*, 218–19.

18. Doris M. Stenton, 'Frank Merry Stenton 1880–1967', in *Proc. British Academy* LIV (1969), 376, 397; Sir Francis Hill, 'From Canon Foster to the Lincolnshire Archives', *Lincs. Hist. and Archaeol.* 13 (1978), 71–3.

19. The excavation report was published by Canon Foster in *Ass. Arch. Reports and Papers* (1926–7), 313–20.

20. *A prospect of Lincolnshire*, 3–5; J. May, *Prehistoric Lincolnshire* (1976), 45–9.

Table 1 *Local authorities in Lincolnshire, 1900-74,* compiled by Owen Hartley

(D = County District, H = Humberside, L = Lincolnshire, RD = Rural District, UD = Urban District)

Status and name	Extensions, amalgamations before 1974	Allocation to present authorities in 1974
COUNTY BOROUGHS:		
Grimsby	Extended 1927, 1959	D in Humberside
Lincoln	Extended 1919, 1959	D in Lincolnshire
COUNTIES:		
Holland		In Lincolnshire
Kesteven		In Lincolnshire
Lindsey		Divided between Humberside and Lincolnshire
MUNICIPAL BOROUGHS:		
Boston	Extended 1932	Into Boston D (L)
Cleethorpes: *see below*		
Grantham	Extended 1931	Into S Kesteven D (L)
Louth	Extended 1936	Into E Lindsey D (L)
Scunthorpe: *see below*		
Stamford		Into S Kesteven D (L)
URBAN DISTRICTS:		
In Holland		
Holbeach	Into E Elloe RD 1932	Into S Holland D
Long Sutton	do.	do.
Spalding	Redrawn boundaries 1932	do.
Sutton Bridge	Into E Elloe RD 1932	do.
In Kesteven		
Bourne		Into S Kesteven D
Bracebridge	Incorporated with Lincoln 1919	In Lincoln D
Ruskington	Into E Kesteven RD 1931	Into N Kesteven D
Sleaford		do.
In Lindsey		
Alford		Into E Lindsey D (L)
Barton-on-Humber		Into Glanford D (H)
Brigg	Extended 1936	do.
Broughton	Into Glan.Brigg RD 1924	do.
Brumby & Frodingham	Into Scunthorpe and Frodingham UD 1919	Into Scunthorpe D (H)
Cleethorpes	Extended 1922, 1927 Municipal Borough 1936	Into Cleethorpes D (H)
Crowle	Into Isle of Axholme RD 1936	Into Boothferry D (H)
Gainsborough		Into W Lindsey D (L)

TABLE 1   363

Table 1 *Local authorities in Lincolnshire, 1900-74* cont.

(D = County District, H = Humberside, L = Lincolnshire, RD = Rural District, UD = Urban District)

Status and name	Extensions, amalgamations before 1974	Allocation to present authorities in 1974
Horncastle		Into E Lindsey D (L)
Mablethorpe, Sutton	Extended 1925	Into E Lindsey D (L)
Market Rasen		Into W Lindsey D (L)
Roxby-cum-Risby	Into Glan.Brigg RD 1936	Into Glanford D (H)
Scunthorpe	Into Scunthorpe and Frodingham UD 1919, Municipal Borough 1936	Into Scunthorpe D (H)
Skegness	Extended 1926	Into E Lindsey D (L)
Winterton	Into Glan. Brigg RD 1936	Into Glanford D (L)
Woodhall Spa		Into E Lindsey D (L)

RURAL DISTRICTS:

In Holland

Boston		Into Boston D
Crowland	Into Spalding RD 1932	Into S Holland D
East Elloe	Extended 1931	do.
Spalding	Extended 1932	do.

In Kesteven

Bourne	Into S Kesteven RD 1931	Into S Kesteven D
Branston	Into N Kesteven RD 1931	Into N Kesteven D
Claypole	Mainly into N Kesteven RD also W Kesteven RD 1931	Mainly do., but also S Kesteven D
Grantham	Into W Kesteven RD 1931	Into S Kesteven D
Sleaford	Into E Kesteven RD	Into N Kesteven D
Uffington	Into S Kesteven RD 1931	Into S Kesteven D

In Lindsey

Caistor		Into W Lindsey D (L)
Gainsborough	Boundaries redrawn 1936	do.
Glanford Brigg	Extended 1924, 1936	Into Glanford D (H)
Grimsby		Into Cleethorpes D (H)
Horncastle		Into E Lindsey D (L)
Isle of Axholme	Extended 1936	Into Boothferry D (H)
Louth		Into E Lindsey D (L)
Sibsey	Into Spilsby RD 1936	do.
Spilsby	Extended 1936	do.
Welton		Into W Lindsey D (L)

Sources: Ministry of Health and Ministry of Housing and Local Government *Annual Reports*; and *Local Government in England and Wales: a Guide to the New System*, HMSO (1974).

Table 2 *Occupations in Lincolnshire 1901 and 1971*

Industrial order	1901			1971		
	Males	Females	Total	Males	Females	Total
1 Agriculture, forestry, fishing	58,756	1,845	60,601	29,290	6,500	35,790
2 Mining and quarrying	1,358	-	1,358	1,150	70	1,220
3 Food, drink and tobacco	3,709	717	4,426	9,520	7,910	17,430
4 Coal & petroleum products and	538	38	570	1,190	90	1,280
5 Chemical & allied industries*				6,380	1,100	7,480
6 Metal manufacture	4,096	10	4,106	19,220	1,830	21,050
7 Mechanical engineering	7,580	1	7,581	16,180	2,270	18,450
8 Instrumentation engineering	318	2	320	210	10	220
9 Electrical engineering	200	-	200	2,200	1,010	3,210
10 Shipbuilding & marine engineering	700	-	700	1,970	110	2,080
11 Vehicles	1,908	18	1,926	3,050	330	3,380
12 Other metal goods	3,859	41	3,900	2,280	190	2,470
13 Textiles	542	682	1,224	2,960	2,470	5,430
14 Leather, leather goods & fur	874	44	918	250	90	340
15 Clothing & footwear	3,088	6,660	9,748	210	2,180	2,390
16 Bricks, pottery, glass, etc.	1,455	11	1,456	2,540	260	2,800
17 Timber, furniture, etc.	2,394	152	2,546	3,100	600	3,700
18 Paper, printing & publishing	1,061	239	1,300	3,650	1,650	5,300
19 Other manufactures	153	44	197	2,150	1,020	3,170

Table 2 *Occupations in Lincolnshire 1901 and 1971 continued*

Industrial order	1901			1971		
	Males	Females	Total	Males	Females	Total
20 Construction	14,611	21	16,632	24,100	1,310	25,410
21 Public Utilities (gas, electric, water)	431	-	431	3,390	750	4,410
22 Transport & communications	16,227	133	16,360	18,080	2,790	20,870
23 Distributive trades	13,589	3,605	17,194	23,500	21,920	45,420
24 Insurance, banking, finance, etc.	1,431	31	1,462	3,580	3,750	7,330
25 Professional & scientific services	3,558	4,122	7,680	10,680	22,650	33,330
26 Miscellaneous services	6,717	27,781	34,498	13,980	19,960	33,940
27 Public administration & defence	2,509	400	2,909	23,110	5,540	28,650
Not classified	8,827	303	9,130	890	1,510	2,400
Total employed	160,473	46,900	207,373	228,810	109,870	338,680
Total population	245,773	254,249	500,022	399,750	409,395	809,145
Crude activity rates(%)	65.3	18.5	41.5	57.2	26.8	41.9

*Coal and petroleum products and chemical and allied industries are calculated together for 1901

Source: C. H. Lee, *British Regional Employment Statistics 1841-1971*, Cambridge UP (1979). Part III, Statistical Tables, Series B. Lincolnshire is county no. 31

Table 3 *Housebuilding in Lincolnshire, 1 April 1945 to 30 June 1966*

Local Authority Areas	Houses built by LAs No	%	by private sector No	%	Total
Urban:					
Grimsby CB	5,386	60.0	3,586	40.0	8,972
Lindsey MBs and UDs	12,735	63.7	7,271	36.3	20,006
Lincoln CBs	5,807	71.8	2,282	28.2	8,089
Boston and Spalding	7,940	50.7	7,729	49.3	15,669
Kesteven MBs and UDs	3,505	55.6	2,797	44.4	6,302
ALL URBAN AUTHORITIES	35,373	59.9	23,665	40.1	59,038
Rural:					
Lindsey RDs	7,205	35.6	13,041	64.4	20,246
Holland RDs	3,830	54.3	3,223	45.7	7,053
Kesteven RDs	4,773	44.0	6,068	56.0	10,841
ALL RURAL AUTHORITIES	15,808	41.4	22,332	58.6	38,140

Source: *Ministry of Housing and Local Government, Appendix to Housing Return for England and Wales, June 30th, 1966,* HMSO, 1966, Cmnd 3068, Table 1.

TABLE 4 367

Table 4 *Population changes in commuter villages, 1901-1971*

(a) **Grimsby area**, villages within six miles of Grimsby town centre, situated outside Grimsby County Borough area at both dates.

Village	Population		Village	Population	
	1901	1971		1901	1971
Immingham	241	10,259	Keelby	658	1,314
Stallingborough	420	714	Healing	227	2,048
Riby	248	139	Aylesby	111	115
Laceby	942	2,408	Bradley	85	153
Irby	176	116	Barnoldby-le-Beck	150	218
Waltham, Old &New	740	6,771	Humberston	234	6,124
Holton-le-Clay	257	2,114	Brigsley	112	280
Ashby-cum-Fenby	204	178	Waithe	61	37
Tetney	636	1,250			

(b) **Lincoln area**, villages in Lincolnshire, within six miles of city centre, situated outside its boundaries at both sides.

Village (N of city)	Population		Village (S of city)	Population	
	1901	1971		1901	1971
Nettleham	953	3,112	Skellingthorpe	772	2,593
Welton	609	1,628	Doddington & Whisby	232	325
Dunholme	289	1,488	Thorpe on the Hill	293	691
Scothern	418	631	N Hykeham	551	9,551
Riseholme	82	209	S Hykeham, Aubourn		
Grange de Lings	57	74	and Haddington	356	548
Sudbrooke	98	478	Bracebridge Heath*	1,215	4,003
Barlings & Langworth	385	444	Waddington*	770	5,367
Reepham	387	991	Harmston*	327	706
Greetwell	55	354	Washingborough	637	2,522
Cherry Willingham	145	2,647	Heighington	655	1,659
Fiskerton	386	787	Branston and Mere*	1,257	2,519
Saxilby with Ingleby	1,055	2,621	Potterhanworth	480	467
Scampton*	253	1,844	Canwick	266	389
North Carlton	94	103			
South Carlton	181	106			
Burton	266	203			

*The institutional populations were included as follows:
Bracebridge Heath, mental hospital, 1901: figure not known, 1971: 940; Harmston, 1971: 395 in mental hospital; Branston, 1971: 80 in sanatorium.
The following institutional populations were EXCLUDED:
Scampton: 530 in 1971; Waddington: 450 in 1971. These are presumably service personnel living in barracks, and not in married quarters, which would be classified as private households.

Table 5 Changing ownership of major Lincolnshire firms

1914	1921	1931	1941	1951	1961	1971	1981

A. ENGINEERING FIRMS

Ruston, Proctor & Co. Ltd (of Lincoln)

Richard Hornsby & Sons Ltd (of Grantham)

- **1918** amalgamated to form Ruston & Hornsby Ltd
- **1930** formed Ruston Bucyrus Ltd
- **1961** taken over by English Electric Co. Ltd
- **1966** taken over by General Electric Co. Ltd Ruston Gas Turbines formed Ruston Paxman Diesels formed (moved 1973)
- **1985** Management buyout renamed RB (Lincoln)

Clayton & Shuttleworth Ltd (of Lincoln)

- **1936** wound up
- **1929** Forge sold to Thomas Smith of Coventry Renamed Smith Clayton Forge
- **1928** Clayton Dewandre Co. Ltd formed Took over Titanic Works
- **1963** Taken over by GKN
- **1977** Taken over by American Standard

Robey & Co. Ltd (of Lincoln)

- **1969** Taken over by Newall Dunford Engineering renamed Robeys of Lincoln (GKN)
- **1985** Purchased by Babcock International ; renamed Babcock–Robey

Wm Foster Ltd (of Lincoln)

- **1927** purchased Gwynnes Pumps Ltd of London
- **1960** taken over by W. H. Allan, Sons & Co. (of Bedford) renamed Allan Gwynnes

Timeline years (top axis): 1914   1921   1931   1941   1951   1961   1971   1981

Clarkes Crank & Forge Co. Ltd
(of Lincoln)

1948 purchased by Mitchell Shackleton & Co. (of Manchester)

Rose Brothers Ltd
(of Gainsborough)

1961 taken over by Baker Perkins Ltd (of Peterborough)

(1967 merged with Forgrove Machine Co. of Leeds to form Rose-Forgrove)

Marshall, Sons & Co. Ltd
(of Gainsborough)

1934 joined Thomas W. Ward group

1966 linked more closely with Wards

1969 merged with John Fowler & Co. (Leeds) Ltd to form Marshall-Fowler

1975 M–F purchased by Leyland Special Products Group; renamed Aveling-Marshall

1979 sold by Leyland; Track Marshall formed

1982 Marshall Tractors formed

1985 sold

1933 Aveling Barford (of Grantham) formed by amalgamation of Aveling & Porter of Kent and Barford & Perkins of Peterborough

1967 taken over by Leyland Motor Corp.

1985 sold; (1996 moved to Scunthorpe)

Blackstone & Co. Ltd
(of Stamford)

1936 associated with R. A. Lister

Associated with Hawker-Siddeley

Known as Mirlees-Blackstone

R. H. Neal & Co. Ltd
(of Grantham)

1837

1959 taken over by Coles Cranes Ltd

B. SCUNTHORPE IRON AND STEEL FIRMS

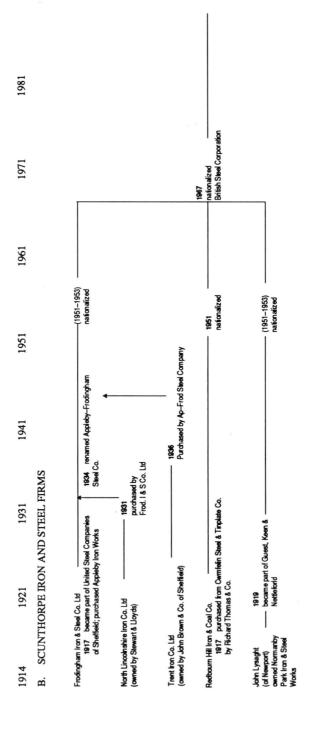

TABLE 6   371

Table 6 *Political control of Lincolnshire constituencies 1885-1983*
compiled by Owen Hartley

Lincoln
Liberal pre 1885, 1892–95, 1906–18
Conservative 1886–92, 1918–24, 1931–45, 1979–
Liberal Unionist 1885–86, 1895–1906
Labour 1924–31, 1945–1973, 1974–79
Democratic Labour 1973–74

Grimsby
Liberal pre 1885, 1892–93, 1895–98, 1910
Conservative 1914–45
Liberal Unionist 1885–92, 1893–95, 1898–1910, 1910–14
Labour since 1945

Grantham
(Borough)
Liberal pre 1885, 1900–1918
Conservative 1885–1900
seat abolished 1918

Boston
Liberal to 1886, 1892–95, 1906–10
Conservative 1886–92, 1895–1906, 1910–1918
seat abolished 1918

Brigg
(1974 Brigg
and
Scunthorpe)
Liberal 1886-94, 1895-1907, 1910-18
Conservative pre 1885, 1894-5, 1907-10, 1918-29,
1931-35, 1979-83
Liberal Unionist 1885–6
Labour 1929–31, 1935–79
seat abolished 1983

Gainsborough Liberal 1885–6, 1892–1900, 1906–18, 1923–24
Conservative pre 1885, 1886–92, 1900–1906, 1918–23,
1924–83
seat abolished 1983

Horncastle
Liberal 1922-4
Conservative pre 1885–1922, 1924–83
seat abolished 1983

Louth
Liberal 1885, 1892–1910, 1910–18, 1920–24
Conservative pre 1885, 1886–92, 1910, 1918–20, 1924–83
seat abolished 1983

Sleaford
Liberal 1906–10
Conservative pre 1885–1906, 1910–18
seat abolished 1918

Table 6 *Political control of Lincolnshire constituencies* cont.

Holland	Liberal 1887–95, 1900–1918 Conservative pre 1885–87 Liberal Unionist 1895–1900 *seat abolished 1918*
Stamford	Liberal pre–1885 Conservative 1885–1918 *seat abolished 1918*
Holland w/ Boston	Liberal 1919–31 (National Liberal 1931–50) Conservative 1924–29, since 1950 Labour 1918–24
Rutland w/ Stamford	Conservative 1918–83 *seat abolished 1983*
Grantham (County)	Liberal 1922–23 Conservative 1918–22, 1923–42, since 1950 Independent 1942–50
Stamford and Spalding	1983 – Conservative
Brigg and Cleethorpes	1983 – Conservative
Glanford and Scunthorpe	1983 – Conservative
Gainsborough and Horncastle	1983 – Conservative
East Lindsey	1983 – Conservative

Sources: F. W. S. Craig (ed.), *British Parliamentary Election Results 1885–1918*, Macmillan 1974; *ditto 1918–49*, Macmillan 1969; *ditto 1950–73*, Macmillan 1971; *ditto 1974–83*; Macmillan 1984. See also Fig. 9.13, p. 241.

BIBLIOGRAPHY

This bibliography is a consolidated list of books, articles, and documents referred to in this volume. For material on particular topics, consult the separate bibliographical notes which immediately follow each chapter. In this bibliography and in the notes, the Lincolnshire Archives Office is abbreviated to LAO.

Newspapers, periodicals, and journals extensively consulted

Architects Journal
Church Times
Grimsby Evening Telegraph
Grimsby News
Grimsby Observer
East Midland Geographer
Industrial Archaeology Newsletter of the Lincolnshire Local History
    Society
Lincoln Diocesan Magazine
Lincoln Leader
Lincolnshire Chronicle
Lincolnshire Echo
Lincolnshire History and Archaeology
Lincolnshire Industrial Archaeology
Lincolnshire Life
Lincolnshire Standard
Louth Standard
Newark Advertiser
Nottingham Diocesan Yearbook
Power Farming

Books, articles, and documentary material

Abercrombie, P. and Kelly, S. A., Report, accompanying Regional
    Planning Scheme, 1936, LCC Parcels 1389/1390/1391, LAO.
Abercrombie, P. and Johnson, T., Outline Plan of Road Scheme, 1922,
    scale 6 in. to 1 mile, in Scunthorpe Borough Museum
Agriculture, Board of, Agriculture, Ministry of, and Agriculture,
    Fisheries and Food, Ministry of, *Agricultural statistics of England
    and Wales*, annually, from 1867

Armstrong, M. E. (ed.), *An industrial island: a history of Scunthorpe*, Scunthorpe, 1981

Armstrong, W. A., *Farm labourers*, Batsford, London, 1988

Baker, A. J., *'The Delaine' of Bourne*, Delaine Coaches Ltd., Bourne, 1983

Baker, F., *The story of Cleethorpes and the contribution of Methodism through two hundred years*, Cleethorpes, 1953

Barber, C., 'The socio-economic impact of the R.A.F. in Lincolnshire', *Trent Geographer*, no. 2, 1981

Barley, M. W., *Lincolnshire and the Fens*, London, 1952

Barley, M. W., 'Plough plays in the East Midlands', *Journal of English Folk Dance and Song Society*, 7, 2, 1953, pp. 68–95

Barnes, F. A. and C. A. M. King, 'The Lincolnshire coastline and the 1953 storm flood', *Geography*, XXXVII, 3, 1953, pp. 141–60

Barnetby-le-Wold WEA, *Aspects of the history of Barnetby-le-Wold 1766–1901*, 1983

Barrow on Humber Civic Society, *Barrow recalled*, Barrow on Humber, 1988

Barry, F. R., *Mervyn Haigh*, London, 1964

Beastall, T. W., *The agricultural revolution in Lincolnshire*, Lincoln, 1978

Bell, Adrian, *Corduroy*, London, 1936

Bibby, H., *The miller's tale*, London, 1981

Birch, N. C., *Stamford – an industrial history*, Lincoln, 1972

Birkbeck, J. D., *A history of Bourne*, Bourne, 1970; 2nd edn 1976

Blake, R., Hodgson M., and Taylor, W., *The airfields of Lincolnshire since 1912*, Leicester, 1984

Boswell, D., and Storey, J. M., *Grimsby as it was*, Nelson, 1974

Bowler, I. R., *Government and agriculture*, London, 1979

Brace, H. W., *Gainsborough, some notes on its history*, Gainsborough, 1965

Brace, H. W., *History of seed crushing in Great Britain*, London, 1960

Bradshaw's railway guide and timetable 1938, London, September 1969

Bray, C., Grantham, K., and Wright, A., *The enemy in our midst: the story of Lincoln's typhoid epidemic 1905*, Lincoln, 1987

Brears, C., *A short history of Lincolnshire*, Hull, 1927

British Railways Board, *The reshaping of British railways*, vol. 1, 1963; vol. 2, 1965, HMSO.

Brocklesby and Marchment, Crosby Housing Scheme for Scunthorpe and Frodingham U.D.C., 1920, Scale 1 : 1250 plan, Scunthorpe Borough Museum

Brown, J., *Agriculture in England. A survey of farming 1870–1947*, Manchester, 1987

Brown, J., 'Agriculture in Lincolnshire during the Great Depression', unpub. Ph.D. thesis, Univ. Manchester, 1978

Bruckshaw, F. and D. McNab, *A century of achievement: the story of Lincoln Co-operative Society*, Lincoln, c. 1965

Buchner, G. E. E., *A reclamation near Wainfleet, Lincolnshire*, Institute of Civil Engineers, Maritime and Waterways Paper no. 12, London, 1949

Burchenall, C. R., *The story of education and the schools of Deeping St James*, Deeping St James, 1957

Burton, H. P. W., *Weavers of webs*, London, 1954

Bygott, John, *Eastern England*, London, 1923

Bygott, John, *Lincolnshire*, London, 1952

Bygott, John, 'Lincolnshire' in A. G. Ogilvie (ed.), *Great Britain: essays in regional geography*, Cambridge, 1928

Byrne, M., *Planning and educational inequality; a study of the rationale of resource allocation*, Windsor, 1974

Carey, W., *Goodbye to my generation*, London, 1951

Carslaw, R. M., 'The economic geography of the eastern counties', *Agricultural Progress*, XI, 1934

Census of England and Wales, 1901 County report, Lincolnshire, HMSO

Chant, C. (ed.), *How weapons work*, London, 1976

City of Lincoln Civic Survey and Housing Exhibition, pamphlet held in Lincoln Central Reference Library, 1944

City School, The, *Lincoln Jubilee 1896–1946*, Lincoln 1946

Clark, R. H., *Steam engine builders of Lincolnshire*, Norwich, 1955

Colsell, L. (ed.), Brooks, R., and Longdon, M., *Lincolnshire built engines*, Lincoln, 1986

Conolly, W. Philip, *British Railways pre-grouping atlas and gazetteer*, London, 1976

Cooper, A. F., 'The transformation of British agricultural policy, 1912–1936', unpub. D.Phil. thesis, Univ. of Oxford, 1980

Coppock, J. T., *An agricultural atlas of England and Wales*, London, 1964, 2nd edn 1975

Coppock, J. T., *An agricultural geography of Great Britain*, London, 1971

Cossey, F., *Grantham and railways*, B.E. Publications, Grantham, 1983

County of Lincoln - Parts of Kesteven - official guide, 3rd edn 1964

Cragg, W. A., (ed.), *Tales of a Lincolnshire antiquary – essays and reminiscences of the late Canon Gilbert George Walker, M.A.,* Sleaford, 1949

Crump, N., *By rail to victory* (the story of the LNER in wartime), London, 1947

Currie, R., *Methodism divided, a study in the sociology of ecumenicalism,* London, 1968

Davies, R. E., George, A. R., and Rupp, E. G. (eds.), *A history of the Methodist church in Great Britain,* London, 1978

Deane, P., and Cole, W. A., *British economic growth 1688–1959,* Cambridge, 1962

Deed, B. L., *A history of Stamford School,* Stamford, 1954

Doran, W. E., 'The Wash', *Geographical Magazine,* 1965, pp. 885–97

Dow, George, *The Alford and Sutton tramway,* 2nd ed., Audlem, 1984

Dow, George, *Great Central,* vols. 2 and 3, Ian Allan Ltd, Surrey, 1965

Eagle, E. C., 'Some light on the beginnings of the Lincolnshire bulb industry', *Lincolnshire Historian,* 6, 1950, pp. 220–29

Education, Board of, White Paper, *Educational Reconstruction,* Cmd 6458, 1943

Edwards, A., and Rogers, A. (eds.), *Agricultural resources,* London, 1974

Edwards, K. C., 'Lincolnshire' in Mitchell, J. (ed.), *Great Britain: geographical essays,* Cambridge 1967, pp. 308–29

Ekberg, C., *The book of Cleethorpes,* Buckingham, 1986

Ekberg, C., *The story of the port of Grimsby and the decline and fall of the deep water industry,* Buckingham, 1984

Elkington, J. R. (ed.), *Alford Drainage Board: 50 years,* Manby, 1987

Elton, Lord, *Edward King and our times,* London, 1938

Elvin, L., *Lincoln as it was, II,* Lincoln, 1976

Employment on leaving school, 1898

Evans, M., 'Report on the economics of bus operation', Papers at Rural Transport Seminar, Polytechnic of Central London, 1972

Field, N. and A. White, *A prospect of Lincolnshire,* Lincoln, 1984

Finn, S., *Lincolnshire air war 1939–1945,* Lincoln, 1973

Finn, S., *Lincolnshire air war 1939–1945,* Book two, Lincoln, 1983

Fisher, A., *History of education in Kirton Lindsey,* Stamford, 1981

Fletcher, Sheila, *Feminists and bureaucrats,* Cambridge, 1980

Fowler, H., *The life and letters of Edward Lee Hicks (Bishop of Lincoln 1910–1919),* London, 1922

Frankenburg, R., *Communities in Britain,* Penguin, Harmondsworth, 1966

Gales, R. L., *Studies in Arcady and other essays from a country parsonage,* second series, London, 1912

Gales, R. L., *The vanished country folk and other studies in Arcady*, London, 1914

Garrod, T. (ed.), *Lincolnshire by rail*, Railways Development Society, Lincoln, 1985

Gasson, R., 'Labour' in Edwards, A., and Rogers, A. (eds.), *Agricultural resources*, London, 1974, pp. 107–33

Gibbon, G., 'The expenditure and revenue of local authorities', *Journal of the Royal Historical Society*, 99 (1936), pp. 457–515

Gillett, E., *A history of Grimsby*, Oxford, 1970

Golby, T. W. P., 'Twenty-two years of education in Kesteven', address given in 1965

Goode, C. T., *The railways of north Lincolnshire*, Hull, 1985

Gowenlock, D., *St Faith's School 1873–1973*, Lincoln, 1973

Green, J. A. S., 'A survey of domestic service', *Lincolnshire History and Archaeology*, 17, 1982, pp. 65–70

Gregg, P., *A social and economic history of Britain 1760–1965*, London, 5th ed. 1965

Grimsby Area Number One Planning Scheme Maps, June 1926, May 1938, South Humberside Area Record Office

Grimsby Area Number One Planning Scheme; Written Statement 1938 in Grimsby Central Reference Library

Grimsby Areas Number Two and Three Planning Scheme Maps, 1937, 1939, in South Humberside Area Record office

Grimsby Tomorrow, 1944. Pamphlet in Pye Collection in Lincoln Library

Grimsby Town Council Minute Book 1937–1938, Grimsby Central Reference Library

Groves, Reg, *Sharpen the sickle*, London, 1949

Grubb, E. H., and Guildford, W. S., *The potato*, New York, 1912

Gurnham, R., 'The creation of Skegness as a resort town', *Lincolnshire History and Archaeology*, vol. 7, 1972, pp. 63–76

Gyford, J., *Local politics in Britain*, London, 2nd ed., 1984

Haggard *see* Rider Haggard

Hallowday, E., 'The Hallowday family and the building of Immingham dock', *Lincolnshire Life*, 27, 4, 1987, pp. 22–7

Hamilton, Owen, *The Lincolnshire landscape*, London, 1939

Hancock, T. N., *Bomber county. A history of the Royal Air Force in Lincolnshire*, Lincoln, 1978

Hancock, T. N., *Bomber county 2*, Lincoln, 1985

Hannam, S. D. J. and D. N. Robinson, 'The end of the Pier?', *Lincolnshire Life*, 18, 11, 1979, pp. 18–24

Hanson, J. W., 'North Sea Camp', *Lincolnshire Life*, 25, 8, 1985, pp. 26–7

Haresign, S. R., 'Agricultural change and rural society in the Lincolnshire fenlands and the Isle of Axholme 1870–1914', unpub. Ph.D. thesis, Univ. East Anglia, 1980

Hartley, Owen A., 'Housing policy in four Lincolnshire towns, 1919–1959', unpub. D.Phil. thesis, Univ. of Oxford, 1969, copy in LAO.

Hartley, Owen A., 'Politics 1883–1919' and 'Politics 1919–1974', pp. 75–83 and pp. 153–60 in Armstrong, M. E., (ed.), *An industrial island*, Scunthorpe, 1981

Henthorn, F. (ed.), *Brigg Grammar School 1919–69*, Brigg, 1969

Hewlett, H. B., *The Quarries – ironstone, limestone and sand*, Stanton, 1935, reprinted Market Overton 1979

Hicks, E. L., *Building in troublous times. A charge delivered at his primary visitation 1912 by the Lord Bishop of Lincoln*, London 1912

Hill, J. W. F., *Victorian Lincoln*, Cambridge, 1974

Hill, J. W. F., 'From Canon Foster to the Lincolnshire Archives', *Lincolnshire History and Archaeology*, 13, 1978, pp. 71–3

Hinksman, B., 'Mission and ministry – ten years ecumenical work in Scunthorpe', 1970 typescript

Hirsch, G. P. (ed.), *Country planning: a re-study*, Oxford, 1975

Hissey, J. J., *Over fen and wold*, London, 1898

Hodson, M. B., *Lincoln then and now*, vol. 1, Lincoln, 1982

Holderness, B. A., *British agriculture since 1945*, Manchester, 1985

Holderness, B. A., forthcoming, in *The English farmer 1900–1970. A social history*

Holderness, B. A., 'Pauls of Ipswich: a business and family history', unpub. but dated 1981, for Pauls and Whites PLC.

Holland Education Committee, Education Works Sub-Committee Minutes

Honeybone, M., *The book of Grantham*, Buckingham, 1980

Horn, P., *Rural life in England before the first world war*, 1984

Jackson, D., and Russell, O., *The Great Central in L.N.E.R. days*, Ian Allan Ltd, Surrey, 1983

Jaeck, P. 'A Yank at Immingham', *Lincolnshire Life*, 27, 4, 1987, pp. 28–9

James, C. H., and Yerbury, P. R., *Small houses in the community*, 1924, Lincoln Central Reference Library

Kelley, T., *History of the public libraries in Great Britain 1945–1975*, 1977

Kelly's Directory of Lincolnshire, London, 9th edn 1919, 10th edn 1922, 11th edn 1926, 12th edn 1930, 13th edn 1933, 14th edn 1937

Kesteven County Council Minute Books, *see* LAO.

Kesteven County Council, North Kesteven Rural District Development Policy, 1966

Kesteven Education Committee Minutes, Elementary Sub-Committee Minutes
Kime, T., *The great potato boom 1903–1904*, Horncastle, 1917
Kime, W., *The book of Skegness*, Buckingham, 1986
Kirby, A. E., *Humberstone, the story of a village*, Humberstone, 1953
Knight, W. P., 'Development of educational facilities in Grimsby 1971–1902', thesis for M.Ed., Univ. Leeds, 1967
LAO., Boultham Hall Estate papers on town planning, 1913
LAO, Holland County Council Minute Books
LAO, Holland, 'Gedney Dyke Log Books'
LAO, Kesteven County Council Minute Books
LAO, LCC Parcels 1640, Scunthorpe Town Planning Scheme 1931–1947
LAO, LCC Parcel 1779, Lincoln and District JP., report of 27 January 1948
LAO, LCC Parcel 1779, Memo 5 January 1944 in file on East Lincolnshire J.P.C.
LAO, LCC Parcels 1783, Lincoln Town Planning Schemes 1923–1950
LAO, LCC Parcels 1941, Skegness Planning Scheme 1921–1943
LAO, Lincoln, Minutes of Housing and Various Committees 1914–1920 (L1/1/21/3) and Minutes of the Housing and Town Planning Committee (L1/1/35/1–4)
LAO, Lindsey County Council Papers, 1902
LAO, S. R. Tetney, 4/1903/2
LAO, Teacher Applications
LAO, Special Minutes of the Lincoln and Grimsby District Synod, 1932–1938
Land of Britain. Report of the Land Utilisation Survey: 69, Smith, C. I., 'Lincolnshire: Holland'; 76, Stamp, L. D., 'Lincolnshire: Lindsey'; 77, Stamp, L. D., 'Lincolnshire: Kesteven'
Leary, W., *Temples of His Grace, being a record of all Methodist chapels in Lincolnshire towns*, Chester, 1979
Leary, W., *Methodism in the city of Lincoln from its origin in the eighteenth century to the present day*, Lincoln, 1969
Lee, C. H., *British regional employment statistics 1841–1971*, Cambridge, 1979
Lee, J. H., *Social leaders and public persons*, Oxford, 1963
Lincoln Cooperative Society, 'A history of Cooperation in Lincoln', c. 1911
Lincoln Diocesan Conference Reports, 1917
Lincoln Draft Town Planning Scheme, scale 1 : 2500, nd, but post-1935, held in Lincoln City Planning Department
Lincoln Central Library MS, Industry I

Lincoln Central Library MS, Industry II

Lincolnshire County Council, Redevelopment on the coast: subject plan, Lincoln, 1981

Lincolnshire County Handbook, London, 1960, 1971

Lincolnshire Education Committee, *Report by County Education Officer, 5 December 1978, Small primary schools in rural areas,* Lincoln, 1978

Lincolnshire Education Topic 1.4, Reorganization of primary and secondary education (Local Government reorganization 1973)

Lincolnshire industrial directory, Gloucester, 1985

Lincolnshire structure plan. Background paper: Employment and industry. Report of view, XXII, Lincoln, 1974

Lincolnshire structure plan. Background paper: Employment and industry. Report of survey: part VIII, Lincoln 1976

Lincolnshire structure plan. The consultation document (issues, analysis, policies, proposals), Lincoln 1977

Lindsey – an official guide, London, 1963

Lindsey County Council, *The Lindsey coast: access and car parking,* 1974

Lindsey County Council, *The Lindsey coast: a policy for conservation,* 1971

Lindsey County Council, *The Lindsey coast: a policy for holiday development,* 1973

Lindsey County Council, *Report of the Survey, Town Map Areas: Immingham and Humber Bank and Cleethorpes, Humberston and Waltham* (c. 1953)

Lindsey County Council, *South-east Lindsey study,* 1967

Lindsey County Council Education Committee, *Report of the Higher Education Sub-Committee on secondary and higher education,* 1905

Lindsey County Council Minutes. *See also* Lindsey Education Minutes

Lindsey Education Committee, *End of a chapter, Education in Lindsey 1970–1974,* Lindsey County Council, 1974

Lindsey Education Committee, *Memorandum by Director, Organisation of secondary education,* 1966

Lindsey Education Committee Minutes

Lindsey Education Committee, *Report by Director of education 1974, Reorganization of primary education*

Lindsey Education Committee, *Report of working party on selection for secondary schools,* Lincoln, 1960

Ludlam, A. J., *The Spilsby to Firsby railway,* Headington, Oxford, 1985

MacGregor, M., 'The rural culture', *New Society*, 9, March 1972

Macksey, K., 'The tank story', *A modern illustrated military history – land power*, London, 1979

Manners, G., Keeble, D., Rodgers, B., and Warren, K., *Regional development in Britain*, Chichester, 2nd edn 1980

Marshall, Sons & Co. Ltd, *A brief history*, Gainsborough, 1985

Marten & Voorheer Associates, *Review of rural settlement policies 1954–80*, prepared for the Directorate of Rural Affairs, Department of the Environment, 1980

Mawer, E. S., *Lincoln Engineering Society 1923–73 Jubilee exhibition catalogue*, Lincoln, 1973

Mejer, E., *Agricultural labourers in England and Wales*, Univ. of Nottingham, 1949

Middlebrook, M., *Boston at war*, History of Boston, vol. 12, Boston, 1974

Mills, D. R. (ed.), *English rural communities: the impact of a specialised economy*, London, 1973

Mills, F. D., 'The National Union of Agricultural Workers', *Journal of Agricultural Economics*, 16, 1964

Mitchell, B. R., *European historical statistics 1750–1975*, New York, 1976

Mitchell, B. R. and Deane, P., *Abstract of British historical statistics*, Cambridge, 1962

Mitchell, B. R. and Jones, H. G., *Second abstract of British historical statistics*, Cambridge, 1971

Molyneux, F. A., 'Geographical aspects of the development of Boston', unpub. M.A. thesis, Univ. of Nottingham, 1968 (copy in Boston Library)

Monks' Dyke School Golden Jubilee, 1929–1979

Moynihan, M. (ed.), *People at war, 1914–18*, Newton Abbott, 1973

Muir, A., *The history of Baker-Perkins*, Cambridge, 1968

Murray, K. L., *Agricultural history of the second world war, Civil Series*, London, 1955

Muskett, P. J., 'Village school closures in Kesteven 1949–79', M.Ed. thesis, Univ. Nottingham, 1979

Newman, B., *One hundred years of good company*, Lincoln, 1957

North, R., *The Butlin story*, London, 1962

Ojala, E. M., *Agriculture and economic progress*, London, 1952

Olivier, E., 'The village at war', *Geographical Magazine*, April 1942

Olney, R. J., *Rural society and county government in nineteenth-century Lincolnshire*, Lincoln, 1979

Orwin, K. S. and Felton, B. I., 'A century of earnings and wages in agriculture', *Journal of the Royal Agricultural Society of England*, 1931

O'Shaunessey, P., *More songs from Lincolnshire*, 1971

Parker, H. M. D., *Manpower. History of the second world war, Civil Series*, London, 1957

Parry-Jones, Brenda, *Magdalen College School, Wainfleet*, Wainfleet, 1984

Pearson, R. E., 'The Lincolnshire coast holiday region', unpub. M.A. thesis, Univ. Nottingham, 1965

Perry, P. J. (ed.), *British agriculture 1875–1914*, London, 1973

Phillips, D. and A. Williams, *Rural Britain, a social geography*, Oxford, 1984

Pinchbeck Local History Group WEA, Spalding Branch, *Pieces of Pinchbeck*, no. 2, Spalding, 1984

Plowden, Lady (ed.), *Children and their primary schools* (the Plowden Report), London, 1967

Pocock, D. C. D., 'Early civic history', *Appleby–Frodingham News*, 1963

Pointer, M., *Hornsby's of Grantham*, Grantham, 1977

Price, J. H. (ed.), *The tramways of South Yorkshire and Humberside*, Light Rail Transit Association, London, 1974

Prospects for the eighties, from a census of the churches in 1979, Bible Society, London, 1980

Rider Haggard, H., *Rural England 1901–02*, vol. II, London, 1902

Roberts, D. E., *The Lincoln gas undertaking 1828–1949*, Leicester, 1981

Robinson, D. N., *The book of the Lincolnshire seaside*, Buckingham, 1981

Robinson, D. N., 'The Clements story', *Lincolnshire Life*, 15, 7, 1975, pp. 32–6

Robinson, D. N., 'Coastal evolution in north-east Lincolnshire', *East Midland Geographer*, vol. 5, pts 1 and 2, 1970, pp. 62–70

Robinson, D. N., 'Gibraltar Point Nature Reserve', *Lincolnshire Life*, 9, 6, 1969, pp. 48–51

Robinson, D. N., 'Humberston Fitties holiday camp: a brief on sea defence and condition of the foreshore', prepared for Grimsby RDC, 1972

Robinson, D. N., 'No. 3 Fish Dock, Grimsby', *Lincolnshire Life*, 24, 4, 1984, p. 22

Robinson, D. N., 'The north-east coast of Lincolnshire: a study in coastal evolution', unpub. M.Sc. thesis, Univ. Nottingham, 1956

Robinson, D. N., 'The Saltfleetby–Theddlethorpe coastline', *Transactions Lincolnshire Naturalists' Union*, XXI, 1, 1984, pp. 1–12

Robinson, Geoffrey, *Hedingham harvest*, London, 1977

Ruddock, J. G. and Pearson, R. E., *The railway history of Lincoln*, 1st ed., Lincoln, 1974

Russell, Rex C., *History of schools and education in Lindsey, Lincolnshire, 1800–1902*, 4 parts, Lindsey County Council 1965–67

Russell, Rex C., *The 'revolt of the field' in Lincolnshire. The origins and early history of farm workers' trade unions*, Lincs. County Committee, National Union of Agricultural Workers, n.d., c. 1956

Sanders, K., 'RAF Wainfleet Air Weapons Range', *Lincolnshire Life*, 27, 6, 1987

Scunthorpe and Frodingham UDC Housing Committee Minute Book in Borough Solicitor's strong room, Civic Centre

Scunthorpe Borough Education Officer, *Education in Scunthorpe 1961–74*, n.d., c. 1974

Scunthorpe and Frodingham UDC Town Planning Committee Book, June 1920–December 1929 in Borough Solicitor's strong room, Civic Centre

Self, P. and Storing, H. J., *The state and the farmer*, London, 1962

Sheail, J., 'The impact of recreation on the coast: the Lindsey County Council (Sandhills) Act 1932', *Landscape Planning*, 4, 1977, pp. 53–72

Skegness and Ingoldmells Town Map, Report of Survey, Lindsey Planning Department, nd [1955], Lincoln Central Reference Library

Smith, A. C., *The South Ormsby experiment*, London, 1960

Smith, A. E., *Nature conservation in Lincolnshire*, Lincoln, 1969

Smith, M., *Blitz on Grimsby*, Hull, 1983

Spencer, C. and Wilson, G., *Elbow room: the story of John Sydney Brocklesby, Arts and crafts architect*, Ainsworth and Watson, nd

Squires, S. E., *West Lindsey yesterday 1880–1980*, Gainsborough, 1983

Stamford Town guide, Stamford, 1967

Stamp, L. D., see *Land of Britain*

Steel, D. I. A., *A Lincolnshire village: the parish of Corby Glen in its historical context*, London, 1979

Stemman, R., *Geest 1935–85*, published by the company, Spalding, 1987

Stenton, D. M., 'Frank Merry Stenton 1880–1967', in *Proc. British Academy*, LIV, 1969

Stevenson, J., *Social conditions in Britain between the wars*, 1977

Stirling, R. L., 'Memoirs of planning in Lincoln and district up to 1947', transcript in LAO and Lincoln Reference Library, 1986

Strandh, S., *A history of the machine*, London, 1984

Sturmey, S. G., 'Owner farming in England and Wales, 1900–50', *Manchester School*, XXIII, 1955

Sutcliffe, A. and J. W. Canham, 'Selection without examination', *Education*, 24 June 1955, pp. 1157–8

Swayne, W. S., *Parson's pleasure*, London, 1934

Sykes, J., *A study of English local authority finance*, London, 1939

Tailby, A. R., *Immingham: the story of a village*, Immingham, 1970

Taylor, M., 'The Fossdyke navigation', *Lincolnshire Life*, November 1986

Teggin, H., 'Britain's Europort: the real treasure in the Wash', *Architects Journal*, 15, 1969, pp. 142–98

Thirsk, J., *English peasant farming – the agrarian history of Lincolnshire*, London, 1957

Turnor, C., *Our food supply: perils and remedies*, London, 1916

UK Fortifications Club, 'World War Two defences of Lincolnshire', unpub. report, 1979

Varley, Joan, *The Parts of Kesteven*, Kesteven County Council, 1974

Vessey, S., *The other side of the track*, Reepham, Lincoln, 1986

Victoria History of the County of Lincoln, vol. II, ed. W. Page, London, 1906

Walker, S., *Great Central lines in Lincolnshire*, Boston, 1985

Walker, S., *Great Northern branch lines in Lincolnshire*, Boston, 1984

Walker, S., *The new line (Kirkstead–Little Steeping)*, Boston, 1985

Wallace, J. C., 'The development of potato growing in Lincolnshire', *Journal of the Royal Agricultural Society of England*, 1954

Walls, J., *Ruston aircraft production*, Lincoln, 1974

Walls, J., *Robey aircraft production*, Lincoln, 1974

Walls, J., *Clayton & Shuttlworth and Marshall aircraft production*, Lincoln, 1977

Walshaw, G. R. and Behrendt, C. A. J., *The history of Appleby-Frodingham*, Scunthorpe, 1950

Warr, H., *Memoirs*, Cheltenham, 1979

WEA, Lincoln branch, *Fancy a man from Pond Street knowing his ABC*, Lincoln, 1986

Webb, S. and B., *History of trade unionism 1660–1920*, 1919

Weekley, I. G., 'Lateral interdependence as an aspect of rural service provision: a Northamptonshire case study', *East Midland Geographer*, 6, 1977, pp. 361–74

Welbourn Parish Council, *The Welbourn story, past, present and future*, Welbourn, 1978

Welch, E., *The peripatetic university, the Cambridge local lectures 1973–1973*, Cambridge, 1973

Whetham, E. H., *The agrarian history of England and Wales, VIII, 1914–39*, Cambridge, 1978

Whetham, E. H., 'The Agriculture Act 1920 and its repeal – the great betrayal', *Agricultural History Review*, XXII, 1974, pp. 36–49

White, D., 'The village life', *New Society*, 26 September 1974

White, F., *A basin full of water*, Kings Lynn, 1968.

White, M. G., 'Fifty years of reunited Methodism: some aspects of Lincolnshire Methodism 1932–82', *Journal of the Lincolnshire Methodist History Society*, 3, 9, 1980

White, P. and Tye, A., *An industrial history of Grimsby and Cleethorpes*, Grimsby, 1970

White, P. R., *A history of bus and coach services in north-west Lincolnshire*, London, 1983 (includes the history of Enterprise and Silver Dawn)

White, P. R., *Passenger Transport in Lincoln*, London, 1974 (also includes an outline history of the Lincolnshire Road Car Co.)

White, P. R., 'Rural Transport: a general review and case study', Papers at Rural Transport Seminar, Polytechnic of Central London, 1972

White, P. R., 'Scartho and the motor bus', *Omnibus Magazine*, October 1969

Wickham, E. C., *Words of light and life*, Oxford, 1914

Wilkinson, A., *The Church of England and the first world war*, London, 1978

Wilkinson, R. B., 'Notes on Old Gibraltar Point', unpub. notes, 1987

Willis, D. and Hollis, B., *Military airfields in the British Isles*, Sherington, 1987

Wilson, I., *Born to blush unseen*, nd, c. 1986

Wilson, M, and Spink, K., *Coles 100 Years*, Uxbridge, 1978

Woods, M. (ed.), *Heckington in the 1870s*, Heckington Village Trust, 1981

Wormell, P., *The anatomy of agriculture*, London, 1978

Wright, N. R., *Lincolnshire towns and industry 1700–1914*, Lincoln, 1982

Wright, N. R., *Spalding – an industrial history*, Lincoln, 1973

Yarnell, D. H., 'The tramways of the City of Lincoln', *Tramway Review*, vol. 8, 1970–71, pp. 163–8 and 195–205, and issue no. 65

Yarnell, D. H., 'The tramways of the City of Lincoln: G.B. System, surface contact', *Tramway Review*, vol. 15, 1983, pp. 48–51

INDEX

Note: this index contains the following collections of items by subject: Acts of Parliament, bishops, churches/chapels, schools. Therefore to find, eg, Laceby Road Methodist Chapel, Grimsby, refer to churches. There are also useful lists within the main text for constituencies: Appendix, Table 6, pp. 371–2; engineering firms: Appendix, Table 5, pp. 368–9; iron and steel firms: Appendix, Table 5, p. 370; local authorities: Appendix, Table 1, pp. 362–3; RAF stations: Tables 6.1 and 6.2, pp. 137 and 140.

Place names have been listed by alphabetical order of the noun element of the name, rather than a preceding adjectival element. Therefore, Cherry Willingham will be found under Willingham, not under Cherry. Names of firms and authorities, however, have been treated in such a way that, for example, East Kesteven RDC occurs under East, and not under Kesteven. References to figures and captions are italicized: thus *224*.

Maitland, Cdr, MP, 218
Major, Kathleen, 359
malting, 64–5, 67
Manby (RAF), 136, 152
Manchester, Sheffield and Lincolnshire
　　Railway, 104–5, 172
Mareham-le-Fen, 2, 28
Market, Common, 15, 46
marketing, agricultural, 42, 46, 63–9
markets, cattle, *40, 75*
markets, corn, *65*
Marklew, Coun., 238
Marsh(es), *7,* 41, 155, 167–8, 176–8,
　　204, 255
Marshall, Sons and Co Ltd, 64, 67,
　　74–5, 77, 80, 89–93, 369
Marshchapel, *246*
Martin, 148, *149*
Martin, Jack, 354–5
maslin, 40
Masson, Miss, 258
masts, mooring, 82
Maugham, Mr, 194
meat, 46, 68
Medical Officer of Health, County, 161,
　　338
Melton Ross, 85
Melville, Canon F. A. Leslie, 322–3
memorials, war, *4,* 285, *310, 324,* 334
Mere, 367
Messingham, 85
Metheringham, 31, 124, 148 (RAF), *149*
　　(RAF)
Methodism/ists, 286–7, 289, 293,
　　295–6, *297,* 313–14, 350–2, *see* also
　　under schools and churches
Methodist Travelling Guild, *310,* 313
Midland and Great Northern line, 115,
　　120
Midland Railway, 115
migration, 2, ch 2 passim, 326–7,
　　*328–*31, 344–5
Milk Marketing Board, 64, 68, *see* also
　　under dairying
mills, flour, 4, 64–5
mills, oil-crushing, 65
mineral extraction, 83–5
Minton, R. C., 250, 263
Mitchell, Dean, *301*
Mitchell, Isaac, *86*
moffrey, *55*

Monson, Lord, 189
Moore, Coun. Alec, 228, 265
Morton (near Bourne), 306
Morton (near Gainsborough), 355
Moulton, 167, 171
munitions, 74–80, 89–90
museums, *5, 47, 55,* 80, *245,* 357–8
music festivals, 172, 350–3

Napier Turbo Chargers, 92
narrow gauge railways, 103–4
National Agricultural Advisory Service,
　　56
National Coal Board, 96
National Farmers' Union, 43, 58–9, 68,
　　226, 359
National Federation of Blast
　　Furnacemen, *86,* 356
National Steam Car Co, 114
National Union of Agricultural
　　Workers, 43, 53, 58–61, 355
nature reserves, 175–8
Navenby, 345
Navenby and District Nursing
　　Association, 338
Neal, R. H., and Co Ltd, 83, 91, 369
'Nellie', 89
Nene, River, *7,* 164, 166, 169
Nettleham, 32, 367
Nettleton, 85
Newson, Sam, 267
newspapers, 1
Newsum, Coun. Clement, 185, 236
Newton, H. I., 198
Nickerson, Charles J., 92
Nocton Hall (RAF), 152
nonconformism/ists, 249, ch. 11 *passim,*
　　especially 291, 293, 295–6, *see* also
　　under churches
Nookin (Welbourn), *320, 325,* 344
Normanby Park, 86–8 (works), *216*
North Kesteven RDC 31, 341
North Lincolnshire Iron Co Ltd, 86
North Lincolnshire Joint Planning
　　Committee, 198
North Lindsey Light Railway, 117
North Lindsey line, 104, 120
North Sea Camp, *167,* 167
Norton Disney, 147
Nunsthorpe, *25,* 113
Nypro chemical works, 88, 96